Reversed Realities

5

Reversed Realities

Gender Hierarchies in
Development Thought

$\blacklozenge$

NAILA KABEER

VERSO

London · New York

First published by Verso 1994
© Naila Kabeer 1994
All rights reserved

Verso
UK: 6 Meard Street, London W1V 3HR
USA: 29 West 35th Street, New York, NY 10001–2291

Verso is the imprint of New Left Books

ISBN 0–86091–384–8
ISBN 0–86091–584–0 (pbk)

British Library Cataloguing in Publication Data
A catalogue record for this book is available from the British Library

Library of Congress Cataloging-in-Publication Data
Kabeer, Naila.
Reversed realities : gender hierarchies in development thought /
Naila Kabeer
p. cm.
Includes bibliographical references (p.   ) and index.
ISBN 0–86091–384–8. – ISBN 0–86091–584–0 (pbk.)
1. Women in development. 2. Feminist theory. 3. Sex role.
4. Households. 5. Birth control. 6. Population policy. I. Title.
HQ1240.K33   1994
305.42—dc20
94–7499
CIP

Typeset by York House Typographic Ltd
Printed and bound in Great Britain by
Biddles Ltd, Guildford and King's Lynn

For Chris

Contents

vii

Preface and Acknowledgements

The chapters in this book were written at different points in time and in response to different requirements. Consequently, most of them could stand on their own and be read in any order. Only the first three would need to be read together, as the arguments in them are built in sequence. The chapters can be broadly grouped into three sections. The first four deal with theoretical debates about feminism and development; the next three focus on key analytical concepts in development thought and practice; and the final three examine the interaction between ideas and practice in relation to some specific examples of practice.

Since all the chapters were written as a result of my own interest in exploring the extent to which feminist critiques of mainstream social sciences in general could be applied to the specific area of development studies, there are a number of common themes which recur throughout the book. These provide an underlying framework and a link between different chapters. One such theme stems from the concern with the assumptions, procedures and practices by which feminist perspectives have been either excluded from mainstream development or else included in a highly diluted or distorted form. A second recurring theme relates to tracking the connections between ways of thinking and ways of doing. Reductionist theories within the social sciences have given rise to reductionist practices, and are in turn a reflection of reductionist methods. The effects of this are seen most clearly in relation to gender issues in development, precisely because women's lives across the world appear to straddle more dimensions and activities than those of men, and are consequently less easy to contain within the compartmentalized modes of thought which characterize some of the mainstream social sciences.

Both gender studies and development studies, the main sources of the ideas discussed in this book, cut across disciplinary boundaries; in the context of the Institute of Development Studies, where I work, both are also concerned with thinking through the practical implications of theory. Consequently, this book should hold some interest for people interested in feminism as well as those interested in development; for people interested in theory as well as those concerned with policy. At the same time, there will be concepts and debates covered here that will be familiar to one group but not to another. This preface is intended to map out the linkages between these different areas in order to make the book more accessible to a broader group of readers.

It would appear logical to begin such a preface by providing a definition of development. However, as some of the chapters in the book make clear, this is not an easy concept to define. Highly ideologically loaded, it means different things to different people. Some see it in terms of a purposive and planned project; others prefer to talk of processes of social transformation. Some define it as the enhancement of individual choice; others see it as the equalizing of opportunities; still others as redistributive justice. Some emphasize ends; others means; and still others focus on the interrelationship between ends and means. These differing perspectives give some idea of the complexity of the term, and rather than putting forward a single definition in this book, we will be exploring the different notions of development embedded in differing perspectives on gender issues in development.

A second important clarification at this stage relates to the key actors in the development field. Some of these actors are immediately obvious. There are the international financial institutions, like the International Monetary Fund and the World Bank, which have become increasingly important in recent decades in determining the thrust of national development policies. There are the multilateral agencies such as those belonging to the United Nations 'family'. There are the various agencies of the wealthier nations which are charged with managing development assistance. There are non-governmental organizations based in donor countries – for example, Oxfam and ActionAid in Britain. Then there are the various governments and non-governmental organizations in what is frequently referred to as the 'developing' countries or the Third World.[1] Finally, there are researchers and consultants in various public and private organizations across the world who play an important role in generating the information which helps to shape how problems are identified and solutions framed.

These different institutional actors cooperate – and conflict – with each other on the basis of their understanding of problems of underdevelopment. How these problems are conceptualized will, of course, have a key bearing on how they are tackled. What is becoming depressingly clear is that the manner of conceptualization has often added to the problem rather than the solution. In particular, abstract and highly formal modes of theorizing, which rule out specific viewpoints of the different unofficial actors in development, have helped to generate the universalistic and top–down approaches which have been the hallmark of much of mainstream development policy so far.

The denial of voice and agency to the unofficial actors of development takes a particularly intense form when it comes to women. Helen Ware, for instance, has estimated that prior to 1975, the UN's International Year for Women, less than 1 per cent of standard textbooks on development referred specifically to women. Development has been about men, by men and for men. Why was this so? Urvashi Butalia, a founding member of India's first feminist publishing press, tells of an Indian journalist who published a series of stories of village life in India, based on his visits to a particular village. He spoke of the men who owned the land and those who laboured on it, of their livelihood strategies, of their livestock and poultry, of the crops and seasons; but he never spoke of the women in the village. When he was asked why not, his answer was simple: he had not seen any. While this is a very literal testament to women's invisibility, it stands as an appropriate metaphor for what many have identified as the basic problem of development for women: policymakers simply did not 'see' women.

The first wave of official feminism within the international development agencies sought, therefore, to make 'women' visible as a category in development research and policy. This has come to be characterized as the WID (Women in Development) approach. There was a conviction that if only planners and policymakers could be made to see women's concrete and valuable contribution to the economy, women would no longer be marginalized in the development process. It soon became clear, however, that there was more at stake than misconceptions and misinformation. The strength, resilience and sheer obstinacy of mainstream ways of thinking have meant that the accommodation of women's issues has often been achieved through a process of pigeonholing. General textbooks might include a chapter on women; development conferences might timetable one workshop on women, perhaps even a speaker at a plenary session; development projects may have a checklist to ensure that 'women's concerns' have been taken into account; government departments set up a 'women's desk'. Neverthe-less, it is generally a symbolic recognition, unsupported by material resources or political commitment.

The shift from 'women' to 'gender relations' as the key focus of analysis in development was an attempt by some feminist scholars and practitioners to bring the power relations between women and men into the picture. The problem with relying on 'women' as the analytical category for addressing gender inequalities in development was that it led to a focus on women in isolation from the rest of their lives and from the relationships through which such inequalities were perpet-uated. The implication was that the problem – and hence the solution – concerned only women. However, while the terminology of gender, gender roles and gender relations has been widely adopted, its implications have not always been fully worked through. For some, it remains just another word for 'women'. Thus the chapter, the workshop and the checklist may speak of gender roles rather than women's roles, but little else has changed.

For others, it has provided an excuse to abandon any measures intended specifically to benefit women. Understanding gender to refer literally to women *and* men, they argue that women-focused policies and projects go against the spirit of a gender analysis. This form of argument was brought home to me during a workshop on gender-aware planning in Bangladesh when one of the women participants asked: 'Do you think we are ready for gender and development in Bangladesh, when we have not yet addressed the problems of women in development?' When she explained how she understood the difference, it transpired that the new vocabulary of gender was being used within her organization to deny the existence of women-specific disadvantage, and hence the need for specific meas-ures which might address this disadvantage. Some organizations have thus embraced the shift to gender because it appears to relieve them of the need to concern themselves with the specific problems that women face within their internal structures, and with the possibility that male interests within the organization may be actively implicated in creating these problems.

Yet a relational analysis of gender inequality within the development process has far-reaching implications. It goes beyond the questions of male prejudice and preconceptions, highlighted in the early WID work, to looking at the institutionalized basis of male power and privilege. It also goes beyond looking at male power and privilege within the domestic domain of families and households, to uncovering its operations within the purportedly neutral institutions within which development policies are made and implemented. Nor does gender analysis imply the symmetrical treatment of women and men. Just as a class analysis can be used to understand and address the problems of the poor, so too a gender analysis can be used to understand and address the problems of women's subordination.

These are the themes of the first four chapters of this book. The first chapter provides a brief overview of the emergence of a Women in Development (WID) perspective within the international development arena. The second chapter deals with the theoretical underpinnings of WID and assesses its contributions to the official policy discourse before pointing to its serious limitations as a politics of change. It suggests that the methodological individualism and liberal-equilibrium world-view which the WID perspective shares with some of the mainstream development theories accounts for its inability to challenge gender inequality in any fundamental way.

The third chapter re-examines many of the same problems which WID advocates had sought to address, but this time from a more structuralist perspective, deriving from, but moving well beyond, the Marxist tradition. Attempts to apply a Marxist analysis to 'the woman question' in development have helped to produce a richer and more questioning framework of analysis within which the structural questions of class and gender (questions missing from the WID analysis) can be located. At the same time, these attempts have exposed the silences and exclusions of many Marxist categories. Feminists working on development issues have had to move beyond the confines of orthodox Marxism to raise the question of 'body-politics' within development discourse, something which had been neglected both by WID scholars and practitioners and by the more traditional Marxist-feminist critics of mainstream development. They have also had to move beyond the preoccupation with structural forces which dominates Marxist thought to looking at how these forces are mediated in people's daily lives. The chapter examines a number of strands of feminist scholarship within this tradition, and pulls together current attempts to ground the concept of gender relations within an institutional framework in order to make it more amenable to empirical analysis. Such a theorization of gender and development focuses on the construction and reinforcement of gender inequalities through the rules, procedures and practices of the key institutions through which development policies are formulated and enacted.

The fourth chapter returns to the question of development, but asks how it might look from this alternative gender perspective. Since gender is present in all forms of social inequalities, such a rethinking would have profound implications for all forms of exclusion. Rethinking development impinges on both the production of knowledge and the allocation of resources. Current methodologies have served the interests of privileged groups, and helped to produce the skewed development practices of the past decades. Knowledge generated by excluded groups would help to transform development thought, extending it to take account of what has hitherto been excluded, deepening it to uncover the interconnections which have hitherto been concealed through compartmentalized modes of analysis and, above all, reversing the order of priorities privileged within it in order that rights and responsibilities, claims and obligations are more closely aligned.

The next three chapters of the book continue the 'deconstruction' of conventional concepts and ideas, but shift from the broader notion of development to more micro-level aspects. Because economics as a discipline has played such an influential role in shaping development thought and steering development practice, its theories and concepts inevitably form a major focus of the critique in this book. Some examples of economic theorizing surface in the broader discussion on development in first section, but it is the central concern of this second section. Attention is now shifted from development in general to microeconomic concepts, such as households and household decision-making, poverty and the poverty line, costs, benefits and cost–benefit analysis, efficiency and equity, all of which figure prominently in the practice of development.

Neo-classical economics provides a powerful illustration of the gender-blindness of development thought in general because it epitomizes more than any other discipline the reductionist procedures through which issues of power and inequality have been kept out of the mainstream social sciences. Paradoxically, it is precisely this reductionism which many economists value in claiming a scientific rigour and clarity for their discipline. Acknowledging that many who have sampled economics will have found it depressing, the economist Mancur Olsen offers this lyrical description of the discipline: 'I plead with them that even if economics seems, when first entered, like a dark cave, it is a cave that if followed *all* the way to the end, leads to the other side of the mountain, and to a magnificent view that includes even terrain that we conventionally associate with other social sciences.'

This, however, is not a description of economics that will receive much support here. A more appropriate metaphor would be that of economics as a bleak and barren terrain in which few plants can flourish (a metaphor which draws on Schumpeter's description of 'Adam Smith, in whose wooden hands, no plant would grow'). The model of human behaviour that economists offer is austere, abstract and formal, totally devoid of the ambiguity, conflicts, noise and mess which characterize the world as we know it, and play a more important role in the more empirically grounded approaches to social reality. In each of the three chapters which make up this section, therefore, I have sought to contrast the economists' version of certain aspects of social reality with the very different version that comes into view when a more relational perspective is adopted. What my analysis makes clear is that economists have generally disposed of feminist concerns with gender power and conflict through the breathtakingly simple device of assuming that they do not exist; their preoccupation with measurability ensures that such issues do not emerge at any subsequent empirical stage of analysis.

Chapter 5 is about households and household decision-making. Economic models of households are premised on the assumption that household members have shared interests ('blood is thicker than water') and decision-making is organized along altruistic principles by the household head, who acts as a 'benevolent dictator'. When the predictions of this model are compared with the empirical realities reported in different parts of the world, it becomes clear that economists have a very odd view of altruism, attributing it most strongly to the household member most likely to monopolize assets, food, prestigious goods and leisure time. The chapter suggests a number of 'patriarchal' dichotomies in neo-classical thought which have helped to produce this incongrous equation of power with altruism and inequality with choice: the dichotomies between individuals and structures, economics and culture, and quantitative and qualitative methodologies.

Chapter 6 deals with poverty, one of the enduring concerns of development efforts. Here the focus is on the dominant conceptualization of poverty, the forms of measurement it leads to and the resulting reduction of poverty to a single statistic. Such an approach provides those responsible for making policy with little insight into who the poor are, what they do and how they perceive poverty and well-being. The fact that women often experience the state of poverty differently from men, and become poor through different processes, is also obscured by this poverty reductionism. One very practical implication of this approach to poverty is that it leads to strategies which target the (male) head of household and do little to address the gender-specific disadvantages that women face. The chapter offers an alternative route to conceptualizing and measuring poverty, one which allows space for the gender dimensions in the state and process of poverty to be incorporated into the analysis.

The final chapter in this section on economic concepts examines the assumptions behind cost–benefit analysis, a key tool in the evaluation of development interventions. Here the challenge is to conceptualize and measure the intangible goals of development – in particular, autonomy and equity. The problem is that economists recognize only the market as the arbiter of value and, by extension, only those costs and benefits which can be given a market price. Consequently, increases in productivity will count as a benefit but increases in autonomy will not; increases in the wage component of the project will count as a cost but the increase in the workloads of women as a result of the project will not. As we have already noted, development is a contested concept; the methodology of cost–benefit analysis privileges an individualistic and production-oriented view of development over a relational and well-being-oriented one.

The last three chapters of the book are also about the relationship between ideas and practice, but focusing here on the way ideas are evolved, clarified or transformed through the experience of development policies and practice. Three different kinds of development practice figure in these chapters. Chapter 8 deals with population policy. It delineates the different meanings of control embedded in conflicting interpretations of the 'unmet need' for reproductive technology. For the population establishment, the issue is control over women's bodies and reproductive capacity; for feminists, it is women's right to control over their own bodies as an essential aspect of their sense of selfhood. However, there are differences among feminists as well in how they see the issue of reproductive control, which mirror their differing political stance in relation to the broader questions of development itself. The chapter traces through some of these debates in order to illuminate how the politics of needs interpretation is played out in one particular policy arena. It concludes by putting forward a set of principles and guidelines which might help to construct a more feminist version of population policy than has hitherto been in evidence. On a broader theoretical level, the chapter adds weight to the argument that choice – reproductive or otherwise – remains at the level of an abstraction unless it is backed up by information, resources, accountability and, in the final analysis, enfranchisement.

Chapter 9 tackles the issues of power and empowerment which have cropped up intermittently in earlier chapters. Attempts to theorize power by social scientists and by feminists working in development are compared and then used to explore the attempts of grassroots non-governmental organizations to operationalize these ideas. The discussion suggests that organizational strategies for empowerment lend themselves to a relational rather than a resource theory of power. In other words, the provision of both economic and welfare resources plays an important part in these strategies, but what distinguishes this from more conventional forms of development intervention is the central role given to changing institutional rules, procedures, identities and relationships. The chapter emphasizes the point (made in Chapter 7) that more conventional approaches to the design and evaluation of development interventions, which privilege certain world-views over others, are unlikely to give rise to projects of enfranchisement and empowerment.

The concluding chapter in this section, and of the book, is about training methodologies. Training can be seen as a particular form of practice whose goal is to change prevailing practice. The chapter compares three approaches to gender issues in development planning which have been disseminated through gender training efforts over the past decade, and draws out what they have to say about gender inequalities in production, labour, resources and power within the official and unofficial institutions of development. The chapter summarizes many of the concerns of the previous chapters. It demonstrates how truncated approaches to social reality tend to overlook the interconnections between different institutional constructions of gender. It suggests the need to link discussions of gender inequality to the rules and practices of the different institutions that interact in the development process. And finally, it moves from looking at the 'gender subtext' of concepts and policies which have figured in the rest of the book to looking at the political subtext of the gender training methodologies under consideration. It reiterates once again one of the central themes of the book: that ways of thinking and ways of doing are inseparable.

As I stated at the beginning of this preface, the chapters in this book were written at different points in time and in response to different requirements. I would like to conclude by acknowledging my debts to colleagues and friends, with the usual proviso that they bear no responsibility for the analysis contained here. The first four chapters were written over a number of years in the course of teaching on the MA in Gender and Development which is run jointly by the Institute of Development Studies and the University of Sussex. I would like to thank the various students who have given me feedback on my lectures, but a particularly warm thank you to MA4.

Chapter 5 was written because of my own interest in household economics, and has appeared as IDS Discussion Paper 288. However, I benefited here from an earlier collaboration with Razia Aziz on developing a teaching module for the Institute of Social Studies in The Hague; I am grateful for her incisive comments on the earlier paper. I am also grateful to Diane Elson for her comments on the discussion paper. Chapter 6 emerged out of a consultancy commissioned by DANIDA on behalf of the Like-Minded Group of donors in Bangladesh. Here I benefited from my discussions with Hussain Zillur Rahman and Shireen Huq. An earlier version of this chapter appeared as IDS Discussion Paper 255, and in the *Journal of Peasant Studies*, vol. 18 (2). I would like to thank them for letting me include a revised version of the paper here. Chapter 7 was written in response to a request from students of the M.Phil. in Development Studies for 'something on gender and cost–benefit analysis'. It has appeared in *Development and Change*, vol. 23, and I would like to thank them for letting me include a revised version of the article here.

Chapter 8 was initially commissioned by the Commonwealth Secretariat for the Commonwealth Ministers' Meeting in Ottawa in 1990. An earlier version of the paper appeared as IDS Discussion Paper 299, and I would like to thank Heather Joshi in particular for her comments at this stage. Chapter 9 was written specifically for this book, as it seemed impossible to produce a book on gender issues in development practice without considering the question of empowerment. Finally, Chapter 10 was written in response to those who asked about the training methodology we have been developing at IDS. This chapter appeared earlier as IDS Discussion Paper 313, and received comments from Gerry Bloom and Ann Marie Goetz. While a number of people have been involved in developing this methodology, I am particularly indebted to those I have trained with most recently: Shireen Huq, Ann Marie Goetz, Ramya Subramaniyam, Shanti Dairiam, Maitrayee Mukhopadhyay and Deborah Kasente. A brief description of the conceptual framework has also recently been published as a chapter in the Oxfam publication *Gender Planning in Development Agencies: Meeting the Challenge* (1994).

In addition, I would like to make more general acknowledgements to a number of people who have helped with their comments, advice and encouragement: Alison Evans, Hilary Standing, Shireen Huq, Diane Elson, Martin Greeley, Henry Lucas, Gerry Bloom, Robert Chambers. I owe special thanks to Ann Whitehead, who has been a source of intellectual leadership for many of us; to Chris Colclough and John Toye for support at the institutional level, and to the Overseas Development Administration for research funding to IDS. At Verso, I would like to thank in particular Robin Blackburn for suggesting putting this book together, Colin Robinson for seeing it through, and Robin Gable for his comments on the draft version. Finally, I have depended enormously on Chris Leaf's help, support and general forbearance. I owe him special thanks.

Notes

1 Most epithets like 'developing countries' and 'Third World' have been rightly criticized for imposing an apparent uniformity on an extremely heteregeneous (culturally, politically and economically) group of countries. Moreover, with the demise of socialist regimes in much of the world, the original rationale for the term Third World as connoting a 'third way' to development for the economies of Africa, Asia and Latin America, different from the first 'capitalist' path and the second 'socialist' path, is increasingly irrelevant. However, it remains the term I am most comfortable with, since it was the basis of my own political education. To replace the term with 'LACAAP countries' (Latin America, Caribbean, Africa, Asia and the Pacific) may be more accurate and appropriate, but it does not come easily to me yet. I have therefore mainly used the term Third World in this book.

1

The Emergence of Women as a Constituency in Development

After a millennium for men, we got a Decade for Women.
(Participant at the Women's Studies Conference, London 1991)

Considerable effort has been made by the majority of countries in furtherance of the objectives of the Decade, but the progress has been insufficient to bring about the desired quantitative or quality improvements in the status of women.
(UN 1980, cited in Maguire, 1984, p. 35)

What has been the impact of all this activity? Not much.
(Tinker, 1982, p. 11, cited in Maguire, 1984, p. 35)

Women's Issues as Development Issues

One way of charting the emergence of women as a distinctive category in development discourse is to monitor their changing significance within the policy declarations and institutional structures of the major development agencies. Changes within the United Nations, a major player in this field, provide an illustrative example. Since the start of the sixties, the UN has marked each official 'decade of development' with a declaration summarizing the lessons learnt from past experience and its priorities for the coming ten years. The declaration that announced the First Development Decade (1961–1970) was devoid of any specific reference to women. A brief reference in the International Development Strategy for the Second Decade to the importance of encouraging 'the full integration of women in the total development effort' hinted at the first glimmerings of a new consciousness. This was

1

further spelt out in the strategy for the 1980s, which declared women
'agents and beneficiaries in all sectors and at all levels of the
development process'. Most recently, the UN has declared that 'In the
1990s the task is to translate greater understanding of the problems of
women into altered priorities. . . . Empowering women for development should have high returns in terms of increased output, greater
equity and social progress' (UN, 1989a, p. 41).

The emergence of this new consciousness was also evident in
changes in the organizational structure of the UN. In its early years,
women's issues were seen primarily in the context of human rights and
confined to the Commission on the Status of Women and to the Third
Committee of the UN General Assembly, which dealt with social and
humanitarian matters (Pietila and Vickers, 1990). By the end of the
eighties, there were several organizations within the UN system
responsible for ensuring that women were integrated into its development efforts. They included the Division for Women within its central
agency, the United Nations Development Programme, along with the
UN Development Fund for Women; the legal Committee for the
Elimination of Discrimination against Women; the International
Research and Training Institute for the Advancement for Women, an
autonomous body within the UN; as well as Women in Development
(WID) units within the various bodies of the UN.

This chapter traces this emergence of women as a recognized
constituency in the development effort and the changes in policy
discourse which it effected. It is customary to begin accounts of this
history by paying tribute to a book by Ester Boserup, published in
1970, which is considered a watershed in thinking about women in
development. Indeed, one WID advocate described it as 'the fundamental text for the U.N. Decade for Women' (Tinker, 1990a, p. 8).
However, the climate might not have been as receptive to Boserup's
ideas if the period when her book was published had not also been one
in which various social movements gathered momentum (Maguire,
1984). The sixties and seventies were marked by protest – in the South
against the injustices of the international economic order, and in the
North against class and race privilege in the universities and factories.
Civil-rights and black-power movements combined with Third World
liberation struggles to heighten awareness of continuing forms of neo-
colonialism across the global landscape. The women's movement itself
emerged out of the questioning mood that prevailed in those times
and mounted a challenge that took on male privilege in the academy,
in politics and in the relations of everyday life.

The questioning mood of the time also pervaded the development
community, leading to a critical re-examination of its own basic

assumptions. Previously held convictions that the gross national product (GNP) sufficed as an adequate measure of development and that the benefits of economic growth would 'trickle down' to households at the bottom of the income hierarchy had been invalidated by the experience of the First Decade of Development. While economic growth rates of over 5 per cent were documented in many Third World countries, they were frequently accompanied by increases in unemployment, inequality and absolute poverty. Dissatisfaction with growth-dominated definitions of development led to a reformulation of development goals to take greater account of poverty, distribution and the meeting of basic needs. In 1970, the UN Development Strategy for the Second Decade declared that 'the ultimate objective of development must be to bring about sustained improvement in the well being of the individual and bestow benefits on all. If undue privileges, extremes of wealth and social injustice persist, then development fails in its essential purposes.'

Various elements made up this new broadened view of development: *Redistribution with Growth* (Chenery et al., 1974); *The Assault on World Poverty* (World Bank, 1975) and the ILO's *Employment, Growth and Basic Needs: A One-World Problem* (1976) were influential publications and epitomized the new sensitivity to the links between economic and social objectives. These changes in the ideological climate of development also resulted in greater attention being given to women's issues. There were two areas where women's role in development received particular attention (Pietila and Vickers, 1990). The first was food. The Food and Agriculture Organization (FAO) nutrition section, staffed mainly by women, had highlighted women's vital role in food production, particularly in Africa. It ensured that the World Food Conference, organized in 1974, recognized women's contributions at different stages of the food chain, along with their role in family food provision and nutrition. The second important area was population. Development studies in the fifties and sixties had been dominated by ambitious macroeconomic models dealing with highly aggregated variables that spelt out how to achieve economic growth. A common assumption of these models (for example, the Coale and Hoover Model [1958]) was that high rates of population growth inhibited a country's investment capacity; potential economic surpluses were used up in consumption and welfare expenditures, instead of being invested in productive capital formation. Supporting this view of 'the population problem' was the work of economists like Enke (1969) who argued that a dollar spent preventing births (through contraceptive measures) added one hundred times more to income per head in a developing country than it would in other forms of aid expenditure.

However, despite the encouragement given to family-planning efforts, birth rates did not go down in the Third World. The limitations of this approach were partly explained by micro-level social science research suggesting that improving the supply of family-planning methods was unlikely to have much impact on birth rates if the conditions that led to the demand for large families remained unchanged (Mamdani, 1972; Epstein and Jackson, 1977). One of the most consistent relationships to emerge out of this body of work was that between different indicators of women's status (for example, education, labour-force participation) and fertility rates. As a study typical of this genre of research concluded, 'the role and status of women is now recognized as a crucial variable influencing fertility decisions, quite apart from the intrinsic human rights aspect' (Jackson, 1977, p. 10). Such research on food and population helped to establish the conceptual link between women's issues and economic development, giving legitimacy to the idea that 'women's issues have development policy implications' (Buvinic, 1983, p. 23). The stage was thus cleared for such issues to be incorporated into the development discourse and to take on increasing instrumental value in the achievement of a variety of development-related goals. The declaration of the International Decade for Women, with the official themes of Equality, Peace and Development, signified the new visibility of Women in Development (WID) in international forums.

It was against this changing, and more receptive, mood within the development establishment that the far-reaching effects of Boserup's book and the work of those scholars and advocates loosely labelled 'WID' have to be understood. The advent of WID in the international arena represented, above all, an infusion of new ideas aimed at influencing prevailing development policy. Its achievements – and limitations – are best assessed by locating them in the context of how women and development had been thought about and 'done' in the years prior, and subsequent, to the WID intervention. In the rest of this chapter, we will be outlining some of the different policy approaches to women in the development arena, before going on in the next chapter to look at the theoretical underpinnings of WID and the limitations associated with it.

From Welfare to Efficiency: Policy Approaches to Women in Development

Buvinic (1983) has suggested that approaches to women in development can be classified as welfare, anti-poverty and equity. (I will discuss Buvinic's equity category in terms of equality, to distinguish it from the equity argument put forward in Chapter 4.) Two further classifications were added by Moser (1989): efficiency and empowerment. Each of these different approaches represented a response to distinct sets of imperatives, but they should not be regarded as either chronological or mutually exclusive. In some agencies, old approaches persisted as new ones were attempted; in others, older ones were returned to as new ones foundered. For analytical purposes, however, welfare and efficiency have been constituted as the two dominant and opposing approaches, located, as it were, at either end of the policy spectrum. The other approaches can be seen as either transitional between them or, as in the case of empowerment, yet to be taken seriously by the official development agencies. We will be discussing grassroots strategies for women's empowerment in Chapter 9. Attention is focused in the rest of this chapter on policy approaches to women and development which have featured more explicitly in the official arena.

WID emerged in the 1970s, not because women had been totally ignored by policymakers in the first decade of development, but rather because they had been brought into development policy on very sex-specific terms. In other words, while men entered the policy process as household heads and productive agents, women were viewed primarily in their capacity as housewives, mothers and 'at-risk reproducers' (Jaquette and Staudt, 1988). Consequently, mainstream 'development' efforts were targeted mainly at the male population, while women were relegated to the more marginal 'welfare' sector. As Buvinic put it:

> Poor women in the Third World had become the main beneficiaries of welfare programs begun by national and international relief agencies soon after the end of the World War II. These welfare programs were designed to relieve poor women's needs exclusively in terms of their roles as mothers and housewives. (Buvinic, 1983, p. 24)

Moser (1989) has pointed to the origins of the welfare approach within development in the notion of 'social welfare' embedded in nineteenth-century European Poor Laws. This helps to explain the continuing 'residual' status given to welfare planning in the development efforts of many of the ex-colonial countries. The Poor Laws came into existence in Europe at a time when individual effort in the marketplace was seen as the recommended route to individual self-improvement. The poor were viewed as the failures of the system, incapable of improving themselves through their own efforts. Their basic needs became the responsibility of voluntary charity organizations. Later, social welfare ministries were set up to effect consumption transfers to meet the needs of 'vulnerable groups' who had been failed by the 'normal structure of supply, the family and the market' (Wilensky and Lebeaux, 1965, p.138, cited in Moser, 1989, p. 1807).

The distinction made by First World policymakers between mainstream *development resources* to be directed to market-oriented productive activity and residual *welfare assistance* for dependent and vulnerable groups was transferred through development planning to the Third World. The 'dependency' connotations of welfare expenditures were further exacerbated where women were concerned because of deep-rooted, normative assumptions about the division of roles between the sexes entrenched within national and international agencies of development. The mutually reinforcing nature of these two sets of preconceptions meant that women were assigned almost exclusively to the social welfare sector, within which interventions for women were further narrowed to address the primarily domestic role assigned to them by the pre-WID development planners, viz. in programmes delivering nutritional training, home economics, maternal and child health care and family planning. As long as economic growth was seen as the overriding objective of development, these welfare programmes were very much of a residual nature, offered only when the requirements of mainstream planning had been met and dispensed with in times of economic austerity. Women entered them passively, rather than actively, as recipients rather than contributors, clients rather than agents, reproductive rather than productive.

Against this background, the publication of Boserup's book in 1970 came as a startling revelation. Writing as an economist and a planner, in language that was familiar to the mainstream development community, she made a strong case for women's productive roles, in direct challenge to the orthodox equation between women and domesticity. She argued that various colonial and post-colonial governments had systematically bypassed women in the diffusion of new technologies, extension services and other productive inputs because of their perceptions – or misperceptions – of what women did. She provided examples of countries where, despite women's critical roles in farming systems, planners had continually operated with stereotyped assumptions about female domesticity.

The initial implication of Boserup's critique, further reinforced by the WID advocates and scholars who came after her, was to shift attention from *welfare to equality* for women in the development process. As Maguire has pointed out (1984, p. 12), the World Plan of Action that emerged out of the 1975 International Women's

Conference contained a 'bold women's agenda' which called for 'the achievement of equality between the sexes within the context of changed relations between North and South'. It also called for a reassessment of the family and societal roles assigned to the different sexes, but focused, in the immediate term, on women's roles and the establishment of socially organized services to free women to contribute equally in economic production. However, this early call for radical change soon evaporated when the time came for implementation. Put forward as an extensive 'shopping list of desirable changes in the status of women', it was left to the piecemeal action of individual governments to put into practice (Maguire, 1984, p. 13). While the process of rationalizing the original list of demands varied between different national and international agencies, some consensus was reached on the main goal: not only to integrate women into the development process, but to integrate them 'more productively'. The key route for this integration was seen as equality of opportunity through education and training.

The Decade rhetoric of equity would have proved difficult to translate into policy because it required a redistribution of resources throughout the development process: 'Focusing on all women, rather than on poor women only, calls for equality at all levels, both among program beneficiaries and among program implementers' (Buvinic, 1983, p. 26). In view of the resistance by predominantly male-staffed development agencies to redistributionist concerns, equal-opportunity programmes, even in their watered-down versions, presented high political and economic costs which undermined their chances of implementation. Instead, the new focus on women was accommodated within the official agencies of development by linking it to the emerging concern with *poverty alleviation and basic needs*. Casting women in the role of managers of low-income households and providers of family basic needs retained a reassuring continuity with earlier welfare approaches, in that it focused on women's responsibility for family and child welfare. However, it also incorporated the WID concern with women's productive roles by recognizing that these responsibilities had an economic component and therefore required income-enhancing measures. In practice, though, this approach generally carried few prospects for changing women's position. Defining women's problems in terms of the family's basic needs rather than their unequal access to resources made a WID policy more acceptable within male-dominated agencies, particularly as measures were designed in such a way as to further minimize any potential for change. Income-generating projects took place in sex-segregated environments, usually near the home and, given the continuing influence of sex-role stereotypes, entailed marginal and financially unviable activities chosen for their compatibility with women's repro-ductive/domestic roles rather than for their profitability.

The focus on poverty alleviation and basic needs represented a transitional phase between the early emphasis on women and welfare and the full-blown concern with *efficiency* which has emerged as the dominant theme in current WID policies. Ironically, the shift to efficiency-led WID approaches and the emphasis on women as economic agents in their own right occurred at a time of large-scale deterioration in the world economy when the ability of whole nations to act as sovereign agents was under threat. The overriding concern of the major donors, under the aegis of the International Monetary Fund (IMF) and the World Bank, became the recovery of Third World debt and the resolution of balance-of-payments crises. Programmes of economic austerity, privatization and trade liberalization were made the conditions on which the international financial agencies were prepared to lend to countries in need of loans. Behind these programmes was a neo-liberal ideology which maintained that the dismantling of bureaucratic controls and greater reliance on free market forces to allocate national resources were the most efficient route to economic recovery (see Colclough and Manor, 1991).

A version of the efficiency argument had always been an important strand in WID scholarship and advocacy: the idea that women were productive agents whose potential had been underutilized under welfare-oriented approaches. With the ascendancy of free market philosophies in donor agendas, there was increased emphasis on this argument. Competitive market forces, free of the prejudices and biases of development planners, were the obvious mechanism to generate gender-neutral opportunities for self-improvement. Women were given increasing recognition as key agents in the development process – as the new micro-entrepreneurs, as the 'nimble fingers' behind the export successes of global market factories and the food farmers who would solve sub-Saharan Africa's food crisis. It appeared that Boserup's plea that women's economic agency be recognized had finally been taken to heart.

Conclusion

As a result of research and policy interventions during the Women's Decade, we now know a great deal more about the commonalities, differences and complexities that characterize women's lives through-out the world. Earlier cultural stereotypes have been scrutinized, statistics are increasingly collected on a sex-disaggregated basis, anti-discriminatory laws have been passed, and the majority of governments now have some form of 'national machinery' for the advancement of women. *And yet*, despite the apparent successes of WID advocacy, women continue to occupy a marginal place in development thought and policy. General texts on development may contain the obligatory chapter on women; general conferences on development may have the obligatory session on women; general policy reports may contain the obligatory references to women. But the mainstream of the development effort remains unreconstructed. Moreover, in recent years, as sections of the Third World undergo a painful process of debt repayment and economic adjustment, it seems that some of the basic gains won by women are being clawed back. The UN's (1989b) *World Survey on the Role of Women in Development* summarized the 1980s thus:

> while some women have improved their position, far more have become poor. Ironically, poverty among women has increased, even within the richest countries, resulting in a 'feminization of poverty'. Poverty particularly afflicted families in which women are the sole income earners, a growing phenomenon . . . Increases in maternal and infant mortality in some developing countries have been observed for the first time in decades as social services have been cut as part of adjustment packages.

Echoing this report is the verdict of a Commonwealth Secretariat report on women's situation in the Third World at the end of the eighties:

> Women have been at the epicentre of the crisis and have borne the brunt of the adjustment efforts. They have been the most affected by the deteriorating balance between incomes and prices, by the cuts in social services, and by the rising morbidity and child deaths. It is women who have had to find the means for families to survive. To achieve this they have had to work longer and harder. (1989, p. 5)

In other words, over a decade of WID policy has achieved a great deal in terms of 'symbolic politics' (Staudt, 1985) but rather less in terms of concrete achievements.

There are, of course, other ways of thinking about the problems of women and development. Critiques of WID strategies have existed almost as long as WID itself, and they continue to challenge the premisses and question the terms on which development institutions seek to 'integrate women into development'. They help to uncover some of the critical omissions and assumptions in early WID thinking which rendered the nature of this 'integration' so problematic. In the next chapter I will provide a brief and necessarily selective account of the theoretical underpinnings of WID, along with some of the important critiques levelled against it, before going on to consider some of the alternative approaches to the question of women and development.

2

Treating Cancer with Bandaid?: The Theoretical Underpinnings of WID

As long as girls remain under the twofold handicap of a family education which suppresses their self-confidence and of training facilities in schools and elsewhere which are inferior to those given to boys, they are bound to be inferior workers. (Boserup, 1970, p. 220)

Teaching women better techniques . . . as Boserup suggests, would have been like treating cancer with bandaid (Beneria and Sen, 1981, p. 287)

Ideology, Pragmatism and the Making of a Field

Different social actors have been involved in the making of the WID perspective in development. Tinker (1990b) distinguishes between three categories. There are the scholars who have helped to compile a wide range of research, of both a theoretical and practical nature, in response to the informational requirements of various development institutions (the UN agencies, the bilateral donors, non-governmental organizations and governments). There are the advocates who have lobbied powerful policymakers to incorporate women more success- fully into the development process. Finally, there are the practitioners, women and men working within the various agencies, whose primary concern is with fulfilling the policy mandate of their institutions to integrate women into development. These groups have different concerns, are accountable to different constituencies and subject to different constraints, all of which shape the nature of their contribu- tions to the interpretation of WID issues. According to Tinker, 'WID advocates and practitioners, because their objective is to influence the

11

development community, tend not to raise basic theoretical issues but rather seek to adjust current development practices to include and benefit women' (1990b, p. 48). Scholars differ in that, 'constrained neither by the existing governmental systems nor by agency bureaucracies, they are free to utilize ideologies or images of the future to test and judge contemporary issues'. Among scholars, however, she distinguishes between those who share the 'pragmatic' perspectives and 'non-ideological' stance of WID advocates and practitioners and those 'who are consumed with theoretical arguments, however far they may be removed from reality' (p.48). The non-ideological stance of WID pragmatists, she suggests, evokes hostility among more theoretically inclined scholars.

Tinker is right to emphasize both the importance of the differing institutional constraints within which WID advocates, scholars and practitioners work and the existence of a common 'pragmatic' agenda unifying many of them. It is misleading, however, to characterize this agenda as non-ideological. It can be perceived as non-ideological only because it reflects a world-view which is dominant in the international development community. The hegemonic character of this world-view, its taken-for-granted assumptions about the nature of social reality, renders it invisible, dispensing with the need to spell out the theoretical premises upon which it is founded. Advocates and scholars who share this world-view are described as 'pragmatic' because they seek reformist goals that preserve the status quo, rather than redistributive ones that challenge it. Attributing a shared world-view to an apparently diverse group of actors, many of whom deliberately eschew all references to theory and ideology, carries the danger of imposing coherence and intentionality where there is frequently confusion and 'ad-hocery'. However, no advocacy, scholarship or policy is entirely free from theory or innocent of ideology. It is necessarily through theoretical lenses that we view social problems, and the world-views of powerful development agencies are likely to have a profound influence on the kinds of research and advocacy they are likely to fund, listen to and act upon (Maguire, 1984). Thus the 'pragmatism' noted by Tinker as a characteristic of the WID constituency in development emerges out of a frequently submerged, but nevertheless powerful, set of assumptions which it shares with the dominant development agencies. It explains certain commonalities in the critiques of development offered by WID scholars and advocates, the policy implications that flow from them, and the vision of progress they embody.

The main elements of this 'liberal-equilibrium' world-view have been summarized by Paulston and cited in Maguire (1984). It envisions a society which constantly strives towards a state of equilibrium. All members of society are assumed to share the basic values of possessive individualism, the pursuit of a greater share of material goods. As long as they are free to pursue their own goals, individuals will be in competition with each other, given that the availability of material goods is always finite. But fundamental social conflict is ruled out; inequalities within the system are the regrettable but necessary price for individual freedom and productivity. Change within this perspective is seen in incremental and evolutionary terms; individuals spontaneously and functionally adjust their behaviour to changes in their environment in ways which converge to a new equilibrium.

The model of the atomized self-interested individual that is at the core of the liberal world-view informs many of the mainstream paradigms of the social sciences and plays an important role in framing official policies and practices. In the rest of this chapter, I will trace the influence of the liberal world-view and the vision of progress it embodies, within some of the key paradigms in development studies. I will argue that while WID scholarship and advocacy sought to reformulate certain ideas associated with the liberal world-view, it shares many of the latter's core assumptions about the role of individuals as agents in the development process. I will conclude by pointing to some of the limitations associated with the WID reformulation for comprehending and transforming the position of women in the development process.

Economic Theory: The Enthronement of Economic Growth in Development Studies

Liberal neo-classical economics has always played a central role in the evolution of development studies and in the formulation of development policy. It can be credited with the persisting emphasis given to economic growth as the primary goal and meaning of development, despite equally persistent attempts at 'dethronement'. In general, liberal market-oriented models of economic growth have set the broad parameters for development planning and framed the fluctuating significance accorded to markets, states and non-governmental organizations as alternative agencies of resource allocation in the development process.

'Economics,' as Lionel Robbins puts it in a widely cited description of the discipline, 'is the science which studies human behaviour as a relationship between ends and scarce means which have alternative uses' (1935, p. 16). His description contains many of the key words of the discipline: *behaviour, science, ends, means, scarcity* and *alternatives*. The simplifying core of economic theory is the assumption that all agents within society are essentially and universally motivated by the attempt to maximise their individual utilities or satisfaction, the 'ends' of economic endeavour. However, because the means at their disposal are limited in relation to their needs, they must decide how to allocate these means between competing alternative uses in order to maximize their utilities, viz. achieve the highest possible level of satisfaction. The ability to allocate scarce means between competing ends in order to maximize utility is referred to as 'rational' behaviour. All agents in the economic universe are utility maximizers although they may define utility differently: for firms, utility may reside in profit maximization, while for households, utility may relate to consumption or leisure.

Given these behavioural principles, the condition for economic growth is seen as individual choice buttressed by the institutions of private property and free markets. Individual choice implies the pursuit of self-defined goals, unimpeded by the value judgements or compulsions of others. Since individual choice is regarded as purely subjective, no external agent can judge what is best for the individual; each agent is the best judge of her own self-interest. Liberal economists are generally reluctant to make evaluative comparisons between individual wants and preferences, the 'ends' of economic activity. These are generally taken as exogenously given, viz. outside the domain of economic analysis. They focus instead on the 'means' by which individuals satisfy their wants as an effective index of choice. Indeed the separation of means and ends is a hallmark of liberal economics: 'The economist is not concerned with ends as such. He is concerned with the way in which the attainment of ends is limited. The ends may be noble or they may be base. They may be "material" or "immaterial" . . . But if the attainment of one set of ends involves the sacrifice of others, then it has an economic aspect' (Robbins, 1935, p. 25). Since the means by which human beings achieve their ends are always limited, individual agents have to compete in order to maximize their share of the available resources through which they will realize their subjectively determined ends.

Private property is seen as a critical institutional support for ensuring rational competitive behaviour. If individuals are not guaranteed rights to the results of their efforts, there will be no incentive for them to seek to maximize their welfare through their own efforts. Markets arise because as societies move from self-provisioning to complex divisions and specializations of labour, prices provide a decentralized mechanism through which exchange takes place and information is disseminated. The 'magic of the market' lies in its potential for promoting choice with efficiency. Market prices signal the existence of scarcities and surpluses within an economy; individual agents are free to respond as they wish. However, failure to respond rationally (increasing supplies of a commodity and reducing demand when its prices are high, and reversing the pattern when prices are low) will carry penalties which will only disappear when individual agents have adjusted their behaviour appropriately. As long as individual agents behave rationally in response to market signals, the market will ensure that a multitude of potentially conflicting choices persistently converge towards a 'Pareto-equilibrium': a condition where no one can become better off without someone else becoming worse off.

By aggregating the operations of the individual units that make up the economy, economists build a theory of the behaviour of the entire economy. Identical behavioural principles are posited as the analytical focus broadens from individual units to nations. If nations specialize within the international division of labour, according to the comparative advantages bestowed by their pattern of endowments, each nation concentrating on those commodities which it produces relatively more cheaply than others and relying on free trade to acquire goods which it produces relatively more expensively, then the same *laissez faire* principles which assure a locally optimal equilibrium will also assure a globally optimal one.

Neo-classical economics thus claims to offer a non-prescriptive or 'positivist' science for predicting how different agents within the economy will, if left to their own devices, choose to allocate the finite resources at their disposal between competing uses in order to maximize both individual and social good. No value judgments are attached to these individual choices. As Solow puts it, 'One of the elegant showpieces of economics is its analysis of the resource-allocation implications of a system of prices or shadow prices. We have learned to free this analysis of ethical overtones' (1963, p. 10).

Modernization Theory and Development by Stages

Sociologists staked an early place in development studies, not so much by questioning the content of the growth models of economists, but by suggesting that they 'presuppose certain social and cultural conditions which sociologists are equipped to analyse' (Bernstein, 1979, p. 80). Modernization theory developed out of this claim. It built on the analysis of the social changes that occurred in the course of Western growth and industrialization to identify and separate out the 'non-economic' factors which are likely either to promote or inhibit economic development. Modernization theory perceived development as an evolutionary, unilinear process of change which took societies from their pre-modern status through a series of stages towards the final destination of modernity. Each stage was different and superior to the previous one, so development was depicted as a cumulative process of improvement in living standards. Modernization implied the 'total' transformation of pre-modern societies: their institutions, their cultures and the behaviours they promoted. Institutions became more differentiated and specialized in their functions, creating a corresponding differentiation and expansion of the possible roles available to individuals within society. Family and kinship lost its central place in the institutional structure as many of its earlier functions were transferred to the now separately constituted and distinct public spheres of economy and state.

Modern societies institutionalized individualism. The new roles available to individuals – and the statuses associated with them – were increasingly *achieved* as a consequence of purposeful individual effort rather than *ascribed* by norms and custom. They involved individuals in impersonal and specialized interactions, governed by universalistic standards, in contrast to pre-modern societies whose systems of caste and patronage brought their occupants into more particularistic and diffuse relationships. Along with the shift from ascribed to achieved roles and statuses, modernization encouraged the flowering of rational self-interest in place of the earlier reliance on superstition and tradition as the guiding principles of individual behaviour.

While modernization theorists used different combinations of social and economic factors to explain the process of change, they generally shared a common emphasis on changes in values and attitudes as a critical prerequisite for the transition to the modern society. They attributed the 'backwardness' of the Third World to the absence of the values associated with rational individualism, together with the socio-economic institutions through which such values could flourish and be rewarded.

Modernization, Economic Growth and the Rise of the Modern Individual

Modernization theory and liberal economics can be seen to offer complementary analyses of the rise of the modern individual in the course of development. Although economists talked of 'economic man' in free-floating, ahistorical terms, they were in fact talking about a very specific kind of individual:

> let us consider the individuals who make up an economy. People have many and varied wants. . . . Until man has reached a fairly high level of attainment, the systemisation of these wants and the ordering of preferences within the possibilities permitted to the individual . . . is not possible. Where this high level has not been reached, man's behaviour will be determined entirely according to custom or impulse (Morishima, 1976, p. 12).

If modern man was defined as 'a being with a systematic will which conforms with rational rules' (Morishima, 1976, p. 13), then certain preconditions ('a high level of attainment') are necessary to bring him into existence. 'Modern man' was the product of the modernization process – Morishima's emphasis is on the educational system as a vehicle of socialization – and was himself a condition for further modernization and economic growth. 'Modern' man and 'economic' man were in fact the same individual and could be characterized by a common set of attitudinal variables which made up rational behaviour: innovativeness, dynamism, competitiveness and risk-taking.

And what about modern woman? Very few of the early development theorists directly addressed the effects of development on women, but those that did offered an optimistic prognosis. It was generally agreed that women would also benefit from the erosion of primordial relationships and superstitious beliefs, but differently from men, because of their different roles in modern society (Tiano, 1984). Modernization and development would lead to a replacement of the traditional extended family, the site of virtually all social activities, by the modern nuclear family, separated off from the public sphere of production. Within the family there would be an increasing division of labour, with women and men specializing in different aspects of household activities. For economists, this division of labour would reflect the principle of comparative advantage (Becker, 1965). Given women's central role in procreation, it would be rational for them to specialize in domestic labour, which was compatible with this role, while men specialized in full-time production for the market. Sociologists, such as Talcott Parsons, interpreted this division of labour in terms of socially functional role-differentiation (see Johnson, 1989). Women and men were socialized into personality types that fitted them for different roles within the family. Men specialized in instrumental roles and acquired the characteristics that went with them: rational, objective, competitive and aggressive. Women were entrusted with the affective, homemaking role within the private sphere of family life. This division into complementary, non-overlapping roles was necessary for the smooth functioning of both family and society: it eliminated competition between husband and wife, ensured the proper socialization of children, and allowed the family to act in unison in relation to the rest of the world.

However, since status was no longer based on ascribed and diffuse relationships, but on individual choice and achievement, women were not necessarily disadvantaged within this system. Technological change would reduce the social impact of biological asymmetry between men and women's physical strength and release women from the time-consuming drudgery of housework, while birth-control technology would give them freedom from the endless cycle of involuntary reproduction (Jaquette, 1982, p. 269). In principle, therefore, women were free to enter the marketplace as long as their jobs were compatible with their primary role as homemakers. Both economists and modernization theorists ascribed a liberating potential to the market: it was seen as the arena where universalistic criteria applied and where individuals were impersonally rewarded on the basis of objective results rather than good intentions, patronage networks or 'ascribed' characteristics such as sex, caste or race. However, even women who chose not to enter the labour force would benefit. Modernization would lead to the spread of liberal, egalitarian values which would help to undermine old, authoritarian structures within the family.

A great deal of early sociological research on women and development was cast in the framework of modernization and sex-role theory. It was premissed, as Jaquette (1982) points out, on the assumption that

> traditional societies are male-dominated and authoritarian, and modern societies are democratic and egalitarian. The process of modernization itself, and the administration of development policies and programs, are perceived as sex-neutral or as particularly advantageous to women, who have been more hemmed in than men by traditional values circumscribing their roles. (p. 269)

There was a proliferation of sociological studies which claimed to measure 'modernity' in women on the basis of changing roles and attitudes. This is typified in the following quotation from a study of modernity in Brazilian women:

Industrialisation encourages new attitudes and behaviour and stresses experiences which enhance [women's] competence and feelings of self-respect, and alters their relationships with others – particularly family members. . . . Everyday experiences in city streets and in stores and shops, sharpen their faculties and sensitize them to the importance of competence and achievement. The opportunities for employment outside the home enrich them intellectually as well as financially. (Rosen and La Raia, 1972, p. 354, cited in Jaquette, 1982, p. 269).

Economists who touched on the implications of development for women offered similarly optimistic scenarios of changing roles, laying special emphasis on the opportunities it would offer women to exercise their rationality – the hallmark of 'economic man' – and thus to attain full personhood. This is how Lewis, an early and influential proponent of industrial growth for the Third World, summarized this view:

Women benefit from (growth) even more than men . . . Woman gains freedom from drudgery, is emancipated from the seclusion of the household, and gains at last the chance to be a full human being, exercising her mind and her talents in the same way as men. It is open to men to debate whether economic progress is good for men or not, but for women to debate the desirability of economic growth is to debate whether women should have the chance to cease to be beasts of burden, and to join the human race. (Lewis, 1955, p. 422)[1]

The WID Critique of Development:
Planners and Prejudice

The WID point of departure from this earlier intellectual tradition stemmed from doubts over the presumed neutrality of the agencies of development and modernization. Contrary to early expectations, women had not been given access to new productive opportunities; technology had not liberated them from domestic drudgery; and market forces had not led to gender-neutral outcomes. Prejudice and preconceptions about women persisted in society in spite of the forces of modernization.

The critiques offered by some of the early WID scholars are worth examining in some detail for what they reveal about their departures from mainstream development thinking – as well as about their convergences. They make clear that WID advocacy in development retained the fundamental premisses of the liberal world-view. It was not the mainstream model of modernization that was under attack, but the fact that women had not benefited from it. It was not the market solution per se that had failed women, but planners and employers – and sometimes women themselves – whose irrational prejudices and misplaced assumptions led to discriminatory outcomes. The problem, therefore, was how to ensure that the benefits of modernization reached women; or, in the language of the UN Decade, how to ensure the integration of women into development. Since these benefits were generated in the modern sector and the cash economy, via the agency of the market, the solution lay in improving women's access to the market and the public sphere. These arguments are best illustrated by examining three influential examples drawn from the WID literature: Boserup's *Women's Role in Economic Development* (1970); Tinker's 'The Adverse Impact of Development on Women' (1976); and Rogers' *The Domestication of Women: Discrimination in Developing Societies* (1980).

Boserup's analysis laid the groundwork for subsequent WID analysis. She drew attention to variations in sex roles across cultures and suggested that, since women were almost always primarily responsible for reproductive work, it was differences in their productive roles that were the key variables explaining differences in their status across the world: where women were confined primarily to reproductive work, their status was likely to be low. In what she termed 'female farming systems', prevailing in much of sub-Saharan Africa and parts of Southeast Asia, women enjoyed 'considerable freedom of movement and some economic independence' (p. 50) based on their significant role in production. This was in marked contrast to the restrictions imposed on women in the 'male farming systems' of South and West Asia whose status was based primarily on their fulfilment of their reproductive roles.

The failure of modernization to benefit women was attributed to a variety of factors reflecting these different cultural contexts. In female farming systems, particularly in sub-Saharan Africa, women had been deprived of access to training, land rights, education and technology by colonial and post-colonial administrators whose biased perceptions led them to favour male farmers. In the market economies of the Third World, employers demonstrated a preference for men, creating a sex-stereotyped job hierarchy, while women's own prejudices and preferences inhibited them from seeking employment in the modern sector. This led to a divergence in attitudes, since 'Employment in the modern sector requires not only formal training, but also a certain attitude to work which may best be described as the capacity to work regularly and attentively. . . . Those who work within the confines of the family are not likely to acquire this attitude' (p. 214). Boserup thus subscribed to the basic elements of the modernization model, but attacked its failure to deliver the goods to women in the Third World. The modern economy being promoted by development planners had brought new resources and opportunities to men, but left women on the margins of development. Consequently, 'the productivity, attitude and outlook of men and women begin to diverge, just as we found happening when commercial farming replaced subsistence agriculture; men become familiar with modern equipment and learn to adapt themselves to modern ways of life, while women continue in the old ways' (p. 139).

Boserup's final chapter, 'The Design of Female Education', contained her main recommendations for policy. She pointed out that 'women's way to employment in the modern sector is barred not only by women's prejudices, but also by their lack of proper qualifications' (p. 212). She condemned the tendency of planners to see women as 'secondary' earners and to train them to be more efficient housewives rather than seeking to improve their professional ability to compete equally with men in the marketplace. She concluded by calling for better-designed education for women to enhance their competitiveness and productivity in the economy.

A similar focus on misinformation and prejudice in the planning process is found in Tinker (1976). She suggested that 'Western stereotypes of appropriate roles and occupations tended to be exported with aid' (p. 33) so that modernization continuously widened the gap between the ability of men and women to cope with the modern world. The problem stemmed from the Western glorification of women's child-bearing roles and the concomitant downgrading of the economic functions associated with child care and housework. These attitudes were then disseminated throughout the world: 'Accepting this stereotype of women's roles, economic theorists in the West imbued their students, indigenous and foreign, with the cliché that "women's place is in the home" classifying them forever as economically dependent' (p. 22).

A major consequence of these stereotypes was the invisibility of women's productive roles in the planning process: 'planners, generally men − whether in donor-country agencies or in recipient countries − have been unable to deal with the fact that women must perform two roles in society, while men perform only one' (p. 22). Planners, Tinker suggested, needed to rethink the 'mythical stereotypes' which led labour-force statistics to be defined only in terms of work performed for money and work located in the modern sector. The definition of work had to include subsistence labour, child care and work in the tertiary and informal sectors, otherwise development would continue to have an adverse impact on women. Three common types of planning errors were identified by Tinker:

- Omission: failure to notice and utilize women's roles in traditional society.
- Reinforcement: projects which merely reinforced pre-existing values that restricted women's roles to domestic and child-bearing activities.
- Addition: superimposition of Western values regarding appropriate work for women upon customary values and practices.

However, while it was clear that Tinker laid the blame for development failures on misinformed and misguided male planners, it was not clear why such errors appeared to be so widespread and systematic. The question raised by her analysis is whether organizations which systematically throw up particular categories of errors and misconceptions are capable, with the right information and training, of producing well-informed and well-designed development for women. The answer would be in the affirmative only if the original problems were indeed products of prejudice and misinformation, rather than stemming from the more institutionalized features of the planning process itself.

Rogers' (1980) investigation of the association between women and 'the fringe area' of welfare in development planning was published ten years after Boserup. It came to a similar conclusion: that existing policy represented a form of discrimination based on the imposition of 'those aspects . . . of external influence and intervention which treat women as different from men, not because of their different "traditional" activities and responsibilities, but because of a very specific Western (men's) model of what women in general should be, and what they should and should not do' (p. 35). However, she probed more deeply into the planning process itself than Boserup had and offered fresh insights into the discrimination practised within the major international development agencies and the biases in their data-collection procedures. She provided examples of sex segregation in development planning which had led to an emphasis on training women in domestic skills ('a woman's place is in home economics') and later, with the advent of WID advocacy, on 'special considerations' projects, mainly handicrafts and small-scale income-generating projects.

Rogers' conclusion contained her recommendations for improved planning for women. She drew strongly on the neo-classical notion of universal economic rationality to strengthen her case against Western male planners. She pointed out that while there was growing acceptance that 'primitive' peasants were far from constituting unsurmountable barriers to change, the 'new awareness of peasants as highly rational decision-makers is still stopping at the last frontier: women' (p. 181). Western planners continued to perceive women as 'illogical' and 'irrational' and saw no reason to offer them incentives to participate in the development process. Instead women were either treated as unpaid family labour controlled by male household heads or as unproductive mothers and wives. Using examples from a number of development interventions, she pointed out how denying incentives to women had undermined project performance: 'in these projects, women are expected to provide a major part of the labour force while rights to land are taken away and all financial incentives withheld from them, and given exclusively to their husbands' (p. 186). The result was dissatisfaction, conflict and unmet targets. Planners needed to stop offering 'special projects' that perpetuated women's marginal status and to seek instead to eliminate gender discrimination in *all* project design, in educational provision and in employment. Ways had to be found to save women's labour, improve their productivity and, most important, to ensure that 'incentives for increased production are channelled to the women as well as the men, in proportion to the contributions made by each' (p. 192).

From Welfare to Efficiency: WID Achievements in the Policy Domain

The efforts of WID advocates and scholars led to some important and enduring shifts in the way in which policymakers viewed women's role in the development process and in the policies that resulted. Sociological sex-role theory had been an important component of modernization theory and had taken firm root in the mindset of the development community. It accounted for the particular model of the household (a nuclear family consisting of a male breadwinner/ dependent housewife and children) which underpinned most development interventions. Feminists had already begun to subvert orthodox interpretations of sex roles, no longer viewing them as an expression of social complementarity, but rather as an aspect of women's inferior status in society (Eisenstein, 1984). Sex-role socialization was seen as a key factor in curtailing women's potential, shaping their attitudes, preferences and expectations. It enforced their conformity to the 'expressive' role within the family, one which dictated passivity, obedience and dependence while endowing men with the ambition, achievement and financial rewards associated with the 'instrumental' role.

To this challenge, WID scholars added their own critique, pointing to the malign influence of sex-role theory in the policy process, shaping the provision of resources and responsibilities through which planners sought to promote the domestic roles of women, even in societies where they traditionally performed the bulk of the productive labour. Empirical evidence of the remarkable diversity in the gender division of labour across the world was used by WID advocates to challenge the idea that the male breadwinner/female dependent division of roles was somehow 'naturally given', and helped to shift the thinking around roles from biological explanations to cultural ones. Boserup herself argued strongly against any attempt to make universal or biological generalizations about the division of labour, pointing out that, 'while the members of any given community may think that their particular division of labour between the sexes is the "natural" one, . . . other communities may have completely different ways of dividing the burden of work among the sexes, and they too may find their ways just as "natural"' (p. 15). Rogers incorporated the distinction emerging in the social sciences between sex as 'physical distinction' and gender as 'social and cultural' explicitly into her analysis in order to attack the biologistic explanations of sex roles which underpinned so much of development planning:

> The assumptions that development planners make about women in society are almost never stated, but are all the more powerful for that reason. It is thought 'natural' that a woman's place is in the home and that she has a very specific set of tasks which are thought to be universal because they are based on the biological imperatives of sex. The most important role for women, defining their entire life, is portrayed as the bearing and bringing-up of children. A man, on the other hand, is seen as the 'natural' head of the family, its representative in the outside world, and therefore the person with whom the planners will deal. Since it is assumed that men control families . . . any new resources intended for everyone should logically be channelled through them. (p. 11)

The imprint of sex-role stereotypes on the data-collection practices of development agencies had played a powerful role in defining women as housewives, regardless of the local reality. One important consequence of WID's challenge to the universality of the nuclear family and the sex-role dichotomy was therefore the call for better data on household structures and on the nature of women's work in the Third World. This has resulted in more systematic disaggregation in data-collection efforts within national and international agencies so that the empirical base for planning is now far more refined. More significantly, however, WID advocacy shifted the grounds for investing development resources in women from *welfare* to *efficiency* or, as Jaquette put it (1990), from *need* to *merit*. At a time when women had been primarily associated with the welfare sector in the planning process, WID advocates used efficiency-based arguments for rescuing women from the margins of development and integrating them into the mainstream. Boserup spoke directly to a market conception of merit claims. She accepted the fundamental wisdom of the market model, but argued that policies based on Western notions of women's roles had 'hobbled' potentially efficient producers (Jaquette, 1990). In contrast to appeals based on women's neediness which could be effective but were likely to be short-lived and subject to the arbitrary whims of charity and political expediency, the shift to merit and efficiency as the basis for women's equality in development promised a more resilient basis for WID advocacy.

The efficiency argument was clearly spelt out by Rogers, who hammered home Boserup's message of women as rational economic agents, constrained by discriminatory planning processes. However, Rogers' book, published in 1980, a decade after Boserup's, contained an interesting reversal in the argument connecting women and development. While earlier arguments had stressed the 'adverse impact of development on women', Rogers stressed the adverse impact of women's exclusion on development. In view of the growing economic crisis in the Third World, she suggested that continued neglect of women's productivity was a costly mistake that planners could no longer afford to make. The issue was not so much that women needed development, but that development needed women. It was this kind of argument which, in the end, was most persuasive among the development agencies, since it appeared to feed directly into their concern with the efficient allocation of resources. It has helped to give the efficiency approach its current prominence in WID policy at national and international levels.

The shifts in policy discourse effected by WID advocacy is evident in the strategy documents of some of the major development agencies. We noted some examples of this in Chapter 1 in relation to the UN Decade declarations. A recent review of Nordic donor agencies also draws attention to the shift from the persistent linking of women and welfare in the policy documents of the early period of Nordic development assistance to its current emphasis on an 'integrated approach, i.e. WID issues are to be incorporated into all aspects of

development assistance be it related to the project cycle or administration' (Lexow, 1988, p. 11). A position paper brought out by the
World Bank at the end of the seventies echoes these concerns. It, too,
makes a strong case of integrating women into development on
grounds of economic efficiency: 'If women continue to be left out of
the mainstream of development and deprived of opportunities to
realise their full potential, serious inefficiencies in the use of resources
will persist' (1979, p. 1).

The efficiency argument for WID is most clearly spelt out in the
USAID document *Women in Development Aid Policy* (1982). The
document declares unequivocally that, 'The experience of the past 10
years tells us that the key issue underlying the women in development
concept is an *economic* one' (my emphasis). The theme of women as
rational agents, responsive to incentives and ill-served by past assumptions of passive dependency, is seen as a major rationale for gender
sensitivity in the planning process: 'Knowledge of these gender-role
patterns will assist project planners to maximise the chance of project
success. . . . Incentives for change which are specifically adapted to
gender roles, and are therefore based on a proper assessment of the
stake the population feels in the outcome of the project, is critical to
success.' WID advocacy has thus helped to dislodge the earlier
equation between women and welfare, and placed women and
efficiency firmly on the development agenda – at a time when the
concern with efficiency was once again in the ascendant among the
major international donors. In practice, however, the neo-liberal
interpretation of efficiency is often at odds with some of the goals of
WID advocacy. The new policy stress on women's economic agency has
occurred at a time when major cutbacks in public expenditure as a part
of structural adjustment programmes were leading to the shifting of
responsibility for welfare services from the paid to the unpaid
economy, often through the intensification of women's labour (Elson,
1991a). The recognition of women's productive potential appears to
have been achieved at the expense of appreciation for their unpaid
workload within the household.

The juxtaposition of the neo-liberal agenda of market-led efficiency
with the WID emphasis on women as economic agents has served to
underscore the 'gender trap' for women within the market solution. If
the market is to be the primary mechanism for allocating resources,
then women, who generally have less purchasing power, will be unable
to purchase the support services they need to reduce their domestic
labour overheads. On the other hand, if they are unable to purchase
these labour-replacing services, then they will be unable to pursue the
range of activities that would help them to increase their purchasing

power. In the rest of this chapter, I would like to return to the theoretical underpinnings of WID analysis in order to uncover its limitations in challenging the paradox of the marketplace for women. These may also help to explain why over a decade of WID advocacy has failed to shift the basic and persistent inequalities that women face in the development process.

WID and the Pitfalls of Individualism: Individual Rationality and Gender Equality

WID has been described as liberal feminism writ global. As such, it shares many of the limitations associated with the liberal world-view (Bandarage, 1984; Maguire, 1984; Jaquette, 1982). WID advocacy drew its ideas about equality from the liberal philosophical belief that, despite differences of culture and class, there is an universal and fundamental argument for equality between human beings. This equality derives from their common human essence, the ability to reason, to choose the best means to achieve their goals. Reason is a 'mental' capacity and the property of individuals who constitute the basic units of society. Liberal theory is a theory of the rational individual who logically exists prior to society and is *essentially* the same across societies.

Jagger (1983) has pointed to the 'normative dualism' embedded in this concept of the human being, in that the mind is seen as separate from, and higher than, the body because it is the site of what is essentially human. A series of binary oppositions flowing from this framework is repeated throughout liberal thought (mind/body, culture/nature, mental/manual, rational/instinctual) and permeates the ways in which value is given to labour, creativity and effort. Human effort that requires the exercise of intellectual faculties is given precedence over manual labour; work that is guided by instrumentalist criteria is given precedence over affective labour. It is the claim of liberal theory that all men are equal because they possess this essentially human ability to reason. Liberal feminists extended this claim for equality to women on the grounds that they, too, are rational beings, but have been denied the opportunity to exercise fully their rationality because of constricting socialization processes. The WID contribution was to extend further the logic of the liberal feminist argument to include explicitly women all over the world. They pointed out that global diversity of gender roles demonstrated that such roles were a product of culture rather than nature. Beyond these cultural

differences, however, women and men everywhere shared the fundamental human capacity for reason and were equally entitled to the
opportunities and benefits of development. However, in accepting the
liberal feminist argument for equal opportunities in development,
WID advocates were also bound into its normative dualisms. They
sought to emphasize women's similarities with men (mental) at the
expense of their differences (biological). The glossing over of biological difference in early WID advocacy was an understandable
reaction to the pre-WID preoccupation with women's reproductive
roles and the concomitant stress on welfare provision. The problem
with this kind of argument, however, is its indifference to the social
implications of biology for individual agency, choice and rationality
(Jagger, 1983).

Human lives are characterized by different degrees of physical
dependency – such as infancy, infirmity, disability, ill health, pregnancy – so that individual choice is differentially constrained. In
particular, reproductive biology still differentiates in important ways
the social experience of women and men. Quite simply, the biological
fact that women bear and suckle children (although there are clearly
historical and cultural changes in the reproductive experience and
process) suggests that they are likely to experience the biological world
differently and to participate in the social world differently from men.
There is likely to be a further differentiation in the life experiences of
women and men, linked to the social arrangements through which
biological needs are met. All individuals require a minimum amount of
labour to meet their basic biological needs – for water, food, clothing,
shelter, health care – before they are in a position to consider making
choices or to engage in the production of material resources. Furthermore, particular categories of human beings – the very young, the very
old, the disabled and the sick – require a greater input of daily labour if
they are to survive. In ignoring the social significance of these
biologically derived activities – the needs of the human species and
how they are met – liberal philosophies devalue the labour, time and
energy of those who carry them out. Since a near-universal feature of
the social division of labour is that women are responsible for most of
the labour necessary to reproduce healthy, active human life, on a
daily and on a generational basis, the devaluation of this labour has
powerful gender implications.

First of all, this devaluation relegates a great deal of the time and
energy in women's mothering and caring activities to the realm of
'instinct rather than institutions'. Indeed, the domestic institutions
within which women carry out most of their reproductive activities
are themselves frequently treated as closer to nature, hence more

universal and resistant to social analysis than other institutions (Harris, 1981). The consequences of this in the context of development planning is that such labour is perceived as an extension of women's natural mothering role and therefore denied policy recognition and the resources that would go with such recognition.

Second, it overlooks the implications of the gender division of labour and responsibilities for how women and men perceive their needs and interests, as well for their capacity to act as rational economic agents maximizing self-interested goals. If men and women demonstrate different degrees of responsiveness to economic incentives, the reason may be sought, not only in the biased provision of these incentives, as WID advocates have suggested, but also in the gendered constitution of rationality and agency. Women's labour in the home relieves men of the tasks associated with maintaining both their own bodies and the domestic locations where such maintenance takes place, thereby freeing them to behave 'as if' they were indeed the disembodied rational agents of liberal theory. However, as Butler (1987) points out, the fiction of a disembodied, implicitly male, rationality can only be sustained on the condition that women are identified almost exclusively with the bodily sphere.

The incorporation of the value-laden dichotomy between mind and body into the WID world-view left intact the dominant hierarchy of development priorities which consistently privileged the domain of production, in which men were concentrated, over the domain of reproduction where women were assigned primary responsibility. The WID espousal of the efficiency argument stemmed from the strategic recognition that these latter activities had little value in competitive market-led growth, the goal of much development policy. The WID objective was to demonstrate that in the marketplace women were as good as men: 'that men could be as good as women did not, in this context, appear to be an important consideration' (Eisenstein, 1984, p. 63). Hence the overriding emphasis on women's capacity to display rational economic behaviour without any equivalent emphasis on men's potential for displaying 'feminine' qualities of caring and nurturing.

The WID agenda of better-targeted incentives and opportunities to women in development was certainly a step in the right direction. However, the quest for formal equality with men on the basis of an imputed common rationality posited a false identity of interests between women and men and denied the implications of their differing degrees of 'embodiment' in the processes of human survival, well-being and reproduction. There was little in WID advocacy to remind policymakers about the implications of women's unique responsibility for reproductive work for their ability to exercise economic agency (Beneria and Sen, 1981). The WID neglect of the interconnections between production and reproduction in women's livers is echoed, for instance, in USAID policy, which in 1979 officially defined WID projects as those which increased women's participation, opportunity and income-earning capacities: 'Explicitly excluded from the WID definitions are those projects in which women are recipients of goods (such as contraception or health projects) or of food and services for themselves or their children' (Staudt, 1985, p. 52). Women were being redefined as the agents of development rather than the recipients, but their agency was premissed on a very truncated understanding of their lives.

A further flaw in the overriding focus on efficiency as the basis for women's access to resources is noted by Jaquette (1990). If women are to be given equal access in development because they are considered to have been equal to men in status and productivity – in pre-colonial Africa or in female farming systems – then the grounds for investing in women could be jeopardized by a convincing counterargument that women have always been subjugated. Jaquette warns that the failure to base claims for women's equality on a firm foundation could backfire; 'equality should be argued on its own merit'. It should not be based on a history of women's equality that is vulnerable to historical refutation or on claims about women's productivity that could be overturned by future studies that 'prove' that men have higher productivity.

Individual Rationality and Global Sisterhood

The emphasis on disembodied rationality as the basis of gender equality which allowed WID advocates to emphasize similarities between women and men also led to an early emphasis on similarities between women. While recognizing, and indeed highlighting, differences in gender roles across the world, WID analysis pointed to commonalities in women's exclusion from market opportunities in both First and Third Worlds, the common denial of their ability to act as rational agents, and the common focus on their domestic/ reproductive roles. The identification of 'malestream' Western planners as the chief architects of the global domestication of women served simultaneously to 'name' a common enemy and to assert a global commonality of interests among women. It is of course true that many aspects of women's exclusion from development could be laid at the door of the Western and Western-educated male elites that devised policies and commissioned research in national and international agencies. However, the selective focus on commonalities in the marginalization of women in the development process served to disguise and deny material differences in power, resources and interests between women themselves. It privileged a particular interpretation of women's needs and interests over others which might reflect more accurately important differences in their social realities.

From the earliest days of WID advocacy, there have been tensions between First and Third World women as to how the problem of women in development was to be conceptualized. The themes of the Women's Decade were, to a large extent, a compromise between the demands of First World women (equality), Third World women (development), and the socialist bloc (peace). The dominance of the voices of First World women in articulating their version of the problems and priorities of Third World women frequently led to acrimonious debates in a number of international forums.

A common feature of the dissent from WID was the insistence that the subordination of women could not be divorced from an analysis of the political and economic structures within which women were located. This, for instance, was the point made as early as 1972 by a high-level commission authorized by the government of India to report on the situation of women in the country. The Commission's Report (Government of India, 1974) drew attention to the fact that, although economic development in India had benefited large numbers of educated and middle-class women, the majority of Indian women lived in increasing poverty. While the findings of the Report that women had been marginalized in the development process converged with those of WID scholars in the North, its analysis differed considerably in that it laid the blame, not simply on ill-informed planning, but on structural inequalities within the development process itself.

This basic conclusion was repeated in a number of subsequent critiques of WID analysis which came from a variety of quarters, but in particular from Third World feminists. In their examination of Boserup's work, Beneria and Sen (1981) challenged her basically benevolent view of modernization and her neglect of the systemic interconnections between social processes of capital accumulation, class formation and the changing situation of women. In the light of these broader processes of inequality, they described the idea that women's declining status could be halted by better education and training as 'treating cancer with bandaid'. Boserup's policy conclusions were all the more paradoxical as she explicitly acknowledged the large numbers of educated unemployed men in Third World cities who had not been absorbed into the modern labour force. She had also dealt at some length with the sex segmentation in the modern sector which led to women's confinement to low-skill, underpaid and casual forms of employment. Consequently her faith in female education as the route to women's integration into the modern sector was remarkably optimistic.

The indifference displayed by many WID advocates to the interlocking structural asymmetries within and between nations and their faith in the reformability of a market-led development process were also challenged by Bandarage. She attributed their optimism to the fundamental belief that women's poverty and subordination were 'simply aberrations within an otherwise just and equitable social system', the results of 'traditional values and male ignorance', rather than 'a structural feature of a social system which puts the profits of a few before the human needs of the many' (p. 499). Her conclusion was that the solutions needed were political rather than merely technical.

DAWN, a network of activists, policymakers and researchers from the Third World, suggested that the problems of development were not unique to the Third World (Sen and Grown, 1985). Within the First World, too, there had always been those who had been marginalized in the processes of market-led growth and whose dissonant voices had not been heard in the mainstream of the Western feminist movement. For poor women and women from racially and nationally disadvantaged groups, the priorities were frequently food, housing, jobs, services and the struggle against racism rather than equality with men: 'Equality with men who themselves suffered unemployment, low wages, poor work conditions and racism within the existing socio-economic structures did not seem an adequate or worthy goal' (p. 18). As DAWN pointed out, many Third World women were caught between their reluctance to separate the struggle against women's subordination from other struggles against poverty, apartheid and neo-colonialism, on the one hand, and their unwillingness to compromise the struggle against women's subordination or to relegate it to some distant future, on the other. Given the very different positioning of Third World women within intersecting structures of oppression, the idea of a global sisterhood defined by First World women, or of integration into a development process initiated by First World donors or the elite classes in their own countries, were viewed as deeply uninviting prospects.

The notion of the global sisterhood was also challenged by AAWORD, a network of African researchers. They rejected the analysis and strategies of Western women 'who insisted on prioritizing problems of inequality between the sexes as the fundamental issue facing all women and argued that the interests of men and women were opposed and mutually exclusive' (AAWORD, 1982). They pointed out that most research on women in Africa, before and during the Women's Decade, was being carried out by Western women academics whose priorities were to challenge the sexist assumptions of male-dominated social sciences, to evaluate the adverse impact of development on women, and to recommend ways of integrating them into the development process. While acknowledging that such research had led to more informed interventions by the development agencies, AAWORD disputed that this agenda sufficed to constitute a global constituency of women in development:

> While patriarchal views and structures oppress women all over the world, women are also members of classes and countries that dominate others and enjoy privileges in terms of access to resources. Hence, contrary to the best intentions of 'sisterhood', not all women share identical interests. (AAWORD, 1982, p. 105)

On the contrary, the unequal world order ensured that WID interventions were also distorted by the politics of development and reflected the divergent experiences, interests, needs and orientations of women from the North. WID scholarship rarely acknowledged that the distortions brought about by colonial penetration in the global distribution of power, privilege and resources also extended to the unequal terms on which First and Third World women entered into the development policy domain, whether as researchers, advocates or practitioners. Nor did the WID agenda offer any challenge to the kind of development that was being promoted by the international agencies and their national representatives; 'African women have begun to ask what exactly is the nature of this "development" from which they alone have been excluded and into which they now should be integrated. Have colonialism in the past and the asymmetrical world economy and political reality been so generous as to put all males in structurally dominant and skilled positions?' (p. 106).

The problem with development was, therefore, not that its benefits had been dichotomously distributed, with uniform benefits for all men and uniform disadvantages for all women. The problem was rather that the development model on offer was itself inherently asymmetrical. Third World countries had little autonomy in determining their own development trajectories as long as power and resources were concentrated in the hands of a few Northern countries. Consequently most men and many women were, and had always been, integrated into the development process, but on asymmetrical terms which were determined by the interweaving of relations of class, gender and the international economic order.

Individual Rationality and Male Power

A final limitation stemming from the methodological individualism of the WID world-view was its failure to consider the question of male power as a property of gender relations. As we noted earlier, WID scholars blamed women's marginalization in the development process on culturally biased stereotypes and preconceptions that had distorted planners' perceptions about the nature of women's contributions. The implication was that resocialization of planners, through well-reasoned argument and more accurate data, would lead to revised attitudes and more equitable planning. One of a series of conversations with various representatives of international agencies recorded by Rogers (1980, p. 55) suggests how this might happen:

> FAO representative: I've just been filling in a questionnaire from head-quarters about women. But you know there's hardly anything to say, because we don't have the sort of projects that would involve them. We have nothing against them, in fact we like to have more for them, but you see all our projects here are concerned with cattle, and it just so happens that women have very few cattle. Of course, we get criticized because cattle are owned by richer people.
>
> Rogers: Is it perhaps more than just a coincidence that all money is going into cattle and almost nothing for crops, when cattle are men's responsibility and crops are women's?
>
> FAO representative: I never really saw it like that. But I suppose that there is a connection.

While this conversation hints at the way in which gender and class interact to shape the distribution of development resources, it is offered mainly as an example of what Tinker called the error of omission: failure to notice and utilize women's roles in traditional society. Rogers suggests that alerting planners to such omissions might persuade them to take them into account in future efforts. However, the idea that better information would result in more enlightened planning was treated with scepticism by AAWORD, which asked: 'Is local recognition of women's vital role in production and reproduction, followed by proper planning, sufficient precondition to solving the multifaceted problems women face?' (p. 106).

Judging from analysis contributed by Dixon (1985), the answer appears to be no, it is not enough. Dixon pointed out that, while definitional and procedural biases had generally led to the invisibility of women's contributions in national statistics, this was not the case in sub-Saharan Africa. Here the agriculture contributions of women farmers had long been documented in labour-force statistics, possibly because independent female farming in the region meant that women farmers were classified as 'self-employed cultivators' rather than 'unpaid family helpers'; possibly because African women often sold their own produce – 'where money is involved, interviewers take notice' (p. 28); or possibly because the temporary or long-term absence of working-age men from some of these regions led interviewers to talk directly to women. Nevertheless, the visibility of women's economic contributions in statistical data had not been matched by a corresponding visibility in the distribution of development resources such as land, livestock, transport, capital equipment, credit, information and training. Dixon concluded:

> It is the blindness to these inequities more than the blindness of invisibility that stands in women's way. The blindness has an institutional and political base. One cannot help concluding that the real issue is who controls the resources distributed to, and deriving from, agricultural households. The reluctance to 'see' women farmers comes not from their invisibility, but from a reluctance to share scarce resources with them. Land, labor, livestock, capital, technology, information, training – all are valued goods that imbue those who own or control them with power and prestige. Why should these resources be shared? Why should institutions be restructured, power bases challenged? (p. 32)

In other words, there are material realities which shape politics and the priorities of planning institutions in ways that a focus on individual bias is likely to miss. The resistance within major planning institutions to any intervention that might 'upset the natural order of things' is explored in some detail in Staudt's illuminating case study of the WID office at USAID (1982; 1985). USAID was one of the first donor agencies to acknowledge its failure to integrate women into its development projects, and it set up a separate WID unit in 1974. The task of the unit was to reorient the agency's programming so as to direct project resources to women in AID-assisted countries. Staudt's analysis of the poor performance of AID's WID policy offers critical insights into the problems that had prevented the WID unit from carrying out what appeared to be a clear mandate. It also suggests the need to go beyond the belief that enlightened planning will result once planners become aware of women's roles in production. Among the problems that the WID office faced were:

- a limited budget ($1 million out of $4 billion);
- a staff of about five women in an agency with around 6,000 employees in the late seventies, and in which men by and large predominated in the professional echelons while women were concentrated in clerical positions;
- ideological resistance from male colleagues, in the form of trivializing comments and personalized attacks on WID advocates' personal appearance and character, jokes, laughter and outright hostility. Accusations of 'exporting women's lib' and destroying the family; tedious jokes about 'developing a woman' or 'what about men in development';
- frequent tendency to discuss women's income-earning or agricultural activities with reference to their own wives;
- lack of veto power or formal authority in the decision-making process. Increasing pressure to make their case in language that mainstream personnel understood, that is, economics and efficiency.

A review by Gordon (1984) on behalf of the Commonwealth Secretariat of Women's Bureaux in six Caribbean countries revealed some degree of similarity in the problems faced: inadequate resources (funds, staff, training); too many demands and unclear policy mandate; inadequate linkages with 'mainstream' ministries; few support staff; reliance on international funding; being caught between political and funding-agency pressures.

It appears, therefore, that setting up WID machineries within donor or government structures to provide accurate information about gender roles is unlikely to guarantee women greater equality in access to development resources. Men's defence of their privileged positions within the agencies is part of the explanation. But there is also an important, but hidden, interpersonal dimension at work here which makes the difficulties encountered by advocates for gender equity within bureaucratic institutions far greater than those encountered in other forms of policy change. It explains the persistent marginalization of WID machineries within their 'host' bureaucracies. Attempting to capture what is at issue here, Staudt makes the following point: 'Those who make policy, predominantly men, live intimately with the group about whom policy is made, and the individual characteristics of that relationship carry over into work relationships and policy thinking in potentially distorting ways' (Staudt, 1985, p. 7). Many of the specific forms of resistance that WID advocates face relate to this fact that, unlike any other form of advocacy aimed at changing institutional norms and practice, advocacy for gender equity impinges directly on the personal beliefs and values, relationships and identities, of those who will have to formulate and implement change.

Thus the principal makers and implementors of policy, primarily men from the elite groups of their societies, do not generally live in intimate power relationship with the poor, with minority groups, or with those whose environments are threatened. The fact that they often live with women leads them to believe that they can generalize from their own experiences: as Lipman-Blum observes, the men who make policies around the world 'have complete faith in their own understanding of women's natures and roles' (1979, p. 6, cited in Staudt, 1985). It also gives them a very personal stake in the existing ideas and practices through which they have acquired their gender identities, and therefore in the outcomes of policies which threaten these ideas and practices. Rogers (1980) noted this earlier on in her encounter with development officials:

> One of the most consistent responses of male planners to the introduction of discussion about women in development is to base their arguments against change on the domestic model familiar to them: 'my wife doesn't work', 'I get on very well with my daughters', 'my mother always said a woman's place is in the home' and other variations on the theme that all women should follow the model of feminine deportment which they consider correct. (p. 50)

Given this deeply entrenched and highly personalized defence of the status quo by agency personnel, it is not surprising that the early WID advocacy for equality of opportunity within the development process met with so little enthusiasm. It also explains why current efficiency approaches (or 'expediency approaches', as Antrobus [1989a, p. 3] has dubbed them) which use recognition of women's productive roles to justify cutting back on resources to them have been so popular within the same agencies. These findings make it evident that the failure to promote gender equity in development policies cannot be attributed solely to a lingering 'irrationality' among planners, but can be seen as a quite rational defence of class and gender interests, both within the planning agencies as well as in the communities 'out there'. As Elson notes, 'policy makers have other goals aside from policy implementation – and preserving male privilege may well be among the more important' (1991b, p. 203).[2]

Conclusion

WID advocacy was grounded in a theory of 'irrational' prejudice and sex-role stereotypes when what was needed was a theory of male power and conflicting gender interests. The concern with individual attitudes, rather than with the larger economic, political and interpersonal power that men exercise over women, is of course inevitable in a theoretical framework which sees the distortions of sex-role socialization as the key explanation of women's disadvantage. However, while sex-role stereotyping partly accounts for the failure of the development agencies to take account of women's productive roles, there were other more material realities as well.

The absence of attempts to devise theories of race roles or class roles is precisely due to the fact that the language of roles cannot capture the exercise of power implicit in racial interactions and class relations. Its very absurdity brings home the contrast between 'the structural and situational perspective used for race and class, on the one hand, and the individualized, essentialist view inherent in the sex roles approach on the other' (Ferree and Hess, 1987, p. 15). Retrospective evaluations of the early WID contribution to development thought and practice have helped both WID advocates and others working in the development field to identify the component missing in the early analysis: the significance of male power as an integral aspect of women's subordination and the need therefore to envisage the WID agenda as a political process.

However, critiques of WID go beyond its neglect of gender politics in the policy domain; they question its theoretical ability and political willingness to address the systemic nature of gender inequality and its connection with other forms of inequality thrown up by the functioning of an asymmetrical world economy. The acceptance by WID advocates of the existing model of development associates them with a particular world-view whose hegemonic status within the development field permits it to be presented as a universally valid and non-ideological agenda. More accurate data may assist in improving planning procedures, but will not bring about the radical revisions that are necessary. Support for WID advocacy within the official agencies of development should not therefore be divorced from a broader political process of transforming these agencies into more accountable, transparent and democratic structures.

Notes

1 I am grateful to Alison Evans for drawing my attention to this quotation.
2 One example of the very real privileges that men within bureaucratic organizations may wish to defend was pointed out to me by Bina Agarwal. She suggests that the Indian women's movement's campaign against dowry

(considered a major underpinning of women's subordination in India), is unlikely to receive much support from male government administrators since men within the Indian administrative service can count on receiving extremely generous dowries, precisely because they are in the bureaucracy. For information on the anti-dowry movement in India, see Palriwala (1989).

3

Same Realities, Different Windows: Structuralist Perspectives on Women and Development

There is no theory which accounts for the oppression of women – in its endless variety and monotonous similarity, cross-culturally and throughout history – with anything like the explanatory power of the Marxist theory of class oppression. (Rubin, 1975, p. 160)

No analysis of the reproduction of labor power under capitalism can explain foot-binding, chastity belts, or any of the incredible array of Byzantine, fetishized indignities, let alone more ordinary ones which have been inflicted upon women in various times and in various places. (Rubin, 1975, p. 163)

Capitalism was partly constituted out of the opportunities for power and profit created by gender relations. It continues to be. (Connell, 1987, p. 104)

Gender, then, like race, is never absent . . . (Whitehead, 1979, p. 11)

Critical Views of Development

While WID scholarship and advocacy became the established voice of feminism within the official agencies of development, there were also other voices in the international arena, dissenting from both the official view of development and the WID perspective within it.[1] Much of this dissent was rooted in a very different analysis of social reality to the one embodied in WID. Described as the critical-conflict world-view, it is summarized by Maguire (1984):

> One assumption of theories within the critical approach is that society is in conflict, not harmony. Societal conflict is rooted in class and group struggles and competition for power and scarce resources. Critical theories seek to explain how domination and oppression are structurally maintained. They expose the function of class-based inequities in systems oriented toward increased production . . . Differential rewards are necessary to keep the working class fragmented and less powerful. . . . Change is explained as an attempt to challenge structural inequities. Unlike the equilibrium approach, the goal of social change is not reform within the existing system but radical transformation of the system itself. Social, political and economic structures should be transformed in order to redistribute power and resources fairly. (pp. 20–21).

The analytical priority given by Marxism to the class struggle in shaping historical and contemporary realities has made it an important wellspring for this world-view. Certain features of Marxist thought have also made it an obvious intellectual starting point for feminists critical of the WID view of development. Its theorization of human nature appeared to promise a perspective on gender that avoided both the biological determinism which WID scholars had argued against, as well as the biology-less individualism which they had adopted. Furthermore, Marxism's concern with the structural basis of exploitation commended it to those feminists working in development who rejected the liberal premiss of complementary and self-equilibrating relations between genders, classes and nations. Bandarage (1984) expressed this position when she wrote,

> Marxists agree with liberal WID thinkers that economic modernization, or more specifically capitalist development, generally marginalizes Third World women. The WID school focuses simply on the outward manifestations of sexual inequality engendered by this process. In contrast, the Marxists claim to understand sexual inequality, structurally and dialectically, as it relates to social class inequality and to the uneven and unequal development of capitalism world-wide. (p. 501)

However, the promise of a more satisfactory analysis of gender inequality in development failed to materialize within the traditional Marxist framework. This failure can be traced to the same reasons that led Hartmann (1986) to describe Marxism as a theory of the development of 'empty places' (p. 10). Marxism helped to explain the hierarchical structures of capitalist production: the emergence of ruling minorities with immense power over the lives of a dispossessed majority, alienated from the means of production; and the persistent reconstitution of reserve armies of labour through which the fluctuating needs of capital could be accommodated. But it manifestly failed to explain why women, rather than men, were systematically located in subordinate positions within the hierarchies of 'empty places' that capitalist accumulation produced. Marxist categories of analysis were, in Hartmann's words, 'sex-blind'. In the rest of this chapter, I will be comparing the traditional Marxist analysis of women's oppression with feminist attempts to use, to extend and to subvert Marxist categories of analysis. I will be pointing to the aspects of women's subordination which these attempts helped to illuminate in a way that traditional Marxism had failed to do, including the gendered composition of institutional hierarchies. I will begin in the next section with a summary of some aspects of Marxism which have underpinned these attempts.

Marxism and the Human Individual

Marxism views human beings as one species among others, with biological needs which, like those of animals, are satisfied in the natural world. Human beings began to distinguish themselves from animals with the first act of *producing* their means of subsistence rather than simply *utilizing* what existed in natural form. By acting on the external world and changing it, human beings also changed themselves and their relationship to the external world, thereby marking an increasing differentiation between themselves and other biological species. Unlike the activity of animals, human labour – or praxis – is reflexive and purposeful; what distinguishes the most clumsy human activities from the most ingenious animal ones is that 'at the end of every labour-process, we get a result that already existed in the imagination of the labourer at its commencement' (Marx, 1970, p. 174). In this view of the human, there is no separation between mind and body; human labour, in the Marxist sense, is *purposeful and reflective activity* rather than blind instinct, on one hand, or the product of a disembodied rationality, on the other.

Recognizing that human biology necessitates some level of interdependence between individuals, Marxism sees human labour as essentially social. The human essence is not some abstract quality inherent in each individual; rather, it is constituted through the 'ensemble of social relations' within which people find themselves in specific historical contexts. The social relations which human individuals form with each other help to organize their activities and to pattern specific modes of production. Human labour is initially directed towards satisfying basic survival needs, but in the process it both produces the means to satisfy human needs and creates new ones. Human beings move beyond biological survival through this dialectical interaction between biological need, human cooperation and the natural environment, interactions which are brought about by human praxis. Since these interactions are subject to historical change, human beings and human consciousness are themselves products of history. In place, therefore, of the liberal view of the human individual existing prior to history, Marxist analysis treats human beings as products of complex, ongoing and interactive processes through which historically constituted needs are met.

The specific mode of organizing labour undertaken in a given society determines the fundamental features of that society and of the nature of its inhabitants: 'It is not the consciousness of men that determines their being, but on the contrary, their social being that determines their consciousness' (Marx, 1968, p. 29). The emergence of language, the accumulation of knowledge through experience, and the institutionalization of practice are rooted in this social character of human labour. However, human labour has the status of an instrument as long as it is harnessed only to meeting the imperatives of physical survival. Only when it has created the conditions which permit the full and free exercise of the human potential does human labour become an end in itself. Two types of condition limit the free development of human potential through labour. The first is that human survival requires a certain necessary labour, the amount and kind varying according to the development of the forces of production. Beyond the realm of necessary labour is the realm of freedom, where the development of human energy and creativity is an end in itself rather than an imperative of survival.

The second condition that curtails the development of human potential is class domination. With the emergence of private property, society has been split into antagonistic classes, defined by their relation to the means of production and hence by their objectively shared conditions and interests. Even when the productive forces are sufficiently developed to release society into a realm of freedom, the existence of exploitative class relations thwarts its emergence. The Marxist critique of capitalism rested on this prognosis. Capitalism was incapable of satisfying basic human need and realizing full human potential because the means of production were in the hands of a small minority who exploited the labour of the dispossessed majority for the accumulation of profit rather than the satisfaction of need. The Marxist view of society is thus one of conflict between classes, rather than competition between individuals. In place of the liberal stress on self-adjusting and stabilizing mechanisms that are capable of reconciling individual competition with the social good, Marxists see the struggle for power and scarce resources as endemic to class society.

Marxism and 'the Woman Question'

Given the significance attached to human labour in Marxist thought, its account of women's oppression, not unexpectedly, begins with the 'original' division of labour in pre-class societies within a two-fold production process:

> According to the materialist conception, the determining factor in history is, in the final instance, the production and reproduction of immediate life. This, again, is of a two-fold character: on the one side, the production of the means of existence, of food, clothing and shelter and the tools necessary for that production; on the other side, the production of human beings themselves, the propagation of the species. (Engels, 1972, p. 71)

According to Engels, 'The first division of labour [was] that between man and woman for the propagation of children' (p. 129). Based on the needs of procreation, it was a 'pure and simple outgrowth of nature'. Men provided the means of subsistence while women were concerned with the production and reproduction of human life. Associated with this division of labour was an egalitarian and complementary division of spheres of responsibility. Both contributions were seen as vital to the community so that both sexes enjoyed equal status. Changes in the relations of production, associated with the development of agriculture and the domestication of animals, led to the production of a surplus and the accumulation of wealth. Men's control over this wealth and their need to pass it on to identifiable heirs led to the overthrow of mother-right on which earlier communities had been based, and laid the institutional foundations of women's subjugation, private property, monogamous marriage and patrilineal inheritance: 'The first class opposition that appears in history coincides with the development of the antagonism between man and woman in monogamous marriage, and the first class oppression coincides with that of the female sex by the male' (Engels, 1972, p. 129).

In later history, the emergence of a generalized market economy, the distinguishing feature of the capitalist mode of production, led to a cleavage between the production of commmodities, which was shifted to the public sphere of the marketplace, and production of human life and labour, which continued in the private sphere of the home. Monogamy remained indispensable to class society since it was one of the main institutional supports of private property. Its persistence prevented women from participating in public life fully and thereby shedding their dependent status. However, there was now an important difference between working-class women and those from the capitalist class. Working-class families had no private wealth to pass on, so that working-class women had fewer constraints and more incentives to enter the labour force. Early Marxists predicted that working-class women (and children) would in fact enter industry in large numbers. As workers, they would be freed from the oppression of their dependent family status and subject only to the same exploitative process as working-class men. Thus the entry of women into the public arena of production would serve both to end their oppression as women and build their solidarity with working-class men. In reality, however, the large-scale entry of women into public production did not occur in much of the capitalist world, and where women entered waged work they did so on persistently less favourable terms than men. Feminists have had to revise Marxist theory, both to take account of the observed marginalization of women in the process of capital accumulation and to address its conceptual weaknesses.

An obvious target of feminist criticism has been the narrow interpretation of production embedded in Marxist thought. Despite ad hoc references to labour and production as encompassing *all* activities necessary to the reproduction of human life, an opposition is often evident in Engels's analysis between the production of things, which depends on the organization of *labour*, and the production of people, which depends on the organization of the *family*. There are also other slippages in Marxist writings, so that production is sometimes equated with the production of people as well as things, but more often with the production of things or, even more narrowly, with the production of things with exchange value (Nicholson, 1987). Consequently, large areas of human activity are overlooked in Marxist political economy, along with the distinctive relationships that men and women have to the various spheres of re/production. The problem stems partly from the treatment of the human body in Marxist thought. Marxism appeared, at first reading, to have restored the human body to a central place in social existence. Human labour, the defining feature of the human condition, was seen as the conscious use of the body – arms, legs, head and hands – to appropriate Nature in a form adapted to human wants. But critical scrutiny revealed that the body that figured in Marxist thought was the body of the proletarianized worker, the producer of surplus value. By equating human labour with the production of objects, and more narrowly, of objects with exchange value, women's bodies and women's labour in maintaining bodily existence are assigned to the domain of nature.

The other major criticism of Marxist thought derives from its overriding focus on the structures of production at the expense of the agency and consciousness of social actors. Within this tradition, women's oppression is reduced to the workings of an abstract mode of production, of benefit only to the abstract category of capital. There is no acknowledgement that men often benefit from women's oppression and that they play an active role in prolonging it, both within the privatized domain of the home but also in the purportedly neutral arena of the capitalist marketplace. Nor can traditional Marxist theory explain the antagonism and resistance expressed by women to *male* (as opposed to class) domination, except as a manifestation of false consciousness or a result of the divisive strategies of the ruling class. If the liberal individual is reduced to pure self-interest, the Marxist individual is defined purely in relation to class interest.

Within development studies, feminists using a Marxist perspective have shared a common starting point in its analysis of capital accumulation as the driving force behind unequal development and social conflict. They have also shared a common view of sexual inequalities as systematically produced by, and indeed essential to, a fundamentally unequal international order. However, they have diverged from traditional Marxism – and from each other – in the place they give to sexual inequalities in their explanation of overall social inequalities. In the rest of this chapter, we will be examining three different Marxist-influenced accounts of sexual inequality in the development process, partly to provide a flavour of the arguments used, and partly to lay the theoretical groundwork for an alternative approach to gender and development to that of WID.

Dependency Feminism and the Needs of Capital

An example of a traditional Marxist feminist perspective on develop-ment is that associated with the dependency critique which dominated Latin American discussions of development in the early seventies. For dependency feminists, the inequalities between women and men could not be understood in isolation from the polarizing tendencies of the capitalist mode of production which placed the 'peripheral' countries of the Third World in a relationship of dependency with the metropolitan centres of the First World. Within an inegalitarian world order, so-called development could not release women from oppressive social, economic and political institutions; it merely defined 'new conditions of constraint' (Leacock, 1977, p. 320).

In a paradigmatic exposition of these ideas, Saffiotti (1977) argued that women's situation resulted from two intersecting contradictions: 'the contradiction between social classes, which is dominant in capitalist social formations, and the contradiction between sexes, which is subordinate in the same type of social formation' (p. 28). Sexual division reflected the legislation and social prejudices of specific societies, which were also divided by class. Class, however, was the fundamental contradiction, since only class antagonism possessed the structural conditions for surpassing the limits of the system. Drawing on Rosa Luxemburg's thesis that pre-capitalist forms of production provided an essential subsidy to capital accumulation, Saffiotti suggested that the family was a primary example of a pre-capitalist form which performed this function. The services carried out within the family, mainly by women, reproduced the commodity, labour power, on a daily and a generational basis. Despite the indispensability of this 'labour rent' to the process of capital accumulation, these services did not assume a capitalist, that is, contractual, form. Rather, the work relations within the family were distinctly domestic ones, remnants of an earlier organizational form in which production was geared to the daily needs of household members. Labour power continued to be produced through these 'pre-capitalist' personalized relations, which were characterized by their voluntaristic nature and the absence of any explicit contracts regulating the distribution of domestic duties, the working time devoted to each of them, or the remuneration of these services.[2]

Although the family operated in this way across capitalist formations, dependency feminists believed that pre-capitalist relations took on greater significance in the underdeveloped regions. Imperialism allowed metropolitan centres to exploit relations with pre-capitalist areas located on their peripheries. This set up differences between women's roles in the two regions. The advantaged position enjoyed by the metropolitan centres gave women there far greater opportunities to enter capitalist forms of production. In the underdeveloped regions, on the other hand, the growth of highly capital-intensive relations of production in the course of economic growth had led to a general process of pauperization and marginalization in which women suffered disproportionately. The analytical primacy given to class contradictions over those of gender within this framework was critical to its contention that women and men shared common class interests: 'It is not men who keep women at home – though they may appear to be the most direct oppressors – but the structure of the capitalist system, which benefits from the unpaid labor of housewives or, in wartime, draws upon this reserve labor supply' (Nash and Safa, 1980, p. xi). However, once dependency feminists moved from the abstract to the empirical, they were confronted with aspects of social life which could be overlooked on the theoretical plane. The dependent position of women within the family and the active role played by their men in perpetuating this dependence raised questions about the extent to which women's status could be attributed entirely to the needs of capital.

To explain this phenomenon without undermining their political priorities, dependency feminists pointed to the pervasiveness of a patriarchal sex-role ideology within the Latin American family at all class levels. Such ideology maintained that women's place was in the home and that she must defer to her husband in all matters relating to the world outside the home. (Nash and Safa, 1980, p. 25). The family was portrayed as a refuge from the hostile world outside, and women were socialized to believe that they were privileged by their husbands to remain within its sheltered confines. In return they were required to obey men and cater to their needs and wishes. Although women enjoyed some autonomy within the domestic sphere, their exclusion from the public sphere explained their inferior status within society at large and their dependent situation within the family.

If many women tended to perceive their husbands, rather than capitalists, as their oppressors, it was because their distance from capitalist relations had denied them the opportunity to develop class consciousness. Thus, researching working-class households in Puerto Rico, Safa found that the 'abuse suffered by many women at the hands of their husbands makes them feel far more oppressed by men and marriage than by their class position. Nearly three-quarters of the women interviewed in 1959 felt that most marriages are unhappy, and blamed it on the man and his vices' (Safa, 1980, p. 78). However, she suggested that it was difficult for women to realize that what they were experiencing was a result of working-class men's inability to take out the frustration and hostility they felt towards tedious, unrewarding jobs except on women and children, who were their only subordinates. 'What women feel most directly is the man as the oppressor, and therefore much of their own hostility is directed against men rather than against the class system' (p. 78). She argued that, despite this sexual antagonism, there was considerable female solidarity among working-class households. They were the mainstay of the family, providing a haven in a heartless world for working-class men:

> though men and women are alienated in their work roles, they have a domestic sphere to which they can retreat and which capitalism has as yet been unable to destroy. . . . This is particularly important to the working class, who have no other source of identity, and who are subjected to extreme exploitation in their relationships with other classes in the metropolis, which are governed by status and market relationships. (p. 80)

Dependency feminists thus offered a very different account of women's marginalization in the development process to that offered by WID scholars. Sexual inequalities were seen as part of larger systems of inequality, created by and essential to capitalist processes of accumulation. Indeed the very term 'development' was revealed as ideologically loaded because of its connotations of a progressive and inevitable improvement in people's lives. In place of the ad hoc treatment given by WID scholars to structural forces and their detachment of information and attitudes from underlying economic structures and power relationships (Elliot, 1977), dependency feminists uncovered the systematic connections between different forms of inequalities at international, national and household levels. Moreover, by analysing women's domestic labour as a subsidy to the process of capital accumulation, they challenged the boundaries of traditional Marxist analysis which located women primarily in the private sphere and therefore as irrelevant to the workings of capital.

However, the strong affiliation demonstrated by many dependency feminists to a traditional Marxist politics limited the analytical scope of their work. In particular, they reproduced the Marxist tendency to refer all social phenomena to the ultimate determining structures of production, private property and class. Gender divisions, firmly treated as a subordinate contradiction to class, were seen to be sustained ideologically by capital in order to weaken working-class solidarity, to subsidize the reproduction of labour power, and to provide itself with a reserve army of labour which it could draw on as required. The fact that women's oppression served the needs of capital was taken to imply that only capital benefited from it. Although dependency feminists recognized the ideological subordination of women within the private sphere, they were reluctant to acknowledge the material extent to which it benefited men, both as a social category and as individuals. They shared the traditional Marxist tendency to focus on women's and men's relationships to the means of production, but ignored the relationship between women and men (Maguire,

1984). As the opening quotations from Rubin suggest, it is one thing to argue that capitalism benefits from women's oppression, but quite another to explain all the 'Byzantine' manifestations of such oppression over the centuries and across cultures in terms of the 'needs of capital'.

The Global Capitalist Patriarchy and Male Violence

Using some of the same analytical categories as the dependency feminists, but disagreeing fundamentally with the prioritizing of class as the 'primary contradiction', was the work of a group of German feminists working in the development field (Mies, 1980, 1982, 1986; Benholdt-Thomsen, 1981; Mies et al., 1988). This group also drew on Luxemburg's contention that capitalism needed non-capitalist forms of production as its surroundings in order to ensure its existence and future development. (Benholdt-Thomsen, 1981). The relegation of women to the unpaid subsistence sector of both First and Third World economies was described as 'housewifization' and seen as part of the same process by which the subsistence labour of the peasantry of the Third World was also used to subsidize capital. The identity posited in the relationship to capital of housewives all over the world – the bourgeois metropolitan housewife, the working-class housewife, the wife of the poor peasantry – led Benholdt-Thomsen to assert: 'Metaphors like – "women, the slaves of our society" or "women, the colonised of our society" – have real meaning from this perspective' (1981, p. 28).[3]

The main point of departure from traditional Marxism for this group was its refusal to accept that class was prior to gender, and its insistence that men, as well as capital, benefited from women's relegation to unpaid subsistence work. To justify this position, Mies (1986) grafted the concept of patriarchy onto the mode-of-production framework, arguing that the contemporary position of women should be seen as the product of a far older system of male dominance over women, nature and, later, the colonies. Consequently, the idea of capitalist patriarchy denoted 'patriarchal civilization as a system, of which capitalism constitutes the most recent and most universal manifestation' (p. 13).

Mies suggested that the rise of patriarchy could be traced to man-the-hunter's original control over the tools of destruction. What Engels had failed to grasp in his account of pre-patriarchal society was the social significance of the fact that women and men acted upon their natural environment with qualitatively different bodies. Women, as bearers of children and carers of the family, experienced their entire bodies as productive, not simply their arms and legs, head and hands, and consequently enjoyed a harmonious relationship between the nature of their bodies and the nature of their environment. Men, however, unable to produce through their bodies, were forced to rely on tools in order to make their productive contributions. However, men's hunting tools were basically means of destruction (rather than production, as Engels suggested) capable of killing humans as well as animals. The full exploitative potential of their control of the means of destruction became apparent with the development of livestock and agriculture and the emergence of an economic surplus. In the struggle to appropriate the surplus for themselves, men's control over the tools of destruction allowed them to domesticate women, as well as animals, and to restrict them to the role of breeding children, particularly sons to inherit their wealth. Women became defined as nature, as part of the physical preconditions for male production. The predatory relationship between man and nature became the model for organizing his relationship with women. This predatory mode of production, according to Mies, has underpinned all subsequent developments. Its latest manifestation, capitalism, has been built on the interrelated processes of colonization and housewifization, both entailing the consignment of large sections of humanity to the realm of nature and therefore to justified exploitation. The 'man-the-hunter' model which gave rise to the original predatory mode of production continues to be the 'base and last resort' of all subsequent modes of production.

It is clear that while Mies uses many Marxist concepts, she unequivocally rejects what she deems the 'old scientific socialist argument' that women's oppression was a secondary contradiction and belonged in the sphere of ideology and superstructure. Where traditional Marxist feminists had shied away from the idea that men might benefit from women's oppression *as men*, rather than as members of the ruling class, Mies declared unequivocally that the 'male–female relation' was fundamentally a relationship of power. In foregrounding male violence as the key to understanding women's oppression, her account represented a radical departure from what has been described as 'the traditional Marxist ploy' of removing the agents of domination from the scene, leaving behind only the blind workings of the capitalist system to explain women's oppression (Campioni and Grosz, 1991). Furthermore, her focus on the sexually differentiated body as an important site for the enactment of patriarchal power relations opened up the analysis of women's oppression to a whole range of issues around body politics that feminists had been working with, but that traditional Marxists had chosen to ignore or play down.

In the end, however, Mies's bold attempt to break from the economic determinism of traditional Marxism suffers from the same problems which beset most accounts that attempt to trace current social phenomena to their root cause in the origins of history. Mies argues that the attempt to uncover the origins of women's oppression is critical to a feminist political strategy: if patriarchy had a beginning, it must have an end. An alternative reading of the quest for origins is put forward by Rosaldo: 'To look for origins is, in the end, to think that what we are today is something other than the product of our history and our present social world, and, more particularly, that our gender systems are promordial, transhistorical, and essentially unchanging in their roots' (1980, p. 392). Or, as Connell puts it, the problem with the claim that knowledge of the origins of patriarchy can inform current oppositional strategies is that it assumes that 'nothing much changes *after* the Origin. Like the Elephant's Child in the Just So Stories having its nose stretched, once you get it you are stuck with it' (Connell, 1987, p. 146). And indeed the impression that emerges from Mies's account is that, despite changes in the modes of production, patriarchy remains much the same. All of history is presented as a catalogue of the various atrocities committed against women. From the earliest practices of kidnapping, raping and imprisoning them in harems, to the hunting, torture and burning of thousands of women as witches in medieval Europe, to the enslavement of the Third World and the rape of nature, men have shaped history in their own violent image. Today the catalogue of violence against women continues in the form of wife battering, rape, sexual trafficking, female circumcision, population control as 'gynocide', dowry murders, female foeticide: 'violence against women, therefore, seems the main common denominator that epitomizes women's exploitation and oppression, irrespective of class, nation, caste, race, capitalist or socialist systems, Third World or First World' (p. 169).

Mies makes sweeping use of monolithic categories such as the global patriarchy, the 'BIG, WHITE MEN', 'women' and 'the colonies' without ever pausing to disaggregate these categories and question the extent to which they are always internally coherent. This allows her to sidestep the potential contradictions in her account. For instance, it allows her to avoid giving the same degree of attention to the role played by women themselves, or by men from the colonies, in perpetuating the oppression of women. Where men's violence against *men* rather than women is touched on, as in her discussion of imperialism and slavery, it is laid at the door of the BIG WHITE MEN, those who currently control the technology of destruction. Where this violence is perpetrated by Third World men against Third World women, she suggests that this is an imitation effect or what she calls 'the BIG MEN–little men syndrome': 'They imitate the Big White Men in the West who are their model of a modern man. . . . Those who have money can buy all those things the BIG Men have, including women. Those who do not have enough money still have the same dreams' (p. 167). Where it is women who are implicated in violence against women – as is often the case with dowry murders in India and female circumcision in parts of Africa – Mies is silent. Her overriding emphasis on the power of men, and the BIG WHITE MEN in particular, denies women any historical agency at all. All men appear as monsters, their culpability in inverse proportion to their location in the global patriarchal hierarchy; all women appear as their victims.

To conclude, Mies's interpretation of the concept of patriarchy leads her into precisely the hopeless political cul-de-sac that Rubin cautions against. Rubin points out that to use the term 'patriarchy' to distinguish male dominance from other social forces is analogous to using 'capitalism' to refer to all modes of production, whereas the usefulness of the term 'capitalism' lies precisely in that it distinguishes one particular system by which societies are provisioned and organized. Similarly, there are many different ways in which societies deal with the organization of sex, gender and babies: 'it is important – even in the face of a depressing history – to maintain a distinction between the human capacity and necessity to create a sexual world, and the empirically oppressive ways in which sexual worlds have been organized' (p. 168). The problem with Mies's usage of 'patriarchy' is that it subsumes both meanings into the same term.

Capital Accumulation and the
Social Relations of Gender

Despite their obvious political differences, both the accounts of women in the international context discussed so far – the dependency version and that of the capitalist patriarchy – are located at similarly abstract and highly aggregated systems of domination rather than in the specific institutions, constraints and practices through which these systems are manifested in people's everyday lives. They represent a form of 'holistic' analysis which effectively reverses the flow of causality found in methodological individualism, so that instead of flowing up from the lowest level of analysis, causality is now imposed top-down from the higher levels (Birke, 1986). While WID scholarship presented women making individual choices in the face of prejudice and constraint, these accounts present women as having no choices at all in the face of overarching structures of power.

However, as Birke points out, an alternative form of 'holism' is possible which seeks to uncover the interconnections between different spheres and levels of society, and between individuals and social structures. A concern with structural forces need not preclude awareness of women and men as historically located actors coping with, and seeking to transform, the conditions of their lives. And while male dominance may be a near-universal phenomenon, it generally operates in more concealed and variable ways than allowed by the global patriarchal model. It may take the form of brute male force (and, indeed, male violence against women is at last being given policy recognition as a 'development' issue), but more often it operates as an aspect of the organization of collective life: 'We see it not in physical constraints on things that men or women can or cannot do but, rather, in the ways in which they think about their lives, the kinds of opportunities they enjoy, and in their ways of making claims' (Rosaldo, 1980, p. 394).

An important contribution to the project of building this less monolithic framework of analysis was made by the Subordination of Women (SOW) Group (see IDS, 1979). Along with an unease with global generalizations about the effects of capitalism and the patriarchy on women, the SOW group were also dissatisfied with the promotion of 'women' as the key category of analysis in the WID discourse. The consequent treatment of women and men as isolable categories had helped to render invisible men's roles in the continuing subordination of women in the development process. The challenge for SOW was to steer a path somewhere between the liberal individualism of WID scholarship and the structural determinism of certain Marxist accounts, so that analysis could move beyond demonstrating the adverse/marginalizing impact of development/capitalism on women to a deeper understanding of the ways in which unequal relations between women and men may have contributed to the extent and forms of exclusion that women faced in the development process.

The central analytical category adopted by the SOW group was the *social relations of gender* which mediated the ways in which individuals experienced structural forces. The concept of gender subordination was used to make the point that power was a general characteristic of these relations (Whitehead, 1979), while the subject matter of analysis was seen to be the domestic arena, from which asymmetrical gender relations sprang, and its articulation with the broader economic arena in which these relations were reconstituted (Young et al., 1981). A useful place to begin a discussion of what is meant by gender relations is with the following quotation from Marx, cited in Rubin (1975, p. 158):

> What is a Negro slave? A man of the black race. The one explanation is as good as the other. A Negro is a Negro. He only becomes a slave in certain relations. A cotton spinning jenny is a machine for spinning cotton. It becomes capital only in certain relations. Torn from these relationships, it is no more capital than gold itself is money or sugar is the price of sugar.

The quotation graphically illustrates a profound insight in Marxist thought – the significance of social relations in ascribing a meaning and a place to people and things – but also its profound limitations. As Rubin points out, 'in Marx's map of the social world, human beings are workers, peasants, or capitalists; that they are also men and women is not seen as very significant' (p. 160). However, the idea of social relations can be usefully extended to the analysis of women's condition, as Rubin demonstrated in her paraphrase of Marx:

> What is a domesticated woman? A female of the species. The one explanation is as good as the other. A woman is a woman. She only becomes a domestic, a wife, a chattel, a playboy bunny, a prostitute, or a human dictaphone in certain relations. Torn from these relationships, she is no more the helpmate of man than gold in itself is money . . . etc. (p. 158)

Gender relations (in this quotation) can be seen as the full ensemble of social relationships through which the female of the human species becomes the 'domesticated woman'. The distinction between sex and gender, referred to in Chapter 3, is further elaborated by Rubin. As she points out, the male and female of the human species are biologically similar in most ways: in their need to eat, sleep and defecate, in their vulnerability in early life and old age, in their susceptibility to diseases and, by and large, in their life expectancies. They are distinguished from each other only by a small range of biological differences: 'from the standpoint of nature, men and women are closer to each other than either is to anything else – for instance, mountains, kangaroos, or coconut palms . . . the idea that men and women are two mutually exclusive categories must arise out of something other than a non-existent "natural" opposition' (Rubin, 1975, p. 178). Thus, while sexually differentiated bodies can seen as an important aspect of the human experience, Rubin suggests that it is in the socially differentiated arrangements of gender that we must seek an explanation for the very different ways in which men and women experience the world. The social rules and practices through which gender relations are constructed constitute a highly selective interpretation of the human body: of its full range of attributes, they privilege only those which are necessary for a specific, sexually based system of human reproduction.

Gender relations therefore simultaneously suppress natural similarities between the sexes and exacerbate the differences, ensuring that the male and female of the human species are channelled into mutually exclusive categories of women and men, based on mutually exclusive traits of masculinity and femininity. However, the translation of biological categories into social ones is not a simple one. While it is generally the case that male and female tends to correlate empirically with men and women, the fit between male/female and masculinity/femininity is more diffuse (Birke, 1986). In the first place, human biology itself is not a constant dimension of human history. Variations in menstruation, menopause, procreation, human fecundity, human size and strength have reflected historical changes in the social organization of production and labour. In fact, new forms of technology now hold out the potential for eradicating the relevance of sex-based categories as the process of human reproduction itself undergoes major transformation; 'biology is "gendered" as well as sexed' (Jagger, 1983, p. 126).

A second reason why biological dichotomies do not translate unproblematically into social ones has to do with the unique quality of human beings to resist, choose and interpret, despite the existence of a multitude of rules and practices to promote just such a translation. What exists in most societies are what Connell (1987) calls 'hegemonic forms' of masculinity and femininity which constrain the actual practices of men and women, but do not determine them. Instead, there are a range of possibilities between the *acceptance* of normative sanctions as the legitimate rules of behaviour, and *conforming* to them (Giddens, 1979). In some societies, the rules and practices which shape gender relations are relatively flexible, leaving room for multiple interpretations; in others, they are severely and punitively enforced. Nevertheless, most societies display a proliferation of gender identities along with normative standards which exercise greater or lesser pressures for conformity.

Finally, it has to be recognized that other social relations mediate the way in which biological difference is translated into gender inequality. Class is clearly an important factor here, along with other forms of social inequality whose significance is context-specific. Empirically, class and gender tend to be mutually constituted; biological differences are always acted upon in the context of intersecting social inequalities. A social-relations approach, therefore, does not give priority to either class or gender as the determining principle of individual identity or social position. Rather, as Beneria and Sen (1982) put it:

> First, a woman's class position structures the concrete meaning of gender for her. The variations that exist between women of different classes are at least as important for the woman's social position as the commonalities inherent in being a women within a given society. Second, class defines the relations among women themselves. That is, class is not simply a differentiating mechanism that places women in varying social boxes. It is an antagonistic social relation that defines, for example, the oppressive social relation between female domestic servants and their mistresses. Class is also antagonistic in broader terms . . . women of different classes often have opposing interests in social organizations and programs for social change. (p. 162)

The Ascribed Relations of Gender

A key set of relations which structure gender both as individual identity as well as social inequality are those of kinship and family, the 'relations of everyday life'. In pre-capitalist societies, kinship was the key idiom of social interaction, organizing economic, cultural and political activities as well as sexual and reproductive practice. Clearly, in such contexts, the domestic domain was the primary site of most social relations, including those of gender. By contrast, one of the pivotal features of contemporary market-based societies has been the institutionalized separation of the 'private' domain of family and kinship from other more 'public' institutions of the market and state. The familial domain still remains a critical site of gender relations in capitalist society, but has ramifications that reach deep into the apparently separate public arena.

One area of literature that remains underrepresented in the field of development is feminist psychoanalysis, which emphasizes the significance of familial arrangements in the early years of a child's life in shaping a sense of selfhood, including a core gender identity. While this literature comes primarily from Europe and North America (Chodorow, 1978; Rubin, 1975; Dinnerstein, 1977), there is no reason why familial arrangements should not have an important influence on individual identities in other cultures as well. Kakar's study in India, for instance, points out how the closeness of the mother–son bond in the Indian family creates an unconscious fear of women's strength in men (1978, cited in Chambers, 1990). Such analysis emphasizes the deep-rootedness of gender identities in people's sense of their place in the world, and the consequent unease which is unleashed by any attempt to question, let alone change, the ideological underpinnings and social arrangements of the family.

Along with individual gender identities, family and kinship relations are systems for organizing rights, responsibilities and resources for different categories of members in different social groups. Whitehead characterizes relationships within the familial domain as gender-ascriptive: 'in them, to describe the position is to describe the gender' (Whitehead, 1979, p. 11). Thus to be a husband, a wife, a mother, a father, uncle, niece, and so forth, is to be either a man or a woman.[4] These relationships are governed by social 'rules' which determine how assets are to be distributed between the occupants of the different relationships, how authority and status are to be assigned, and how labour allocated. Familial relationships are a primary mechanism through which social meanings are invested in, and social controls exercised over, womens' bodies, labour, sexuality, reproductive capacity and life choices. Although varying across different classes and social groupings, the rules and practices governing marriage, procreation, inheritance and parenting all combine to ensure that, in much of the world, the care and nurture of the family is seen as primarily women's responsibility, while entitlement to material resources is mainly invested in men – hence the 'monotonous similarity' of women's oppression in different parts of the world. On the other hand, the rules and practices through which familial relations are constructed, and the scope that they give to women to challenge, negotiate and transform them, are 'endlessly variable', taking different forms over time and in different settings. Instead of positing a universal structure of patriarchy, a social-relations approach suggests that apparent commonalities in gender subordination across the world are constructed through historically specific class and gender relations, and consequently have very different implications for what men and women can and cannot do.

Gender Relations and the
'Hierarchy of Empty Places'

While gender is an obvious constitutive principle of family and kinship relations, empirical research demonstrates the reconstitution of gender relations through the rules, procedures, practices and outcomes of other institutions of society, including those of the market and state. Given the analytical importance of labour in Marxist theories of social relations, the role given to the gender division of labour in feminist analysis of different institutions is not unexpected. The feminist reworking of this concept offers a powerful tool for analysing the complexity, the pervasiveness and the deep-rootedness of gender as a facet of human endeavour.

At its simplest, the gender division of labour can be seen as the allocation of particular tasks to particular people. It becomes a social structure to the extent that this allocation poses a constraint on further practice (Connell, 1987). This happens in a number of interrelated ways. Prior divisions of labour become sedimented through practice so that they take on the significance of social rules: in most cultures, women look after children because they have 'always' looked after children. What may have started out as a way of organizing labour takes on a normative significance so that values become embodied in the tasks and in who does them. The routine assignment of women and men to specific tasks becomes intimately bound up with what it means to be a 'man' or a 'woman' in specific contexts (Whitehead, 1991). To challenge the gender division of labour within a social order is to challenge the basis of core gender identities. Motherhood, for instance, is such a crucial component of women's gender identity in most cultures that it is seen as the 'natural' expression of womanhood. As Butler (1987) suggests, this representation of motherhood as instinctual, rather than an institutional, helps to disguise the possibility of motherhood as an optional practice: 'If motherhood becomes a choice, then what else is possible? This kind of questioning often engenders vertigo and terror over the possibility of losing social sanctions, of leaving a solid social station and place' (p. 132). Equally, there are powerful norms about masculinity that work against men taking on the role of 'mothering' and domestic work; to do so would be to risk emasculation.[5] As these divisions of labour become sedimented, they form the basis of new constraints on practice because they are associated with a particular gender division of skills. The persistent allocation of certain tasks and activities to women and men on the basis of their 'natural' aptitudes and capabilities leads them to acquire these aptitudes and capabilities through routine performance of these activities. In contrast to most material endowments, human skills are generally enhanced rather than depleted through routine use. The recruitment of women and men into different tasks, activities and occupations consequently ends up as a rational response to socially constructed, but nonetheless real, differentials in their skills and aptitudes.

We referred at the beginning of this chapter to Marxism's failure to explain the hierarchies of 'empty places' created by the organization of production. A structural analysis of the gender division of labour helps to explain why these organizational hierarchies translate in practice into gender hierarchies. Deliberate and direct gender discrimination is rarely an adequate explanation; more often, such hierarchies are created as the hidden, unintended, but generally inevitable, outcome of institutional dynamics. As Acker points out (1990), the organizational logic of public institutions, both in terms of hierarchies and in terms of their basic units, jobs, is to create abstract categories, 'empty places' devoid of occupants, bodies and genders. The different levels of skills, complexity and responsibility used to define organizational hierarchy are seen as products of organizational logic rather than expressions of management values and preferences. However, these abstract categories are constructed on the premiss of a disembodied worker who exists only for the job:

> Such a hypothetical worker cannot have other imperatives of existence that impinge upon the job. . . . The closest the disembodied worker doing the abstract job comes to a real worker is the male worker whose life centres on his full-time, life-long job, while his wife or another woman takes care of his personal needs and his children. . . . The woman worker, assumed to have legitimate obligations other than those required by the job, did not fit with the abstract job. (p. 149)

Thus the concept of a job, while presented as gender-neutral, already contains the gender-based division of labour and the separation between work within the family and work in the public sphere. Hierarchies within organizations are also gendered because they, too, reflect these assumptions: those whose bodies, lives and skills that mesh most closely with the requirements of organizational logic are rewarded with pay, responsibility and authority.

The enactment of rules of recruitment, reward, allocation and evaluation in purportedly gender-neutral institutions systematically reconstitutes gender inequalities, ensuring that women and men are always brought into them as bearers of differently rewarded attributes and capabilities. Gender does not have to be a contractual aspect of particular positions within the occupational structure for it to enter nonetheless through implicit rules and practices. In the UK, for instance, women tend to be crowded into the service sector, and within it into nursing and teaching jobs in the lower echelons of the occupational ladder. Men are found in larger numbers in traditional heavy industry and in the financial end of service sector; they also dominate in senior managerial positions. There is nothing inherent in these sectors, occupations or positions that make them male or female. Rather, they reflect the fact that women and men enter the market bearing the different attributes associated with their gender – ascribed attributes of masculinity and femininity as well as acquired ones of education and skills – which mesh with the different objective requirements, routinized practices and subjective expectations that dominate in the workplace.

The result is a hierarchial distribution of the genders across sectors, in different occupational segments within the sectors, and at different levels of the occupational structure, characterized not only by different kinds of activities but also by different rewards. The fierce resistance by men to women entering previously male-defined arenas of responsibility, and their defence of the existing gender distribution of jobs, makes more sense, as Connell (1987) points out, when it is realized that it is also about men's defence of their privileged access to resources. Empirical research (Cockburn, 1983; Phillips and Taylor, 1980; Chhachhi, 1983; Humphrey, 1987) attests to the amount of effort that goes into protecting gender hierarchies in the division of labour, both within the home and in the marketplace. It documents the struggles over definitions of qualifications and skills, training, wage differentials and occupational grading through which the more privileged sections of the male working class have defended their privileges within national and international labour markets.

To sum up, therefore, the concept of gender relations tends itself to what might be described as a feminist theorization of institutions. Institutions provide the framework for specific organizational forms[6] which, through the operation of tradition, custom or legal constraint, tend to create 'durable and routinized patterns of behaviour' (Hodgson, 1988, p. 10); gender is seen to be an aspect of *all* organizational relations and behaviour, more distinct and explicit in some institutional locations than others, but always interacting to shape the identities, practices and life-chances of different groups of women and men in quite specific ways. An analysis of the rules, norms and practices through which different institutions construct gender divisions and hierarchies helps to uncover the underlying shared ideologies which govern apparently distinct and separate institutions. Despite the separation of domestic institutions from the public domains of production and exchange, familial norms and values are constantly drawn on to construct the terms on which women and men enter, and participate, in public life and in the marketplace. At the same time, because different social institutions are organized around quite specific objectives and have their own rules and practices, gender hierarchies are not seamlessly and uniformly woven into institutional structures, but produced dynamically through the interaction of familial gender ideologies and distinct institutional practices. Both within and across institutions, gender operates as a pervasive allocational principle, linking production with reproduction, domestic with public domains, and the macroeconomy with the micro-level institutions within which development processes are played out: 'Gender', as Whitehead points out, 'is never absent' (1979, p. 11).

Gender Relations and the Development Process

In the context of development studies, a gender-relations framework seeks to establish an inductive mode of analysis in place of highly abstract theorizations which lead to empirically ungrounded generalizations: 'The form that gender relations take in any historical situation is specific to that situation and has to be constructed inductively; it cannot be read off from other social relations nor from the gender relations of other societies' (Young et al., 1981, p. vii). As a general project, this perspective has been associated with the study of the variable, sometimes contradictory, outcomes of the interaction between specific forms of gender subordination and different processes of production. Whether pitched at the level of larger structures or located in more micro-level realities, a social-relations approach is concerned with exploring how the relations of class and gender mediate social realities, translating broader processes of change into concrete gains and losses for different groups of women and men. Nor is change seen as unidirectional. While the drive for capital accumulation does impose a powerful logic on the possibilities open to individuals and groups, the diverse ways in which people organize their working and family lives also exercise upward pressures on the capacity of global capitalism to shape these possibilities. The consequences can be seen in the multiplicity of outcomes that emerge from the workings of capital in different parts of the world, some of which carry an emancipatory potential for women while others intensify the conditions of their subordination (Elson and Pearson, 1981).

Beneria and Sen (1982) provide an example of a macro-structural analysis of gender relations within the international workings of capital. They point out that the single most powerful tendency of capital accumulation is to separate direct producers from the means of production and make their conditions of survival more insecure and contingent. However, capitalism is not seen as a single homogenous structure of surplus extraction, but rather as different regimes of accumulation which employ 'qualitatively different' mechanisms of exploitation in plantation economies, small-holder commercial farms, labour-intensive or capital-intensive industries, export-oriented or inward-looking growth. Its implications for the gender division of labour and for women's subordination will depend, therefore, on the specific forms that accumulation takes in different social formations.

Such analysis points to the inadequacy of the WID view that women were adversely affected by development because of unequal access to new technologies and skills. It suggests, rather, that technical change was itself embedded in changing class relations of production. It was accompanied by the alienation of the mass of direct producers, both women and men, from the means of production and by their growing reliance on the sale of labour power, large-scale migration in search of work and the resultant growth of unemployment in the urban slums. The authors conclude that the problem was not that women had not been integrated into development, but that they had been integrated at the bottom of an inherently hierarchical and contradictory structure of production and accumulation. While apparently widespread, this outcome reflected differing configurations of accumulation regimes, processes of class formation, and gender relations. Some of the factors behind women's subordinate position were related to gender; others reflected specific patterns of capital accumulation and the forms of inequality which they systematically created or exacerbated. For poorer women, the results might be overwork and undernourishment, even in relation to men of their class. For wealthier women, concentration on reproductive work might free them from direct class-based exploitation, but generally meant greater economic dependence on men.

Beneria and Sen offer a number of examples to demonstrate the variety of effects that the spread of capitalist relations have had internationally. In many parts of sub-Saharan Africa, where poorer peasants and labourers have lost rights over land and common property resources, women have had to intensify their labour in searching for fuel, carrying water and processing food. This is exacerbated in areas where men have either shifted to cash-crop production or migrated to towns in search of work, leaving subsistence production entirely to women. In urban Latin America, the entry of commercial capital has displaced women as independent artisans. While the introduction of plantation agriculture provided work for the local population, women were employed at the bottom of the labour hierarchy because of the demands of their reproductive work. Finally, the setting up of global market factories in a number of Southeast Asian countries has led to the feminization of their labour force and the increased migration of young women to urban areas as waged labour.

Also from a gender relations perspective, Kandiyoti's analysis (1985) focuses on the interaction between different forms of household organization and economic transformation in different parts of the world. She suggests that the spread of capitalist relations of production represents the combined and uneven workings of national governments, international agencies and multinational corporations. The so-called 'traditional' sector, the target of the modernization project, is in most cases the product of highly 'modern' interventions. It reflects the distortions wrought by colonial penetrations of the economies, and the coercion of peasants into producing cash crops on smallholder farms or in plantations. A comparison of rural commoditization processes in different regions of the world suggests that production relations between the sexes, prior to capitalist incorporation, both shaped the subsequent division of labour and 'set limits' to its variability. The interests of capital in cheap and plentiful labour were not necessarily in harmony with the survival strategies adopted by individual household units, or with the division of labour and power within them. Resistance at the household level could thwart the smooth operation of capital accumulation.

At a still lower level of analysis, Whitehead (1981) provides a detailed account of the intra-household division of labour and resources between men and women in the very different economic systems of rural Ghana and industrial Britain. In one context, households relied on subsistence production; in the other, they relied on the sale of labour power and the purchase of wage goods. Whitehead suggests that the conjugal contract, or the terms on which husbands and wives exchange goods, services, labour and income, is a useful focus for the study of intra-household gender relations, although clearly exchanges based on parental and other familial relations within the household were also important. Her analysis demonstrates how cultural rules about the division of resources and responsibilities operated through very different householding arrangements, but with the effect of loading the terms of exchange in favour of men in both contexts.

Conclusion

While these authors locate their analysis at quite different levels of abstraction, they demonstrate some of the contributions of a gender-relations approach to understanding the situation of women in the development process. We will conclude this chapter by noting what these contributions might be. First of all, the focus on gender relations extends the Marxist concept of social relations beyond the production of objects and commodities to the production and care of the human body and human life: procreation, child care, care of the sick and elderly, along with the daily reproduction of labour power. It entails the theorization of the relations of everyday life and their interconnections with the relations of re/production in the changing local and world economy.

The use of gender relations as a category of analysis also shifts the focus away from the earlier one on women. A focus solely on women tended to imply that the problem – and hence the solution – could be confined to women. A focus on social relations extends the analysis from women – and men – as isolable categories to the broader interconnecting relationships through which women are positioned as a subordinate group in the division of resources and responsibilities, attributes and capabilities, power and privilege. Moreover, treating gender as one aspect of social relations reminds us that it is not the only form of inequality in the lives of women and men. While 'gender is never absent', it is never present in pure form. It is always interwoven with other social inequalities, such as class and race, and has to be analysed through a holistic framework if the concrete conditions of life for different groups of women and men are to be understood.

A second important contribution of this approach is its concern with the complex processes by which the simple 'facticity' of biological difference become socially constructed as gender difference and gender identity. While a concern with the making of gender identities may appear far removed from the concerns of development policy-makers and activists, it is in fact a critical starting point. It helps to challenge the notion that women and men are somehow naturally suited to certain tasks and activities. Women's ability to pursue their claims within the policy process has been closely bound up with pushing back the boundaries of what is 'natural' about their lives and revealing its socially constructed basis. Furthermore, understanding how deeply gender identities are rooted in our consciousness will also help us to understand and anticipate the resistance that women, as well as men, can display towards policies which threaten to change the symbolic and material arrangements that make up prevailing gender relations.

Finally, a gender-relations approach seeks to avoid the universalist generalizations that characterize the more structuralist approaches which see women's oppression as produced by the capitalist mode of production or by a global patriarchy. It offers instead what Connell

describes as 'a gentler, more pragmatic but perhaps more demon-
strable claim that with a framework like this we can come to a
serviceable understanding of current history' (Connell, 1987, p. 97). It
points to the pervasiveness of male dominance, but suggest that men's
control over women's bodies and lives – their labour, sexuality,
reproductive capacity and life choices – operates through taken-for-
granted asymmetries about what is possible for, and available to, men
and women, rather than solely through the exercise of force or the
threat of violence. Power in this analysis does not inhere in any single
aspect of the social system, but in the social relations which enable men
to mobilize a greater range of resources – symbols and meanings,
authority and recognition, objects and services – in a greater range of
institutional domains: political, economic and familial.

Related to this last point, the strategies for change suggested by this
approach are very different from those which stemmed from the more
traditional Marxism of dependency feminism or from the global
patriarchy perspective. Early Marxist feminism was generally associated with a refusal to have any truck with any of the official agencies
of development, seeing them primarily as agents of international
capital. The focus was on building the solidarity of the working class
and seeking to meet women's demands through the struggle for
workers' rights. Autonomous women's organizations were frequently
regarded with suspicion, and accused of diverting attention from the
'real' struggle.

An even stronger antipathy to the official agencies of development is
to be found among those who lay the failures of development at the
door of the capitalist patriarchy. Mies's account of history as the
unfolding of a single relentless patriarchal logic does not lend itself to
any half-way measures that simply deal with the problems that women
face on a day-to-day basis.[7] She proposes instead an alternative vision
of society based on a feminist conception of labour, involving direct
and sensual interaction with nature, unmediated by technology. This,
she suggests, requires that certain nations gain greater economic
autarchy to rectify the unequal world order; autonomy for women
over their lives and bodies, and rejection of any state or male control
over their reproductive capacity; and finally men's participation in
subsistence and nurturing work so that they too can experience unity
of body and mind. The problem with such a strategy, as with the
intermediate steps that Mies suggests, is that it is not one that can be
implemented in the foreseeable future. It assumes a global solidarity
among women which in fact has to be the object of struggle.

To some extent, the strategies stemming from both these

approaches are a logical reflection of their construction of the problem. Only total transformation will suffice when power is viewed as an all-encompassing structure within which national and international agencies are merely one of many manifestations of imperialist or patriarchal capitalism. Short-term measures through such agencies can be dismissed as, at best, ameliorative, and at worst, a co-opted form of feminism. However, this is not a satisfactory position, if only because we cannot *afford* to ignore the official agencies of development. Women all over the world face a critical shortage of resources to meet their own and their families' needs, and the official agencies remain powerful mechanisms of resource allocation, potentially capable of meeting or exacerbating this deprivation. Whatever our final vision of a society organized on feminist principles, we still need transitional strategies to bridge the present and the future. We need a more complex strategy than one of militant disengagement with official development efforts. In this context, a gender-relations analysis offers a more nuanced view of official policymaking institutions because it draws attention to the rules, relations and practices through which institutions are constituted. It becomes apparent that while these institutions do undoubtedly embody class and gender privilege, they do not automatically represent a uniform set of interests; capitalism, racism, patriarchy and underdevelopment may be interdependent, but they are not the same. Their contradictory pressures within the agencies create the space for a feminist agenda. The success of the WID project of making women visible to policymakers was precisely due to one such contradiction: that between the expressed policy goal of efficiency and the neglect of women's productive roles in practice; or, put another way, that between the interests of patriarchy and the interests of capital. Such contradictions have to be used strategically to push forward a feminist development agenda.

As Sen and Grown (1985) have argued, we need to use these contradictions strategically. An alternative to militant disengagement might be engagement with a view to transformation – through research, advocacy and political strategies that challenge the assumptions of neutrality which permeate the goals, objectives, rules and practices of influential development agencies and help to disguise the partial nature of their vision of development. Beyond these necessary critiques, alternative visions also have to be worked out by constantly monitoring and evaluating the assumptions, procedures and outcomes of all policies and programmes, and working out who gains and who loses in the different processes of development and why.

Notes

1 For another discussion of the different views of women and development, see Rathgeber, 1990.
2 As we shall see in Chapter 5, this view of 'the household' has a remarkable similarity to that contained in orthodox neo-classical economics.
3 A collection of articles from this perspective published in 1988 is in fact called *Women. The Last Colony* (Mies et al., 1988).
4 The only example of gender-ascriptive relations outside the familial domain that Hilard Standing and I were able to think of was that between monks and nuns in a religious order.
5 For examples from the Indian context, see Ramu (1989/90); from the British context, see Cockburn, 1983.
6 North (1990) makes a useful distinction between institutions as distinct frameworks of rules for doing things and organizations as the specific structural forms that institutions take. Thus the state is the larger institutional framework for a range of legal, military and administrative organizations; the market is the framework for firms, corporations, farming enterprises; the 'moral economy' of the community provides the framework for patron–client relationships, village tribunals, lineage organizations etc. We will be using the term 'institution' to refer to the broader site on which specific organizations operate.
7 The political stance and practical implications associated with this view are touched on in the context of reproductive rights in Chapter 8.

4

Connecting, Extending, Reversing: Development from a Gender Perspective

'[I]n systems of domination, the vision available to the rulers both will be partial and will reverse the real order of things. (Hartsock, 1990, p. 36)

The best way to separate out scientific ideas from ideology is to stand the ideology on its head and see how the ideas look the other way up. (Robinson, 1962, cited in Waring, 1989, p. 44)

Reversal is used to describe a direction, away from normal practice and towards its opposite. (Chambers, 1992, p. 40)

Power and Resources in the Development Process

In this chapter, I would like to return to the concept of development, but this time to approach it from a gender perspective. The earlier discussion of the differing views on women and development makes clear that development is by no means an unproblematic concept. In its narrow meaning, it refers to the *planned* process by which resources, techniques and expertise are brought together to bring about improved rates of economic growth in an area variously designated as the Third World, the developing world, the periphery, the South, and so on. In its broader sense, it refers to a purposeful project, no doubt, but one with unacknowledged assumptions and unanticipated outcomes. Development then becomes the broader processes of social transformation unleashed by the attempts of diverse development agencies at local, national and international levels, both within the official domain and outside it, to achieve various, and often conflicting,

69

goals. Given this broader meaning, development can carry negative as well as positive connotations. For some, it is synonymous with the gradual and progressive expansion of individual choice; it has helped to eliminate life-threatening diseases and to prolong human life expectancy, to harness the energy of rivers for human use, to promote new and hardier miracle crops, and to reclaim the deserts and marshlands. For others, however, development has simply defined new conditions of constraint, enriching a few, impoverishing the many, and in the process eroding both cultural and biological diversity across the world. At the heart of these contradictory outcomes is what Gandhi pointed out many decades ago: that there are enough resources in the world to meet the basic needs of all, but not enough to satisfy the greed of a few. Yet it has been the greed for profit of the few, backed up by control over the levers of power, that has shaped the patterns of distribution in development. Power in this field, as elsewhere, derives from control over resources and control over ideas, each form of control reinforcing the other. Control over resources enables those in power to determine the parameters within which debates and controversies in development can be conducted, which problems are to count within the development agenda, and which subset of solutions will be considered.

The power exercised through control over resources is particularly evident in the international financial institutions where voting is weighted by contributions rather than on the basis of one member, one vote. In the World Bank and the IMF, the industrial market economies share more than half the weighted decision-making process, with the United States alone allocated almost a fifth (Staudt, 1991). The UN agencies have geographically representative staff. While this does not guarantee that the UN represents the interests of all its potential constituencies, it is generally seen as more independent of Western interests than the Bretton Woods institutions.

The US also dominates in terms of overall development assistance, followed closely by Japan. Control over the flow of aid ensures that development priorities in national and international agencies reflect donor priorities. Donor assistance rarely goes to the poorest countries or to those most able to use it effectively or equitably. Rather, it flows to countries which are most likely to represent donor interests. US aid, for instance, is directed mainly to countries of key strategic importance (for example, Israel and Egypt) while British and French aid goes disproportionately to their former colonies. Israel and Jordan, which received the highest aid receipts per capita in 1988 (282 and 108 dollars respectively), also had higher per capita GNP (8,650 and 1,500 dollars respectively) than any other country except Syria, which had

1,680 dollars per capita, but received 16 dollars per capita (World Bank, 1990, p. 129). Ethiopia and Bangladesh, the countries with the lowest per-capita GNP (120 and 170 dollars respectively) received 21 and 15 dollars respectively. Of the various Western donors, the Nordic countries are considered to be most concerned with poverty reduction and contribute the highest proportion of their GNP to foreign assistance.

There are other ways in which sectional interests are promoted within the international development arena. Grants and loans are frequently tied to the purchase of goods from the donor countries, to the use of their shipping companies, and to staffing, planning and management by their technical experts. Recipient countries would benefit far more from such assistance if they were free to go through competitive tender rather than being tied to donor facilities. Among six bilateral donors in 1982, the percentage of tied grants ranges from Canada's high of 83 per cent, Britain's 78 per cent, the United States' 55 per cent, France's 47 per cent, and West Germany's 34 per cent, down to Sweden's 16 per cent (Staudt, 1991, p. 162). In the USA, AID routinely uses the argument that 80 per cent of US foreign assistance is spent within the United States to obtain Congressional approval for its budget requests.

The call for a New International Economic Order in the early 1970s stemmed from a recognition of some of these inequalities: 'An international economic order controlled by a few rich countries . . . cannot be a just development order. All nations must have effective access to resources and a share in effective decisions governing their use' (cited in Arndt, 1987, p. 142). At a time when the international agencies were stressing poverty alleviation and basic needs, the countries of the South saw the global redistribution of resources as an essential prerequisite for this internal redistribution to take place.

While it is the case that the NIEO gave at least rhetorical attention to issues of class and poverty, it was conspicuously silent on gender inequalities; the UN Resolution calling for the NIEO included only one reference to women − it concerned women's biological role (UNDP, 1980, cited in Maguire, 1984). Thus, despite its radical agenda, the meaning given to inequality within the discourse of the NIEO was a very partial one, itself a product of other underlying relations of inequality which remained unacknowledged. In this sense, while the goals of development might have varied between different agencies, between countries and between the North and the South, they were still premised on certain core assumptions which allowed them to recognize certain kinds of inequalities in the development process but to overlook or deny the existence of others.

Power and Knowledge in the Development Process

Along with the promotion of particular policies, power in the development arena has also been associated with the promotion of a particular world-view. As we noted in Chapter 2, there is an intimate relationship between the world-view of powerful development agencies and the kinds of knowledge that they are likely to promote, fund and act upon. Excavations of the methodological foundations of this world-view have helped to uncover the underlying hierarchy of knowledge upon which it is constructed, a hierarchy which privileges certain kinds of information (scientific, positivist) over others (local, experimental); and certain kinds of knowers (neutral, detached) over others (committed, involved). The origins of this hierarchy lie in the liberal epistemological tradition which views reality in an essentially atomistic way, typified, for instance, in the Cartesian formulation of scientific method (cited in Shiva, 1989, p. 29): to 'reduce involved and obscure propositions step by step to those that are simpler, and then starting with the intuitive apprehension of all those that are absolutely simple, attempt to ascend to the knowledge of all others by precisely similar steps'.

This reductive approach to the production of knowledge implies that the complexities of nature and society can be broken down into their constituent components, and the separate parts studied in isolation from each other. It operates with a hierarchy of explanatory levels. Simpler, lower-level events assume priority in terms of causality as well as sequence over higher-level phenomena: 'According to this line of thought, it is both possible and desirable to build solid foundations to knowledge by isolating basic components within the social system and subjecting them to detailed investigation. Once the component is understood, we can build upon it as if it were a fixed and immutable foundation for subsequent enquiry' (Harvey, 1982, p. 2). Objectivity is essential to scientific method, so that knowledge is only considered valid when it is undertaken in a value-free and disinterested fashion – 'the so-called Archimedean standpoint somewhere outside the reality that is being observed' (Jagger, 1983, p. 370). The strength of theories which are produced by such a methodology is that they can be verified by anyone and will provide the same results, regardless of who is testing them.

Reductionism has survived as a methodology because it offers an accessible route to knowledge. Its treatment of social phenomena as analogous to natural phenomena has a powerful appeal to common-sense views of how things work (Birke, 1986). Its satisfying simplicity as a form of analysis, its promise of determinate outcomes based on a linear and hierarchical sequence of causality, commencing logically upwards from the lowest 'foundational' level of analysis to the highest aggregated one, explain why it survives as the dominant form of knowledge-construction. But reductionism is also an approach to knowledge that is fraught with problems. It works as a metaphor of nature and society as machine, rather than as organic whole; all systems are seen in terms of the same basic constituents, discrete, unrelated and atomistic (Shiva, 1989, p. 22). It neglects complex interactions between units, the interactions between the unit and the whole, as well as the possibility that a phenomenon can be simultaneously a unit and part of a larger whole (Birke, 1986, p. 61). Concepts and units of analysis are reified, frozen into universal and unchanging categories, robbed of the historical or analytical contexts from which they originally arose (Weisband, 1989, p. 4). One consequence of methodological reductionism is the isolated and piecemeal analysis of problems and solutions, resulting in the frequent confusion of surface appearance with underlying reality, symptoms with causes.

As a form of knowledge about *nature*, methodological reductionism has served dominant interests well. It promotes a view of nature broken down into its constituent parts, each of which can be treated as separate from the whole and separately exploited without appearing to impinge upon the whole. '[I]f the world is viewed as consisting of an aggregation of bits, some of which can be directly exploited for financial gain, then the overall effects of exploitation are likely to be overlooked. The effects on the global ecosystem of capitalism's piecemeal exploitation of resources bears witness to this' (Birke, 1986, p. 74). As a form of knowledge about *society*, methodological reductionism has also promoted dominant interests. Originally a method for understanding natural phenomena, it has been transferred wholesale into the social sciences where it plays an essentially conservative role, appearing to offer a neutral and objective analysis of 'how things work'. Extension of the metaphor of the machine to the study of society has led to the partitioning of social reality into its component parts and an insistence on the separability of these parts – of politics, culture and economy. Suppression of the interconnections between these spheres has helped to conceal the extent to which those who command material resources also exercise enormous command over the lives of others and over the ideas of their times. It has promoted a narrow focus on piecemeal inequities, led to a separation between 'means' and 'ends' in policy analysis, and blocked out consideration of the exploitative nature of the social system itself.

The fragmented view of society contained in the dominant world-view is mirrored in the compartmentalization of the social sciences into a number of separate and apparently self-contained disciplines, each concerning itself with one aspect of the whole. Within the social sciences, economists consider their discipline the most 'scientific' precisely because they have gone furthest in the reduction of society to atomized individuals, and knowledge production to 'parsimonious' models which are presumed to have universal application. However, neutrality, objectivity and scientific rigour are also claims made by the other social sciences for their own theoretical endeavours.

The dominant development paradigms outlined in Chapter 2 all bear the hallmarks of this reductionist approach to knowledge, helping to explain both why gender was excluded as a category of analysis and why this exclusion was obscured from the view of so many development thinkers. As Elson observes, most models informing development policy are couched in abstract and apparently gender-neutral concepts (the economy, the gross national product, the market, the formal sector, the informal sector, and so on). 'It is', she remarks, 'only on closer analysis that it becomes apparent that these supposedly neutral terms are in fact imbued with male bias, presenting a view of the world which both obscures and legitimates ill-founded gender asymmetry' (1991a, p. 9). In the rest of this chapter, we will take a closer look at some of these key concepts in order to demonstrate how reductionist forms of analysis help to disguise and legitimate the gender asymmetries which are embedded within the central concepts of development.

Confusing Means and Ends

'Why do we confuse development with economic growth?'
(Seers, 1979, p. 9).

Despite vigorous attempts at 'dethronment', economic growth remains fundamental to the most influential models of development thought. There have been extensive debates as to how such growth is best achieved: physical capital formation, human capital formation, and technical innovation have all gained, lost and then regained favour as possible ways forward. There was a brief respite in the seventies with the shift in focus to basic needs and distributive concerns, but the eighties saw the reassertion of the primacy of economic growth, with the emphasis on 'getting the prices right' and rolling back the frontiers of the state.

Proponents of economic growth argue that without such growth, 'development' in the broader sense of human well-being would be impossible to achieve. They recognize, of course, that economic growth is a 'means' rather than an end in itself, but tend to argue that achieving economic growth is the first priority. Once this has been achieved, additional redistributive measures may be necessary to ensure that it serves the real ends of development – improvements in human well-being and expansion of choice. Unfortunately this separation of means and ends, a hallmark of the liberal paradigm, has allowed more attention to be paid within such thinking to the *rate* of economic growth than to its *pattern*. Consequently, redistributive measures have never been seriously implemented either at the national or international level. There are, of course, exceptions that demonstrate what it is possible to achieve by way of human development when attention is paid to distributive measures. As Emmerji (1992) points out, Sri Lanka has higher adult literacy than Saudi Arabia, despite the fact that its per-capita income is fifteen times lower. Child mortality in Brazil is four times higher than in Jamaica although its per-capita income is twice that of Jamaica. But these remain the exceptions.

The confusion between means and ends, between growth and development, has served a very real political agenda. Preoccupation with maintaining the conditions of economic growth has detracted energy and resources from attempts at redistribution to meet the basic needs of all. Instead, economic growth has been pursued for goals that have little to do with equity. Redistribution tends to get postponed on various pretexts: because economic inequality is considered necessary to provide incentives, because countries need to build up domestic industry or military power, or simply because ruling groups consider the current distribution a just one. The extent to which there is a trade-off between equity and growth has been – and will continue to be – passionately debated and will not be dealt with here. What is relevant to the concerns of this chapter is that the neglect of distributional issues on political and economic grounds is reinforced by their neglect on conceptual grounds, with serious implications for gender equity. This illustrates graphically how 'ill-founded gender asymmetries' are woven into the core concepts of development thought.

Writing at the end of the sixties, Seers suggested that the persistent confusion between development and economic growth could be traced to the common practice by planners of measuring a country's level of development by its gross national product (GNP). The GNP was a convenient indicator since it provided a single, comprehensive measure of the wealth of a nation. 'It provided economists with a variable which can be quantified and movements which can be analysed into changes in sectoral output, factor shares or categories of expenditure,

making model-building feasible' (Seers, 1979, p. 9). Per-capita GNP
was therefore used as an indicator of a country's level of development,
and GNP measures formed the basis on which powerful national,
bilateral and international agencies formulated policies and monitored performance. However, it had become clear by the time that
Seers wrote his article that economic growth was not solving the
problems of development. Social and political difficulties continued to
beset countries with rising per-capita GNP as well as those with
stagnant or falling rates of growth. It was time to 'dispel the fog'
around definitions of development and to clarify what it meant. What
Seers put forward was a viewpoint of development that was in
complete opposition to the claims made for 'positive' neo-classical
economics. 'The starting point,' he suggested, 'is that we cannot avoid
what the positivists disparagingly refer to as "value-judgements."
Development is inevitably a normative concept, almost a synonym for
improvement. To pretend otherwise is just to hide one's value
judgements' (Seers, 1979, p. 10).

The problem lies in how the GNP is perceived: 'One defence of the
national income is that it is an objective, value-free indicator' (Seers,
1979, p. 14). It relies on apparently neutral market forces to assign
values to every type of product and service in an economy. The market
is seen as neutral in the sense of being morally random: it distributes
rewards and penalties on the basis of results, rather than effort or
intentions. In reality, however, the GNP is rarely a value-free measure
because the market itself is a highly partial mechanism for assigning
value. A fairly familiar issue in economics is the adequacy of income as
a measure of demand when the income distribution is unequal and
highly concentrated. However, further 'deconstruction' of the GNP
reveals a deeper, gender subtext to this question. First of all, it is
important to recognize that while GNP is intended as a measure of the
value of a nation's productive activities and resources, what it actually
measures are those activities and resources that are exchanged in the
market. In other words, the GNP equates the *value* of goods and
services in an economy with the *prices* they command or could
command in the marketplace.

Despite the claim by economics that the pricing mechanism is a
neutral arbiter of values, it is in reality deeply value-laden: it creates a
constant slippage in development thinking between using prices to
measure value to using them to *confer* value (Waring, 1989). Thus the
value of a 'good' is seen to lie, not in its ability to satisfy human need,
but in the price that it commands through the interplay of supply and
demand in the marketplace. A further level of disaggregation reveals
the gender bias implicit in this practice. The forces of demand and

supply are themselves extremely selectively defined when the market is the defining arena. Supply does not refer to the full range of goods and services that satisfy human needs within a society, but *only to goods and services which are offered for sale in response to market signals*. Similarly demand does not refer to the full range of goods and services that may be needed or wanted by people, but *only to 'effective' demand, or demand backed by purchasing power*.

An immediate effect of these selective definitions is that a major section of the working women of the world disappear into a 'black hole' in economic theory. A significant proportion of women's activities, produced as a part of their familial obligations ('housework'), does not enter the marketplace, does not earn an income, and is therefore excluded from GNP estimates. It has no value as far as planners are concerned. On the other hand, since these dimensions of women's labour are either unremunerated, or else ensure their confinement to the casual and low-paid sectors of gender-segregated labour markets, the 'effectiveness' of their demand is also curtailed. They do not command the purchasing power that would allow them to meet their needs through the marketplace and must rely instead on the benevolence and efficacy of non-market forms of provision: households, states or community organizations. Thus, within a market-led framework of development planning, certain categories of 'demand' and 'supply' are given secondary status in defining the means and ends of economic growth because the market is not capable of assigning a value to them. As a corollary, a major category of the working population is also accorded a secondary status in the allocation of development resources. The blindness of national accounting systems to significant aspects of women's work gives rise to various kinds of absurdities in economic analysis. A textbook example, familiar to most students of economics, points out that when a man marries his housekeeper, there will be a decline in the GNP since he now enjoys for free services which he had previously to purchase. This is treated as an amusing but trivial aberration in economic theory, unlikely to undermine its fundamentally sound principles. Yet inclusion of 'housework' would throw economic theorizing into considerable disarray and woefully complicate its claims to make predictions about the state of the economy. In the revealing words of an American labour economist,

> There is considerable warrant for considering such work (e.g. housework) as not less real – and far more vital – than work outside the home. However, there would be little analytical value to measures which always showed about 100% of women in the labour force, varying not at all through the

business cycle or through time. (Lebergott, 1964, p. 56, cited in Ciancanelli
and Berch, 1987, p. 247).

Nor is it domestic labour alone that is excluded from economic
analysis, but all aspects of human endeavour and the natural environment which have not been subjected to the same market-oriented
rationality: 'The current state', writes Waring, 'of the world is the result
of a system that attributes little or no "value" to peace. It pays no heed
to the preservation of natural resources or to the labour of the majority
of its inhabitants or to the unpaid work of the reproduction of human
life itself – not to mention to its maintenance and care. The system
cannot respond to values it refuses to recognise' (p. 4).[1]

The conflation of prices and value is by no means restricted to
macroeconomic concerns with economic growth; it permeates all levels
of development planning, starting with the GNP and other macro-
level statistics and moving all the way down to micro-level project
planning (this will be discussed further in Chapter 7). It generates a
hierarchy of production which dominates development policy and
determines how resources are allocated. The concern of development
planners has been, first and foremost, with the measurement, evaluation and promotion of marketed goods and services. However,
formally marketed goods and services are only the visible tip of the
iceberg. As a form of production, they rely critically on the performance of all kinds of other activities which are carried out beyond the
boundaries of formally recognized markets: the informal sector, the
parallel economy, the black markets. Beyond marketed activities are
the subsistence and networking activities through which most poor
people assure their livelihoods and support systems. The extent to
which these activities *can* be included in GNP calculations will depend
on the extent to which values, based on market-derived 'shadow'
prices, can be imputed to them.[2]

However, all these activities, whether carried out in the official or
unofficial economy, require the expenditure of human labour and
human creativity. They are premised, therefore, on a prior set of
activities which is concerned with the production, care and well-being
of human labour itself, both daily and across generations. By and
large, these activities are unlikely to be responsive to market prices
because they embody a set of values which has no place within a profit-
maximizing calculus. The tendency of economists to treat human
labour as somehow 'given' like any other factor of production tends to
obscure this point.[3] The result is that the care and reproduction of
human beings, undertaken largely outside the marketplace, will
always be excluded from any planning framework which relies solely

on the market to determine value. It is not simply that the system refuses to recognize certain values, as Waring suggests. It is also that it is *unable* to recognize certain values. As Robinson pointed out in 1962, the system fosters the ideology that values which can be measured in monetary terms are the only ones that should count. The same point appeared more recently in Jodha (1985):

> The first step is to measure whatever can be easily measured . . . the second step is to disregard what can't be measured . . . the third step is to presume that what cannot be measured easily is not very important . . . the fourth is to say that what cannot be easily measured really does not exist. (p. 1)

The hierarchy of production within the development discourse – and the resource allocation that it legitimates – begins to make sense if we consider the hierarchy of interests served by such a representation. In particular, we should note that women are underrepresented in activities at the 'tip of the iceberg', where development efforts and resources are concentrated; they appear in larger numbers in informal-sector and subsistence activities. They are predominant – particularly poorer women – in the reproduction and nurturing of human life and labour, the neglected sectors in the policy domain. This skewed representation demonstrates graphically the convergence of power and ideas in the field of development. It ensures that women are positioned within the policy debate as unproductive 'welfare' clients, and that their claims on the national development budget, based as they are on activities and resources which are excluded from calculations of the GNP, are rarely heard in debates over budgetary allocations. The unvarying labour of women and the continued exploitation of natural resources are taken for granted, providing what Waring calls a 'shadow subsidy' to economic growth.

Reversing the Hierarchy of Knowledge

Transformed possibilities for development come into view if we undertake a process of expanding conventional categories of analysis, revealing their interconnections and reversing the hierarchy of values embedded within them. Although the 'reversals' we will be suggesting in this chapter are specifically from a gender perspective, they have wider implications. Development processes have generated many different kinds of social inequalities, but gender is present in some form in all of them. Understanding the ideas and practices by which this most pervasive form of inequality is sustained contributes to the broader project of development built on respect for humanity and nature. As we noted at the start of the chapter, the 'ways of knowing' that have dominated the production of knowledge in development studies (and generally in the social sciences) have played an important role in defining and legitimating particular viewpoints and methods. The production of knowledge is therefore a logical place to begin the project of reversals.

Our knowledge of the world is constructed rather than discovered. It is therefore likely to be shaped and limited by the location of the knower in the social world. Marxist epistemology recognizes that in a hierarchically organized society, where the production of knowledge is controlled by a dominant class, hegemonic forms of knowledge will always be partial because they are likely to reflect the interests of the dominant class: 'Because the ruling class has an interest in concealing the way in which it dominates and exploits the rest of the population, the interpretation of reality that it presents will be distorted in characteristic ways. In particular, the suffering of the subordinate classes will be ignored, redescribed as enjoyment or justified as freely chosen, deserved or inevitable' (Jagger, 1983, p. 370).

Feminist contributions to this analysis recognize that oppressed groups may sometimes be duped into acquiescence, denial or collusion in their oppression. However, they also maintain that the reality and relentlessness of their suffering can give the oppressed a very different consciousness about the justness of the social order to that held by dominant groups. It is not in the interests of the oppressed to hold on to a partial view of society, but rather to see it in all its complexity and its distortions: 'whereas the condition of oppressed groups is visible only dimly to the ruling class, the oppressed are able to see more clearly the ruled as well as the rulers and the relation between them' (Jagger, 1983, p. 371). Citing Nandy (1986), Shiva makes the same point: 'one must choose the slave's standpoint not only because the slave is oppressed but also because he represents a higher order cognition which perforce includes the master as a human whereas the master's cognition has to exclude the slave except as a "thing" ' (p. 53).

This suggests that a very different form of knowledge and practice is likely to emerge if it is based on what Hartsock (1987) describes as the 'feminist standpoint', based on the distinctive experiences associated with women's lives in a gendered social world. It is specifically the character of women's labour – their caring and manual labour – that provides them with this distinct standpoint in relation to social reality. However, the plea for a more situated knowledge based on a 'feminist standpoint' carries the danger of positing once again the universalism of women's interests. As the DAWN group argue, 'feminism cannot be monolithic in its issues, goals and strategies, since it constitutes the political expression of the concerns and interests of women from different regions, classes, nationalities and ethnic backgrounds' (Sen and Grown, 1985, p. 13). The group proposes instead that it is from the vantage point of the most oppressed – women who are disenfranchised by class, race and nationality – that the complexities of subordination can be best grasped and strategies devised for a more equitable development. This argument for a new paradigm for development with equity was supported by Jain (1983), a founding member of DAWN, who pointed out that gender inequality pervaded all other forms of inequality – economic, racial, ethnic, religious – so that any attempt to address it would also address these other forms. It was also supported by Antrobus, who said, 'the strongest case for the focus on the poor Third World woman is that in her we find the conjuncture of race, class, gender and nationality which symbolizes underdevelopment' (1989b, p. 202).

This idea that development theories and practice should start from the vantage point of the poor Third World women should not be taken to imply that somehow this figure is more knowledgeable than all others, but rather that she offers the viewpoint from below, a viewpoint that can help to realign development paradigms more closely to 'the real order of things'. Nor should it be taken to signify that only the dispossessed women of the Third World matter, but rather that without a structural transformation of the lives of the poorest and most oppressed sections of all societies, there can be neither development nor equity.

Because reversals in the hierarchy of knowledge are in the interests of all oppressed groups, feminist researchers, advocates and practitioners are likely to find allies among others who share their critique of the dominant paradigms. While the various grassroots movements, environmental lobbies and social-action groups working directly with the poor and dispossessed do not always share feminist priorities, there are many overlapping elements in their critique of the knowledge produced and validated through official development practices in relation to the environment, to indigenous forms of knowledge, to evaluation techniques, and to the perceptions and priorities of the poor (see Agarwal, 1985; Mitra, 1982; Fernandes and Tandon, 1981; Chambers, 1992). Within this body of work, the feminist critique has been the most far-reaching, asserting that hostility to women is woven into the very fabric of scientific method; that 'scientific objectivity' is merely male subjectivity in disguise (Merchant, 1980; Keller, 1985; Shiva, 1989).

Discussing these diverse critiques, Kloppenburg, Jr. (1991b) suggests that they have a shared point of departure: 'the central insight that the mental productions that we call scientific knowledge are no less subject to social influences than are the products of any other way of knowing' (p. 8). Just as gender was a socially constructed representation (rather than a precise reflection) of sex, so too was science a socially constructed (rather than a precise) reflection of nature. What also unifies these critiques is the central place they give to a development based on local, rather than universal, claims to knowledge. Locally produced knowledge is knowledge which emerges out of experience rather than theory, although it may inform and improve theory. It is derived 'from direct experience of a labor process which is itself shaped and delimited by the distinctive characteristics of a particular place with a unique social and physical environment'. As examples, Kloppenburg, Jr. suggests:

> It is *local* knowledge that informs the birthing skills of the sages-femmes studied by Bohme (1984). It is *local* knowledge that enables the competent farmer to master the 'intricate formal patterns in ordering his work within the overlapping cycles – human and natural, controllable and uncontrollable – of the life of a farm' (Berry, 1977, p. 44). It is *local* knowledge that allows Robert Pirsig to keep his bike running through *Zen and the Art of Motorcycle Maintenance* (Pirsig, 1974). It is *local* knowledge that enables machinists to 'make out' on the shop floor (Burawoy, 1979). And it is *local* knowledge produced by workers that is the object of appropriation and control in both Taylorist and 'postindustrial' strategies of industrial management (Kloppenburg, Jr., 1991b, p. 14).

However, a cautionary note is necessary here. While there are many convergences between different critiques of the dominant form of knowledge production, there are also many divergences, particularly in relation to how alternative paradigms are to be produced. Such divergences are also apparent among feminist critics. There are those who believe that all formal methods for gathering knowledge are oppressive, that objectivity is impossible to achieve, and all that can be done is to accept a plurality of views that are essentially incommensurable. As Eichler points out, 'the logical consequence of such a principled stance is that research, including the implied cumulative knowledge it generates, is impossible', a conclusion that is tantamount to throwing the baby out with the bathwater (1991, p. 11). It has particularly disastrous implications for those who have to take policy decisions, since it denies the possibility of a theoretically informed practice.

Eichler argues that it is possible to be critical of existing definitions of objectivity without sinking into 'the morass of complete cultural subjectivism' (p. 13). This would require a distinction to be maintained between 'objectivity', which is based on recognition that a material reality exists outside of the observer, and 'detachment', the idea that the observer can step outside the reality being observed. Values are an inherent aspect of the production and application of knowledge, but need to be made explicit rather than being shrouded in neutralizing and technicist discourse. Eichler's criteria for a more situated objectivity ('an asymptotically approachable, but unreachable goal, with the elimination of sexism in research as a station along the way' [p. 14] entail a commitment to look at contrary evidence; the aim of maximum replicability through accurate reporting of all processes employed, including clear distinctions between reporting and interpreting; a commitment to truth-finding or veracity; and clarification and classification of values underlying the endeavour.

Reversing Allocational Priorities

The production of knowledge has been an important site of struggle for feminists working in development, but it is only one such site. Such knowledge has to feed into the struggle for 'reversals' in the development budget if it is to have a practical effect on people's lives.[4] The arguments for undertaking a reversal of allocational priorities in the planning process become compelling once we step back from the taken-for-granted assumptions of dominant development paradigms and ask ourselves once again what exactly the 'ends' of development are supposed to be and what are the means to these ends.

The stark suffering of the past decade provides a fresh and urgent reminder that development, in its best sense, must be about the development of the well-being and creativity of all members of society. The poor are poor precisely because they lack the means to live healthy, active and secure lives. They are poor because they must run down their only asset – their bodies – simply to survive. A 'reversed' development which starts from the priorities of the poor places human life and human well-being at the forefront of the planning process, so that the 'means' of the development process are valued in terms of their contribution to this goal. All human endeavour, whether concerned with the production of goods or services, tangibles or intangibles, is valued to the extent to which it leads to the immediate satisfaction of human need or assures its future satisfaction. The most valued activities, then, become those concerned with the care, nourishment and well-being of human life. Since human labour is necessary to activate all forms of production, human resources are unique in being both the ends and the means of development, of instrumental as well as of intrinsic value. People cannot be planned for in the same way as things.

While it is clearly the case that investment in human welfare is not possible without economic growth, it is also the case that economic growth requires – and is intended to achieve – the health and well-being of people. If economic growth is slowed down by greater investments in human welfare, then this should be seen as a trade-off between different kinds of development. The terms of this trade-off can only be calculated if we have, along with the GNP, indices of sustainable human welfare that monitor those 'goods' which are valued as ends in themselves rather than in terms of the prices they command.[5]

If the satisfaction of human need rather than the exercise of market rationality is taken as the criterion of production, then clearly a much more holistic view of development becomes necessary. Development is no longer measured by the volume of *marketed* goods and services alone, but by the extent to which human well-being is assured. Activities which contribute to the health and well-being of people would be recognised as productive, regardless of whether they are carried out within the personalized relations of family production, the commercialized relations of market production, or the bureacratized relations of state production. Markets would take their place as simply one of a variety of institutional mechanisms through which human needs can be met, rather than as the sole arbiter of 'value'. Such an approach would promote both class and gender equity: women, particularly poor women, would take their place as key actors in the development process because of their contribution to human survival and well-being among those who have been most disenfranchised by growth-dominated development strategies.

Such reversals in allocational priorities are unlikely to occur without a sea-change in the way in which policymakers make their decisions. But as the extreme forms of hostility to state intervention that marked the 1980s give way to policies which seek a judicious mix of markets and state allocation, new opportunities for a feminist reformulation of the development agenda become possible. There appears to be a growing recognition in international policy circles (where hostility to state interventions was most marked) that both economic growth and poverty alleviation are better served by 'governed', rather than untrammelled, market forces. While the arguments which have roused greatest interest predictably relate to the need for 'market-friendly' interventions for greater economic growth, there is also an increased interest in a 'human development' (UNDP, 1990) which combines labour-intensive growth strategies to generate employment opportunities for the poor with public provision of key welfare resources. While this offers a more hospitable environment for a 'reversed' agenda than a neo-liberal driven one, we need to continue to argue for policies that go beyond 'market-friendly' interventions to policy approaches which are designed to equalize access to market opportunities as well as to welfare provision; for what Elson (1988a) calls 'the social management of the market'.

Connecting Welfare and Efficiency: Another Perspective on Gender Equity

Within this reversed hierarchy of development priorities, a different notion of gender equity to that promoted through early WID advocacy becomes possible, one grounded in the interdependence between people, resources and activities. It suggests that the opposition posited in WID advocacy between welfare and efficiency needs to be re-thought. Although welfare ultimately relates to the state of human well-being, there has been a persistent confusion within the develop-ment discourse between *welfare* as a desirable outcome of human endeavour and *welfarism* which refers to the stigmatizing relations associated with the public provision of welfare goods, especially to the poor. The treatment of recipients of state-provided welfare goods as dependent and passive clients has resulted in an unfortunate and false polarization between 'welfare' and 'efficiency' so that any state provision of social services is automatically deemed to create depen-dence and undermine the efficiency of the economic system. Nor is this peculiar to developing country contexts. As US Senator Daniel Moynihan wrote:

> If American society recognised home-making and child rearing as produc-tion work to be included in the national economic accounts the receipt of welfare might not imply dependency. But we don't. It may be hoped the women's movement of the present time will change this. But as of the time I write, it had not. (Cited in Waring, 1989, p. 8).

Although early WID advocacy was important in displacing the old policy equation between women/reproduction/welfarism, the new policy equation between women/production/efficiency has been con-structed on an equally impoverished view of women's lives. It has defined women's economic agency as equivalent to that of men, ignoring their greater embeddedness in familial and domestic responsibilities. If the care of human life and well-being were to be given the same value in development priorities as the production of material resources, then the provision of welfare services would be seen as complementary to development goals rather than antithetical to them. It would free women to pursue economic livelihoods if they chose to, or were compelled to by their circumstances, rather than imposing a predetermined set of life choices on them. Planning for gender equity on the basis of social justice, rather than of formal equality, requires recognition of the full weight and implications of the gender division of labour in the lives of women and men, and of the different needs, priorities and possibilities that it gives rise to. Gender equity requires that welfare is seen as complementary, rather than in opposition, to efficiency.

However, a gender equity based on recognition of difference rather than similarity, has implications that go beyond equality of opportunity. Adapting a simple metaphor about foxes and cranes used by McAllister (1984) in arguing for gender equity will help to indicate why. If market competition for scarce resources is represented as a race across a stretch of land to get to a single saucer of food, then market equity (reliance on free market forces) will favour foxes who are swifter on land than cranes. Equality of opportunity entails the removal of discriminatory barriers to market participation so that everyone is treated the same: both foxes and cranes are to be fed from saucers. However, the fox still has an advantage over the crane since the saucer is better adapted to its feeding requirements. Equalizing agency requires recognition of different needs and requirements so as to ensure equity of outcomes; foxes are fed from saucers, while cranes are fed from vessels. We need not stretch the metaphor too far, but it does help to draw attention, not only to the unequal terms on which women and men enter the public domain, but also to the formidable barriers within public institutions. The earlier stress on equality of opportunity for women was premised on the belief that the problem lay in discriminatory barriers to women's employment and their lack of educational credentials to compete with men. However, as we noted in the last chapter, public institutions have not evolved neutrally but in deeply gendered ways. They reward certain kinds of skills and abilities over others, and certain kinds of economic agents (those unencumbered by bodies, families or sexual identities) over others. Consequently, problems of sexual harassment, the need for separate toilets or breast-feeding facilities, provision of paid leave to have children, absenteeism due to illness in the family, only emerge as problems when women join the workplace. Training women in marketable skills and abilities will not give them the same degree of agency as men in the public domain as long as public institutions do not accommodate the different bodies, needs and values that they bring to the workplace. Gender equity thus goes beyond equal opportunity; it requires the transformation of the basic rules, hierarchies and practices of public institutions.

Building Alliances:
The Bureaucratic–Activist Divide

Clearly, the official agencies of development, both within national machineries and at the international level, have the resources and social weight to play an important role in implementing this broader vision of gender equity. However, this brings us back to the question asked in Chapter 2: to what extent can institutions that have systematically displayed prejudiced and stereotyped views about women be relied upon to implement the goal of gender equity? There has now been sufficient research into these issues to suggest that the institutions responsible for development planning and administration are not exempt from the gendered processes identified in the public domain at large (see the review of this literature in Goetz, 1992). Bureaucracies do not passively reflect the values of the wider society, but are actors in their own right, with a stake in upholding the hierarchical organization of gender. Research into gender relations within bureaucratic organizations suggests that, despite differences in the cultures in which they are located, and the resources which they command, there is a remarkable similarity in the way in which bureaucratic rules and practices actively reconstitute gender hier-archy. Women and men are positioned differently and unequally both as the agents of policy administration and as objects of policy attention. There are few women at the top levels of decision-making within policy to transform this state of affairs, and even fewer who are willing to challenge dominant agency practice (Goetz, 1992). Consequently, even organizations that have adopted goals of gender equity have frequently failed to implement them.

The continuing marginality of women's concerns is revealed in the organizational structures of national and international development bureaucracies. As we noted in the first chapter, increasing awareness of women as a category of development led to the setting up of national machineries of women's affairs and WID units in the bilateral and multilateral aid agencies. However, these tend to be 'often perched on the peripheries of "mainstream" development concerns' (Goetz, 1992). They are never located in the crucial 'technical core' of rule-making, budgeting and personnel policy within bureaucratic processes. The so-called 'women's desks' attached to many ministries are often literally no more than a desk (Staudt, 1985, 1990). WID units usually operate with minimal budgets, staff and authority. As Staudt (1990, p. 9) has estimated, 3.5 per cent of the projects of UN agencies, representing 0.2 per cent of budget allocations, benefit women; less than 1 per cent of FAO projects specify strategies to reach women farmers (figures cited in Goetz, 1992). The limited resources and authority given to most WID units provide little leverage for carrying out their mandates.

Staudt's analysis of the WID office in USAID (cited in Chapter 2) pointed to the important support given by its outside constituencies in its battles to convince a 'recalcitrant bureaucracy' to allocate more resources to women in AID-assisted countries. At the same time she noted the ambivalent situation of women constituents, caught as they were in the dilemma of criticizing, yet supporting, an agency that was dominated by men and continued to direct resources to men at the overwhelming rate of 96 per cent of programme funds. This is a familiar dilemma for many feminist activists, a dilemma further sharpened for Third World feminists working at grassroots level where they confront on a daily basis the disastrous effects of male-dominated, frequently donor-supported, development efforts. There is a strong, and understandable, temptation to eschew all forms of interaction with these officially sanctioned vehicles of gender inequality. Yet, as we argued in the previous chapter, it is important that feminist activists do not turn their back on the official agencies of development, which remain the most powerful mechanisms for resource allocation, with the potential capacity to satisfy or to exacerbate the desperate imbalance in resources and responsibilities that underpins women's subordinate position in most societies. While donor agencies are rarely accountable to the populations of the Third World, national governments are, at least in principle, supposed to be. What is needed, therefore, is a critical scrutiny of official agencies for the possibilities that they might offer. Such analysis can provide important insights for attempts to forge networks and alliances between those working within and those working outside these agencies. Reviewing the WID record of a number of development agencies, Kardam observes: 'Understanding the structural constraints under which development agencies operate and what they can and cannot do to empower women is very important . . . it enables staff members who act as change agents to use appropriate strategies to incorporate WID, and Third World women to find allies among development agencies' (Kardam, 1989, p. 150).

WID practitioners within the agencies may be governed by their institutional rules and incentives, but they are also charged with the mandate of ensuring greater opportunities for women.[6] Their vision of development may differ from those of grassroots activists, but they share a concern for meeting women's basic needs. This can form a creative basis for coalitions, networks and alliances. WID advocates within the agencies can help to expand the 'room for manoeuvre' available to feminist activists by helping to channel resources and create the enabling infrastructures that women need. They can also provide an important link for feminist activists outside the official agencies with powerful decision-makers within, so that the pressures of a wider political constituency for a transformed agenda of development are felt by the agencies. Activists can play a valuable role, not only in seeking official support for women's basic needs, but also in ensuring that these needs are met in ways that help to transform the conditions of women's lives rather than merely reinforcing their dependence. In other words, ends and means have to be seen as interrelated aspects of the development effort, rather than as distinct and separate. To quote Beneria and Sen (1982, p. 173), 'because the principal outcomes of the tensions between class and gender are the differential overwork and ill-health of women, we must support measures such as systems of water provision, electrification, sanitation, and medical care and other similar policies, but with a strong emphasis on *how* such programs are implemented and *whom* they benefit.' Seeking allies within official agencies offers the opportunity to influence the 'hows' and the 'whoms' of basic needs provision.

Beyond Planning: Strategies for
Women's Empowerment

The concern with the politics of basic-needs provision is now an important theme in feminist development practice. Molyneux's discussion of the concept of women's interests has proven particularly useful in helping to outline a transformational politics that begins with the day-to-day problems faced by poor women (1985). Since it will feature in subsequent chapters, a brief summary is provided here. Molyneux suggests that the concept of 'women's interests', while central to feminist evaluations of social policy, is a dubious one because it assumes that such interests are a given entity that can be either ignored or overridden by policymakers:

Although it is true that at some level of abstraction women can be said to
have some interests in common, there is no consensus over what these
interests are or how they are to be formulated. This is in part because there
is no theoretically adequate and universally applicable causal explanation of
women's subordination from which a general account of women's interests
can be derived. . . . A theory of interests that has an application to the debate
about women's capacity to struggle for, and benefit from, social change
must begin by recognizing difference rather than assuming homogeneity.
(pp. 231–2).

A recognition of difference – not just between women and men, but
also *within* categories of women and men – makes the concept of
'women's interests' highly contentious. 'Because women are positioned
in their societies through a variety of different means – class, ethnicity
and gender – the interests they have as a group are similarly shaped in
complex and sometimes conflicting ways' (p. 232). Consequently,
Molyneux suggests that the concept of gender interests be reserved for
those that 'women (or men, for that matter) may develop by virtue of
their social positioning through gender attributes' (p. 232). However,
these may be practical or strategic, 'each being derived in a different
way and each involving different implications for women's subjectivity'. Women's strategic gender interests are derived in the first
instance deductively: 'from the analysis of their subordination and
from the formulation of an alternative, more satisfactory set of
arrangements from those which exist' (p. 232). Practical gender
interests, on the other hand, are given inductively and derive from 'the
concrete conditions of women's positioning within the gender division
of labour . . . Practical interests are usually a response to immediate
perceived need, and they do not generally entail a strategic goal such
as women's emancipation or gender equality' (p. 233). Thus, by virtue
of their responsibility for family welfare within the domestic division
of labour, women may be seen to have a practical gender interest in the
provision of resources that meet basic welfare needs.

Embedded within this distinction between the practical and the
strategic is a distinction between policies that address the concrete
conditions of women's daily lives, which are imposed by existing
divisions in resources and responsibilities, and those which seek to
transform women's *position*[7] within a structurally unequal set of social
relations. The structural inequalities of gender in different contexts
define both how men and women perceive their day-to-day practical
needs as well as giving them differing and possibly conflicting stakes in
the longer-run transformation of these inequalities. Examples of

strategic measures suggested by Molyneux that could help to transform women's position include the abolition of the gender division of
labour; alleviation of the burden of child care and domestic labour on
women; removal of institutionalized forms of discrimination; measures against male violence, sexual exploitation of women, and
coercive forms of marriage.

The distinction between practical and strategic, between women's
condition and position, is useful because it suggests a way of looking at
the question of women's empowerment. We will be considering this in
greater detail in Chapter 9, but there are a number of points worth
making here. While most mainstream development agencies have
recognized the *efficiency* of factoring gender into their policy design,
and while some acknowledge the *equity* arguments for meeting
women's practical gender needs within the existing division of
resources and responsibilities, few are prepared to address the
underlying inequalities frequently associated with this division. The
distinction between practical and strategic helps to unpack the very
real tension between policies which seek to distribute resources in ways
that preserve and reinforce these inequalities and those which use
women's everyday practical needs as a starting point for challenging
these inequalities.

As Molyneux points out, when official policymakers (she takes the
example of the Sandinista government in Nicaragua) seek to address
women's concerns, it is generally the practical gender issues, particularly those that serve the policymakers' own predefined agendas,
which are both 'safer' to implement and have an instrumental value.[8]
If there is a single important lesson for feminists to learn from the past
decades of development, it is that the political will for taking on more
politically controversial issues which address women's strategic gender
interests is contingent on women themselves organizing to demand
and promote change. However, solidarity around strategic gender
interests does not come naturally into existence. What has given
women's disenfranchisement its intractable character is not only their
exclusion from the main sources of power, privilege and prestige
within their societies, but also the ideological construction of such
exclusion as biologically determined, divinely ordained or rationally
and voluntarily chosen. Such beliefs are deeply rooted in the consciousness of both women and men, since they are acquired along with
their sense of selfhood and identity. Nor are gender identities unitary;
they are cut across by class and other social divisions. Solidarity is likely
to be most effective when it is built from the bottom up, in response to
locally identified needs and priorities, rather than imposed by some

false universalistic notion of sisterhood (Beall et al., 1989). Feminist activists working in development have consequently often taken women's given practical gender concerns as an entry point for initiating a longer-term process of transformation, a strategy which has been described as 'subverting welfare for equity'.[9]

In the final analysis, therefore, women's collective strength and creativity remains the main hope of a transformative politics; and here there is scope for optimism. Despite the reversals and setbacks that the economic crises of the past decade have wrought in the lives of women − and men − throughout the world, there have also been important and enduring changes. Throughout the world, it has become apparent that women's formal and informal lobbies, organizations and movements have formed the backbone of struggles to resist the predations of a top-down development process. Perhaps the key achievement of the Women's Decade is that is has helped to create an important political space for the proliferation of both informal grassroots associations and nationwide movements which seek to improve women's condition and position. As Moser (1992) notes, taken individually, these organizations appear weak, underfinanced and disparate. But together they represent a diverse and rich movement for changing women's lives well beyond what is envisaged by the official agencies of development. This can be seen as the most important legacy of the Women's Decade. We will conclude this chapter with the tribute paid by the DAWN group to the resourcefulness and resilience of women, all over the world, despite the odds against them:

> It is important for us in the women's movement to understand and acknowledge our own achievements and strengths . . . It is easy to be discouraged about the concrete improvements in women's economic and social position. They appear to have been as meagre as the resources which agencies and governments have actually directed to women. But let us look at our experiences in another way. We know now from our own research how deeply ingrained and how far back historically is the subordination of women. What we have managed to do in the last few years is to forge *worldwide* networks and movements, as never existed before, to transform that subordination and in the process to break down other oppressive structures as well . . . Starting from little knowledge and training, and having to challenge the full social, economic and psychological weight of gender (and often class, national and ethnic) oppression, we have acquired skills and self-confidence and the capacity to organize for change. (Sen and Grown, 1985, p. 15)

Notes

1 A more immediate example of the distortions wrought by reliance on the market to calculate the production of value within an economy was reported by David Nicholson-Lord in the *Independent*, 31 May 1993. It relates to the doubling of rates of skin cancer in the UK compared to twenty years ago, due largely to the growing hole in the ozone layer which is letting in carcinogenic radiation. Profit margins on suncreams are about 50 per cent and the market is growing at 4 per cent a year. Noting the alliance between Boots Chemists and the Cancer Research Campaign to promote 'sensible sun behaviour', he suggested that Boots' interests in the campaign lay partly in the fact that three of the five guidelines for sensible sun behaviour entailed purchasing products (sun hats, sun cream and sunglasses). Boots sell sunglasses and account for 47 per cent of the lucrative sun-protection market. Nicholson-Lord goes on to comment, 'When the Treasury does its sums, that portion of the £110m sun-protection market arising from worries about UV radiation will be added to the gross national product and will count as economic growth. Thanks to the hole in the ozone layer and the skin cancer epidemic, we will all be that little bit *richer*.'

2 However, the adoption of imputation procedures entails leaving behind the relative transparency of market prices in favour of a murkier territory of assumptions and arbitrariness. As Pittin (1987) points out in her study of Nigerian census data, measuring the status and value of women's work is fraught with difficulties, many of which are related to the 'implicit challenge to male domination inherent in the kinds of questions asked' (p. 41). The absurdities which result from attempts at imputation generally err on the side of underestimating women's contribution. Bangladesh census data classified men who are engaged in field-based stages of rice production as economically active while women engaged in home-based processing of the same rice crop are excluded from labour force statistics. Rice is generally counted in the GNP, whether it is consumed or marketed, but kitchen garden crops were for a long term excluded from GNP calculations regardless of whether they were marketed or not. The Fiji 1974 Labour Force Survey defined anyone involved in raising fewer than ten chickens as economically inactive, while anyone raising ten or more chickens was considered economically active.

3 Orthodox economics shares with Marxist political economy the apparent assumption that an individual is born at the time of applying for 'his' first first job (Jagger, 1983, p. 77).

4 Some examples will help indicate priorities within national budgets. In South Asia, education accounts for 6.7 per cent of public expenditure; in Southeast Asia it is closer to 13 per cent. Throughout Asia, health accounts for 3 per cent of public expenditure. Economic services (transport and communications, infrastructure and power) account for around 36 per cent of public expenditure in South Asia. ESCAP calculated at the end of the seventies that minimum basic needs could have been met within all low-

income communities in Asian countries if governments had raised their social services outlay by at least 20 per cent of total public expenditure and raised the proportion to at least 33 per cent as income grew over the next decade (taken from Rao et al., 1991).

5 There is an attempt to develop such an index for Britain by the New Economics Foundation (*Independent*, 31 May 1993).

6 Indeed in contexts where there is no strong grassroots women's movement, WID advocates within the government may be critical for safeguarding women's practical gender needs and for creating the environment for women's future political participation. This, for instance, is argued by Keller and Mbewe (1991) in the Zambian situation where structural adjustment policies threaten to undermine women farmers' ability to earn an income and to ensure household food security.

7 Naripokkho, a women's organization in Bangladesh, uses the distinction between the condition and position of women as a way of clarifying the distinction between womens practical and strategic gender interests. Personal communication, Shireen Huq.

8 In the case of the Sandinista government, Molyneux points out that, despite its initial commitment to an emancipatory agenda for women, counter-revolutionary forces, economic scarcity and military threat eroded its ability to carry out its promises. A study of its policies make clear that it was only able to implement those measures which fitted in with its general goals, enjoyed popular support and could be realized without arousing strong opposition. Sandinista policies which addressed their domestic responsibilities through mother-and-child health-care programmes obviously met women's practical gender interests. In addition, the government also carried out campaigns to encourage women to conserve their domestic resources so as to prevent pressure building up over wage demands which might undermine its broader economic programmes. However, a conservative clergy, linked with the Catholic Church, constituted a powerful force in favour of traditional family life and the division of labour which characterized it. They actively opposed all measures that had strategic implications for women's position, such as educational and family reforms, the conscription of women, legalization of contraception and birth control.

9 The phrase was coined by Dorienne Wilson-Smilie to describe her strategy as Director of the Women and Development Programme within the Commonwealth Secretariat in the late eighties.

Benevolent Dictators, Maternal Altruists and Patriarchal Contracts: Gender and Household Economics

The assumption that the family integrates the welfare of its members into an internally consistent family-utility function attributes a role to the family that undoubtedly exceeds its capacity as a social institution. (Schultz, 1973, p. S10)

Schultz has argued that a household manager or decision-maker will internalize the utility functions of family members through a high level of concern or caring for other members and will also be more informed than other (particularly younger) members. This is pretty much where the theory rests at this point. (Evenson, 1976, p. 89)

Home is the place where, when you have to go there,
They have to take you in. (Robert Frost, cited in Pollak, 1985)

The control and allocation of resources within the household is a complex process which has to be seen in relation to a web of rights and obligations. The management of labour, income and resources is something which is crucially bound up with household organization and the sexual division of labour. (Moore, 1988, p. 56)

Introduction

The previous chapter discussed some of the value-laden concepts through which gender inequalities have been ignored or obscured within the macroeconomic development discourse. The analytical focus in this chapter will be located at the other end of the spectrum. It will compare conceptualizations of the household within microeconomic analysis with its treatment in (mainly feminist) anthropology in order to explore in greater detail the ways in which different theoretical lenses shape – and limit – our insights into the nature of social reality. The household has a particular relevance for this attempt since many of the basic allocational activities that economists are concerned with are organized through the 'intimate' relations of marriage, parenthood and kinship, the traditional domain of anthropologists. On a more practical note, economists' assumptions about the household have informed and shaped a range of different policies, which, as subsequent chapters will show, explains why women's needs and interests have so often been overlooked by policymakers.

Broadly speaking, two different approaches to the household will be considered: that which treats the household as a unit of altruistic decision-making, and that which considers it a site of bargaining and conflict. I will examine how economists have dealt with these alternative views, starting with the 'altruistic' version which continues to exert a powerful influence on how households are thought about and data collected within the development field. I will then go on to examine other social-science contributions to see how they represent domestic modes of resource allocation. Such a comparison inevitably touches on questions of method, given the very different approaches to knowledge production to be found in these different disciplines.

Economists and Others:
Dissent over the Household

An astronomer once suggested that students of the 'human' sciences had problems distinguishing irrelevant information from genuine, that is, 'signals' from 'noise':

> Instead of separating the noise – throwing it away as the physicists do – they spend their energies chasing through every detail of the darned stuff . . . Students of sociology might indeed be described as the ultimate students of noise. (Hoyle and Hoyle, 1971, cited in Sprey, 1990, p. 25).

A sociologist's rejoinder to this was, 'This is a somewhat naive, but also worthwhile observation. Naive, because after all, one person's noise may be another's signal; worthwhile, because it alerts us to the fact that the world of marriage and the family is a noisy one indeed' (Sprey, 1990, p. 26). Although these diverging viewpoints come from the natural and human sciences, they capture remarkably well the methodological differences between neo-classical economists (still the mainstream within the discipline) and 'others' within the field of social sciences.

The simplifying core of neo-classical theory, as we saw in Chapter 2, is the assumption of rational choice, so that all human behaviour is explained as the attempt to maximize individual utilities in the face of economic scarcity. The economic problem is reduced to making non-prescriptive, 'positivist' predictions about how scarce resources are likely to be allocated between alternative uses to meet this maximization criterion. Neo-classical economists claim simplicity, parsimony and elegance for their approach; they achieve these through a process of theoretical and methodological reductionism. The bewildering and contradictory complexity of 'everyday lived reality' is compressed into a few, tightly bounded concepts which lend themselves to quantitative approximation, econometric manipulation and determinate outcomes; the rest is discarded as so much 'noise'. The pre-eminence of positivist thinking within economics explains the privileged status granted to 'value-free' quantitative verification of theoretically derived hypotheses.

Criticisms of the neo-classical approach have existed almost as long as the approach itself, directed primarily at its aggregating, averaging and universalizing tendencies, and at the impoverished construction of social reality which results. Structural constraints, institutional processes and cultural variations – the 'noise' which neo-classical economists discard – have all been invoked to challenge and 'unpack' the tightly bounded concepts which constitute the neo-classical model of the universe. Other disciplines have, of course, their own limitations. Sociologists, as we saw, have been described as 'the ultimate students of noise'. Similarly, the relentless focus on ethnographic minutiae of many anthropologists lays them open to charges which reverse those levelled at economists, namely, an antipathy to generalizable 'rules' and a preoccupation with 'exceptions'; an unease with certainties and an emphasis on uncertainties; indifference to the larger picture and immersion in the details of daily existence – too much noise, in other words, and not enough signals.

While it is indeed the case that social reality is infinitely diverse and contradictory, theoretical paradigms need to possess boundaries and limitations if they are to be useful. The economist's concern with stripping human behaviour down to its bare essentials may be justified if it can be shown that what is excluded is random or anomalous. If, however, some of the 'noise' discarded by economists turns out to throw a new or different light on the very phenomena which economic models purport to explain, then economic explanations must be regarded as misleading or incomplete.

The New Household Economics: 'From each according to ability; to each according to need'?

Neo-classical theory has not always had a great deal to say about households. Early versions tended to approximate household behaviour through the behaviour of individuals, either in their capacity as consumers (demanding goods) or as workers (supplying labour). The household collectivity was thus left as a 'black box' in economic theory, its internal relations and processes excluded from the economic explanandum.

A major obstacle to incorporating the collective nature of households was that economic modelling had been developed to deal with individual preferences and behaviour. In an early exposition of what he called the 'Mr and Mrs Hyde problem', Samuelson (1956) articulated the conundrum of intra-household issues for economists: how could the preferences of individual household members be collapsed into a single aggregated order of preferences so that households could continue to be treated within economic models as internally undifferentiated (and therefore mathematically tractable)? Samuelson demonstrated that the family would behave 'as if' it maximized a joint welfare function *only* if joint consumption and interdependent utility functions within the family could be ruled out. Unfortunately, both these features might be considered precisely what distinguishes the family as an institution. Samuelson's way around this problem was to assert that the 'natural' altruism of the family would be sufficient to override any deviations from the technical conditions for joint-welfare maximization:

> since blood is thicker than water, the preferences of the different members are interrelated by what might be called a 'consensus' or 'social welfare function' which takes into account the deservingness or ethical worths of the consumption levels of each of the members. The family acts *as if* it were maximizing their joint welfare function. (p. 10)

The problem of Mr and Mrs Hyde was addressed in greater detail subsequently by Becker (1965, 1976, 1981) who laid the foundations of the New Household Economics. Becker's main contribution was to integrate the production and consumption activities of the household economy and to extend maximization principles to its internal workings. In his version, 'Mr and Mrs Hyde' come together in marriage because of their complementarity in biological reproduction (Becker, 1974). Once they have formed a household, they behave 'as if' they were a single entity, maximizing a joint welfare function, subject to the household production function. They combine goods and services purchased from the market with domestically available inputs, primarily the labour of the family, in order to produce a bundle of 'Z-goods', the direct objects of utility (for example, health, nutrition, recreation, child services, and so on). In order that the welfare-maximizing bundle of Z-goods is produced, productive resources at the disposal of the household are allocated to those activities in which they are likely to make the greatest contribution. Family labour is also allocated on this principle of comparative advantage so that each member specializes in those activities which give them the highest relative returns. However, households could only be portrayed as a welfare-maximizing unit if efficiency in production was matched by a distribution process which also maximized the welfare of its members. Here a problem arose. Unlike productive inputs like household labour and assets, which were potentially, if not actually, marketed, individual utility could not be given a transaction price. Nor was it generally acceptable within the positivist tradition to make comparisons between subjectively formulated utilities of different individuals.

Once again, the problem of assuring joint welfare maximization in household distribution was resolved through the ingenious ploy of *assuming* that this was precisely what happens. Some versions proposed full altruism: 'the welfare of each member of the family is normally integrated into a unified family welfare function' (Schultz, 1973, p. S6). Willis (1973) suggested reversing Samuelson's argument; in other words, 'the family exists as an institution because, given the existence of altruism and nonmarket mechanisms for the allocation of commodities and welfare among its members, it has both the incentive and the capacity to resolve allocative problems' (p. S19). Thus the existence of joint consumption and inter-dependent utilities which, in the impersonal environment of the market, would lead to maximization failures was irrelevant within the household where altruism was the paramount decision-making principle. In other versions of the model, selective altruism was assumed to ensure joint welfare maximization. Becker (1981), for instance, accepted the possibility of 'rotten kids', but posited the 'benevolent dictatorship' of the household head to ensure welfare maximization: 'the household welfare function is considered to be identical to that of the benevolent dictator who heads the household and ensures that welfare resources are optimally allocated between households members' (p. 192). The benevolence of the head was such that, according to one economist, he would 'feel the disutility of labour, say of his wife, as much as that of his own' (Nakajima, 1970, cited in Evans, 1991).

Altruism within the household does not rule out welfare *differentials* within the household; those who produce more may have a greater claim on household consumption (Evenson, 1976). But it does rule out welfare *inequities* in the sense of unequal weighting being given to individual utilities within the aggregated welfare function. If intra-household welfare differentials are observed, they are inferred to be the outcome of a voluntaristic decision-making process, that is, 'household members agree to certain household management rules regarding the distribution of income within the household, and the allocation of household members' time' (Evenson, 1978, p. 2). The dichotomous depiction of household decision-making as one of market efficiency in production and altruism in distribution has been compared to 'the primitive communist rule governing the allocation of the work-load and the distribution of consumption', viz. from each according to ability; to each according to need (Saith and Tankha, 1972, p. 351, cited in Ellis, 1988).

While some modifications are made to adapt this household model to conditions in other parts of the world, neo-classical economists are prone to making powerful claims for the universality of their theory. Becker, for instance, claims that rational-choice theory provides a unified framework for *all* behaviour involving scarce resources,

> be it behaviour involving money prices or imputed shadow prices, repeated or infrequent decisions, large or minor decisions, emotional or mechanical ends, rich or poor persons, men or women, adults or children, brilliant or stupid persons, businessmen or politicians, teachers or students. (1976, p. 8)

However, there is scepticism about these claims, even within the discipline. Sceptics have pointed to the fallacies of aggregation which underpin the Beckerian representation of the household as an essentially altruistic collectivity: the aggregation of individual utilities into a joint welfare function; of individual incomes into a common budget; of individual family labour into an abstract pool of household labour; and of aggregating individual members into a single decision-making unit (Galbraith, 1974; Folbre, 1986a, 1986b; Evans, 1991; Sen, 1990). I will deal with these in turn.

Fallacies of Aggregation: Gender and
Household Welfare

Some of the earliest criticisms of the Beckerian household were levelled at its assumption of an internal harmony of interests. Galbraith, for instance, condemned neo-classical theory for 'burying the subordination of the individual [woman] within the household' (1974, p. 35) and suggested that 'the household, in the established economics, is essentially a disguise for the exercise of male authority' (p. 36). Sen pointed out the absurdity of believing that only the household head's view of the collective welfare should count and asked why the views of 'subordinated' and 'subjugated' members regarding their own and family welfare should be given no status (1984, p. 373).

The growing literature on distributional inequalities within the household in both advanced capitalist as well as Third World countries (see Folbre, 1986b) appeared to provide a further empirical refutation of the idea of intra-household welfare maximization. The conflicting interpretations given to these findings are usefully illuminated by a debate sparked off by the Indian sex-ratio question. Macro-demographic studies had drawn attention to the marked regional pattern of sex ratios in the South Asian subcontinent, with more 'masculine' sex ratios in the northern plains and more 'feminine' sex ratios in the south (Visaria, 1967; Bardhan 1974; Miller, 1981; Dyson and Moore, 1983). Micro-level research confirmed the existence of gender bias in intra-household distribution. It documented not only the existence of excess female mortality among younger age groups and among women in their reproductive years, but also provided evidence of gender-related differentials in household health-seeking and nutritional behaviour (Chen et al., 1981; Miller, 1981; Kynch and Sen, 1983; Mahmud and Mahmud, 1985; see also Jain and Banerjee, 1985).

One attempt to reconcile this apparent disjuncture between the assumption of intra-household welfare maximization, on the one hand, and evidence of intra-household welfare inequalities, on the other, is found in Rosenzweig and Schultz (1982). They suggested that the observed sex differentials in mortality rates in India could be seen as a rational response by parents to observed gender differentials in employment rates: 'children who are expected to be more economically productive adults receive a larger share of family resources and have a greater propensity to survive' (p. 814).[1] The challenge to this interpretation made by Folbre (1984a), and the authors' subsequent rejoinder, neatly encapsulated some paradigmatic dissensions within the field of economics. Folbre pointed out that, while discrimination against female children might be compatible with parents maximizing the total *income* of the household, it was difficult to see how it could be seen as maximizing total *welfare*. Not only was the welfare of non-surviving female members excluded from the calculation, but the productivity of surviving girl children was also undermined by lower investments in their 'human capital'. Their continued disadvantage within the market place was thereby perpetuated. She offered an alternative hypothesis that mothers in Indian households might benefit more directly than fathers from the survival of female children, since daughters commonly assisted their mothers in domestic chores. However, mothers' preferences would not be reflected in household outcomes if women did not participate on equal terms in household decision-making. In place of shared preferences and voluntaristic decision-making, intra-household inequalities could just as easily reflect conflicting preferences and differential decision-making power. The same set of outcomes was compatible with more than one explanation.

Folbre's alternative interpretation was rejected by Rosenzweig and Schultz (1984) on the grounds that it required a more complex theoretical structure, when the more 'parsimonious' assumption of a joint welfare function offered a perfectly satisfactory prediction of household behaviour. What was interesting about this response was what it revealed about some of the stated and unstated preferences of neo-classical economists. First of all, it revealed what economists valued about their theoretical models. While acknowledging that their assumptions '[did] violence to reality' (Rosenzweig, 1986), economists appear to give priority to the accuracy of prediction over adequacy of explanation. The problem with this is summarized by Akerlof (cited in Swedberg, 1991, p. 73):

> I think this maximization business leads to slightly interesting exercises and it all looks very elegant when people do all this mathematics and so forth. But it may not make people wiser. And in the last analysis we all want something that makes people a little bit wiser.

Second, and less explicitly, it revealed the strength of the neo-classical attachment to voluntaristic interpretations of behaviour, at least within the family. The explanation offered by Rosenzweig and Schultz had the virtue of protecting the private domain of the household from charges of gender discrimination, relegating such discrimination to the marketplace. It was the 'given' gender inequalities in market returns to labour that dictated that parents, as rational price-takers, invest more in male children. While this may have resulted in what economists would call a 'greater propensity to die' among female children, it still served the collective interests of the household.

Folbre (1986a) later pointed to the untenable paradox at the heart of neo-classical household economics: the belief that individuals who were guided by competitive self-interest in the marketplace became selfless altruists when it came to intra-household behaviour. Scepticism about the prevalence of purely altruistic principles within the household does not necessarily rule it out as an aspect of household behaviour. Indeed, the greater evidence for altruism within the household domain than in most other institutions explains the remarkable convergence between the neo-classical depiction of intra-household relations as akin to 'primitive communism' (Saith and Tankha, 1972) and the conventional Marxist depiction of the household as a haven in a heartless world, a 'miniature utopian socialist society, untroubled by internal conflict' (Folbre, 1986a, p. 6). However, the evidence of widespread intra-household distributional failures suggests that the possibility of conflicting interests between household members must be allowed for in household analysis.

Fallacies of Aggregation: Gender and Household Income

The postulate of joint welfare maximization is itself premissed on the underlying assumption that all household resources are (at least notionally) pooled. They are then reallocated according to the principle of Pareto-optimality, viz. a situation where no member of the household can be made better off without someone being made worse off. The identity of the household member earning or owning resources is rendered irrelevant, since all resources will be merged and then redistributed according to this basic decision-making rule.

Once again, empirical research has contradicted this premiss. In particular, the gender of the person owning wealth or earning income appears to have a systematic effect on patterns of resource allocation within the household. The actual form of this effect varies in different contexts. Thomas (1990) found in Brazil that the effect on the probabilities of child survival was nearly twenty times greater when non-earned income accrued to women rather than to men. Research in the Philippines (Senauer, 1990) documented men's small but consistent advantage over women in the distribution of calories and found that increases in women's wage rates led to an increase in the share of household calories consumed by women and children, apparently at the expense of men.

Studies of contract sugar farming in a Kenyan district found that, despite the increased prosperity of sugar farmers, increments in household income did not translate into significant changes in the nutritional health of women or young children (Kennedy and Cogill, 1987; Kennedy, 1989). Examination of decision-making within these households revealed that women were responsible for food expend-itures and were more likely to allocate resources under their control to consumption with observable nutritional benefits. Consequently, women-controlled income had significant and positive effects on household food consumption. Sugar income, along with income from the non-farm sector, was mainly controlled by men, and spent on male areas of responsibility with no obvious nutritional benefits. Evidence that children from female-headed households did better nutritionally than children from other households supported the idea that where women's preferences dominated in household distributional patterns there were likely to be positive nutritional effects.

Other studies confirm this picture of gender-differentiated patterns in the disposal of income, with male income more strongly associated with personal forms of consumption or what economists termed 'adult goods' (alcohol, meals eaten out, cigarettes and 'female companion-ship') while a higher proportion of women's income was spent on goods for their children and for collective household consumption (Hoddinott, 1992). Reviewing these findings for Côte d'Ivoire, Had-dad and Hoddinott conclude that 'to the extent that increasing women's share of household income increases the purchase of "good" goods (and reduces the expenditure on "bad" goods) . . . there are strong reasons for raising women's incomes' (1991, p. 61).

The empirical picture thus contradicts the assumption that the identity of the member earning or controlling resources is irrelevant to final patterns of resource allocation; rather, it lends credence to the idea that household members have different preferences – or obliga-tions – which lead them to allocate resources within their jurisdiction in systematically different ways. If altruism exists within the house-holds so that 'parents . . . care about the health, earnings potential and/or food consumption of each member' (Rosenzweig, 1986, p. 235), such altruism appears to be generally more associated with one parent, rather than both, and with maternal, rather than paternal, preferences.

Fallacies of Aggregation: Gender and Household Labour

One of the major contributions made by the New Household Economics to the economic analysis of household behaviour was its recognition of labour time as a key resource at the disposal of households, and of the allocation of household labour between multiple uses: market production, home production and leisure.[2] However, enlarging the potential number of uses to which household labour could be allocated has not undermined the fundamental premiss that allocation occurs through a unified decision-making process. The Beckerian model treats individual members as essentially disembodied units of labour, differentiated from each other only by productivity-related characteristics, and allocated to different activities on the basis of comparative advantage. Thus, as Evans points out (1991), 'family labour time is treated like any other factor of production which can be flexibly allocated on the basis of its comparative costs in market and non-market activities' (p. 55). If women specialize in unpaid domestic chores within the household, it is because returns to their market activities are lower than those of men. Within this model, changes in returns to any member's time will induce the household to reallocate its labour resources so as to restore equality in the marginal returns to different labour units (Rosenzweig, 1986). Thus an increase in women's market earnings will lead to their increased participation in market work; their unremunerated domestic responsibilities can be accommodated in a variety of ways. Previously idle labour (of children, the elderly or unemployed members) may be drawn in to take up these chores; or other members in less well-paying market activities will be reallocated; or there may be an overall reduction in women's domestic workload and purchasing of these services from the market.

That is the theory. What is observed, in practice, are various forms of rigidities within the household division of labour, reflecting these social characteristics, and acting as brakes on the equilibrating process. The most widely observed 'stickiness' is in the extent to which male labour substitutes for female in domestic and child-care activities. Data from India and the Philippines, for instance, led Rosenzweig (1986) to note (but not explain) an apparently 'closer substitutability' between the labour of women and children, particularly girls, in domestic chores. Consequently, increases in female wages lead to children being withdrawn from school – and girl children from the market – to take up women's domestic chores. However, other studies from the Philippines identify women's time as the key adjusting factor. They show that increases in women's market participation is accommodated by reductions in their leisure time; the time devoted to domestic work and child care remains roughly the same (Folbre, 1984b). As Popkin notes, 'there is close to a one-to-one correspondence between increase in maternal work time and the decrease in maternal leisure time' (1983, p. 166). Even fathers who are unemployed, underemployed or engaged in home-based income-earning activities devote very little time to child care. Folbre concludes from her findings that men not only appeared to have no 'preference' for child care, but revealed an active aversion to it. Furthermore (and contrary to Nakajima's suggestion cited earlier), it appeared that while altruism within the household might, in principle, result in male heads gaining some utility from their wives' leisure time, they appeared to gain even more from their own.

One result of these gender-related rigidities in the intra-household substitutability of labour is that women all over the world, particularly those from poorer households, have to balance a multiplicity of demands on their time. In sub-Saharan Africa, where women are the mainstay of the agricultural sector, responsible for around 60 per cent of agricultural production and 80 per cent of food production, there is widespread evidence that women work longer hours on average than men; in Uganda and Zimbabwe this is true even if only farm labour is compared (Agarwal, 1985; Cleave, 1974). In the Indian context, Sen and Sen (1985) found that poorer women were most likely to combine waged labour, income-replacing work (provision of fuel and water, care of livestock and poultry) and domestic labour (cooking, cleaning and child care); specialization in purely domestic work was largely the province of women from wealthier households. A review of six village studies in Nepal suggested that women worked longer hours in economic and domestic activities combined and had less time for leisure and social activities than men of an equivalent economic stratum (Bennett et al., 1981). Nor is this stickiness in intra-household labour allocation restricted to the Third World. In the United States, 'despite "help" from husbands, the average working woman spends 80 hours a week on her paid employment and on housework combined, compared to 50 hours for the average man' (Jagger, 1983 p. 70). A recent government survey from Australia reported that women did over 70 per cent of housework, whether or not they were in paid employment.

The reality behind these findings is that human labour, and particularly family labour, is not just another factor of production. It is different from other factors of production in that it has a gender, age and status (Evans, 1991). It is also differentiated in that it has consciousness, interests, preferences, obligations and differing amounts of power and agency, all of which reflect its social characteristics. The allocation of labour within the household cannot be treated as completely analogous to the allocation of other resources.

Beyond Unified Welfare Maximization: Disaggregrating Decision-making Power

Taken individually, each of these empirical challenges to the neo-classical model can be reconciled with the idea of 'altruism' within the household. Brought together, however, they mount a serious challenge to the idea of the altruistic household. Asymmetries in intra-household distribution can be reconciled with altruism in household decision-making by positing differences in individual preferences. Preferences, in the neo-classical model, are generally taken as exogenously given, stable and randomly distributed. Inexplicable behaviour due to taste differences is allowed for, but is believed to be either trivial or idiosyncratic (Amsden, 1980). It is therefore perfectly feasible that some household members will display an idiosyncratic preference for depriving themselves of food, medical attention and leisure time in favour of others.

However, when (a) the subordination of personal needs in favour of the well-being of others appears to be systematically the property of the less powerful category of individuals (women and/or children), while the beneficiaries of such preferences appear systematically to belong to another more powerful category (men), and when (b) the consequences of such behaviour are life-threatening levels of ill-health and malnutrition, then the notion of voluntaristic decision-making becomes patently absurd. The tendency to treat the household as an anthropomorphic entity within the neo-classical literature detracts attention from the reality that,

> the household can neither decide not think, since analytical constructs are not so empowered. Rather certain people within the household make decisions. One or more persons with enough power to implement then makes decisions and other less-empowered household members follow them. (Wolf 1990, p. 60).

It is clear that if the distribution of decision-making power between household members is to be opened up to analysis, then the household welfare function, budget, labour supply and, above all, the decision-making unit itself will have to be disaggregated. Attempts to do this are examined in the remaining sections of this chapter.

The New Institutional Economics: Implicit
Contracts and Household Bargaining

Not all economists make a fetish of parsimony in their analysis; many
subscribe to Sen's view that, 'like any virtue something is sometimes to
be gained by making things more complicated'. A different perspective on the household is evident in recent attempts by economists to
look at the role of institutions in structuring complex, long-term
economic relationships. Here attention is paid to the boundaries,
structure and internal organization of different institutions, concerns
which are conspicuously absent in the new household economics.
Whereas conventional explanations of economic behaviour focus on
the production costs of economic activity, institutional economics is
also concerned with costs of transactions between different economic
actors. In market-based societies where needs are met through
specialization and exchange rather than through production for use, a
number of institutional modes exist for organizing production,
provisioning and exchange. The household is recognized as one such
mode – others are firms, governments and non-profit institutions.

Households can be seen as a specific institutional response to the
problems of meeting needs and organizing behaviour in an uncertain
world. They are based on 'long-term, implicit exchange contracts
between individuals of different generations related by birth or
marriage. These individuals, who have distinct preferences and
personal economic constraints, pursue their self-interests through
family exchanges in a world of risk and uncertainty' (Todaro and
Fapohunda, 1987, p. 3). What makes the household distinct as an
institution is the close intertwining of economic and personal in intra-
household relationships. The opportunistic misrepresentation of risks
and costs that is likely to occur in the impersonal arena of market and
state institutions is less likely or possible in the more intimate domain
of the family. This gives it a comparative advantage in organizing
certain kinds of transactions, particularly those where loyalty, personal
knowledge and some amount of altruism count for more than
technical competence and scale economics (Pollak, 1985). The familial
relationships of marriage, households and extended kin networks can
thus be seen as specific institutional responses to the desire of
individuals for long-term stable environments in which to live, to bring
up children and cope with the uncertainties of illness, disability and
old age.

Institutional economics does not require households to display the
same degree of responsiveness to price signals that characterize

Beckerian households. Behavioural outcomes are likely to reflect contractual rights and obligations as well as economic incentives. The nature of household relationships means that such contracts are long-term ones, rather than renegotiated periodically, giving a certain degree of stability (or 'inertia') to household behaviour. Nor does the approach require altruism and consensus in intra-household relations. As Todaro and Fapohunda pointed out, 'the terms of domestic trade need not be equal but may vary, as in market transactions, with the relative bargaining power of participants' (p. 3). The bargaining process thus generates intersecting contractual relationships between different household members, specifying their rights and obligations to each other, as the basis of household cooperation. Individual members are likely to observe the terms of the contract as long as they are better off than they would be should the contract break down. Attempts to renegotiate – and achieve success at renegotiation – will reflect changes in individual circumstances which in turn impinge on relative bargaining power within the household. Decision-making within the household is thus seen as the resolution of potentially conflicting preferences through a process of negotiation between unequals.

Some versions of bargaining models tend to retain the voluntaristic underpinnings of mainstream economics. Inequality between members is reduced to their individual characteristics and endowments and they are able to choose non-cooperation as a possible solution should the bargaining process not prove satisfactory. However, household bargaining cannot be treated as analogous to bargaining between unrelated individuals within the marketplace. The incentive for members to cooperate is not simply individual need but also powerful normative pressures backed up by the threat of social sanctions, which make the 'choice' of household membership a social, rather than a purely individual, one. The neglect of these factors reflects the larger problem of the neo-classical tradition, that 'it has too little structure'. An attempt to remedy this is made by Sen (1990), who offers a version of the household which retains the basic bargaining format, but extends it in ways that address more explicitly issues of gender and power within the household. Sen's household is a site of cooperative conflict. In common with other bargaining models, he assumes that cooperation between household members will take place as long as it leads to outcomes that are preferable to those that prevail in the absence of cooperation. The bargaining problem arises over the choice between alternative cooperative outcomes, on the one hand, and whether to cooperate at all, on the other.

The prosperity of the household depends on the totality of various activities – getting money incomes, purchasing or directly producing food crops and other goods, producing edible meals out of raw food materials, and so on: 'the members of the household face two different types of problems simultaneously, one involving *cooperation* (adding to total availabilities) and the other *conflict* (dividing the total availabilities among the members of the household (p. 129). The final selection between alternative outcomes – that is, 'the particular pattern of division of fruits that emerge from such cooperation' – will reflect the bargaining power of different members within the household (p. 131). Differences in bargaining power between members (or categories of members) are the product of interlocking asymmetries, including the range of options facing members, should household cooperation break down (the fall-back position); the perceived significance (illusory or otherwise) of their contributions to household prosperity; the degree to which members identify their self-interests with their personal being (and therefore the extent to which they are prepared to subordinate their own well-being to that of others); and finally the ability of some members to exercise coercion, threat or violence over others. Where these different bases of power coalesce, as they do for men in many cultures, clearly the ability to shape, and indeed impose, cooperative solutions on subordinate members of the household is immense.

Women's 'perceived contribution' is an important factor affecting women's bargaining power within the household. This is likely to be related to the visibility and extent of 'gainful' work. The greater visibility of remunerated, outside work is seen as a crucial factor in determining women's fall-back position. Sen cites Bhatty's research (1980) with women workers in the Indian *beedi* industry whose outside earnings appear to have strengthened their role in household decision-making and their claims on household resources. He also notes that the home-based lacemakers of Narsapur studied by Mies continue to be perceived as dependent housewives, both by themselves and by their families. The 'invisibility' of their work weakens their ability to bargain for higher wages from their employers and for a greater share of household resources.

On a broader level, Sen points to Boserup's contrast between women's dependent status in the male farming systems of South Asia and their greater autonomy in the female farming systems of sub-Saharan Africa as further support for his model. It suggests that women's bargaining power, manifested in the degree of equality observed in intra-household welfare indicators, is related to the extent of their involvement in field-based and/or waged agriculture in different farming systems. He also provides statistics from Africa and

Asia showing that female life expectancy, relative to male, is positively related to female activity rates, relative to male. Thus sub-Saharan Africa has the highest ratio of female to male activity rates, as well as the highest female life expectancy relative to male; South Asia and northern Africa have low relative rates of female activity and low relative levels of female life expectancy. East, West and Southeast Asia are intermediate regions.

A similar relationship explains the north/south contrast in sex ratios and gender differentials in mortality rates within the Indian subcontinent noted earlier. Thus the northern states of India where women's labour-force participation is recorded as low is also a region of 'masculine' sex ratios, with men outnumbering women (106–114 men to 100 women) compared to the southern states (97–107 men to 100 women) where women have much higher rates of participation in agriculture and trading. The relationship between gender differentials in well-being and labour-force participation is thus given a very different interpretation by Sen to that offered by Rosenzweig and Schultz. The Sen model shifts the emphasis from gender differences in the *fact* of productive contributions to gender differences in its *visibility*, suggesting that women's participation in outside gainful employment improves their bargaining power within the household and is therefore associated with greater gender equality in the distribution of household resources. Sen's formulation goes further than other bargaining approaches in taking account of structural factors that mediate between the individual and the rest of society. Such factors can drive a wedge between personal choice and personal welfare, a possibility that is not envisaged in the Beckerian universe. He also extends the necessary empirical base for analysis well beyond the prices-and-incomes requirements of formal household models. Information from both within and outside the domestic domain are brought into the analytical framework, thus helping to open up the 'black box' of the neo-classical household and allowing it to interact with its immediate and broader environment.

Altruism versus Bargaining in Household Economics: The Limits to Inferred Preference

Bargaining models of the household have a number of advantages over altruistic models for the study of gender relations. Although concerned with the same allocational decisions, they accommodate greater diversity in decision-making behaviour. They do not rule out altruism as the basis of such behaviour, but treat it as one possibility among others. They also introduce the idea of unequal power within the household, thus raising issues of conflict which were missing when only altruistically unified memberships or benevolent patriarchs made decisions. Moreover, despite their roots in methodological individualism, bargaining models have the potential for accommodating the idea of gender asymmetry as the product of structural rather than purely individual inequalities in power, privilege and resources. As Folbre points out: 'Because major differences in bargaining power derive from objective differences in the economic position of men, women and children outside the family, this approach leads rather inevitably towards a more structural analysis of patriarchal inequalities' (1986b, p. 6). However, from the Beckerian perspective, the greater open-endedness and complexity of the bargaining approach is precisely what constitutes its weakness: it does not generate hypotheses that are easily tested through conventional econometric methodology. Its critics object that 'it is difficult or impossible to test, refute or falsify, claiming that it explains everything and, therefore, explains nothing' (Pollak, 1985, p. 584).

As it happens, the same criticisms have also been levelled at the more traditional economic models, despite their claims to greater parsimony and rigour. Utility, for instance, the cornerstone of neo-classical theory, was described by Joan Robinson (1962) as a 'metaphysical concept of impregnable circularity; utility is the quality in commodities that makes individuals want to buy them, and the fact that individuals want to buy commodities shows that they have utility' (p. 47). By extension, 'the principle of utility maximization is also "impregnable" because utility is defined as whatever is being maximized' (Folbre, 1986, p. 246). Consequently, it is not always clear what kinds of evidence would be inconsistent with the theory of utility maximization (Hannan, 1982).

At the level of formal hypothesis testing, a major problem in selecting between altruistic and bargaining explanations of household behaviour is that they do not generate hypotheses that can be easily distinguished from each other. Household decision-making principles are inferred from observed outcomes, but the same set of outcomes is compatible with more than one set of explanations. For instance, an empirical correlation between wages earned and welfare differentials among household members is compatible with both joint welfare maximization (maximizing household income by investing in productivity of higher earners) and the bargaining model (higher earnings enhance bargaining power within the household). Similarly, observed gender differences in the disposal of income may reflect gender differences in preferences. Or they may reflect an attempt to match gender-differentiated categories of income (continuous flows versus lump sums; irregular versus regular; income in cash versus income in kind) to different kinds of expenditure requirements. Or it may mean that there are different (but equal) spheres of influence and power. Finally, the greater amount of time women spend in child care can be attributed to their choice, reflecting greater maternal altruism, or to the absence of choice, a reflection of greater paternal irresponsibility.

The difficulties of distinguishing definitively between competing explanations of household decision-making are likely to persist as long as empirical verification is restricted to formal hypothesis testing. As Robinson (1962, p. 23) pointed out, the general problem with hypothesis testing in the social sciences is that 'we have not yet established an agreed standard for the disproof of an hypothesis. Without the possibility of controlled experiment, we have to rely on interpretation of evidence, and interpretation involves judgement; we can never get a knock-down answer.' Hypothesis testing can tell us whether or not the empirical data is compatible with a given hypothesis, but it cannot rule out its compatability with an alternative hypothesis.

In the absence of knock-down answers, we will turn to other data and other disciplines for insights into some of these questions. We will examine how this other literature, mainly from feminist anthropology, deals with issues of gender, labour and welfare within the household, and in particular what light it can throw on the question of cooperation and conflict within household decision-making. We will return in the concluding section of the chapter to reconsider the earlier economic concerns through the very different lenses offered by an inter-disciplinary perspective.

Anthropological Households: Socially Constructed and Empirically Diverse

The first impression that leaps out from the anthropological literature on households is the sheer cross-cultural diversity of household forms. Indeed, some anthropologists have been led to question the very validity of the concept of 'the household' (see Roberts, 1991). They challenge the conflation of units of residence, reproduction and production into a single unified entity, the result of which is that 'the domestic group is often seen as monolithic, clearly bounded and unchanging, except in so far as the domestic cycle produces changes in personnel' (Pittin, 1987, p. 26). What they offer instead are 'shifting, flexible structures in which boundaries are difficult to discern . . . a diversity of family and household composition and social relations, mediated through marriage and kinship, creating a variety of conjugal and residential arrangements' (Evans, 1991, p. 54).

Anthropologists have also questioned the conflation of families and households, pointing out that while familial rules are important means of recruitment into households in most cultures, there are also other routes to membership such as pawning, adoption, purchase, domestic service and temporary residential sharing. Finally, they reject the notion that familial ties necessarily imply purely voluntary and altruistic interactions, pointing to the contractual nature of household relations: 'persons related through descent and affinity may collaborate in joint household activities under more or less explicit contracts which specify obligations and the resources each brings to such enterprises' (Roberts, 1991, p. 62). Despite the scope and validity of these criticisms, there is a difference between abandoning the concept of 'the household' as it is defined in most economic textbooks, and abandoning the concept altogether. The empirical significance of household relationships in the daily management of resource entitlements, and as the routine context of people's lives, suggests that it has a certain facticity, despite its shifting guises. Moreover, as Moore (1988) argues, 'households are important in feminist analysis because they organize a large part of women's domestic/reproductive labour. As a result, both the composition and the organization of households have a direct impact on women's lives, and on their ability to gain access to resources, to labour and to income' (p. 55).

A useful strategy would therefore be to abandon the ideological baggage of the new household economics and to seek instead generalizable approaches to kinship-mediated economic flows which could accommodate the empirical diversity of household forms. A valuable contribution to this is Friedman's formulation (1979) of households as a 'dual specification', viz. as internally diverse institutions, embedded within and interacting with a wider array of networks and institutions beyond their boundaries. One aspect of this dual specification relates to the internal structures of rules and resources within the household, including those relating to marriage and parenthood, property and production, authority and dependence. The other specification deals with the market and non-market institutions which jointly constitute the external context within which households reproduce or transform themselves. The household is then seen as a useful analytical construct whose content and boundaries are determined by the wider social and political relations in which it is embedded. We will use the term 'household' in the rest of this chapter to refer to the bundle of relationships in a society through which its primary reproductive activities are organized, recognizing that these frequently involve principles of kinship and residence. The economy of the household, then, refers to the rules, relations and practices which govern household production, acquisition and distribution of the valued resources essential for meeting the needs of its members.

Households as Institutions of Resource Management

While anthropological research has helped to uncover cross-cultural *variations* in the boundaries of domestic groups, it has also pointed to the existence of certain regional *uniformities* in the social relations that govern production, distribution and consumption within the household. It suggests typologies of 'ideal-typical' household forms, based on observed patterns of household rules, norms and practices, the contractual basis of intra-household relationships (Caldwell, 1982; Kandiyoti, 1988; Goody, 1976; Cain, 1984; Boserup, 1970; Dyson and Moore, 1983). These typologies highlight the different degrees of corporateness in household organization and their implications for gender relations within the household. At one end of the spectrum are the more corporate forms of householding, centred around the conjugal bond, characterizing what Caldwell called a belt of 'patriarchy–patriliny–patrilocality' stretching from northern Africa to Bangladesh, across the Middle East and the northern plains of India. These household structures roughly approximate those described in Boserup's 'male farming systems'. They are organized around cultural rules which focus on male responsibility for the protection and provisioning of women and children. The practices of female seclusion, patrilineal inheritance and patrilocal residence interlock to produce corporately organized, patriarchal household forms. The social norms of male breadwinner/female dependent are reflected in men's privileged, albeit class-differentiated, claims to material and labour opportunities.

Such household systems contrast with the weaker cohesiveness of the conjugal unit in the Caribbean, parts of Latin America and in sub-Saharan Africa (Caldwell, 1982; Cain, 1984; Goody, 1976; Guyer, 1981; Guyer and Peters, 1987; Youssef, 1974). In sub-Saharan Africa in particular – the region of Boserup's female farming systems – the empirical literature suggests the prevalence of non-coterminous units of production, reproduction, consumption or residence and the significance of lineage, rather than conjugal, ties. Here women and men are assigned responsibilities for separate aspects of household provisioning and assigned separate resources to enable them to discharge their obligations. These responsibilities usually include supplying all or most of the family's food, while resources include usufructuary rights to land from the husband's or mother's lineage groups (Palmer, 1988). In general, women and men tend to cooperate in producing the obligatory component of collective subsistence needs and to use their residual time to pursue their own-account activities. The picture that emerges from this literature is of varying degrees of economic autonomy for women, based on the gender-specific assignment of resources and responsibilities. In Palmer's words,

> There is strong evidence in many African countries of what might be called a gender division of management of crops (or fields). . . . Management here is defined as responsibility for mobilising the variable factors of production to be applied to a piece of land . . . If inputs are purchased the manager pays for them with cash, labour, produce or any other means. Consequently, the manager has the right to dispose of all or the bulk of the returns to the outlay. This is what is meant by women and men within the household drawing on the household-level stock of resources to form their own economic accounting units. (Palmer, 1988, p. 7)

This contrast between household forms in different regions is not intended to suggest a rigid and unchanging typology. Households are constituted historically in the context of changing economic and social transformations: such transformations will be reflected in household relations and produce regional forms which break with past patterns. For instance, increasing commercialization of agriculture and changing land distributions in parts of Africa have led to the emergence of proletarianized peasant households which bear a striking resemblance to those associated with South Asia.

Clearly, most households fall somewhere between these 'ideal-typical' extremes. Within the South Asian context, households which approximate the 'ideal-typical' corporate picture described earlier occur most frequently in the northern plains of India, among Muslim groups, among caste Hindus and among landowning classes. In southern India, on the other hand, rather different organizations of households and gender relations are evident. Female seclusion is less emphasized, virilocal residence (setting up a separate establishment after marriage) is common, women are able to interact more regularly with, and draw on the support of, their natal kin and sometimes inherit and/or transfer property rights. Dyson and Moore (1983) suggest that India is the meeting point for two larger socio-cultural formations: a

'West Asian' kinship system charactering the northern plains, and the more egalitarian Southeast Asian kinship system in the south.

In sub-Saharan Africa, Palmer (1991) suggests, separate accounting units are more likely to be a feature of West African households where women are most likely to be provided with independent farming land. In East and Southern Africa, women farmers are more often a combination of 'squatter on their husbands' (cash crop) land and their husbands' farming agent' (p. 21). Their contributions are more likely to be subsumed in the cultivation of household fields where ultimate control over productive decision-making lies in the hands of husbands.

The delineation of ideal-typical cases has a heuristic value. It helps to focus attention on the key insights from feminist anthropological research that the issues of *appropriability, control* and *autonomy* at different stages of household resource management are likely to be critical in shaping decision-making processes, with implications for the extent and form of cooperation and conflict. We will examine how these features are manifested in different household forms and consider their relevance to the economists' concern with distribution of labour, income and welfare within the household.

Gender, Labour and Income within Household Systems

Anthropological research draws attention to the importance of more or less explicit contracts within household systems which serve to structure the distribution of rights, resources and responsibilities between members in systematically different ways. Whitehead draws specific attention to 'conjugal contracts' in different contexts as one important aspect of household resource management, since they specify 'the terms on which husbands and wives exchange goods, incomes, and services, including labour, within the household' (1981, p. 88). In place of the 'free' and flexible allocation of resources in response to economic incentives envisaged in the Beckerian household, economic behaviour within the household is seen as embedded in contractual relationships between household members. As Moore (1988) puts it, 'the control and allocation of resources within the household is a complex process which always has to be seen in relation to a web of rights and obligations' (p. 56).

The contractual nature of household relations structures the ability of its members to cooperate, acquiesce or dissent in household decision-making processes. It ensures some degree of cooperation between members as a necessary condition for their daily reproduction, but it also shapes the potential for conflict. Bargaining over the terms of the contract, then, reflects the kinds of resources different members are able to bring to bear on the process. However, the feminist analysis of household bargaining shifts attention away from the economists' emphasis on 'value and visibility' of labour contributions to the hierarchies of control and command embedded within different labour relations. Whitehead (1985) has pointed to two 'form' aspects of the division of labour which are implicated in these hierarchies. The first relates to the *nature of interdependence* in the production process. Women, she suggests, appear to enjoy less managerial autonomy over production processes in which tasks are shared, either jointly or sequentially, with male members than in those where production processes are segregated. While both forms are observed in the sub-Saharan context, Palmer (1991) suggests there is an underlying pattern: 'Women help their husbands in a more corporate manner if husbands have responsibility for finding the family's food. It is when women are allocated land to grow the family's food that divisions of labour (and quid pro quos) are more in evidence. That is to say, the more pronounced are separate accounting units the sharper the division of labour' (p. 29).

The significance of sequentially or jointly shared labour processes stems from the fact that there are certain critical stages in production where decision-making authority has implications for the division of resources and responsibilities beyond that specific stage. For instance, a study by Burfisher and Horenstein (1985) of the Tiv people in Central Nigeria suggests that the responsibility for planting was one such critical stage. There was a close correlation over nine different crops between who planted a crop and who managed it and the proceeds from it.

Women's greater decision-making roles in female segments of the production process will count for little if critical distributional decisions about workloads or the proceeds from production are associated with different and male-dominated segments of production. In any case, there is generally a less clear-cut basis for assigning value-added in production to the effort of various members when contribution is on a sequential basis. It is consequently more difficult for a women to increase her share of the gains that result from extra effort or to resist male decisions about its allocation without challenging the basis of the conventional division of labour (Whitehead, 1985).

The implications of gender-sequential labour processes are most clearly illustrated in the northern plains of the Indian subcontinent where female seclusion is a widespread practice among landowning households. Male labour, whether family or waged, carries out field-based supervisory or labouring tasks. Men are also dominant in the marketing of produce. Women from such households are generally responsible for the homestead-based processing of crops as well as for income-replacing and domestic work. A significant feature of such a division of labour is that it is not possible for women individually to calculate or appropriate the products of their labour. Sen and Sen (1985) sum up the implications: 'As long as women's claims to the household resources continue to be exercised through men (husbands or sons), their contribution disappears without a trace, as it were, into the household' (p. WS-55), in this case into a joint conjugal budget which is under male management.

By contrast, women are better able to control the proceeds of their labour where production processes are gender-segregated. Such segregation can take a variety of different forms: separate fields, separate crops, separate sectors or separate accounting units. The contractual terms characterizing segregated labour processes tend to protect female family members from arbitrary demands on their labour time and arbitrary claims on their produce from other more powerful members. Gender-segregated labour processes are most marked in the West African context. It is evident in the division of crops cultivated by women and men among the Kusasi in northeast Ghana. Men grow millet, the mainstay of the local diet, and it is the household head's obligation to ensure that the granaries are filled through collective family effort on 'household' fields. Both men and women also have 'independent' plots on which the former grow millet, guinea corn, rice and groundnuts, while women grow rice and groundnuts (Whitehead, 1981).

Jones's research (1985; 1986) among the Massa in Cameroon suggests that segregation occurred by field rather than by crop. Both men and women were expected to contribute to household supplies of red sorghum, the main staple crop. Except for their labour obligations on the compound, sorghum was usually cultivated by women and men on separate own-account fields with little exchange of labour. Married women had their own sorghum granaries which were drawn on first, followed by the husband's supply of sorghum. The sorghum from the compound field was generally saved for the hungry season.

The Mandinka in The Gambia also had a system of separate as well as jointly managed fields (Dey, 1981, 1982). In addition, there was some gender division of labour by crop. Women and men both contributed labour for compound food provision but specialized in different crops. Men tended to grow millet and sorghum for compound consumption, while women grew rice. In addition, they had separate access to own-account holdings which they had cleared themselves. Here men were most likely to grow groundnuts as a cash crop, while women grew rice and groundnuts to meet their personal needs or to supplement their contributions to family consumption needs. However, the introduction of modern irrigated rice has blurred its status as a 'women's' crop.

In certain contexts, gender segmentation in the household economy can give rise to what Palmer (1991) calls 'internal markets', in that redistribution between members takes the form of explicit economic transactions. In Tiv households in Nigeria, women are remunerated for their labour on men's fields with millet, which they process and sell; men receive yams for their labour on women's fields. Foodstuffs may also be sold within the household: women buy millet or sorghum from their husbands to make beer. There are also loans between spouses, often with interest. Secluded women in northern Nigeria earn money by processing the unsold part of their husband's crops or other farmers' crops. Husbands have no claims to their wives' earnings. Women may charge interest on loans of money or grain to their husbands to provide the family food. Some buy grain from their husbands after the harvest and sell it back later at a higher price to provide the meals which they share with their husbands. Manure from household livestock is sold to husbands for use on food fields.

The second aspect of the division of labour relevant to the distribution of decision-making power within the household relates to the differing potential for control or autonomy embodied in different *labour relationships*, such as unpaid family labourers, disguised or direct wage labour, membership in patronage networks, or own-account work. As Whitehead says, 'clearly the very notion of labour for others, even within family relationships, carries with it the potentiality for the control and command of work to lie with the user of the labour rather than its provider – a potentiality over and above the technically implied control discussed above' (1985, p. 44).

Many studies report that women control, or believe that they control, income which they earn directly, much more than that earned by, for instance, their husbands. However, these findings appear to hinge not merely on the incidence of earnings or the identity of the earner, but also on the form of social relations within which income is earned. As Mies's Narsapur study testifies, the constraints associated with seclusive norms in India compress the range of options available to women (particularly those from higher castes and landowning households) to forms of work which are least likely to enhance their bargaining power, viz. unpaid family labour or home-based earning activities. Income per se appears less important to women's bargaining power than access to new social networks outside the household which certain forms of income-earning provide. While this point is implicit in

Sen's model, it is not brought out in his discussion of Mies's study. Instead his emphasis is on *perceptions* of lacemaking as a part-time and insignificant activity, carried out inside housework boundaries and between domestic chores, despite the reality that it was often a main source of income in an area of high male unemployment. These women earned less than did female agricultural labourers from lower-caste households, but were reluctant to give up their secluded status for public manual labour. However, the isolated conditions of home-based lacemaking denied them access to the intangible but critical extra-household resources of solidarity with other workers in the same situation, an access which might have improved their bargaining power vis-à-vis their employers as well as vis-à-vis the men of their households.

In contrast, Hart (1991) notes the use made of collective bargaining power by female agricultural work gangs in rural Malaysia to drive up their wages. She points out its implications for women's bargaining power in relation to other household members: 'women workers' capacity to contest the ideology of male responsibility in the domestic sphere . . . is, I suggest, reciprocally linked with their capacity to define themselves as workers, and to organize collectively in opposition to their employers' (p. 115). In terms of the bargaining framework, women's higher earnings combined with their membership of these newly emerging extra-household forms of cooperation improved their fall-back positions vis-à-vis other household members: 'some of the women in these groups were either widowed or divorced, but the married women also operated in considerable independence from their husbands. Even where husbands were present in the village, these women maintained separate budgets (and wherever possible, savings) rather than pool their income into a common fund (1992, p. 821).

Guyer (1981) has argued strongly for extending the concept of resources beyond the conventional ones of land, labour and capital to include what she calls political or social resources: 'much evidence shows that where resources are not commodities, people have to invest in the mechanisms which assure them continuing access. One needs social and political resources to get material resources' (p. 102). Rights and claims on people or groups of people can be acquired, transferred and accumulated, often through participation in various inter-household networks and associations (Fleming, 1991). The resource implications of access to different kinds of extra-household relationships are also pointed out in March and Taqqu's review (1986) of women's informal associations in developing countries. They conclude that, in general, women's esteem and influence within a community is closely connected to the extent of their participation in extra-domestic associations, but they distinguish between 'defensive' associations based on women's exclusion from male networks and more 'active' associations with clear economic roots and purposes and organized along horizontal rather than vertical ties. The latter, based on 'the shared economics of being female', include rotating credit or labour associations and can provide an important avenue to autonomy and control for women, demonstrably improving, rather than merely protecting, their position within their households and communities.

Gender and Intra-Household Welfare Differentials

Focusing on the gender divisions of resources and responsibilities among household members also deepens our understanding of intra-household welfare differentials. As noted earlier, both altruistic and bargaining models posit a correlation between welfare levels and economic contributions of household members, but offer different explanations for it. In the former, the correlation is considered to reflect the economic rationality of favouring more productive members; in the latter it is attributed to the greater bargaining power of more visibly productive members. The relational approach to the household outlined above is clearly closer to the bargaining view because of its stress on unequal power relations. However, it also encourages attention to other dimensions in the link between well-being and contributions which are not addressed in the competing economic explanations. While it is the case that what women and men do within the division of labour influences their individual *claims* on household resources, it also influences their individual *requirements*. This point will be explored through illustrative data from Bangladesh and The Gambia as examples of corporate and segmented household systems.

At first sight, the data from these countries appear to support the idea of a correlation between the visibility of women's labour-force participation and their claims to household welfare resources. In Bangladesh, 13 per cent of women are estimated to be in the labour force and they make up around 10 per cent of the agricultural labour force. Here there are widespread findings of female disadvantage in basic well-being (see review in Mahmud and Mahmud, 1985). In terms of nutritional status, there is female disadvantage in almost all age groups; it is particularly marked among women and children from landless households and women who are pregnant and/or lactating. There is also excess female mortality in most age groups. Overall female life expectancy is lower (46:47 years in 1980 [Seager and Olson,

1986]) in keeping with the pattern in most of South Asia, but is the reverse of the pattern of lower male life expectancy in the rest of the world (Sen, 1990).

The picture in The Gambia is very different. Seventy-one per cent of women are estimated to be in the labour force and they make up at least half the agricultural work force. In the region as a whole, there is little evidence of female disadvantage in nutrition, and at least one study notes greater female advantage in nutritional indicators among children as well as adults (Svedberg, 1988). Estimates from The Gambia show higher female life expectancy than male (35:32 years [*New Internationalist* 1985]), unlike the pattern in Bangladesh and South Asia in general, but in line with the rest of the world. However, while there are obvious differences in the 'visible' labour of women in these countries, certain similarities in their 'invisible' responsibilities tend to be less obvious. In both contexts, women have primary responsibility for the post-harvest processing of food grains and their transformation into edible form; for collecting fuel and water, and cleaning the house; in other words, for a relatively constant 'overhead' of domestic chores which have to be performed, as a part of their contractual obligations within the family, regardless of other respons-ibilities. Furthermore, in both regions, women have high rates of fertility (an average of 6.7 children in Bangladesh and 6.4 children in The Gambia in 1980 [*New Internationalist*, 1985]) and are given main responsibility for child care.

Juxtaposing these 'invisible' labour obligations with the more widely acknowledged 'visible' ones draws attention to the very different work burdens entailed for women in The Gambia compared to Bangladesh. In Bangladesh, purdah restrictions limit women's contributions in market-oriented production and field-based agriculture, accounting for their low levels of 'visible' labour-force participation. In The Gambia, on the other hand, gender divisions in the labour process operate to assign women and men to different crops and fields rather than to restrict the range of activities permissible for women. Second, while women undertake the tasks of gathering fuel and carrying water in both countries, it is unlikely that the distances travelled to carry out these tasks in Bangladesh are as great as those in The Gambia, simply because of the ecological differences between the two countries. In The Gambia, fetching water requires women to carry between two and four gallons per trip, the number of trips being determined by their age, household size and distance to water source: 'drawing water and its porterage are energy-demanding activities especially where wells are deep as in the Gambia' (Haswell, 1981, p. 18). Third, in both contexts, women carry out the manual processing of staple crops, and in both it is regarded as one of the most burdensome of their responsibilities. Yet the amount of time and energy required is very different. In Bangladesh it has been calculated that an average of around forty-five minutes a day is spent on paddy dehusking ('the most arduous female task') for the average rural family (Greeley, 1987, p. 223). However, the arduousness of the task has a very different connotation in the West African context, where Nath (n.d.) calculated that 'A woman must spend six hours to get 6 kg. of processed grains, the quantity consumed by an average household of six or seven persons for one of the two daily meals and for leftovers for the next morning's breakfast.' Haswell estimates that in The Gambia, this activity was the highest energy user of women's non-farming activities (4.9 k.cals per min.) compared to 'drumming and dancing' (that is, leisure), the highest energy user of male non-farm activity (5.5 k.cals per min.). Women interviewed by Nath described the hand-pounding of grains as 'the worst part of being a woman'.

When it is recollected that Gambian women provide around 60 per cent of total energy expended in 'visible' farming activities (Haswell, 1981), and that their less visible but routine domestic and child-care activities are 'relentlessly performed even during periods of high energy expenditure in the production of the staple food crop' (Haswell, 1981, p. 17), clearly another look at well-being indicators is called for. Disaggregating and expanding on the earlier indicators reveals aspects of female disadvantage in The Gambia which remain concealed if the focus is only on the value and visibility aspects of their labour contributions. One difference that emerges, of course, is in the length of women's working days, both cross-culturally, and in relation to their men. A review of time-allocation studies from different rural areas in Bangladesh (Hamid, 1989) reports little difference in the hours worked by women and men. In general, both men and women worked nine to ten hours a day, with men predominating in direct income-earning and women in subsistence and reproductive activities.

In The Gambia a very different picture emerges. During peak periods of agricultural activity (May to December), 'pounding of foodgrains begins before daylight between 5 and 6 am and women retire to bed between 9 and 10 pm after the evening meal' (Haswell, 1981, p. 17). During the agricultural season, it was estimated that women worked just over twice the number of hours in farming that men did (1,073 hours compared to 595 hours [p.12]). When non-farm work is added to these estimates, it was clear that leisure and low-energy-consuming activities have a smaller place in the lives of women than men. Men spent a greater part of the year with positive energy balances than women (257 days compared to 201 days). During the agricultural working day, aside from energy spent in agricultural work, men spent 28 per cent of their energy expenditure in leisure activities and 9 per cent in routine chores (primarily fuel collection), while women spent 27 per cent of their energy in routine chores and 9 per cent in leisure. During non-farm working days, men spent 21 per cent of their energy in routine chores (housebuilding) and 59 per cent in leisure. Women spent 40 per cent of their energy in routine chores and 40 per cent in leisure.

These demands on Gambian women's time and energy show up in forms of female disadvantage which resemble those observed in Bangladesh. In both cases, this disadvantage is concentrated in women's child-bearing years. While Gambian women have a higher life expectancy overall than men, there is marked excess female mortality among women in the reproductive years (15–50), a less marked excess when the 5–60 age group is considered, and excess male mortality only among the under-fives and 60+ age group (World Bank, 1980a). In both countries, maternal mortality rates are extre-. mely high. In Bangladesh, there are five to seven maternal deaths per thousand live births; around a third of deaths to women in the reproductive ages are from maternal mortality. While the percentage of deaths among women in the reproductive years from maternal mortality (that is, 29 per cent) in The Gambia is of the same magnitude as Bangladesh, (Maine et al., 1986), the risk of dying in pregnancy appears much higher in The Gambia, that is around ten per thousand live births (WHO, 1987). Nutritional indicators also point to this pattern of female disadvantage during the reproductive years, a situation that is more severe in The Gambia. There appears to be a considerable shortfall in the calorie intake of pregnant and lactating women in The Gambia (around 60 per cent of WHO/FAO norms), compared to a shortfall of 75 per cent for the rural population as a whole (World Bank, 1980a, p. 74). In Bangladesh, 66–70 per cent of women in the reproductive years suffered from nutritional anaemia compared to 80 per cent in The Gambia (*New Internationalist*, 1985, Table 10).

Clearly differences in the relationship between women's contributions and well-being in Bangladesh and The Gambia cannot be established purely on the basis of this data. Differences in poverty and social infrastructure would have to be taken into account. But these findings do signal that women's work/well-being linkages work through a wider complex of routes than allowed for by many economic models of the household, and have to be taken into account in understanding household welfare differentials. In the Bangladesh case, the shortfalls appear to be a product of gender discrimination in the distribution of welfare resources, while in the Gambian case, they appear more closely related to the distribution of women's work burdens and energy expenditure. In both case, women's 'illfare' – the imbalance between requirements and claims – is exacerbated during their reproductive years, when the additional energy requirements posed by child-bearing and breastfeeding are not acknowledged in the distribution of energy resources or work responsibilities among household members.

The discussion also highlights the need to go beyond minimalist definitions of well-being in the analysis of women's status. Broadly aggregated indicators of the kind used in Sen's analysis provide a first and necessarily crude picture of patterns of gender disadvantage. For instance, while female disadvantage in nutrition and life expectancy is certainly more apparent in Bangladesh than in The Gambia, data on time allocation would probably reveal greater gender differences in leisure and sleep in the latter context. Female longevity does not necessarily imply a better quality of life: as we concluded in an earlier article (Kabeer and Aziz, 1990), 'rural men in the Gambia no doubt have a heavy workload, but their extra minutes or hours of leisure per day compared to their wives may well represent the difference between well-being and exploitation.' If differences in well-being are used as indicators of gender disadvantage, they need to be sensitive to the specificities of gender inequality in different social contexts.

Rethinking Household Decision-making: Dichotomous Rules or Structural Incentives?

How do the insights provided by anthropological research on households help to illuminate the economic debates discussed earlier? One important contribution they make is to challenge the separation between production and distribution evident in both the economic conceptualizations of household decision-making. In the Beckerian household, a dichotomy is posed between competitive self-interest in the marketplace and altruistic consensus within the household. Sen's formulation effectively reverses this, juxtaposing cooperation in production – 'adding to total availabilities' – with conflict in distribution – 'dividing total availabilities'. Cooperation in production is induced by the interdependence implicit in the social organization of production: 'technological interdependences make it fruitful for the different parties to cooperate in production. In particular, the pattern of division of fruits which emerges from such cooperation reflects the "bargaining powers" of the respective parties' (p. 131). However, there is no *a priori* reason why interdependence should be seen as automatic-ally cooperative; it can also carry potential for conflict, bargaining and negotiation. Obviously, some degree of cooperation is necessary if households are to remain intact; persistent non-cooperation is likely to lead to disintegration. What is of interest is why conflict arises between household members and the form that such conflict takes. Detailed examination of intra-household relations suggests that, since women and men are differently positioned in relation to the division of resources and responsibilities within the household, they are likely to have different, and often conflicting, priorities in production, distri-bution or both. However, inasmuch as households can be seen as risk-mitigating mechanisms, it also suggests that the actual management of this conflict, the extent to which it is suppressed or overt, will reflect the structure of risk faced by different members should household cooperation break down. As the analysis in this chapter suggests, the interacting gender asymmetries within and outside the household domain set up gender-specific regimes of risk in different contexts, including the risks faced by women and men in the context of household conflict and breakdown. As Kandiyoti (1988) observes: 'forms of patriarchy present women with distinct "rules of the game" and call for different strategies to maximize security and optimize life options with varying potential for active or passive resistance in the face of oppression' (p. 274).

The dual specification of households in different cultural contexts can help to spell out how the interaction between intra- and extra-household relations shapes the risk environment – and hence risk-minimizing strategies – for women and men. Broadly speaking, households which are organized as corporate patriarchal entities are more likely to generate material pressures – and incentives – for women to acquiesce, however reluctantly, in a centralized decision-making process. Such 'cooperation' represents their best risk-minizing strategy, given their lack of extra-household options, should the bargaining process break down. Conversely, segmentation of the household economy and a more dispersed distribution of intra-household resources tends to be associated with greater access by women to resources within the household and to extra-household resources. Such systems are likely to entail fewer penalties for explicit and overt gender conflict, and women may be as likely as men to withdraw cooperation from the male-headed households, to live separately and head their own households.[3] We will explore this point by returning to our comparison of different household systems.

Cooperation and Conflict in Corporate Household Organizations

This literature suggests that the more corporately organized household systems of northern India, Pakistan and Bangladesh – where men own most of the household's material assets, control the labour of women and children, and mediate women's relations with the non-familial world – are most likely to be characterized by an absence of overt conflict in household decision-making. Within such systems, women are socially constructed as passive and vulnerable, dependent on male provision and protection for their survival. Women's well-being tends to be tied to the prosperity of the household collectivity, and their long-term interests best served by subordinating their own needs to those of male family members. Women's position in north Indian peasant households has been described by Bardhan (1985, p. 2208):

> They have to depend on male sanction and mediation for the work they do, and its remuneration . . . even for the security of claim to a share of the subsistence they work to generate. . . . The crucial reason for this is that men control property (land, equipment and other productive assets), cash flows and the vantage points in the marketing chain, and women even when forced to hard work for a living must constantly be guarded in conduct so as not to risk incurring severe penalties from family and society. . . . Destitution, women cut off from the male-mediated order, is an ever present spectre.

Households in this context are characterized by strong systemic sanctions supporting, possibly enforcing, cooperation in decision-making and by minimal incentives for women to engage in open conflict over these processes. Bardhan points to the way in which patriarchal household contracts reward female compliance and inhibit open conflict and struggle over household objectives (p. 2265). Indeed when cooperation breaks down, as in times of economic crisis, it is men who are most likely to abandon their households; cooperation becomes unviable if the cost of maintaining dependents is perceived as too high. The 'patriarchal risks' (Cain et al., 1979) associated with women's dependent position lead them to adopt overtly cooperative strategies which maximize their longer-term security, often at the cost of their personal well-being. As Kandiyoti points out, 'women's strategies to maximize their security always involve gaining and keeping the protection of their men; through the adoption of attitudes of submissiveness, propriety and self-sacrifice' (1988).

Material pressures and incentives to cooperate extend to distribution and there is little evidence of overt conflict over distributional processes. Instead there is a hierarchy of decision-making, needs and priorities (associated with age, gender and lifecycle), a hierarchy to which both men and women appear to subscribe. Thus women appear to acquiesce to – and indeed actively perpetuate – discriminatory practices in intra-household distribution in order to assure their own longer-term security. Denied access to extra-household relationships and resources, it is in their material interests to subscribe to the general son-preference which characterizes this culture, and they invest in a great deal of 'selfless' devotion in order to win their sons as allies and insurance against an uncertain future. 'Maternal altruism' in the northern Indian plain is likely to be biased towards sons and can be seen as women's response to patriarchal risk. Women are not entirely powerless, of course, but their subversion of male decision-making power tends to be covert. The use of trusted allies (relatives or neighbours) to conduct small businesses on their behalf, the secret lending and borrowing of money, and negotiations around the meaning of gender ideologies of purdah and motherhood, are some of the strategies by which women have resisted male power (Abdullah and Zeidenstein, 1982; Kabeer, 1990; White, 1992). That their resistance takes this clandestine form reflects their lack of options outside household cooperation and the concomitant high risks associated with open conflict.

Such corporately organized households resemble in form the altruistic household model of neo-classical theory, but apparent unity in decision-making is imposed by the considerable power invested in male family members rather than being adopted through a democratic consensus: dictatorship without benevolence. Sen notes the possibility of enforced cooperation, although he does not pursue it:

> Not only do the different parties have much to gain from cooperation; their individual activities have to take the form of being overtly co-operative, even when substantial conflicts exist. . . . Although serious conflicts of interests may be involved in the choice of 'social technology', the nature of the family organisation requires that these conflicts be molded in a general format of co-operation, with conflicts treated as aberrations or deviant behaviour. (p. 147).

Cooperation and Conflict in Segmented
Household Organizations

A rather different picture emerges from the segmented household economies of sub-Saharan Africa where women and men have separate but interdependent responsibilities in production, and separate but interdependent obligations to their families. Here there are risks associated with patriarchal relations, 'the insecurities of African polygyny' (Kandiyoti, 1988). However, the household arrangements which give rise to them appear to offer scope for openly expressed conflict to coexist alongside areas of cooperation. Gender conflicts in household decision-making in such contexts are often overt, rather than covert, and arise out of the struggle by different household members to pursue their individual priorities and interests, rather than being expressly associated with either production or distribution. It is worth noting that the main axes of Mandinka domestic life, as noted by Carney and Watts (1990, p. 230), conform closely to the decision-making principles we are discussing here, viz. *badingya* (cooperation, obligation and harmony) and *fadingya* (ambition, selfishness and conflict).

West Africa offers the most widely cited examples of household systems where conflictual forms of decision-making are in evidence. As Hill (1975) points out, 'It is abundantly clear that West African husbands and wives seldom form a unified production unit. Of course, this is not to deny that there is much mutual dependence and complementarity within the household' (p. 123). Roberts (1989) has chronicled the sexual politics of production among Yoruba households in Nigeria which are neither units of corporate ownership nor collectivities of labour. Here, for most women, farming means working for men, usually husbands, while trading means working on their own account. Women undertake domestic tasks in return for food provisions from husbands; if they scale down their domestic labour, husbands reduce contributions to their subsistence. Farm tasks are compensated separately and this recompense is used to finance women's independent trading activities. The pursuit of a separate enterprise strengthens women's negotiating position with their husbands and allows them to insist on compensation for their farm services. 'Ultimately. . . . a woman can withdraw from a household in which neither her domestic nor her farm services are rewarded' (p. 36), and Roberts notes that women successful in trade do frequently separate from their husbands.

Jones's work in Cameroon details the conflicts over production among the Massa which resulted from the absence of a 'joint household rationality'. The introduction of an irrigated rice scheme led to the emergence of a new contractual relationship, alongside the pre-existing ones governing sorghum production. Women now worked on primarily male-owned rice plots in return for remuneration in the form of paddy and cash. While it would have maximized joint household income for both women and men to devote more resources to paddy cultivation – women by allocating more labour to rice production and men by offering women higher rates of remuneration to induce them to do so – neither sought to achieve allocative efficiency at the household level. Women who were unhappy with the remuneration offered for their work on the rice fields would refuse to prepare their husbands' food as a sign of their displeasure. Some were beaten as a result. They were also beaten if they refused to work on their husbands' rice fields when not working on their own. The long hours that women chose to spend on their own fields, rather than on their husbands', reflected not so much the relative returns to labour (which would have been higher on the rice fields) but the fact that they enjoyed greater control over crops from their own fields. As Jones suggests, the household internal market operated 'as if' it was a bilateral monopoly, created by marriage and the associated sanctions made available to each partner. Husbands and wives confronted each other as the sole 'buyers' and 'sellers' of a particular kind of labour. In the absence of joint rationality at household level, there was little incentive to achieve allocative efficiency at the household level.

The potential for gender conflicts over production goals were also brought out into the open in The Gambia by a series of irrigated rice projects which sought to turn over irrigated rice land – a crop that had previously been cultivated by women – to men in the compound. Since women had no customary obligation to perform free labour on their husbands' own account holdings, they were protected from these demands from their husbands. The gender struggles within the household which ensued concerned 'who would work and under what conditions' and the extent to which wives' labour could be mobilized on male-controlled plots (Carney and Watts, 1990, p. 226). Some women withheld their labour and pursued their own independent economic strategies. Others agreed to work (often for their husbands) on the irrigated land in return for compensation in the form of wages, a share of the yield or usufruct rights over land elsewhere.

Separate productive activities may be combined with complementarity in consumption. As Guyer (1988) notes, among the Beti in southern Cameroon men and women are involved in separate spheres of productive activity, but acknowledge complementary obligations in certain areas of consumption, including food provisioning and expenditures on children (feeding, education, initiation and bride-wealth). However, the extensive literature on conflictual distributional processes within West African households signals that such obligations are not smoothly effected through pooling and sharing but may be the subject of exchange and bargaining. Jones, for instance, notes from in her work among the Massa in Cameroon the prevalence of 'frequent and pronounced conflict' between women and men over the division of income from rice production. Men's interest in using their wives' income, usually for the purchase of livestock for bridewealth pay-ments, conflicts at the margin with women's interest in using the income to purchase consumer goods which have become increasingly more available and socially necessary (1985, p. 451). Whitehead points out that, despite interdependencies in male and female familial obligations and hence expenditure patterns, differing obligations can lead to differing distributional priorities and frequent domestic conflict, especially in conditions of economic stress: 'Rural women complain at the selfish way men spend; men complain reciprocally at the constant financial demands from their wives' (1990, p. 67).

Conflicting priorities over production and consumption can lead to a perceived divergence between women's own interests and household interests, as evidenced in women's investment strategies. Roberts (1989) notes how women in rural Hausa Niger invest part of their 'pitifully small' earnings in reciprocal gift-giving with other women in order to build a significant network of credit and security. Hill (1975) comments that in West African farming households, women's invest-ments, 'far from complementing their husbands'' or being incorpor-ated into a general household fund, 'may be geared toward setting up an insurance against divorce', often by investing in their natal kin groups after marriage (cited in Guyer, 1988). Leach also reports how young married women in Sierra Leone prefer not to invest their labour in growing trees on their husbands' land because they do not consider themselves to be 'permanent residents' in their married homes (Leach, 1990).

Thus, women's responses to marital risk and uncertainty often militate against cooperation in the disposition of household labour and promote their greater investment in extra-household networks. While 'ideologies of maternal altruism' might account for the closer associ-ation between women's incomes/crops and children's welfare noted in an earlier section, Whitehead suggests that motherhood itself creates special sets of circumstances and interests so that women's fortunes are bound up with particular forms of altruistic behaviour towards their children. As in South Asian households, 'maternal altruism' in West

African households may also be a way of dealing with 'patriarchal risk', although here there is no evidence of, or material basis for, marked son-preference.

Conclusion: Overcoming Conceptual and Methodological Dichotomies

At the beginning of this chapter it was noted that economists had achieved the formal elegance of their models by sacrificing the bewildering and contradictory complexity of everyday reality. This chapter has sought to reverse this process, sacrificing elegance for a noisier, messier understanding of social processes. This has involved bridging a number of normative dichotomies which define and limit economic thought. The first is the dichotomy that privileges individuals at the expense of structures. The concentration on the individual and the exclusion of the social relationships which connect different categories of individuals and help to organize their activities explains to some extent the relentless voluntarism of neo-classical explanations of individual behaviour. There is no space here to consider power as a structural relationship, as socially entrenched asymmetries in rules and resources that enable some categories of individuals to constrain and shape the options and actions of others. Inequality is perceived only in terms of individual endowments; conflict takes the form of competition between individuals; and power implies decision-making power. The structural dimensions of gender and other inequalities are not merely ignored in mainstream neo-classical economics, but are *inconceivable*.

The second dichotomy relates to the distinction economists make between 'economic' and 'cultural'. 'Culture' is generally used within this literature to refer to all those norms, customs and practices that prevent full and certain prediction of people's behaviour by principles of economic maximization alone. Culture, it could be said, is the other things people value aside from scarce good and services. One version of economics denies that culture is at all relevant to economic problems; all behaviour can be explained in terms of prices and incomes (Stigler and Becker, 1977). An intermediate version acknowledges that 'non-economic' factors are important, but argues that 'the net effect of economic factors should be perceptible while allowing for the non-economic' (Cassen, 1978, p. 75). A third position acknowledges that culture can constrain the 'rational' allocation of resources within the household: 'Where this is the case the subordination of women may sometimes be found to have a practical economic effect on the material conditions of survival of the household, quite apart from its meaning in terms of the inferior social status of farm women' (Ellis, 1988, p. 183).

The argument here suggests that the dichotomy between 'economic' and 'cultural' is one of methodological convenience rather than empirical accuracy. In practice, economic processes frequently work through cultural relations, and cultural 'rules' have concrete, material effects. Rather than leaving cultural phenomena to 'whoever studies and explains tastes (psychologists? anthropologists? phrenologists? sociobiologists?)' (Stigler and Becker, 1977), or explaining them purely in terms of prices and incomes, this chapter has sought to demonstrate that an inclusion of allocative rules, aside from those of the market, would considerably improve our understanding of household processes and outcomes.

A final dichotomy, and one that is closely related to the other two, is the methodological one between quantitative and qualitative analysis. The positivist tradition is not unique to economics, but economists have demonstrated the greatest faith within the social sciences in the scientific status of quantitative knowledge and the least respect for qualitative insights. However, there are significant dimensions of the human experience that do not lend themselves to enumeration. One such dimension that has figured prominently in this chapter is that of power. Quantitative approaches may be able to measure 'statistically important' areas of decision-making power for women and men, but the elusiveness of power lies precisely in its resistance to 'objective' observation. This point has been made repeatedly in feminist scholarship, but also appears in other analyses of power. It is contained in Foucault's observation that 'power is tolerable only when a good deal of its workings are concealed' (cited in Wilson, 1991). The divergence between personal well-being and perceived interest that Sen posits in his household model not only undermines an individual's ability to bargain for a favourable share of household resources, but is itself indicative of an already unequal division of power among household members. This is not, however, an insight that can be easily quantified.

The elusiveness of gender power within the household is the greater because of its embeddedness in the most intimate arena of human relationships, that of the family: in no other institution are relationships 'so extended in time, so intensive in contact, so dense in their interweaving of economics, emotion, power and resistance (Connell, 1987, p. 121). It is highly unlikely that the subtle and concealed nature of such power will reveal itself through the format of a highly structured and standardized questionnaire. It is frequently the 'silences' and 'absences' within the research encounter, the information that is withheld rather than that which is volunteered, which signal the presence of disempowering relations (see, for instance, Wilson, 1991). By their privileging of individuals to the exclusion of structures, of the economic over the cultural, and of 'objective' quantitative predictions over qualitative explanations, neo-classical economists have succeeded in drawing a veil over the power dimension of intra-household relations. They demonstrate the core of truth in Robin Morgan's (1977, p. 15) blunt assertion that, 'the either/or dichotomy is inherently, classically patriarchal'.

Notes

1 There is a theoretical circularity in neo-classical explanations of the link between gender inequality within households and within markets. In this example, lower investment in women's 'human capital' is attributed to their poorer employment prospects. Elsewhere, however, lower investment in women's human capital (specifically education) is blamed for their lower rates of labour-force participation (Appleton et al., 1990). In other words, in some explanations, market differentials are taken as given and explain women's disadvantage in intra-household resource allocations; in others, intra-household resource allocations are taken as given and explain women's disadvantage in the marketplace. As Amsden (1980) points out, divorced from the underlying social realities, maximization principles become little more than justifications for an unjust status quo.

2 Unlike the New Household Economics, which distinguishes between home production, leisure and market work, previous neo-classical models treated household/individual labour supply decisions as a choice between paid employment and leisure. As Dex observes, the practice of describing all activities other than paid employment as 'leisure' was a peculiarly male choice of label (1985, p. 64).

3 'Voting with their feet' was how a student from Botswana explained the high proportion of women who chose to head their own households in her country.

6

Beyond the Poverty Line:
Measuring Poverty and
Impoverishing Measures

The most common approach in defining a poverty line is to estimate the cost of a bundle of goods deemed to assure that basic consumption needs are met. (Lipton and Ravallion, forthcoming, p. 20)

The value of the living standard lies in the living, and not in the possessing of commodities, which has derivative and varying relevance. (Sen, 1987, p. 25)

Introduction

In this chapter I would like to pursue further the connection between concepts and method, focusing this time on the question of poverty and poverty measurement. There are two major challenges in developing an appropriate approach to the evaluation of living standards and they pull in different directions (Sen, 1987, p. 20). The first is the challenge of relevance, which demands that we recognise the inherent complexities of the idea rather than reducing it to some convenient, but arbitrary, index. Chambers has written eloquently on the tendency to define poverty in a way that 'blurs distinctions and sustains stereotypes of the amorphous and undifferentiated mass of the poor' (Chambers, 1989, p. 1). On the other hand, the approach needs to be practical in the sense of usability for actual assessment of living standards, a requirement which necessarily imposes a restriction on the kinds and quantities of information which can be incorporated. 'Relevance wants us to be ambitious; usability urges restraint' (Sen, 1987, p. 20).

Some form of measurement is central in monitoring exercises since the objective is to compare the incidence of a particular phenomenon at intervals over a period of time in order to determine the direction and magnitude of trends. Monitoring entails the conceptualization of the relevant phenomenon, the development of appropriate measures, and then the assessment of changes in this measure. In the next section, I will be discussing the conceptualization of poverty in mainstream development literature and the forms of measurement it has given rise to. I will be pointing to some of the exclusions entailed in this conceptualization and their roots in a particular ideology of intra-household relations. The rest of the chapter outlines an alternative framework for conceptualizing poverty, one which is less prone to these selective exclusions. The analysis in this chapter is based on my involvement in developing a methodology for monitoring poverty in rural Bangladesh, and I will be using empirical examples from rural Bangladesh both from my own field visits and from the existing literature to demonstrate the significance of gender relations within such a framework.

Alternative Conceptualizations of Poverty

A useful starting point for discussing different ways of looking at poverty is the idea of deprivation: the poor are those who are deprived of basic human needs. Poverty can then be captured in terms of an 'ends' perspective – the actual levels of deprivation – or a 'means' perspective – the adequacy of resources to avoid deprivation. As we noted in Chapter 2, economists tend not to concern themselves with ends as such, but with the scarcity of the means by which these ends are realized. Consequently, the conceptualizations and measures of poverty offered by economists tend to focus on the scarcity of means rather than the achievement of ends. The poverty line, one of the most widely used measures of poverty, exemplifies this approach. The poverty line identifies poverty with shortfalls in household purchasing power. It is represented by the average amount of income necessary to purchase enough food for all members of an 'average-sized' house-hold to meet their average daily recommended calorie requirements. Households are classified as poor or non-poor depending on whether their income is below or above the poverty line. While any attempt to reduce poverty to quantifiable dimensions necessarily entails simplifi-cation, there are particular dangers in reducing it to a single undimensional index.

First of all, the dichotomous classification system of the poverty line means that it is insensitive to changes in the absolute levels of poverty and to changes in the distribution of poverty on either side of the line (Sen, 1982b). Its focus on purchasing power rather than achieved consumption rules out non-market consumption possibilities (for example, self-provisioning, barter, state provision or common property resources). Yet these are likely to be of some significance in the partially monetized economies of most Third World countries, particularly among the poor. Second, its concern is entirely with measuring the extent to which household income is sufficient to achieve an 'acceptable' level of household welfare. How households choose to allocate this income is seen to be a matter for private choice rather than public policy. As long as altruistic principles of distribution within the household prevail, they will ensure that the burden of poverty is equally distributed so that all household members are equally poor. However, if the arguments of the previous chapter are accepted, then it becomes clear that choice is selectively, not equally, exercised by the household membership so that welfare outcomes reflect relations of power rather than democratic consensus. In fact, the evidence cited in the previous chapter of a systematic gender, and age, bias in intra-household welfare distribution suggests that women and children are likely to be disproportionately represented in the ranks of those below the poverty line. It also suggests that where women are denied control over productive resources, such biases are likely to be more marked.

The problem with household-based measures of poverty, therefore, is that they render invisible inequalities within the household with respect to ends as well as means. A more effective methodology for capturing the 'constitutive plurality' (Sen, 1987, p. 2) of poverty might be the use of key human indicators along with a composite household-based index. Key indicators make room for the varying experiences and priorities of different poverty groups and for varying rates of change in different dimensions of poverty. Their potential for capturing human as well as household poverty characteristics is valuable in contexts where gender differentials and the more qualitative aspects of poverty are considered important. However, a conceptual framework is still necessary if the indicators are to be selected on a theoretically informed, rather than an ad hoc, basis.

Poverty as 'Ends': A Basic Needs Perspective

The idea that the 'means' available to the poor – as measured by their purchasing power – can be separated from their 'ends' – the satisfaction of basic needs – stems from the belief that whatever these needs are, they can be satisfied through a sufficient level of purchasing power. Purchasing power can therefore be taken as an adequate index of needs satisfaction. However, this is premissed on a very narrow interpretation of need. In its most reductionist version, it refers only to the imperatives of physiological survival. This is the view embedded in many versions of the poverty line which define the poor as those who are not able to cover their basic calorie needs. However, basic needs can be given a wider range of different meanings than the ability to purchase a minimum recommended daily allowance of calories. Human need is about more than physiological survival; it is also about living a healthy active life and participating in the life of the community. These are the 'beings and doings' that people value and that Sen (1987) calls 'agency achievements'. A more inclusive definition of basic needs would therefore encompass culturally defined levels of physical well-being (health, housing, clothing, sanitation) while a still broader definition results· if the concept is stretched to cover the more intangible aspects of deprivation – powerlessness, dependence, isolation (Chambers, 1988).

As a preliminary hypothesis derived from his own research, Chambers (1988) suggests the idea of a 'hierarchy of basic needs' among the poor in the sense that basic survival needs have to be satisfied before security, and then self esteem, can become important.[1] My own field investigations offer a different perspective on this proposition. In the words of one of the women I interviewed:

> What need have the poor for self-respect or propriety. Everything is dictated by scarcity [abhab]: scarcity of food, scarcity of clothes, scarcity of shelter, there is no end to the scarcity . . . there are mothers who cannot feed their children, can they afford propriety?

Her statement conveys the clear message that for those living on the margins of physical survival, the struggle to stay alive appears to be an overriding priority. However, it also contains the suggestion that for poor women, the notion of self-esteem itself might be more closely tied to the ability to feed their children than to middle-class ideals of female propriety, which would hamper their survival strategies.

Conflicting notions of self-esteem were also evident in the different responses to the attempts of a development project in one of the villages I visited to provide landless women with earth-cutting and other non-traditional forms of work. According to the village mattabars (leaders), the spectacle of women from 'their' village engaging in public forms of manual labour would bring shame on the community.

A few husbands also objected to their wives joining the project, using arguments about their own self-esteem and honour. For many landless women, however, the project offered a route to independent resources and they chose to defy both village opinion and their husbands' threats. In speaking, therefore, of self-esteem and autonomy as 'basic' human needs, it is important to remember that such needs are socially constituted and cannot be assigned *a priori* meanings. Poor women may value self-esteem and autonomy, but define it very differently both from men in their own households and from women from more prosperous households.

If these less tangible aspects of well-being are taken into account, it becomes clear that means and ends are no longer separable. Different ways of ensuring command over material resources are likely to carry different implications for poor people's self-esteem and autonomy; and there may be gender differences in what these implications are. But these cannot be assumed. The assessment of poverty must therefore make space for considering the extent to which the tangible and intangible basic needs of the poor women and men are met.

Poverty as Means: The Entitlements Perspective

The idea of entitlements comes from Sen (1982b) and draws attention to the different basis of claims on resources which prevail in a society. The distribution of resources in any society occurs through a complex system of claims, which are in turn embedded within the social relations and practices that govern possession, distribution and use in that society (Sen, 1982b). Poverty occurs because the value of the two main parameters – endowments and exchange entitlements – that constitute the basis of household or individual claims to the social product is not sufficient to cover basic needs. While entitlements pertain to individualized command over resources, the literature on poverty in Bangladesh suggests that it has a structural basis. The prevailing distribution of entitlements emerges out of institutional processes which effectively 'disenfranchise' certain groups from participating in decisions about entitlements and hence from challenging their distribution (Appadurai, 1984). The causes of poverty are therefore not simply a question of inadequate entitlements, but also of structurally reproduced distributional inequities. There is an extensive class analysis of impoverishment and polarization in rural Bangladesh (Hossain, 1987; North–South Institute 1985; Rahman, 1986a, 1986b); far less attention is given to gender-based forms of disenfranchisment and poverty (see Feldman and McCarthy, 1984; and Adnan,

1988 for some exceptions). In the discussion that follows, the social relations of gender are considered at least as significant as those of poverty and class in generating entitlement inequities.

Sen's concern with the legalistic basis of entitlements (the formal rules that govern who can have the use of what) in his earlier work led him to overlook the very different basis of claims which were inscribed in what we discussed as the 'implicit contracts' of intra-household relations in Chapter 4. This was rectified in a later paper (Sen, 1990) where the concept of entitlements was extended to encompass those intra-household distributional processes which rest on 'perceived legitimacy' – norms and conventions – rather than legally binding contracts. These extended entitlements have a special significance for women in a country like Bangladesh, where they are in effect classified as dependent minors along with children, and their welfare entrusted to male guardians and breadwinners. Powerful beliefs and practices, sanctioned by the norms of religion and community, produce a highly unequal division of social and economic space. Women's ability to mobilize resources, including their own labour power, independently are severely curtailed. Instead, their claims to the means by which they meet their basic needs are embedded to a large degree within the contractual relations of family and kinship. Even when women have apparently independent entitlements, for instance through ownership of assets or sale of their labour power, they prefer to realize them in ways that do not disrupt kin-ascribed entitlements, their primary source of survival and security.

The gender dimension of poverty occurs, therefore, because women and men experience poverty differently and unequally. They are also likely to become impoverished through processes that sometimes (though not always) diverge. Conceptually, there are two distinct processes by which women become impoverished. They can become poorer along with the rest of the family-based household through a deterioration in its collective entitlements; in such cases women's interests are bound up with the collective interests of the household. Alternatively, they can become poorer with the breakdown of the family unit itself, and with it the 'accepted legitimacy' of their specific claims. Here situations may emerge where women's interests diverge from, and may indeed conflict with, those of male members of the household. Empirically, these different processes are closely intertwined; the impoverishment of a household is often accompanied by the simultaneous disintegration of its 'core' family structures and the erosion of women's normative claims on their kin.

The starting point for our framework for analysing poverty is, consequently, that ends and means are interrelated. We therefore need information on both household 'ends', the meeting of basic needs, and household 'means', its command over the resources by which these needs are met. Second, means and ends may mean different things to different people; in particular, women and men may have very different priorities and possibilities. There are important methodological implications to such a premiss. First, it implies that data will have to be disaggregated to take account of intra-household differentials in 'beings and doings'. Second, it implies the need for indicators which recognize that women's lives are governed by different and often more complex social constraints, entitlements and responsibilities than those of men, and are led to a far greater extent outside the monetized domain. The rest of this chapter analyses the gender dimension of poverty in rural Bangladesh in terms of basic needs and resource entitlements, using examples from the available literature as well as from my own field investigations.

Gender and Basic Needs: Food Security

Severe physical deprivation is at the core of poverty in Bangladesh. It takes the form of chronic malnutrition, widespread hunger and low levels of life expectancy. In most studies of poverty, nutritional status is taken as an unequivocal statement about the level of individual well-being. Data on nutritional status among the rural population in Bangladesh indicate the magnitude of the problem. Only 5 per cent of the population consume an adequate quantity and quality of food, while 58 per cent of the rural population suffer from long-term malnutrition (UNICEF, 1987). The centrality of this dimension in determining absolute deprivation suggests that it will also be a critical area in which to locate and understand female poverty.

Nutritional indicators, like indicators in general, are only as reliable as their underlying assumptions. The earlier belief that all human beings have a predetermined minimum level of nutritional requirements (modified by such variables as activity levels, pregnancy, breastfeeding, and so on) is being challenged by more recent arguments that populations are able to 'adapt' to low energy intake (see Payne and Cutler, 1984). While there is no conclusive evidence in favour of either position, the relationship between *severe* malnutrition and increased risk of morbidity and mortality is not an issue. Bearing these caveats in mind, a brief account of the available evidence is presented.

One set of evidence relates to dietary intake vis-à-vis recommended minimum requirements. One of the problems with this is that estimates of minimum requirements which rely, among other things, on body weight and activity levels, tend in the case of women to incorporate and reproduce past nutritional discrimination and are, furthermore, based on unreliable estimates of women's activity levels (Chen et al., 1981). Consequently, findings from the 1981–82 Nutrition Survey that there is a female disadvantage at adult ages 'only' in so far as the higher calorie requirement of pregnant and lactating women is not met (Mahmud and Mahmud, 1985) may underestimate the real levels of female malnutrition. Nevertheless, as the authors point out, the findings still suggest significant female disadvantage in a context where two-thirds of women in the reproductive ages (15–45) are pregnant, lactating or both. A major cause of female malnutrition in Bangladesh is therefore the superimposition of early, frequent and closely spaced child-bearing on already high levels of malnutrition.

Aside from pregnant and lactating women, the other category which suffers severe nutritional disadvantage is the young, especially young girls. The Nutrition Survey of 1985–86 provides anthropometric evidence of widespread chronic and acute malnutrition among rural children (58 per cent and 8 per cent). Both problems affected girls more frequently than boys (UNICEF, 1987). Fifty-nine per cent of girls and 56 per cent of boys suffered chronic malnutrition, while 10 per cent of girls and 7 per cent of boys suffered acute malnutrition. A more recent national survey conducted by the Bangladesh Institute of Development Studies (BIDS) found that there has been a significant improvement in the average weight of boys during the eighties, but little improvement for girls (Choudhury, 1991).

While the most pressing reason for widespread malnutrition in Bangladesh is 'simply that people do not have enough food' (UNICEF, 1987, p. 36), the interpretation of female malnutrition is complicated by the interaction between gender and economic factors. Practices which lead to inequitable gender distribution of food in the family include feeding males first, particularly adult males, and giving them the choicest and largest servings. The norms and values justifying such dietary practices are subscribed to by both men and women and reflect cultural beliefs about the relative needs and contributions of different household members, fears about the consequences of violating accepted practices, and ideologies of female altruism and self-sacrifice:

When I can, I give my husband and sons more. Men don't understand if food runs short, so I wait till they have eaten.

A good wife is one who makes sure her husband has enough to eat.

If a woman eats before her husband, she shortens his life.

Men work harder than women, they need to eat more.

How can you explain to children that there is not enough food . . . ? When my son cries, I feed him. It is easier to make my daughter understand.

If there is less, I eat less. You have to feed the men more or they beat you. Even my son beats me if there is not enough food. (Fieldwork notes, 1987/8)

Conflict over food is a frequent source of violence within the family; women can be beaten if food falls short, if there is too much salt in it or too little salt, or if they are found tasting the food before others have eaten. Hartmann and Boyce (1983, p. 89) note other flashpoints: because the chicken stole some grains of rice, because the wife forgot to buy milk. They quote a sharecropper's wife in their village study: 'When my husband's stomach is empty, he beats me, but when it is full, there is peace.' The authors point out that wife-beatings were frequently an outlet for men's powerlessness in the face of grinding hunger. Anecdotal evidence from Greeley's fieldwork suggests that the incidence of wife-beating may have a seasonal component as it appears to increase in the 'hungry' months.[2] To the extent that this is a general phenomenon, women's apparent acceptance of their subordinate claims on household food resources may be based as much on the implicit threat of male violence as it is on internalized social norms.

Inequities in the intra-household distribution of resources are not confined to the poor, but operate in a modified form across the economic spectrum giving gender a significance independent of class. Thus, while malnutrition decreases as family income and mothers' education rise (UNICEF, 1987), the disadvantages associated with gender and age persist. Data on calorie intake vis-à-vis requirements show that children suffer from substantial deficits even in the richest households, while female adults suffer from larger deficits (relative to male adults) in the poorest and enjoy smaller surpluses in the richest households (Mahmud and Mahmud, 1985).

It is clear that in the narrowest sense of basic needs, women suffer deprivation to a greater extent than men within households. However, food is as much about security and status as it is about shortfalls in calorie consumption. A great deal can be learnt about household poverty by comparing the *source, frequency* and *content* of meals. Where a household can rely on a stable, reliable and well-established bundle of entitlements, the acquisition of food is unlikely to require a great deal of management or foresight. A different picture prevails among those whose access to food is insecure and who do not know where their next meal is coming from. Here considerable ingenuity and effort is spent, frequently by women, to stretch out the meagre resources available to the household. Women's activities in this area include, for instance, gleaning the fields after the harvest; gathering edible wild plants, fuel and fodder from common property reserves; negotiating and begging rice or lentils from neighbours; bringing home the discarded stalks and leaves of vegetables from the kitchens of wealthier households. Another aspect of women's contribution is the practice among labouring women who receive meals as part of their wages to share it with their children, either taking their children along to the employer's house or bringing the meal home. This does not occur as frequently among male labourers paid in the same way. One explanation offered was that it was considered too revealing of their poverty and therefore demeaning to their role as breadwinners.

Diversity of diet also enters into social definitions of well-being. Food occupies an important role in the social life of rural communities and there is a distinct hierarchy of preference for different kinds of food. Rice, especially the finer grain variety, is generally preferred to *rooti* (wheat-based bread) as the staple item in the daily diet. Most other items can be placed on a scale from 'luxury' or 'status' foods to 'famine' or 'poverty' foods. Meat and certain larger varieties of fish can only be afforded by affluent sections of the community. Chicken used to be considered the ultimate status food (Aziz, 1979) and the only one prestigious enough to offer a visiting son-in-law. Similarly, consumption of cigarettes (rather than *biris*, hand-rolled tobacco leaves) and tea with sugar and milk is also more common among affluent households.[3] Poverty diets, on the other hand, include various wild plants, – *kolmi saag* (an aquatic plant); *shapla* (water hyacinth) stems; young jute leaves; the fleshy trunk of the banana tree; *bon kochu* (wild arum) – many of which can be gathered from common property reserves. Very frugal meals such as rice with chillies and salt alone, a gruel made with rice and the water in which it is cooked, rice cooked only with lentils (no oil or spices), also make up the diet of the poor. Finally, frequency of meals per day is a particularly stark indicator of food security. The poor can seldom afford more than two meals a day, the very poor make do with one. In a village study conducted in 1980, I found that 63 per cent of landless households ate two or fewer meals a day compared to 30 per cent of households owning at least half an acre of land. (Kabeer, 1986). In the 'hungry' months, some of the poor report going to bed without eating all day, perhaps chewing on tobacco or betel leaves or drinking water to blunt their hunger.

Age and gender differentials in food indicators can arise because meals are acquired through different sources or because of straightforward discrimination. Gender differences in agricultural wage labour and patterns of remuneration may lead to more frequent meals for male members, with a greater likelihood of preferred items, like rice, lentils, and vegetables, in the diet. The greater ability of this group to visit tea shops, attend social gatherings and go into the towns also suggest other possibilities for diversifying their diets. By contrast, women eat at home more often and their meals are more likely to consist of 'poverty' foods, particularly when male members are absent. Differentials can also emerge through straightforward discrimination. The custom of giving male members the choicest and largest servings of food has already been noted. On some occasions this was revealed through direct observation of food distribution during my interviews. Not only was there a clear disparity in the amount of rice served to male and female members, but male members were also privileged in the distribution of the accompanying items, such as vegetables and lentils. Women and young girls made do with chillies and salt.

Gender and Basic Needs: Health

The issue of health graphically illustrates the artificiality of separating means and ends in the analysis of development problems. As Chambers puts it, 'The main asset of most poor people is their bodies' (1989, p. 4). Consequently, poverty can be seen both in terms of shortfalls in basic bodily needs as well as in the ability to translate labour endowments into adequate command over resources. Low levels of health and nutrition reduce labour productivity, which in turn devalues returns to labour and future capacity to improve physical well-being. Bodily well-being is thus simultaneously means and ends.

Although health is the key to productivity among the poor, they are least likely to enjoy it. As a UNICEF report observes, 'In reviewing the pattern of mortality and morbidity in Bangladesh, one is struck by . . . the extent to which the risk of illness and death is linked to poverty' (UNICEF, 1987, p. 33). Illness appears to be a normal rather than an exceptional event for the poor and can have profound reverberations in their lives. The BIDS national survey found that after natural disasters, illness-related expenditures and losses were the most frequent form of crisis reported by rural households (Rahman, 1991). In households where the physical labour of members is the basis of entitlements, days of work lost or productivity lowered by illness often constituted the starting point of its gradual descent into greater poverty. Many women working outside the shelter of purdah had been precipitated into this form of labour by the illness of a male breadwinner (Chen and Ghuznavi, 1979).

There is evidence of gender discrimination in access to health care. For instance, Chen et al. (1981) show that boys are more likely to be brought in to clinics and hospitalized than girls, despite equal incidence of infection and the availability of free clinical care in the area under study. According to another study (Sabir and Ebrahim, 1984), equal proportions of boys and girls were afflicted with diarrhoea, but 66 per cent more boys than girls were taken to health facilities for treatment.

Gender differentiates the link between health and poverty in other ways. While child-bearing in itself may be considered a 'normal' biological event for most rural women, it can have fatal consequences when it is juxtaposed with women's disadvantaged access to nutrition and health care. Maternal mortality in Bangladesh is among the highest in the world (around five to seven per thousand live births) and accounts for nearly a third of deaths among women in their reproductive years (Chen et al. 1974). There are other more hidden mechanisms at work. Maternal mortality rates are highest among the so-called 'poor reproducers'. These are women who have not been successful in producing a live birth or healthy children, particularly healthy sons, and who are usually under intense pressure to undergo a succession of closely spaced births; as Mahmud and Mahmud point out, 'in a woman who is undernourished and anaemic to begin with, this can create a life-threatening condition leading to premature death' (Mahmud and Mahmud, 1985, p. 17).

Cumulative discrimination against women probably underlies their lower life expectancy relative to men. The effects of discrimination begin early. In their study of mortality differentials, D'Souza and Chen (1980) demonstrate that female biological advantage is only evident in the first month after birth, when it may be assumed that social discrimination has not yet had effect. By the end of the first year, the biological pattern is reversed. In the first four years of life, half as many more girls are likely to die as boys. In fact, apart from death by drowning, UNICEF notes that girls in this age group accounted for a greater number of deaths from all other causes. Female mortality exceeds male in almost all subsequent age groups, thereby reversing the phenomenon of higher female life expectancy found in most other countries (Sen, 1990).

There is one other route through which a gender dimension in basic health needs is manifested. It relates to the question of perception. A study of health-seeking behaviour in village households noted that men, particularly among heads of households, were most likely to report on their own illness (UBINIG, 1987). The reporting of illness in the case of women was poor, even where interviewers found that the women were clearly sick. The study makes a distinction between reporting and recognition, in that some health problems are not reported because they have not been recognized. It concludes, however, that women's illnesses are doubly ignored. They are frequently not identified as illnesses that require treatment and, where they are so identified, women have no clearly recognized entitlement to necessary health care. Women themselves bolster this value system by ignoring their own ill health, seeing it as their role to continue to work as long as they are physically able to.

Gender and Basic Needs: Personal Security

Vulnerability, along with deprivation, is endemic to poverty. It may take many different forms but is often associated with the trade-offs that poor people are often forced to make in order to survive. Frequently, the struggle for survival and security can only be assured at the expense of autonomy and self-reliance; for example, many poor families are forced to become clients of powerful local patrons, offering loyalty and unpaid labour in return for protection and assistance in times of crisis. Furthermore, the intense competition for scarce and dwindling resources, combined with struggles for economic and political power among a small group of wealthy landlords, give rise to situations of random as well as systematic violence between different competing factions where it is the poor who are most frequently the victims.

The vulnerability of the poor stemming from various class-based antagonisms has received some attention in the literature (BRAC, 1980; Hartmann and Boyce, 1983). It is manifested in the police harassments, property feuds, false litigations, forcible evictions, extortion, assault and sometimes murder, all of which are more likely to characterize the lives of poor people and reinforce their dependency on more powerful sections of the community. The ability to manipulate, as well as violate, community norms and customs adds to the control exercised by these sections over the lives and choices of poor people. Thus in one case, powerful neighbours bent on driving a widow, living on her own, from her land, were able to harass her by letting loose their livestock on her homestead plot; in another case, a landless women was beaten and had her goats confiscated by a local landlord who claimed they had wandered into his fields.

What has been less documented in the available literature are the specifically gender-based forms of vulnerability that affect women. In particular, questions of sexual harassment of women and domestic violence have barely been touched on, although they were repeatedly referred to in my interviews and conversations with village women. Consequently their link with poverty can only be speculated on here. Vulnerability to sexual harassment and domestic violence is an aspect of the gendered nature of poverty because poor women, in particular, are most exposed to the risk of harassment and least able to remove themselves from violent situations. Women may have to stay with violent husbands, or accept sexual abuse from their employers, because the alternatives to such behaviour are even more bleak. It is also the case that women who move in 'public space' are perceived to be transgressing the boundaries of female propriety and are therefore a sexual provocation, to be teased, harassed or assaulted. Poorer women and girls are least able to afford to remain within the shelter of the homestead or to purchase forms of transport that would maintain their purdah, and are consequently most exposed to harassment by strangers. Moreover, in a society where family honour is linked to the virtue of its female members, sexual harassment and rape are often used in property feuds and factional disputes to humiliate opponents.

Domestic violence against women (and children) is also a widespread but poorly documented phenomenon. Husbands figured most frequently in my interviews as the perpetrators, but brothers, uncles and sons were also mentioned. Conflicts over resource distribution often sparked off these incidents. Food-related conflicts have already been noted; women also reported beatings when they refused to sell their patrimonial property at their husband's insistence; an orphaned girl was beaten by her uncle when she asked for her share of fruits from family-owned trees. Harassment and sometimes murder of women also occurred over dowry-related conflicts.

The incidence of violence, particularly domestic violence, is of course extremely sensitive information and difficult to collect. However, a record of the number of suicides, murders, sexual assaults and 'unnatural' deaths in an area may help to provide at least some indication of the link between poverty and gender-specific forms of violence. Certainly there is some 'anecdotal' and some statistical evidence to suggest that women's experience of personal insecurity may differ significantly from that of men and may need to be given specific recognition in the documentation of poverty. A few examples of this evidence are cited below.

A village study by Hartmann and Boyce (1983) points out what many village-level development workers can confirm: that the list of suicides or 'accidental death through drinking pesticides' in many villages in Bangladesh is predominantly female. When violence and ill-treatment are persistent features of a woman's life, suicide represents final escape and 'tragic revenge' (p. 97). Blanchet (1988) cites a study from Matlab thana in Bangladesh which found that 'violent deaths in women of reproductive age is highest for unmarried girls. . . , the first cause being complication of induced abortions, followed by suicide and homicide. There are indications that suicide and homicide in this age group are often associated with illegitimate pregnancy and rape' (p. 7). Another micro-level study, this time based on interviews with prostitutes in Dhaka city, found that they were disproportionately drawn from the poverty-stricken rural districts of Bangladesh and that forty-five of sixty prostitutes interviewed reported rape, divorce or remarriage by husbands, allegations of immorality by neighbours, or sale into prostitution, as the major factors behind their entry into the brothels (NORAD, 1988).

In terms of larger-scale statistical data, a noteworthy finding from BIDS study of rural poverty relates to perceptions of injustice reported by women and men (Rahman, 1991). The form of injustice most frequently reported by men was 'physical insecurity': 49 per cent, compared with 36 per cent among women. For women, the most frequently reported form of perceived injustice was 'immorality' (42 per cent compared to 22 per cent of the men). As the study notes, women's concern with immorality as an issue of insecurity reflects the fact that they are most often the victims of it. Also worth noting are the findings of the Government of Bangladesh Statistical Bureau (1992) whose sex-disaggregated data on causes of mortality in Bangladesh show that 'unnatural deaths' was the single greatest cause of death among adult women, higher even than maternal mortality, and higher than the equivalent figure for men. Unfortunately, the category 'unnatural deaths' does not distinguish between suicide and murder, on the one hand, and burns, poison, drowning, snakebites and accidents, on the other. The information provided by both these national statistical surveys is consequently limited by the highly aggregated nature of the categories used.[4]

Gender and Labour-Based Entitlements

We have so far focused on the 'needs' aspects of poverty. A focus on entitlements shifts our attention from the manifestations of poverty to its causes. In particular, it spells out in greater detail the range of options that poor women and men have access to and helps to explain gender differences in the regimes of risk and vulnerability that were touched on in the preceding section.

As noted earlier, the primary cause of poverty in rural Bangladesh is the absence of any entitlement to the social product, other than what can be acquired through the use of unskilled labour power. Gender is relevant here because it differentiates both the conditions under which men and women can dispose of their labour and the returns to their labour power. Men dispose of their labour in a variety of ways, but are able to orient most of their effort to income-earning activities. Women's ability to dispose of their labour power is constrained within the narrower parameters imposed by purdah and by their domestic obligations, is less likely to be remunerated, and generally receives lower returns when it is. National data show that women earn 40 per cent of the wage rate earned by men (Rahman and Sen, 1993).

One of the characteristics of poor households is the existence of multiple earners – women, men, the old and the young – and often in multiple occupations, since no single occupation is stable enough or well-paid enough to guarantee the household an adequate livelihood. Women's participation in income-earning activities need not violate purdah norms, since many forms of income earning can be carried out within the homestead precincts. Cultivation of the homestead plot and livestock rearing are common examples. The practice of 'share-rearing' allows poor women to transform their only resource, labour power, into a productive asset. By this arrangement, they rear livestock and poultry on behalf of wealthier households. This entitles them to keep every alternate offspring or half the profits from sale of stock. Purdah can also be preserved when income is earned on a putting-out basis. In some districts, the local tobacco industry employs women to roll cigarettes on a piece-rate basis in their homes. Elsewhere, women are supplied by local subcontractors with palm leaves which they weave into mats, returning one mat in every two and selling the other themselves. Similar arrangements operate for other craft products: quilts, jute goods, and so on.

Performing domestic chores and post-harvest processing of crops in wealthy households is considered an acceptable form of wage labour for women because it is still homestead based. However, the value of returns on this activity is diminishing because increasing numbers of women are competing for employment in a field where opportunities are being eroded by the spread of mechanized milling.[5] While meals still constitute a common form of remuneration, the amount and quality of food offered has deterioration: the previous custom of allowing women to eat a 'full stomach' worth of rice is giving way to predetermined quantities; *rooti* (less preferred wheat-based bread) is replacing rice for one or more meals; lentils and chillies are appearing more frequently in place of vegetables. Furthermore, bran and husk from the paddy, which had formed part of the wage for paddy processing in earlier times, is increasingly retained or sold by the landlord as fuel.

The erosion of employment opportunities through mechanization of post-harvest processing of crops at a time when poverty is making female dependence increasingly unviable has put considerable strains on the customary division of labour. Women are entering in large numbers into public rural works projects, small mills and workshops, and petty trading activities in the bazaar economy. Changes are also evident in the agricultural process itself. Hitherto strictly enforced proscriptions on women weeding, transplanting and, more recently, harvesting are showing signs of crumbling. In one area women, usually working in small gangs, have been harvesting paddy since the floods of 1981. The attraction of female labour is obvious: women can be paid less, ostensibly on the grounds of differential ability to carry bundles of paddy – women carry fifteen or twenty compared to thirty by men. However, not all the women are impressed with this argument. One pointed out:

> I can match the men when it comes to harvesting and beating the paddy. Maybe they can carry more bundles of paddy, but we don't spend all day just carrying bundles so why should that be the criterion. Besides, when the men are carrying the bundles, we don't just sit around doing nothing, we go on cutting the paddy. Men take more time off to smoke and gossip.

The restructuring of the gender division of labour and the increasing presence of women in areas of work outside the boundaries of purdah have contradictory implications for women's well-being. On one hand, it might be argued that purdah is still a powerful norm, so that public forms of physical labour are associated with considerable stress, shame and insecurity for women. The presence of women in brickfields, road construction and bazaars is generally indicative of 'distress sales of labour' (Elson, 1988b), since they will enter such public forms of manual labour only under extreme economic stress. On the other hand, since it is precisely the ideology and practice of purdah that creates and legitimates women's material dependence, there is an emancipatory potential to their emergence from seclusion and entry into segments of the labour market hitherto barred to them. It gives them access, perhaps for the first time in their lives, to entitlements other than those associated with socially ascribed relations of dependence.

The contradictory effects of social change serve as an important remainder that the relationship between income and well-being contains subjective evaluations as well as financial considerations. For example, outdoor, manual or 'dirty' work, hired status, arbitrary, casual or personalized terms of employment, are all qualities that are generally less valued by both men and women than 'clean', indoor or desk jobs, self-employed status, and secure, well-defined conditions of employment. Many landless households prefer to trade off the higher earnings from agricultural wage labour for the greater independence associated with farming sharecropped land. Evaluation of employment options for women is likely to be more complex because purdah norms link their social status (and that of their kin) with their public invisibility. Certainly most of the women interviewed expressed a preference for home-based activities because of their compatibility with purdah norms. Nevertheless, there were noteworthy exceptions to the general rule, which suggested that below a certain level of poverty, or among women who had already made the break with purdah, considerations of convenience, the demands of the work and financial gain, similar to those which concern men, become predominant.

Gender and Capital-Based Entitlements

Capital is used here in the broad sense to encompass tangible and intangible assets which embody claims on future consumption. Land remains the most important tangible asset in a predominantly agrarian economy, enabling command over different types of resources. It enhances a household's productive base, and hence its capacity to meet its longer-term consumption requirements, as well as offering the possibility of meeting more immediate needs. However, poverty highlights the potential fungibility of most objects, and there are a wide range of household possessions – productive assets as well as consumer items – which can also serve to secure basic needs among the landless through pawning, exchange, sale or as a collateral in times of crisis.

The constraints on women's mobility and earning power described above also limit their ability to purchase assets or raise credit. Their main access to tangible property is through kinship entitlements: inheritance and marriage gifts. Daughters inherit land, though less land than sons, under Islamic law. However, women seldom enforce their entitlement to land, preferring to waive it in favour of their brothers in exchange for a claim to their protection in case of widowhood, abandonment or divorce. The value of assets accruing to women at marriage is also being overshadowed by the shift to the dowry system. In the past, a woman was entitled at the time of her marriage to various kinds of moveable assets (utensils, jewellery, cash, and so forth) donated by both her own and her husband's family. However, the direction of exchange now favours the groom and his kin, who demand productive assets or consumer durables as a precondition to the marriage.

Inequalities in capital-based entitlements are also manifest in access to credit. While the wealthy are able to tap into most sources of credit, including officially subsidized programmes, the poorest sections of the population are confined to the informal market where interest rates are several times higher. Even credit at the local village store is offered on discriminatory terms to the poor: it is rarely for more than a few days and often consists of inferior goods which they do not dare return. Moreover, it is more likely to be extended to households with regular income earners, a practice which in effect discriminates against female-headed households where income is predominantly earned through casual forms of labour. It is not simply the lack of collateral and riskier nature of extending credit to the poor which accounts for their confinement to the more unfavourable segments of the credit market – the standard economic explanation – but characteristics pointed to by Pearse (1974) and taken up by Whitehead (1985). Poor villagers may find themselves competing for credit with the local elite who have city houses and political connections and may even belong to the institutional bodies that distribute public sector credit: 'illiterate, ill-clad cultivators must argue their case in town offices with status conscious officials' (Pearse, 1974, p. 77). As Whitehead (1985) points out, the 'contractual inferiority' in the capital market which characterizes the relations of poorer peasants to richer ones is also likely to characterize those between poor women and elite male officials. Gender-based 'contractual inferiority' in rural Bangladesh derives from women's greater material dependence within the household, greater illiteracy, poorer clothing, fewer collateral-generating assets, coupled with their general inexperience in the domain of public institutions. (This point is succinctly made by a poor slum woman, interviewed in a study of female informal sector workers in Bombay, talking about bank lending: 'If we go alone, who will listen to us? We don't know who to meet, what to ask for? People are rude to us, they think we are dirty and talk to us badly. They don't try and explain anything to us' (Everett and Savara, 1983, p. 116).

Women consequently engage in informal rather than formal credit transactions through their neighbourhood networks. There is a long-standing practice among rural women to keep aside a 'fistful' of uncooked rice, often clandestinely, every day before the main meal. This builds up into a small but important savings fund and forms the basis of informal borrowing and lending activities within the neighbourhood. These networks are the source of important intangible resources for women since they provide them with contacts, information and security in the absence of access to formal credit institutions. However, the plight of the ultra-poor in the sphere of credit was summed up by a young girl from an all-female household: 'We don't dare to take loans from anybody, because we know we could never pay them back'.

Gender and Household-Based Entitlements

The ideologies, norms and practices embodied in the 'implicit' contracts of household and kinship relations interlock to produce a situation where women's control over material assets and labour power, including their own, and their ability to mobilize resources outside the household, are severely curtailed. Women's experience of poverty is differentiated from that of men as a result of this asymmetry in their entitlement systems. Implicit household-based contracts are neither symmetrically distributed nor legally enforceable. Women's claims to support and shelter consequently tend to be normative, embedded to a large extent in socially ascribed obligations associated with marriage, family and kinship. This is in contrast to male entitlements, which have a material base. Even men who have no assets to their name have at least the freedom to sell their labour power to the highest bidder, unconstrained by the ideological boundaries of purdah. There is therefore a fundamental asymmetry in the distribution of material and normative entitlements within the household: 'male authority has a material base, while male responsibility is normatively controlled. Normative control, while powerful, is nevertheless relatively malleable in the face of economic necessity' (Cain et al., 1979, p. 410).

The gender asymmetry in entitlements and claims has various repercussions. The data on nutrition and health status within the household already cited suggest that the distribution of resources does not correspond to the actual needs of members. Instead it appears to be determined by the individual's position in the various intersecting hierarchies of age, gender and kinship status which characterize household relations. Inequalities in the distribution of material entitlements consequently translate into inequalities in the satisfaction of basic needs. Furthermore, asymmetrical entitlements produce important difference in the trajectories by which different categories of household members become poorer. The gender dimension in poverty processes stems from women's limited access to material entitlements and their disproportionate dependence on normative ones. The failure to make a successful transition from the status of daughter to wife to mother, each status bearing specific claims on a male guardian and breadwinner, entails a specific diminution of women's economic and social well-being. The death of a husband, for instance, can precipitate an abrupt descent into poverty for a woman if there are no surviving adult sons to take over her protection and support.

Marriage itself is becoming a less secure option for women: 'the normative obligations of men toward women – the principal protection women have against loss of status – have probably never been universally honoured, but there are indications that under the pressure of increasing poverty, male normative commitment has eroded' (Cain et al., 1979, p. 408). There is now a greater tendency among men, particularly poorer men, to walk out of marriages, thus abdicating their financial responsibility to dependent wives and children. A variety of sources attest to the strains placed on familial obligations in the process of impoverishment. Development workers in one district spoke of 'seasonal divorce', referring to the increase in the incidence of desertions in the hungry season, while a number of writers have noted the higher rate of divorce and desertions among poor and landless groups (Miranda, 1982; Chaudhury and Ahmed, 1980; Kabeer, 1985). My own study found that the single most important reason given by women for marital dissolution was the failure of husbands to feed their wives, that is, the collapse of conjugal entitlements (Kabeer, 1985).

The growing numbers of female heads of households are also indicative of the erosion of male normative commitment. Micro-level and national statistics document this departure from the social norm of patriarchally organized households and establish its links with poverty· (Cain et al., 1979; Kabeer, 1985; Alam, 1985). The 1981 Population Census and the Agricultural Sector Review (Safilios-Rothschild and Mahmud, 1989) both showed that 15 per cent of rural households were female headed, while the latter also noted that the incidence of female headship was highest among the landless (25 per cent) and diminished with increasing landholdings. The BIDS study (Hamid, 1991) cited earlier found that while 8 per cent of male-headed households fell into the category of 'hard core poverty', the figure for female-headed households was 33 per cent. Moreover, female-headed households had an income which was on average 40 per cent below that of male-headed households.

A final observation relevant to the breakdown of normative entitlements is the increasing significance of migration, both permanent and temporary, as a component in household survival strategies. The poverty dimension in migration patterns is revealed in various studies; its direction is generally from poorer districts of Bangladesh to more prosperous rural areas, or else to the urban conglomerations, where employment opportunities might be higher (see Rahman et al., 1987). Migration rates were also found to be higher among landless households, particularly during the famine of 1974 (Rahman et al., 1987). In earlier national statistics, female migration appeared primarily as a result of women moving at marriage to their husbands' villages. Independent female migration was rare. The increased presence of women in the urban areas documented in the 1974 Census was dismissed as the product of better coverage than earlier censuses, though it did not exclude 'greater female migration to cities to join their husbands'. However, smaller-scale studies in urban slums and brothels (Farouk, 1976; NORAD, 1988) show that a significant proportion of recent migrants were divorced/deserted women from poor rural families who sought employment in towns because of its greater acceptability and availability compared to rural areas. Detailed migration data from one area in Bangladesh estimated that independent female migration, in pursuit of livelihood strategies or subsequent to marital dissolution, constituted nearly a third of all female migration (Matlab Surveillance System, 1979). The rise of independent female migration, like the emergence of female-headed households, can be taken as signalling both household and female pauperization because it signifies the breakdown of family-based entitlements and impinges most severely on women and their dependents.

There do not appear to be any studies in Bangladesh that seek to establish what migration might mean in the lives of the poor in general, and for poor women in particular. However, qualitative evidence from India testifies to the disruption and insecurity it creates in the lives of those who have to resort to migration. Using participatory appraisal techniques, Meera Shah reports how women described the experience of having to work as migrant casual labour for a few months every year: 'they had no place to stay and would camp in different places, carrying the barest of necessities with them, and most of the time slept under the open sky' (1993, p. 10). Mazumdar (1989) also reports how migrant women agricultural labourers in West

Bengal declared that, far from acquiring a taste for high living in the more prosperous regions (as the local bureaucracy believed), migration was resorted to only in conditions of extreme distress since it entailed long journeys in extremely arduous circumstances, sexual harassment by employers or their recruiting agents, search for temporary shelter and highly exploitive conditions of work, compared to regular attached labour.

Gender and the Processes of Poverty

So far we have offered a static presentation of poverty in Bangladesh, one that would be evident in a 'snap-shot' of the poor at any point in time. However, poverty is also a dynamic phenomenon, a process that reflects changes in the underlying causal mechanisms which determine the distribution of claims and entitlements. There are, of course, a variety of different processes by which people slide into greater poverty. Some of these are abrupt – a one-off event which wipes out a family's savings or destroys its assets. Others occur more gradually; assets are sold off one by one and the productive base of the household slowly disintegrates. Some are specific to a household: deaths, divorce, business failures, illness of breadwinner. Others may result from a more generalized set of circumstances: floods, drought, cutbacks in government subsidies, a rise in the price of essential foods. Whatever the event that begins the process, at the core of each process is the deterioration, loss or failure of individual or family entitlements to the social product. This is likely to be met by a series of adjustments in the sphere of needs and entitlements which either help to return the household to its former state or push it further down a relentless spiral of poverty. The crisis-coping capacity of households serves to summarize the resilience and reliability of their entitlement relations, since it is in times of crisis that these are most tested and that shifts in standards of living are likely to occur. Monitoring the household's crisis-coping mechanisms will reveal most effectively the processes by which households/individuals either succeed in weathering crises or else simply slide downwards into greater poverty. What also becomes evident in such a monitoring exercise is that gender is an important factor differentiating the processes by which women and men become poor.

One feature of household-coping strategies noted by Dreze (1988) is the precedence given to the protection of the long-run productive base of the household over short-term consumption standards. Widely reported as a first response to crisis by those interviewed was greater austerity in consumption: reducing the amount of food and number of meals consumed daily, letting illnesses go untreated and huts unrepaired. This is frequently accompanied or followed by other strategies: intensifying income-earning efforts, going into debt, or turning to neighbourhood networks. In a persisting crisis, a gradual divestment of assets takes place in order of their dispensability to household survival and security; non-productive assets tend to be disposed of before productive ones. Land is generally held on to as long as possible, final dispossessions being postponed through mortgaging arrangements. Ownership of homestead land has an independent significance for the poor, since it offers scope for productive effort and also anchors the household unit to a stable place in the community. Its loss propels family members into the ranks of the floating and rootless poor and may be the beginning of the disintegration of the core family unit.

At some stage in the divestment process, members of the household who are not normally in employment – women, the very old and the very young – will be forced into seeking their own livelihood. The final stages of impoverishment are characterized by desertions and crisis-migrations, along with the visible breakdown of the 'moral economy' of rights and obligations which bind the family unit together. Able-bodied male earners become increasingly reluctant to shoulder the burden of non-earning dependents. They are likely to be the first to abandon the family unit, leaving women to look after the very young and very old. At extreme levels of destitution, mothers abandon their children in orphanages or leave them to fend for themselves in the informal 'bazaar' economy. Thus, after the 1974 famine, women who had been deserted by their husbands migrated to the cities and began to fill the vagrant homes, while in one district special homes had to be set up for deserted children (Alamgir, 1980).

As long as family-based entitlements are respected, women's interests are very much bound up with the fortunes of their family unit and they are likely to experience poverty processes in much the same way. There are certain points, however, in the downward spiral of poverty when conflicts become apparent between the interests of male and female members. At such points, the manner in which conflicting interests are resolved will critically shape women's subsequent experience of the impoverishment process. For instance, the finding that increased mortality during disaster was disproportionately experienced by young girls (D'Souza and Chen, 1980) suggests that the austerity response in times of crisis is not neutrally distributed within the household, but bears more heavily on some categories of members than on others. Demographic responses – migration or dissolution of the family unit – often give rise to female-headed households, which are frequently more vulnerable to the risk of further impoverishment.

Gender differentials are also manifested in household divestment strategies. As we noted earlier, divestment strategies are generally devised to protect the household's productive base so as not to endanger future recovery. The gender of the owner of the different household assets may be an additional consideration in determining the sequence of disposal. There is some suggestive evidence on this possibility. In his study of the Bengal famine in 1943, Greenough notes, 'One of the first signs of economic distress in rural Bengal was the sale of women's jewellery and ornaments' (1982, p. 197). With continuing crisis, household utensils, cooking implements, brass pots, tin roofs all found their way into the market (Greenough, 1982, cited in Agarwal, 1990, p. 404 n. 940). Jiggins has also suggested, on the basis of case studies from Bangladesh, as well as Sri Lanka, that 'whatever women's personal earnings or assets, these are consumed *before* the point of family breakdown' (1986, p. 14).

The village interviews threw up a number of exceptions to the practice among rural women of waiving their rights to their fathers' property in favour of their brothers. Some of the women interviewed had been driven by family poverty or by their husband's threats to lay claim to their share of the patrimonial assets. From the information offered, it appeared that husbands frequently used the threat of desertion to force wives to sell off their share of inherited land. Sometimes the husbands left anyway, having appropriated the proceeds of the sale. One abandoned woman had incurred her husband's wrath for refusing to sell her share of land, at the same time as alienating her brothers for agreeing to sell trees from the same piece of land.

According to Jahangir (1986), the ideologies governing property rights in rural Bangladesh distinguish between male property rights, which refer to *sampatti* (where ownership is embedded in conjugal, familial and kinship systems), and female property rights, which refer to *jinish* (delegated, hence confiscable, rights over items or things). If such ideologies are used to justify the sale of women's assets earlier on in a household's divestment strategy (and we need firmer empirical evidence on this) it means that further down the poverty spiral, when family-based entitlements begin to break down, women have fewer resources to fall back on than men. Their only recourse is to sell their labour in the worst paid, highly casual and most subservient forms of income-earning activities.

Conclusion

The way in which we choose to 'know' and measure poverty has implications for how we deal with it. Our discussion of a gender-differentiated framework for analysing poverty highlights some of the problems with more conventional approaches. First of all, focusing solely on household-level poverty gives rise to poverty-alleviation strategies which target only (male) heads of household, on the assumption that the welfare of other members is thereby assured. Second, the separation of means and ends in conventional approaches, the preoccupation with means rather than ends, and with the physical aspects of deprivation rather than the more intangible ones, all tend to encourage strategies which focus only on 'efficient' delivery mechanisms. They fail to consider that the terms on which resources are offered have profound implications for people's sense of dignity and control over their own lives.

A gender perspective on poverty reminds us that household income cannot be equated with individual well-being. It signals the need for the disaggregation of information and strategies in order to ensure that poverty-reduction strategies are translated into equitable outcomes within the household. It also suggests that such a translation requires attention to means as well as ends. A concern with gender equity will entail recognizing that needs may be prioritized differently by women and men and that entitlements may carry different implications for their self-esteem and autonomy.

Expanding the definition of basic needs to include more qualitative dimensions such as self-esteem, autonomy and participation suggests other ways of rethinking anti-poverty strategies. These dimensions are most likely to elude quantification and hence most likely to be overlooked in the measurement of poverty (Chambers, 1988). This will have serious implications for the way in which poverty is addressed. Tackling poverty only in its observable and measureable dimensions carries the danger of leaving intact those dimensions which arise out of the 'deep-rootedness' of poverty in the social structure. Anti-poverty strategies, to be sustainable as well as equitable, will have to go beyond a practical concern with welfare to a more strategic analysis of the political economy of class and gender. However, such strategies are not easy to devise or implement. On the policy side, they seek to address the more intangible aspects of women's empowerment, their lack of autonomy and self-esteem, aspects which take policy-makers well beyond routinized delivery of welfare or income-generating resources into territory that they may be both unfamiliar as well as uncomfortable with. On the community side, such strategies are more difficult to implement precisely because they threaten the established hierarchy of class and gender interests. In the final analysis, such strategies must rely on the self-organization, management and leadership of poor women themselves since they have the strongest stake in their success and sustainability.[6]

Notes

1 There is of course a strong logic to putting physical survival before other aspects of well-being. As Michael Lipton puts it, you have to 'be' before you can 'well-be' (personal communication).
2 Personal communication, Martin Greeley.
3 Given the value attached by all sections of the community to the social obligations of hospitality, the material condition of a household is often evident in the food that is offered to guests. During my own visits to village households, when offerings were usually of an impromptu nature, wealthier households offered tea with milk and sugar and elaborate snacks while poorer households shared betel leaf, some betel nut or tamarind from a nearby tree.
4 My thanks to Shireen Huq and Ann Marie Goetz for drawing my attention to the Bureau of Statistics' findings and to Blanchet's study respectively.
5 The World Bank (1983) estimated that employment opportunities for landless women were being destroyed at a rate of 3.6 to 5.1 million days a year.
6 Chapter 9 contains a discussion of examples of such strategies.

7

'And No-one Could Complain at That': Claims and Silences in Social Cost–Benefit Analysis

The basic notion is very simple. If we have to decide whether to do A or not, the rule is: Do A if the benefits exceed those of the next best alternative course of action and not otherwise. If we apply this rule to all possible choices we shall generate the largest possible benefits, given the constraints within which we live. And no-one could complain at that. (Layard, 1972, p. 1)

CBA is a method for assessing not just the identifiable cash profit or loss of a public project, but also elements of 'intangible' social cost and benefit. In principle this might seem a progressive innovation . . . but in CBA all these are compressed onto a single dimension – money. Qualities which had previously been assumed as inalienable are now given a price tag. (Rosenhead and Thunhurst, 1979, p. 300)

Introduction

The significance of social cost–benefit analysis as a tool of public-sector planning is related to the kinds of objectives which distinguish public decision-makers from private ones. Public policy objectives differ from those of the private sector because public planners are entrusted with ensuring the social good in situations where private profitability considerations are unlikely to bring it about. However, it is not sufficient for planners to have the right intentions. Like all other actors in the economy, planners need decision-making rules that help to distinguish between efficient and inefficient uses of limited resources. As a practical application of standard welfare economics, cost–benefit analysis (CBA) claims to provide an appropriate, coherent and theoretically grounded set of decision-making rules to assist in this selection process. It is now widely used in development planning to decide whether a project is worth embarking on (appraisal) or whether it has achieved what it set out to do (evaluation).

The actual guidelines vary according to the particular goals that an intervention is intended to achieve. Where the goal is financial profitability, cost–benefit analysis requires that the market value of the benefits that flow from a project over its life cycle exceed the market costs of its inputs. Discount rates are used on both sets of flows to allow for the fact that costs and benefits incurred in the future might be valued differently from the same costs and benefits incurred now: the bird-in-hand principle. However, development planners recognize that for a variety of reasons, private costs and benefits may diverge significantly from social costs and benefits. For instance, an economy may be protected by tariffs and subsidies from international competition so that its domestic market prices do not reflect the true scarcity value of its resources. Where foreign exchange has to be earned or allocated in such an economy, reliance on market prices will not assure an efficient set of choices. The broader goal of economic efficiency, rather than the narrower one of financial profitability, requires that costs and benefits of all planned interventions are assigned 'shadow prices' which reflect their real scarcity value, in place of imperfect market prices which distort it. In our example, this entails using international market prices as 'shadow' prices for all goods and services.

Finally, social cost–benefit analysis (SCBA) extends the analytical framework still further. Premissed on the assumption that the aim of public policy is to maximise the social welfare or the public good, SCBA takes explicit account of the distribution of costs and benefits, weighting them differently when they accrue to disadvantaged individuals/groups/areas. The use of distributional weights to incorporate equity objectives is the main contribution of SCBA to the field of project analysis.

The Claims for SCBA: Gender and Efficiency

The apparent breadth of SCBA's reach in addressing both efficiency and equity objectives suggests that it is a promising approach to ensuring a more central place for women's concerns in development planning in general. Supportive measures for women, like all forms of planned intervention, require decision rules because they use scarce resources in order to produce desired outcomes. Interventionist policies on behalf of women tend to fall into the domain of SCBA because they are generally undertaken by agencies that pay at least rhetorical attention to equity issues along with efficiency objectives. This dual concern is summarized, for instance, in a USAID position paper on women and development, which declares:

> To pursue a development planning strategy without a women in develop-
> ment focus would be wasteful and self-defeating – wasteful because of the
> potential loss of the contribution of vital human resources and self-
> defeating because development which does not bring about its benefits to
> the whole of society is self-defeating (1982, p. 2).

SCBA can be used to justify greater attention to gender issues in the project cycle on efficiency grounds if, for instance, it can be demonstrated that market prices do not reflect the benefits produced by women or the costs incurred by them. Any development project which neglects either of these dimensions runs the risk of allocating resources without due regard for the real structure of costs and benefits. This is a point which finds a sympathetic audience in many planning agencies. To quote USAID again, 'the misunderstanding of gender differences, leading to inadequate planning and designing of projects, results in diminished returns on investment' (1982, p. 3).

The efficiency case for taking gender dimensions seriously in project planning is supported by a series of case studies that document the failure of projects to achieve their efficiency objectives because they neglect the gender distribution of costs and benefits. Much of this failure was premised on a view of the household which did not mesh with the reality on the ground, a view rooted in the 'transcultural' assumption of unified household decision-making promoted in orthodox neo-classical economics. A number of these examples have been touched on in Chapter 4, but it is worth reiterating the underlying policy assumptions that led to project failure. In the case of The Gambia, between 1966 and 1980, not one but *three* successive groups of foreign donor agencies (the Chinese government, the Taiwanese government and then the World Bank) sought and failed to bring about the anticipated reduction in imported rice through the promotion of double-cropped irrigated rice production. As the World Bank report on this project (1977) points out, the actual acreage (1,934 acres) of irrigated rice cultivated between 1973 and 1975 fell well short of the planned acreage for this period (3,000 acres).

Dey's research (1982) provides an interesting and illuminating study of the assumptions that underpinned this project misbehaviour. The critical factor lay in the planners' failure to recognize (a) that the local Mandinka system of rights and obligations required women as well as men to contribute to their family's food requirements, thereby offering the former some insulation from arbitrary demands on their labour time by their husbands; and (b) that women were primarily responsible for rice farming, which they undertook on compound holdings as well as on land they had cleared for their own use. Using a misconceived model of the gender division of labour and obligations within the household, planners targeted their efforts entirely at men, giving them cultivation rights over the irrigated land and offering them credit, inputs and extension services. Rather than working on newly irrigated ricelands where they had no recognised rights, women preferred to clear new swampland plots and continue their independent cultivation of rice. Consequently there was a shortage of labour at critical times of the year, forcing many men to pay women (sometimes their wives) wages to secure their labour inputs.

Jones's study of a World Bank project to increase irrigated rice production in Cameroon (Jones, 1983, cited in Horenstein, 1985) offers other examples of misplaced incentives in project planning. Once again it was assumed that Massa 'household' labour would be available to work on the irrigated rice fields. In this case, what the planners overlooked were 'the traditional patterns of production and distribution which denied women access to rice fields of their own and control over the products of their labour' (Horenstein, 1985, p. 27). As we saw in Chapter 5, in the Cameroon case Massa women and men had individual sorghum fields which they cultivated separately, but rice fields were almost invariably cultivated jointly by husband and wife, with husbands controlling the disposition of the crop. Although women working on the irrigated rice fields received some financial compensation for the labour they provided to their husbands, it was not large enough to persuade them to cultivate the additional fields necessary to meet targeted output levels (Jones, 1983).

A third example of efficiency losses through gender-biased misconceptions comes from Western Kenya. Staudt's (1978) research points out that government extension officers seeking to encourage the adoption of new hybrid maize assumed the gender of farmers to be male and concentrated their attention on households where men were present. While around 40 per cent of farms were female-managed, these were consistently bypassed. Nevertheless, female farm managers used their own information networks to increase their rates of adoption and frequently proved to be more innovative than farms where men were present. According to Staudt's calculations, a third of the female-managed farms that were classified as early adopters of hybrid maize had no administrative support or advice for such a move; among farms with men present which had been similarly neglected, only 3 per cent adopted early. She concluded that ignoring women's productivity potential had slowed down the diffusion of innovative farming practice: 'Denying access to capable groups because of norms which support male preference represents an inefficient use of scarce resources' (Staudt, 1978, p. 452).

The Claims for SCBA: Gender and Equity

A powerful case can also be made for the use of SCBA to promote gender equity in development planning. The goal of gender equity has gained an increasing legitimacy among policymakers. Empirical measures show that women do less well than men according to many of the conventional indicators of human well-being: lifetime income, nutrition, education, wealth and leisure (UN, 1980a; Sivard, 1985; Seager and Olson, 1986; Buvinic et al., 1983; Folbre, 1986b; Bruce and Dwyer, 1988). The now widely cited declaration by the UN that women do nearly two-thirds of the world's working hours, but receive only a tenth of its income and own less than 1 per cent of its wealth, summarizes for many the case for greater gender equity in development. Since equity goals demand that specific attention be paid to the welfare of those who are relatively worse off, large numbers of women would qualify on these grounds to participate in development interventions which help counteract gender-specific disadvantage.

SCBA, with its emphasis on equity objectives, appears particularly appropriate in this context. The objective of improving the lives and status of women could be treated as what welfare economists call a 'merit good' — an area of activity in which the government is better equipped than individuals or the market to act in the best interests of society. In principle, therefore, a strong case can be made for the use of SCBA in advocating supportive investments for women. It appears capable of taking cognizance of both women's vital role in sustaining economic production and the inequitable practices which prevent them from fully sharing in the fruits of development.

Not everyone accepts the claims made by the proponents of SCBA (Stewart, 1975; Chambers, 1978; Oakley, 1990; Hokesbergen, 1986). Among the objections raised to SCBA procedures are its silence on the intangible and qualitative aspects of development; the illusory nature of its claims to neutrality; and its underpinnings in a particular, conflict-free world-view. While these limitations are likely to under- mine its usefulness as a planning tool whenever the interests of subordinated groups are at stake, they take on a particular form when gender issues are involved because of the specific nature of women's subordination in many societies. The rest of this chapter spells out in greater detail some of the flaws of a market-driven development paradigm that were touched on in Chapter 4.

The Silences in SCBA: Gender Segmentation in the Labour Market

The first limitation of SCBA stems from the overwhelming market bias of its valuation procedures. As noted earlier, it requires the conversion of all the costs and benefits associated with intended interventions into commensurable sets of values, but values as measured by the market. As Donahue explains, 'values are slippery, and this goes far to explain the appeal of an automatic mechanism for setting values – market prices' (1980, p. 3). The use of market prices to measure the value of goods and services is premised on the free operation of competitive market forces. Although market imperfections are recognized in SCBA and dealt with through shadow pricing procedures, these only work if an alternative set of prices, free from distorting factors, can be identified. As we saw, the use of world market prices in place of domestic prices in protected national markets is one conventional example of shadow pricing; the use of wages in unprotected rural labour markets to value labour in protected formal sector employment where wage rates are artificially high is another (Irvin, 1978).

In reality, however, the 'free' market is an analytical – and ideological – construct, rarely encountered outside economic text- books. More often, markets operate as an arena for the interplay of political power and the expression of cultural norm (Basu, 1986; Mackintosh, 1990):

> markets concentrate information, and hence power, in the hands of few: some participants are 'market makers' while others enter in a position of weakness; . . . profits of a few, and growth for some, thrive in conditions of uncertainty, inequality and vulnerability of those who sell their labour power. (Mackintosh, 1990, p. 50)

And among those who sell their labour power, there are further inequalities. In particular, there is strong evidence from a variety of contexts to suggest that gender is a major dimension in labour-market inequalities; that powerful ideologies of masculinity and femininity, of appropriate gender roles, government legislation and male protectionism, create and sustain systematic distortions in the relative prices and mobility of male and female labour. The problem often does not lie in overt wage discrimination between women and men working on the same jobs, but rather in the creation of incommensurable segments in the labour market: gender cuts across sectors, occupations and tasks as an 'axis of segmentation' (Scott, 1991, p. 128) so that competition in the labour market occurs more strongly within, than between, its male and female segments.

The process by which this segmentation is produced is among the best-documented insights of feminist scholars. They have pointed to the powerful way in which the gender division of labour operates as a system of ideas and practices to suppress and deny the comparability of 'male' and 'female' activities (Edholm et al., 1977). Ideological preconceptions about differences between men and women – their so-called 'natural' propensities, preferences and attributes – determine their assignment to very different tasks and activities. Furthermore, most cultures tend to use very different criteria in their evaluations of male and female activities. Men are seen to engage in activities which require purposeful effort, instrumental rationality and the expenditure of energy. Women's work, by contrast, is associated with caring and nurturing qualities and 'affective' rationality. Such an association has served to devalue women's labour effort because it is seen as a 'natural' extension of their familial roles rather than purposive or demanding work.

While prevailing ideologies of gender may appear to echo the gender division of labour within the familial domain, they are also continuously acted upon and reconstituted in other forms of productive activity, including urban and rural labour markets (Phillips and Taylor, 1980; Kumar, 1982; Chhachhi, 1983; Evans, 1993; Humphrey, 1987; Standing, 1991). We noted in Chapter 3 the extent to which apparently gender-neutral public organizations of production privilege certain kinds of workers, bodies and skills over others. Women and men are treated as non-substitutable labour, entering production and the market through separate channels, recruited into gender-specific segments and assigned to various tasks in accordance with preconceived gender stereotyping rather than by efficiency criteria. Market forces are, in other words, saturated with gender norms and practices. These are not simply imposed by employers in their pursuit of profit, but actively supported and defended by the male workers who are direct beneficiaries. Men's fierce defence of existing gender divisions at work can be understood in terms of the privileged – and protected – access it gives to opportunities for which they would otherwise have had to compete with women. In this context, Safilios-Rothschild's observation is apposite:

> that the previously privileged group – men – will be discriminated against as a result of transitional measures favouring a previously oppressed group – women – is a fear typical of groups resenting the loss of their monopoly of advantageous and desirable options. The transition, for example, from a monopoly on exclusivity of options for high-prestige and high-paying jobs to the necessity to compete with equally, or better qualified women will be painful for men, especially mediocre and average men. (1974, cited in Staudt, 1985, p. 4)

The complexities of gender within the marketplace are evident in a study by Snell (1979) of working women and men in fifteen British workplaces. She noted that employers' non-compliance with new legislation upholding equal pay for work of equal value was frequently not even recognized by women workers. The extent of gender segregation between jobs meant that women were not aware of the content of men's jobs. She also documented the diversity of ways in which employers sought to resist implementation of the new legislation. In the words of one personnel manager:

> Legislation doesn't mean a company will act differently. We won't change our personnel decisions, just how we go about them . . . Just as we keep a 'good' mix on race by finding reasons to reject most Asians, so we will find reasons to reject women for some jobs. (p. 49)

Nor were employers the only agents in perpetuating these gender (and race) stereotypes. One important factor behind employer tardiness in implementing equal-pay legislation was fear of the male workers' reactions:

> During implementation, men in several organisations who objected to women being brought up to their rates put pressure on management for upgrading and additional bonus pay. In one case they went on strike. In almost every case, management conceded to the men's demands in order to avoid possible disruption and conflict. (p. 46)

Phillips and Taylor (1980) have used historical and contemporary examples from Britain and the US to document the collusion between unionized male workers and management in upholding the stereo-typing process in order to protect male privilege. This collusion has meant that

> the equations – men/skilled, women/unskilled – are so powerful that the identification of a particular job with women ensured that the skill content of the work would be downgraded. It is the sex of those who do the work, rather than its content, which leads to its identification as skilled or unskilled. (Phillips and Taylor, p. 85)

A study of global market factories came to the conclusion that the widespread association between women and unskilled jobs on the assembly line could be attributed to the fact that women enter the labour market already determined as 'inferior bearers of labour' rather than because they are 'bearers of inferior labour' (Elson and Pearson, 1981, p. 150). Finally, a review of the literature on women's employment in India and the Philippines pointed out how ascribed characteristics like caste and gender are frequently used to screen workers prior to more conventionally recognized devices of education and other acquired qualifications (Kabeer, 1987). Productivity tests are seldom carried out; rather, women and men are automatically assigned to particular tasks and occupations on the basis of ascribed caste and gender attributes.

To sum up, we would suggest that gender hierarchies in the occupational structure – with women primarily 'crowded' into less well paid, more casual and informal areas of economic activity – should not be seen as the outcome of individual responses to impersonal market phenomena, as many orthodox economists seem to believe. They result from a more complex combination of factors. As Scott points out,

> the key to the segregation between male and female labour markets lies in recruitment, but this has to be conceived broadly. Several factors may be involved here: the process whereby particular jobs become sex-labelled; the effect that sex-labelling has in deterring potential applicants form applying for jobs of the 'wrong' sex, and in creating discrimination on the part of employers; the presence or absence of any explicit exclusionary mechan-isms; and finally, the degree to which the content of education and vocational training is 'gendered' and therefore fails to equip women for competition with men for 'male' jobs. (Scott, 1986, p. 355)

In the light of these findings, how reliable are wage differentials as a measure of gender differentials in the marginal productivity or opportunity costs of labour? I would argue that pervasive gender-based imperfections in the labour market have serious implications for measuring the true productivity, opportunity costs and wage elasticity of male and female labour; what is even more serious is that we have few ways of knowing what the extent of the bias is. The cleavage in the labour market into 'male' and 'female' sectors leads to the persistent undervaluation of women's labour – and the concomitant overvaluation of men's – making any clear-cut comparison of the true value of labour across the sectors nearly impossible.

However, some suggestive estimates of the economic implications of labour-market segmentation have been thrown up by simulation exercises carried out with UK data (Tzannatos, 1988 and 1990; Pike, 1982). Assuming for the sake of the argument that gender differentials in wages apply to otherwise indentical labour and are *entirely* due to the discriminatory confinement of women to a few low-paid occupations, these estimates suggest that employment in male dominated occupations would have to increase by around a third to achieve equality of wages. Interestingly, the findings also suggest that competitive-labour-market outcomes would lead to significantly increased wages in the few previously female-dominated occupations (by around 50 per cent), reduction by only a few percentage points in previously male-dominated occupations, and substantial output gains. Similar estimates are also reported for a number of Latin American countries (Psacharopoulos and Tzannatos, 1991). As Tzannatos (1990) puts it, 'There are efficiency gains to be obtained from the elimination of crowding' (p. 200).

To return to the question of SCBA in development planning, the problem faced derives, therefore, not so much from straightforward discrimination (that is, unequal pay for work of equal value) as from the creation of incommensurable forms of labour, the widespread confinement of women to low-paid sectors of the economy, and the consequent curtailment of direct competition between the sexes. Faced with this situation, project planners have two courses of action. They may decide to accept the given distribution of wages on the grounds that it is the relevant measure of the value of labour; as Evenson (1976, p. 92) suggests, 'strictures about female labour force participation do not negate the implications of economic theory, they only influence the value of women's time'. In doing so, however, they help to preserve an inequitable status quo and probably miscalculate the real value of production forgone through the employment of women. On the other hand, if they decide to pay female labour on 'equitable' wage, then the elaborate process of cost–benefit analysis may be rendered redundant. As we argue below, CBA has particular difficulties in accommodating the notion of equity within its framework of analysis.

The Silences in SCBA: The Valuation of Non-marketed Goods

The problem of 'incommensurables' dealt with so far refers to the problem of using market prices as the measure of value in situations of restricted competition and segmented labour markets. Market bias works differently when benefits or costs *cannot* be assigned monetary prices because they do not enter market transactions at all. Without monetary prices as the common numeraire, there is no meaningful basis of comparison between costs and benefits. The issue of these non-marketed activities is not a trivial one, particularly in the Third World. It is generally true that the poorer a nation, class or household, the more critical is the role of self-provisioning and other non-market activities to its survival. The gender bias to this preoccupation with marketed goods stems from the fact that a significant proportion of women's labour in most developing economies takes place outside the market.

Within the general category of non-marketed goods, there are further sub-categories. Some goods are potentially marketable; others, however, *by their very nature* do not enter the marketplace at all. Where the products of women's labour are at least potentially marketable (for example, subsistence crop production, fuel and water porterage), some form of shadow pricing may be possible – although clearly the procedure of imputing prices on the basis of 'equivalent' activities in gender-segmented labour markets is fraught with simplifying assumptions and *ad hoc* guesstimates.[1] It is difficult, however, to imagine how the logic of shadow pricing could be extended to women's labour in activities for which markets do not exist. The most obvious example of such labour is in the domestic reproduction, maintenance and care of human resources: child-bearing and child care, care of the sick, disabled and elderly, and the daily maintenance of all household members. These activities are at least as important to household survival and well-being as the production of material resources; but, as we pointed out in Chapter 4, to treat them as analogous forms of production would be to ignore the very different values that govern them. Elson summarizes this point well when she says:

Unpaid domestic labour is not carried out entirely for love, ignoring the economic costs and benefits; but neither is it simply another economic activity. The process of the reproduction and maintenance of human resources is different from any other kind of production because human resources are treated as having an intrinsic, not merely an instrumental value. Women may to some extent weigh up the costs and benefits for themselves of the amount of services they provide without pay to other family members, but they do not regard their children as just another crop, to be tended if the benefits are high enough, and to be left to rot untended if the benefits become too low. (Elson, 1991b, p. 176)

On the one hand, therefore, there are limits to how far women themselves will apply an economic calculus in determining how much of their time they spend in unpaid domestic labour. On the other hand, their ability to do so is in any case constrained by the implicit contractual obligations that characterize intra-household relations. As we noted in Chapter 5, many aspects of the gender division of labour within the domestic domain appear remarkably resistant to change (Folbre, 1984b; Standing, 1991; Beneria and Roldan, 1987). There is little evidence to show that men take on a greater share of child care or domestic labour when women increase their marketed labour. Women are only able to participate in market-oriented activities by intensifying their overall labour effort. The 'double burden' of labour involved in caring for the family and making a living is the basis of the widespread finding that, on average, women work longer hours than men.

In terms of project design, the apparently lower opportunity costs of women's time, as measured by their market wages, ignores both the value – and the contractual basis – of their labour contributions within the family. Development interventions premissed on the availability of female labour time are likely to 'misbehave' unless they are able to integrate a recognition of the amount and flexibility of women's domestic overheads. This is one of the points made in Leslie's review (1992) of maternal health and family-planning provision, both examples of interventions targeted primarily at women. She cites a study from Ethiopia by Ayalew (1985) which found that failure of government health provision could be traced to the failure to understand and accommodate women's time use within the community and suggested that community time budget be used to address this planning deficiency. She also notes that Coreil (1991) found that the combined effects of maternal time constraints and absence of alternative caretakers within the family limited women's use of child health services, particularly those (for example, immunization) which had to be used outside the home.

The conceptual problems of integrating non-marketable 'reproductive' work into a cost—benefit framework are further compounded by the unreflecting biases on the part of some analysts. This was clearly exemplified in the proceedings of a Working Group convened in London by the Commonwealth Secretariat and WHO in 1983 to consider ways of appraising investment in supportive measures for working women in developing countries. Influenced by the apparent success of an earlier conference held in Zimbabwe in utilizing conventional cost—benefit considerations to reinforce the case for implementing the Code of Marketing of Breastmilk Substitutes, some members of the Working Group suggested that policy advocacy on behalf of women would have more impact among planners if couched in the familiar language of CBA. A paper presented earlier at the Zimbabwe Conference advocating breast-feeding in place of bottle-feeding on the basis of costs and benefits, was circulated for the benefit of the participants of the London Workshop (Greiner 1983, appended in Thomas, 1984). Among the national and family-level costs of switching from breast-feeding to bottle-feeding identified by Greiner were the substantial extra demand for foreign exchange to cover imports of dried milk; loss of contraceptive effect connected with breast-feeding and resultant increase in population; impaired health status of babies and young children as a result of early cessation of breast-feeding, and the associated rise in health-related expenditures. In Ghana, Greiner estimated that a reduction of only 1 per cent of the estimated national annual breast-milk feeding would have cost about US$1 million for milk powder alone, while the cost of simple rehabilitation of even the small number of resulting cases of malnutrition would have probably approached US$1 million. The consequences of women switching from breast-feeding to bottle-feeding were spelt out in apocalyptic terms: 'Developing countries which simply stand by and allow breastfeeding to decline in coming years will risk economic havoc as a result' (Greiner, 1983, p. 53).

However, the case for promoting breast-feeding and the case for supportive measures for working women are by no means parallel. As Heather Joshi (1983)[2] one of the members of the London Working Group, pointed out, the apparent 'success' of conventional economic considerations in reinforcing the case for promoting breast-feeding stemmed partly from the fact that an unpriced commodity (breast milk) was being compared with manufactured milk powder − a product of the monetized economy and, furthermore, a 'traded' good on which scarce foreign exchange was directly incurred. The time and energy of the mother needed to produce breast milk was rightly or wrongly treated as costless. The converse applied when investment in support measures for working mothers, for example, child-care centres, was being considered. Here resources from the cash economy – investment in child-care centres – had to substitute for non-cash resources (namely women's labour and energy) so that it was as easy to make day care look artificially costly as it was to make breast-feeding look artificially costless.

The asymmetrical evaluations of these different components – internationally traded goods, marketed goods and non-marketable goods – by cost–benefit analysts is linked to the point made earlier that many aspects of women's labour, particularly those connected with caring and nurturing, are so steeped in familial ideologies that their costs and benefits are rendered invisible. Greiner's perceptions of breast-feeding as costless springs from such ideologies. 'Breastmilk', according to him, 'is a natural resource of almost unequalled importance . . . It is the only food available almost equally to rich and poor alike' (Greiner, 1983, p. 55). The consignment of breast-milk production to the realm of 'natural' activities meant, of course, that it did not need to be subjected to economic analysis. Yet breast-feeding is not a costless activity; it makes considerable demands on women's time and energy. Nor does it 'cost' the same for rich and poor. Leslie observes that time demands of exclusive breast-feeding are undoubtedly more intense than any other health service or health-care practice targeted at women. For poorer women, the need to contribute to household survival strategies may necessitate long and uninterrupted hours of absence from the home, and it is not always possible for women to take their babies with them. A study of women farmers in Western Nepal found that most were unable to take their infants to the fields, because of the steep terrain and long distances to be travelled and because of fears about the safety of the infant (Levine, 1988, cited in Leslie, 1992).

If the nutritional demands that breast-feeding makes on women's energy reserves (lactating women require a supplement of several hundred extra calories daily to maintain their energy reserves) are juxtaposed with the levels of malnutrition documented among poor women in many parts of the world, then its purported 'almost equal availability' to rich and poor women must also be juxtaposed with its very unequal costs. As was pointed out in Chapter 5, pregnant and/or breast-feeding women suffer from shortfalls in their nutritional requirements in many different parts of the world, possibly because of similar views of these aspects of their labour as costless. In fact the World Health Organisation has pointed out, in relation to women who are malnourished during pregnancy or whose workload is too heavy, that 'lactation in these cases will involve the depletion of the mother's own tissues; thus, although malnourished women can successfully breast-feed, it is at their own expense' (WHO, 1980, p. 11).

A partial solution to situations where no meaningful monetary valuation can be made of costs and benefits would be to rely on non-monetary indicators of projected benefits and use *cost-effectiveness analysis* to decide how to achieve them. Social indicators, such as reduction in infant mortality rates or increase in per-capita nutritional intake, may serve to approximate the qualitative aspect of benefits. However, while the use of cost-effectiveness takes care of the problem of non-monetary benefits, the danger of treating monetized and non-monetized costs in an asymmetrical fashion still remains. Furthermore, cost-effectiveness analysis is not considered as powerful as CBA because, while it points to the least-cost method for achieving a given objective, it is silent on whether the objective is worth the investment in the first place (Haverman, 1976). It opens the door to subjective and political criteria rather than depending on economic ones alone. The assumption that CBA is somehow uncontaminated by such considerations is one we will return to later.

The Silences in SCBA: Pricing the 'Intangible'

The difficulties we have addressed so far relate to the problem of relying on money as the numeraire for measurement in situations where markets either do not exist or exist imperfectly. The incorporation of equity objectives into cost–benefit planning raise a whole new set of problems. The notion of equity has a far more ambiguous status than efficiency in welfare economics, not only because it is difficult to put a monetary value on it, but because it is often impossible to *quantify*. Unlike some categories of 'incommensurables', which may at least be approximated through qualitative indicators, there are equity-related objectives that do not lend themselves to numerical representation. CBA has no procedure for dealing with these 'intangibles'. The problem of equity tends to be resolved in SCBA by assigning higher weighting to benefits accruing to subordinated groups. Thus Project A may be selected over Project B because it provides additional income to poor women. However, this is a very conservative version of equity. SCBA would still find it difficult to evaluate projects which tackle the underlying *causes* of women's lower earnings relative to men of similar class or educational backgrounds. A notion of equity that focuses only on outcomes, and ignores processes, will leave intact the structural inequalities in material resources, influence, contacts and organizational capacity which underlie gender inequalities in earning power.

There is another dimension to the question of 'intangibles' which concerns values other than those of the market. The disutility of lowered consumption has a measurable component in a way that the disutility of increased dependence does not. Yet, as we noted in the previous two chapters, there is a considerable literature to suggest that these intangible aspects matter. In fact, women may prefer to work on their own enterprises or for wages rather than on household or male-managed fields, regardless of relative returns on the two activities, because they value their autonomy from the men in their households over the prospect of enhanced household income over which they had little or no control (Jones, 1985, 1986; Dey, 1981, 1982; Jackson, 1978).

In terms of our earlier distinction between 'practical' and 'strategic' , planners relying on CBA are far better at dealing with women's practical gender interests – those arising out of their preassigned tasks and activities within an unequal gender division of responsibilities and resources – than with their strategic gender interests which would require a transformation of these unequal gender divisions. An added complexity is that strategic gender interests are not always 'transparent' to women themselves, let alone to planners, in the way that needs deriving from existing daily routines and responsibilities might be. Rather, they emerge out of a process of analysing and understanding the structures of women's subordination in specific societies and the strategies necessary to transform them.

If women are to increase their capacity to analyse, question and act upon their subordination – in other words, to empower themselves – they must be given access to the time, resources and space to do so. Their practical needs are obviously an important precondition to this: women who are overburdened with work, who must walk many miles for clean water, or whose children are hungry are unlikely to prioritize the longer-term project of self-empowerment. However, the manner in which these practical needs are addressed have important implications for the transformatory potential of different kinds of projects. The question of ends and means become inseparable. Women's practical needs can be provided for in ways that leave their dependent and subordinate status intact: income-generating projects which are unviable without the intervention of project officials (Van der Laan and Krippendorf, 1981); health-care provision offered on welfarist or elitist principles (Shatrugna et al., 1987); or potable water distributed through powerful members of the community (Bunch and Carrillo, 1990, p. 76). Alternatively, the needs can be addressed in ways which increase the collective strength and organizational capacity of women – what we referred to earlier as the subversion of welfare for equity.

Here the limitations of SCBA-defined notions of equity become manifestly clear. Projects which seek to address these longer-term strategic considerations are likely to fail by SCBA standards because the processual nature of empowerment eludes quantification. How would one measure the costs and benefits of the strategies of 'conscientization-organization-mobilization' which a variety of grass-roots development organizations in different parts of the Third World have adopted in response to this challenge (see Chapter 9)? How would one measure the growth in awareness among women that disempowering practices such as male violence, enforced child-bearing and inequalities in the distribution of resources and respons-ibilities within society are not divinely ordained or biologically deter-mined, but historically produced and hence can be challenged and transformed? Agencies that claim to support such social action programmes will have to plan and assess them according to criteria which are likely to fall outside the evaluative domain of SCBA.

The Silences in SCBA: Conflicting Interests in the Social Welfare Function

The problems discussed so far stem from gender biases inherent in the methodology of SCBA itself. In addition, there is a separate set of problems that stem from the political economy within which most SCBA exercises are conducted. It relates to the conflictual nature of gender relations we touched on in the preceding section. SCBA is capable of recognizing certain kinds of inequalities – namely, inequal-ities in the distribution of income in a population and the existence of poverty groups. However, it maintains a deafening silence on the power relations that produce these inequalities, despite the fact that such relations persistently impinge on the interpretation of the social welfare function. This can seriously limit the usefulness of SCBA as a planning tool. In her critique of CBA, Stewart (1975) points to is underlying assumption of a neutral and benign decision-maker entrusted with the task of measuring project costs and benefits in relation to 'the' social welfare. The question of whose interests help to define what constitutes the social welfare is not considered problem-atic. Yet the construction of a social welfare function is fraught with problems if it has to accommodate heterogeneous sets of interests, where each set of interests generates a corresponding set of shadow prices. In place of the unique set of values, shadow prices and distributional weights visualized by SCBA, there is likely to be an array; 'if used for project evaluation, a different set of projects would be chosen according to whose values, and hence which shadow prices, were being used' (Stewart, 1975, p. 33). When there are conflicting interests at stake, overt or covert struggles will ensue over whose interpretation of the social welfare function – and hence whose values – will prevail. In the final analysis, the outcome that emerges is unlikely to be one which seriously threatens the underlying distribution of power in society.

If 'class' is used in a broad sense here to refer to groups that share structurally similar life options, then our earlier discussion of strategic gender interests becomes relevant. It is not necessary to believe that all women will prioritize the same set of interests: they are by no means endowed with a natural solidarity stemming from their biological attributes. Their needs and priorities are the product of a number of intersecting relations, including their relationship to the means of production. Nevertheless, in given contexts, women and men may have different and conflicting interests, arising out of the inequalities of power and privilege embedded in concrete relations of gender. Once these relations are brought into the analysis, they provide compelling reasons why male-dominated policymaking bodies may favour certain kinds of interventions over others. Men's strategic gender interests help to shape, however unintentionally, the meaning given to 'the social welfare function' within the policy domain, as well as the design and implementation of the projects which flow from these interpretations. Male interests are evident at a number of different levels within the project cycle, setting limits on the 'control areas' available to planners, defining the assumptions and values which shape project design, and subverting the implementation process. We will consider briefly how this works in practice.

SCBA is implicitly premised on the assumption that good project design can be used to correct for distortions in the broader environment (Stewart, 1975). Thus the use of weights and shadow prices is intended to ensure that project-level calculations are freed of distortions in prevailing market prices or biased income distributions. Yet the same forces that prevent action being taken to correct distortions at the national level are also likely to operate at the lower level of communities and governments. In relation to gender, there is no reason why planned interventions will be able to override at the local level the forces that constrain women's opportunities in the broader arena. Men's strategic gender interests are an intrinsic part of the process by which the 'control areas' within which planners operate are demarcated. This was a point implicit in a cost–benefit exercise carried out by Greeley (1987) on mechanized rice milling in Bangladesh, which had improved rural labour productivity, but had also led to the erosion of one of the few employment opportunities available to poor, landless women. Although by SCBA criteria, the welfare costs of mechanized mills exceeded their benefits, Greeley concluded that curtailing the spread of such mills could not be contemplated because, among other reasons, it was unlikely that the regulations could be effectively policed. In Greeley's word, 'Planners who find that the value judgement of [SCBA analysis] is acceptable and that intervention to stop huller mills is desirable in principle will also be aware that the control areas they command and policy implementations cannot be juggled into shape in the same way that a social cost–benefit analysis can' (1987, p. 292). This is another way of saying that when the interests of a powerful group, however small (wealthy farmers and traders, mainly men), are evaluated against the interests of a disempowered group, however large (poor, landless women), it is unlikely that recommended interventions which favour the latter have much chance of being implemented.

However, the problem is deeper than one of powerful sections of the community demarcating planners' 'control areas'. Gender politics are woven into the planning process itself. Male privilege is frequently protected in the design of policies and projects through the use of normative assumptions which permit women's independent interests to vanish through their association with – and subsumption under – socially acceptable 'others'. The classic assumption of this kind is that men are the primary or sole breadwinners and economic decision-makers. Women are cast in the role of financial dependents, responsible only for family welfare. This permits the distribution of employment and productive resources to male heads of households; women enter as 'unpaid family labour' or are assigned to small-scale, unproductive income-generating projects which do little to challenge the power relations of the household. The case studies of agricultural projects from The Gambia, Cameroon and Kenya cited earlier are examples of this type of assumption.

A second common assumption by which women's interests are made to vanish is by conflation with their children. As Buvinic notes, 'potential conflicts between women's and children's welfare are customarily resolved in [welfare-oriented] programs by emphasising women's motherhood roles, thereby making children's welfare the ultimate objective' (Buvinic, 1983, p. 25). The same point is made in an article entitled 'Where is the M [mother] in MCH [Mother Child Health]' where the authors point out that the bulk of funds in mother–child health programmes in the Third World are spent on children's health on the general assumption that 'what is good for the child is good for the mother' (Rosenfield and Maine, 1985). This certainly appeared to have been Greiner's assumption; as we noted, his advocacy of breast-feeding rested on the welfare of the infant and the invisibility of the mother. In reality, important biological and social synergies make the reverse relationship equally significant; women's nutritional status affects the birth weight of infants (WHO, 1980), and women's control over resources can have a beneficial effect on children's nutritional and health status (Longhurst, 1988; Kennedy and Cogill, 1987). Referring back to our discussion in Chapter 5 on the long hours that women work in rural Gambia, there is striking evidence to demonstrate the link between the well-being of mothers and children. According to The Gambia's census, 30 per cent of children in the rural areas die by the age of two; a detailed village study indicates that more than half die before their fifth birthday. Sixty-eight per cent of these deaths occur in the busy rainy season when women's workload is at its peak. Lower birth weights – and hence higher probability of infant deaths – are especially likely when the last trimester of a pregnancy occurs in the rainy season. The World Bank (1980) attributes the 'extremely high infant and child mortality rates' in The Gambia to the 'unsatisfactory situation of their mothers, who usually are badly nourished and heavily overworked' (p. 19).

Finally, there are other, more active ways in which men protect and promote their strategic gender interests within the policy process. The earlier WID literature concentrated on the assumptions underlying policy formulation. More recent research has uncovered the implications of largely covert forms of male resistance for the implementation, and hence for the actual outcomes, of policies ostensibly geared to gender-aware efficiency or equity goals. As Staudt observes:

> Bureaucratic officials increasingly confront policies which, if implemented, prompt the redistribution of resources and values between men and women, a threatening prospect that incurs political conflict in ways no different from politically provocative class redistribution. However, such conflict occurs behind the closed doors of bureaucracy, as threatened officials personalise such prospects and resist, deflect and/or undermine those policies. The bureaucratic resistance to women's programmes that comes from redistributive threats is a critical phenomenon. (Staudt, 1986, p. 329)

Consequently, even where gender redistribution features as an intended objective in the project design, it is unlikely to feature in project outcomes if those responsible for their implementation are able to subvert these goals. Analysing why projects for poor women which had started out with explicitly production-oriented goals frequently assumed welfarist features in the process of implementation, Buvinic (1986) concluded that welfare-oriented action was seen as promoting 'appropriate' roles for women and (most importantly) as not taking away resources from men. Underlying the fear that poor women might compete with poor men for development resources appeared to be the anxiety that there might be 'unwelcome' social changes within the family. She quotes a high-level official in a planning ministry who supported income-generating projects for women as long as they did not lead to women earning more than men, since he perceived this as having undesirable consequences within the family.

Equity goals at policy level are even more likely to be subverted in practice. I will summarize here Carney's findings (1988) from the latest chapter of the epic saga of Gambian irrigation schemes, which documents how men's gender interests have operated in the implementation process to subvert the apparent commitment to gender equity expressed in project goals. This scheme was begun in Jahally Parchar in 1984 as a large-scale, centralized operation seeking to introduce double cropping in rice through a system of contract farming. The project donors and management sought to reverse the effects of earlier schemes by awarding rights to the newly irrigated plots to the original female rice farmers. While the scheme was successful in increasing real incomes in the area, 87 per cent of the plots were registered in male names. An assessment of the scheme by von Braun et al. (1989, p. 10) concluded that gender distributive goals were difficult to enforce through 'bureaucratic means such as land titles, which have little relevance in the field'. Carney's study (1988), elaborating why 'bureaucratic means' had failed, draws attention to the issue of male resistance in the implementation process. She notes that international publicity around women's grievances after a first round of land distribution had led to IFAD, the major donor this time round, assuming direction of the second distribution. The second distribution dramatically increased the number of plots registered in women's names. However, subsequent research revealed that, despite being registered in women's names, the irrigated plots were being designated as compound holdings. Consequently, despite the project's objectives, women had no individual rights to the land. Carney traces this partly to the continuing struggle over land rights between women and men, sparked off by forty years of government disruption of customary rights in favour of men. That male claims carried weight locally had already been revealed in the first distribution.

A second reason put forward by Carney was the management's willingness to acquiesce to existing political hierarchies in the area. IFAD's registration of land in women's names had been made possible because project managers made a formal distinction between registration and control, listing the name of the male compound head alongside the name of the female 'owner', suggesting that the compound enjoyed rights over the land. Male resistance to the second distribution was also overcome by management agreement that land would not be lost to compound males in the event of divorce, but transferred to another female within the compound. Both these practices ensured that de facto control over the irrigated crop was centralized in the hands of the male compound head despite the project's avowed intention to respect women's rights. Carney points out that women did not become impoverished as a result of the project, but they become increasingly more dependent on their husbands to meet their needs. Mandinka women suffered most from this erosion of their autonomy. Other groups of women still had access to own-account upland plots and therefore greater capacity to bargain over the question of remuneration for labouring on men's irrigated fields.

Aside from political considerations, there was a strong economic rationale for designating the land as compound land, since only this category carried claims to unremunerated family labour necessary to meet contract-farming production demands. The need to make family labour available for cropping dominated the equity goals of the project management. However, instead of seeking to address labour shortages by designating irrigated plots as compound plots, project managers could have targeted the fundamental production unit of women rather than that of men. Aligning control over plots with the work unit that most closely resembles the actual labour force in cultivation could have resulted in a more equitable outcome. Project managers could also have defended women's usufructuary rights, if not on the pumped plots, then at least in the tidal irrigated areas where these rights had a prior existence. Carney concludes by pointing to the difficulties of implementing equity goals in rural development projects: 'powerful ideological forces are at play in maintaining existing rural, political and economic alignments. The challenge for policy-makers and donors interested in implementing equity goals is to identify a framework to enhance that possibility' (p. 75). Commitment, vigilance and innovative approaches to project design, implementation and monitoring, as well as to evaluation, are essential.

Conclusion: Horses for Courses?

Bearing these points in mind, how useful is CBA in gender planning? The reality is that CBA, like any other evaluative methodology, carries within it an implicit set of goals which it is best equipped to deal with. If a typology of evaluation methods were constructed according to the policy goals they were best suited to evaluate, CBA would perform best with interventionist, rather than participatory, projects; with projects that have single objectives, preferably related to efficiency, rather than those with multiple or equity-related objectives; and with costs and benefits that can be assigned market values, or at least clear shadow prices. Once qualitative objectives are introduced and the principle of commensurability is abandoned, the clarity and power of CBA starts to leak away. Clear specification of distributional weights will only partly compensate for the move from the realm of the objective, or at least the observable, into the realm of the subjective and more explicitly political. Cost-effective or Logical Framework analysis, which allow more explicit recognition of non-monetary and non-quantifiable considerations in the project planning cycle, are other options to SCBA in these situations, but they retain a common bias towards quantifiable indicators.

Focusing more specifically on projects dealing with gender equity considerations, cost—benefit methodology is still likely to be useful for those that confine themselves to women's daily practical needs and are therefore unlikely to encounter male resistance. Here, SCBA can help to spell out the resource implications of alternative ways of meeting these needs for the benefit of decision-makers. The difficulties begin when projects seeking to implement redistributive or empowering strategies have to be appraised or evaluated by decision-makers who do not share – and may be threatened by – these objectives. Here the use of SCBA is an altogether more dubious practice. It is unlikely to capture benefits and costs as envisaged by those proposing the project, but it offers decision-makers a facade of neutrality in rejecting the project.

For those policy-making agencies who wish to encourage and promote women's empowerment, more participatory forms of planning and evaluation, based on analysing the objectives, successes and problems of a project as seen by the various stake-holders in the process and in partnership with those the project is intended to serve, might be a more appropriate approach (see contributions to Rahman, 1982; Fernandes and Tandon, 1981; Greeley et al., 1992; Dighe and Jain, 1989). While participatory approaches to evaluation may appear to be unduly subjective and politicized, their advantage is that they are undisguisedly so and are therefore open to scrutiny and challenge. The problem with CBA is that while it frequently makes the same political judgements and partisan assumptions, these are disguised in the seemingly clinical and frequently impenetrable jargon of the economic technocrat (Chambers, 1978).

In conclusion, therefore, there are strong arguments for not regarding CBA as a neutral and foolproof guide to all project selection or evaluation. The fist step has to be to conduct a cost–benefit analysis on CBA itself (Chambers, 1978). CBA is often a costly exercise, requiring scarce managerial and analytical skills that might be put to better use elsewhere in the development effort. If a project concerned with empowering women is to be evaluated for the benefit of a policy-making agency that has no real commitment to gender equity, then carrying out an expensive CBA is likely to be a waste of scarce resources. In this case, the cheaper and more honest option might be what CBA analysts term the 'universal alternative' of doing nothing: the agency can simply reject the project outright without seeking to hide its biases behind an expensive and time-consuming cost–benefit exercise.

Notes

1 I would like to thank Heather Joshi for permission to quote from her presentation to the Commonwealth Secretariat Workshop on Support to Working Mothers in a Cost Benefit Framework held in London in 1983.
2 Particularly if one bears in mind the point cited earlier from Phillips and Taylor (1980) that it is frequently the sex of those who do a task, rather than its content, which leads to its grading as skilled or unskilled. The tasks that women do at home frequently mirror the tasks they are assigned through the labour market, and both are generally seen as unskilled. Using shadow prices to value women's non-market activities may simply reproduce the undervaluation of female categories of activities by market forces.

8

Implementing the Right to Choose: Women, Motherhood and Population Policy

The Independent on Sunday: Which world event are you most worried about?

David Bellamy (naturalist): My main concern is that there are one and a half billion women in the world of child-bearing age. If they all got pregnant at one time the world population would go up by one and a half billion – something very few people think about. (17 January 1993)

Women know that child bearing is a social, not purely personal, phenomenon: nor do we deny that world population trends are likely to exert considerable pressure on resources and institutions by the end of this century. But our bodies have become a pawn in the struggles among states, religions, male heads of households, and private corporations. (Sen and Grown, 1985, p. 42)

Introduction

Population policies in the past few decades offer an excellent illustration of why merely targeting women, without considering the broader social relations in which they live, is unlikely either to change their lives or to achieve intended goals. As the pressure of population on limited resources becomes identified in many minds as the major cause of world poverty, women are being seen as both the cause and therefore the potential solution. I have used the quotation from David Bellamy to open this chapter because it appears to crystallize both past and present features of this state of mind. The present is evident in the growing involvement of environmentalists in population debates,

leading to new versions of the old link between population growth and global disaster. But the past continues in the singling out of women as the cause of overpopulation. If Bellamy's fears are realized and all billion and a half women in the reproductive ages get pregnant at the same time, some acknowledgement needs to be made of the contribution that men have made to this outcome. Yet men are generally invisible when it comes to considering issues of reproduction.

Feminists in this field have long been aware of the contradictory ways in which motherhood and mothers are treated within the policy discourse. Motherhood as a 'role' for women is given a visibility and significance that is not attached to fatherhood as a 'role' for men. It is treated as the reason, rationale and realization of women's nurturing instincts, and most policy concerned with family welfare and family planning tends to be targeted at women. At the same time, women as mothers or would-be mothers are rarely perceived as competent actors, capable of making responsible choices in their own and in their families' interests. Instead they are subjected to agendas which have been determined elsewhere by policy-makers who have little or no accountability to them. This chapter discusses shifting perspectives in population policy over the past decades as well as important continuities. It also outlines some different feminist responses to the official population policies before going on to outline a feminist case for an alternative policy.

Changing Perspectives on the Population Question

The importance given to population control is evident in the resources currently allocated to population-related programmes. Each year, about US$1 billion is spent on family planning in the Third World. About $100 million is spent by individuals themselves on contraception, $400 million is spent by Third World governments, and $500 million by the Western population establishment (cited in Hartmann 1987). The United States alone spent $235 million in 1988 (Germain and Ordway, 1989), and accounts for about 50 per cent of all population assistance (UNFPA, 1989).

Concern with population control has figured prominently on the development agenda at least since the early 1960s, when India became the first developing country officially to set up a Department of Family Planning in its Ministry of Health. However, like all other aspects of development, perspectives and paradigms in the population debate have undergone several shifts over the years. The first decades of development were dominated by fears that population growth in the

Third World would literally eat into the fruits of economic progress, leading to deepening poverty on a global scale. Financed initially by the US and other Western governments, and later adopted by a number of Third World governments, the massive dissemination of contraceptive technology was the hallmark of this period.

The 1974 World Population Conference at Bucharest took place at a time when the entire growth-dominated paradigm was under great strain. A number of Third World and socialist countries suggested that the narrow focus of Western governments on the 'population prob-lem' was a way of distracting attention from the underlying inequalities in the international economic order. They also pointed out that it was the spread of economic and social progress in Europe at the beginning of the twentieth century which had brought about sustained and widespread declines in fertility. The lesson to be drawn from this was that 'development was the best contraceptive'. The World Population Plan of Action adopted at Bucharest reflected a new and broader international awareness of population issues. It declared that popula-tion programmes were constituent elements of socio-economic deve-lopment policies rather than substitutes for them. It specifically recognized the right of all couples and individuals to decide freely and responsibly the number and spacing of their children, and to have access to the information, education and means to do so. The Bucharest Conference marked a decade when, alongside the continu-ing dissemination of contraceptive methods, greater attention began to be paid to the underlying social context which led to high rates of fertility.

The late 1970s also saw changes in policy approaches to the related question of health service delivery. Most post-colonial governments in the developing world had sought to model their health services on those of the advanced industrialized countries. The result was highly centralized health systems which were state-financed, hospital-based and relied on a small number of highly trained physicians. This approach came under increasing criticism for being too expensive, reaching too few people, being biased toward the urban sector, and placing too much emphasis on curative services.

In a major attempt to reorient health systems to the needs and resources of developing countries, 134 countries endorsed the new Primary Health Care (PHC) approach at the Alma Ata conference in 1978. Two central elements in PHC are its focus on the preventive management of illness, infection and nutritional deficiency and its reliance on auxiliary health workers and community participation. PHC does not require dramatic changes in community infrastructure, but concentrates instead on improving community practice in certain

areas considered critical to preventive health care, viz. health, nutrition education, mother and child health, family planning, water and
sanitation, immunization, essential drugs and treatment of common
diseases and injuries. However, while PHC was widely endorsed and
seemed to hold out the promise of a revolutionary new approach to the
health problems of the Third World, other developments on the
international stage intervened to prevent the full realization of this
promise. By the end of the seventies, the widespread debt crises,
recession and structural adjustment policies had precipitated cutbacks
in state expenditures on social services in many developing countries;
population assistance to the developing world currently represents 1.3
per cent of total Official Development Assistance compared to around
2 per cent in the 1970s (UNFPA, 1989). Declines in social service
expenditures were particularly drastic in sub-Saharan Africa and
resulted in a severe deterioration of health-care provision: shortages
of vehicles, fuel and maintenance services, understaffing of clinics and
hospitals, and shortfalls in supply of critical drugs and medical
equipment (Commonwealth Secretariat, 1989; Leslie et al., 1988). The
human cost of this adjustment was, as we noted in the first chapter, a
slowing down and in some cases a reversal in the previous steady
progress in social indicators.

A consequence of this crisis in the health systems of the Third World
has been a growing preoccupation with achieving economies in the
delivery of health care. The increasing emphasis on cost recovery or
user fees is one clear response to constrained government and
international funds for the health sector. There has also been a
tendency to focus on selective primary-health-care provision which
deals only with a limited number of 'cost-effective', vertically delivered
elements of PHC (for example, family planning and the child survival
revolution based on the GOBI strategy: growth monitoring, oral
rehydration therapy, breast-feeding and immunization) rather than
on the full range of measures considered necessary for preventive
health care. As we shall argue in the next section, cutbacks in family
planning and health-care provision have implications for the broader
context in which fertility behaviour is located.

Women and Population: A Long-Standing Link

Women have always received a disproportionate amount of attention
in population-control programmes. This is in marked contrast to their
negligible presence in other spheres of development research and
policy; according to Ware (1981), for instance, prior to International

Women's Year in 1975, less than 1 per cent of sixty development texts specifically referred to women. The prominent place accorded to women in the population literature reflects the very real significance of motherhood in most women's lives. It overlooks, however, the fact that women's lives encompass more than just child-bearing and child-rearing; that women all over the world balance a greater multiplicity of roles and responsibilities than male members of their households. The equation of *womanhood* with *motherhood* embedded in early population policy is a construct of policymakers rather than a reflection of reality.

The focus on women in the development debate began to widen beyond family-planning and welfare concerns in the 1970s. As we noted in Chapter 1, one reason for this was that social-science research had begun to highlight the fertility-reducing impact of enhancing women's status, as measured by indicators such as literacy, education, employment and decision-making power. Furthermore, the designation by the UN of two successive years as World Population Year and International Women's Year (1974 and 1975) encouraged members of the international development community to think about the two issues simultaneously and to take an interest in the connection between woman's roles and population growth (Newland, 1977). Recognition of this important relationship had considerable ramifications for population policy. Women's contributions in arenas other than that of biological reproduction received greater attention and resulted in the promotion of projects to enhance women's earning power. Unfortunately, while such activities may have increased women's access to cash incomes, there is no evidence that it transformed their dependent status within their families and communities, or even that it had the expected effect on their fertility behaviour. As the World Bank points out, 'employment seems to have an independent effect on fertility only for women in well-paid, modern jobs' (1984, p. 110). In general, the forms of employment generated by women's projects over the past decade were neither 'modern' nor 'well-paid' and focused on income generation rather than sustainable employment.

Moreover, changes in the international economy over the past decade, and concomitant changes in the provision of social services, have highlighted more sharply than ever the contradictions entailed in creating mainstream employment opportunities for women. These contradictions stem from the conflicting demands made on women's time by their roles in the production and care of human resources juxtaposed with their involvement in the production of material and financial resources for their households. Both economic crisis and adjustment policies have made women's contribution to household income critical to the survival of poor and middle-income households.

The freezing of salaries and wages, the erosion of real incomes through rising prices of essential commodities, and the application of user fees to compensate for reduced government expenditure in health and education have combined to 'push' women from both chronically poor and newly impoverished households into intensifying their inputs into income-enhancing activities. On the positive side, structural adjustment policies have also increased opportunities and 'pulled' women into some sectors of production, such as cash crops and export-oriented manufactures (UN, 1989).

At the same time, other developments have increased the load of reproductive work in the household. First of all, the increased emphasis on the primary health care approach, while more in keeping with the resource endowments of poorer countries, made particular demands on women's time. It has been estimated that at least 75 per cent of all health care takes place at the family or individual level (Leslie et al., 1988) and it is women, particularly in their role as mothers and wives, who have the greatest responsibility for promoting the family's health and nutrition. The 'community participation' essential to the success of PHC strategies was premised on the unpaid labour of women (Leslie et al., 1988). Second, cuts in government financing of social expenditures, together with the imposition of user charges, have further increased pressures on women's time, either through the need to earn additional financial resources or else to compensate for cutbacks in the public provision of health and education services. Longer waits at understaffed clinics, reduced supplies of drugs, deterioration in cheap public-transport services all contribute to the time and opportunity costs of using public health services and force women to take on further responsibilities in the area of family health.

We have noted in previous chapters that multiple demands on women's time lead to exceedingly long working hours. While such time is to some extent 'fungible' between productive and reproductive labour, there is generally a minimum fixed overhead of daily domestic chores which they have to complete before they can undertake any other tasks. Initiatives to transform women's productive opportunities – and hence their reproductive strategies – are unlikely to be successful if they take no account of women's existing domestic labour overheads. The conflicting labour demands that women experience in their roles as health carers, producers and mothers have not been helped in the past by the sectoral approach that characterizes policymaking in both national and international agencies. Like the other aspects of development, a gender-aware population policy must be firmly grounded within a holistic framework.

Population Policy and the Politics of
Needs Interpretation

The continuing controversy over population policy attests to the contradictory meanings that it assumes for different actors in the development field. A useful framework for discussing some of these differing meanings is suggested by Fraser's discussion of what she calls the 'politics of needs' (1989, p. 164). She points out that discourse about needs has been an important element of public interventions, particularly in relation to social welfare. How needs are perceived, prioritized and met has functioned as a medium for making claims and distributing resources. The politics of needs can be seen to comprise three moments, analytically distinct but closely interrelated. The first is the struggle to secure the political status of a need, that is, to establish that an identified need is a legitimate area for policy concern rather than a matter for the 'private' domestic or market spheres. The second is the struggle over the interpretation of this need and hence how to satisfy it. The third is the struggle to secure or withhold the resources needed for the satisfaction of this need.

Both the official population establishment and many women's health advocates agree that there is a 'need', largely unmet and particularly in the Third World, for contraceptive technology. But there are substantial differences in the way in which this need is interpreted. Most feminists have struggled to give women's need for reproductive technology a political status as one element of their broader rights to exercise control over their bodies and their lives. This, however, has not been the status given to the need for reproductive technology within the population establishment, although reproductive choice is more frequently invoked now as a secondary rationale for their programmes. Rather, the official interpretation has been to conflate women's needs for reproductive choice with the policy needs generated by long-standing concerns with population control. Consequently, official population policy has frequently operated as a denial of women's choice, rather than as an enhancement. In addition, the vagaries of First World politics juxtaposed with the asymmetrical nature of political accountability in donor funding have led to politically driven shifts and reversals in official definitions of reproductive choice for Third World women. This is well illustrated in an examination of US population policy, summarized here from Jaquette and Staudt (1988).

In the sixties, the publications of an influential book by Paul Ehrlich (1968) predicting global apocalypse as a result of unrestricted population growth, combined with fears of political instability in the Third

World as a result of such growth, had led to USAID support for the theory that 'overpopulation' was the primary cause of Third World poverty. From the title of Ehrlich's book (*The Population Bomb*) to the close association posited between the population explosion in the Third World and US security interests, to the militaristic terminology used to describe it, this support was manifested as a 'war' on population. Ravenholt, then director of USAID, adopted what he called a policy of 'contraceptive inundation' to deal with 'the people epidemic', with women singled out as its biological 'first cause'.

US policy was strongly criticized for its preoccupation with the population problem by Third World countries at the 1974 Population conference. It also came in for strong attack within the US by the women's movement as a result of the publicity given to its practice of dumping unsafe contraceptives on the Third World. AID subsequently modified its single-minded focus on the dissemination of contraceptives and began devoting more resources to investigating and addressing the social conditions that gave rise to the demand for children. However, by the time the Second International Conference was held in Mexico in 1984, positions had reversed. Third World countries were now generally committed to the idea that their resources could not support unrestricted population growth, while the US position had swung around radically in deference to developments in its domestic politics. The neo-liberal stance of the Reagan regime led to the attribution of poor economic performance in Third World countries to excessive state intervention rather than to over-population; private enterprise and market-led growth were now seen as the best contraceptive. The Reagan government adopted a 'neutral stance' on population growth but withdrew all support from any development agency that was associated with provision of abortion. 'With this one stroke the Reagan administration was able to pay a debt to the moral majority . . . underline its rejection of Third World demands for a New International Economic Order . . . and reinforce its message that capitalism is the only model that works' (Jaquette and Staudt, 1988, p. 226).

Jaquette and Staudt point to the lack of accountability built into foreign-assistance flows so that the definition of population as an issue and its translation into US development assistance occurs outside the 'political feedback loop' which might have helped to soften policy excesses: 'one of the virtues of a *pluralist political process* – that those affected by policies are actively involved in setting those policies and monitoring their implementation – was absent' (p. 215). In fact, the absence of women's interests in the shaping of population policy has been one of its enduring characteristics across the world. In some contexts, women enter the policy process only as the targeted clients of family-planning services which frequently violate the principles of human rights and reproductive choice. In others, they are denied the ability to curtail their fertility on the grounds of religious doctrine or because the national interest is deemed to be served by high-growth demographic regimes.

Examples of coercive practices – and a concomitant indifference to human rights – abound in the literature on family planning. Occasionally official attempts to enforce particular forms of fertility behaviour have taken the form of overt violation of human rights. This, for instance, occurred during the Emergency in India in 1975/76 when central government pressure on family-planning workers to meet sterilization quotas led to the setting up of vasectomy camps and police raids to round up 'eligible' men for forcible sterilization (Gwatkin, 1979; Banerji, 1980). More often, however, coercive measures are brought to bear on targeted populations in other, more hidden ways: through the highly selective promotion of contraceptive technology, through the use of incentives and disincentives, or through the selective dissemination of particular methods. Thus a team of demographers working in South India noted that local family-planning clinics gave wealthy villagers a choice of contraception, but offered the poor no alternative to sterilization (Caldwell et al., 1982). An editorial in a prestigious Indian weekly commented in 1985: 'The family planning program is beginning to resemble a giant, over-developed and hyperactive limb growing out of an inefficient health system which is incapable of supervising and controlling it' (*Economic and Political Weekly*, vol. 20, no. 4, p. 1668).

The Puerto Rican example is discussed in Mass's critique of US population assistance. Economically integrated into the US since the start of the century, Puerto Rico passed a law legitimizing sterilization in 1937. By 1968 around a third of Puerto Rican women of child-bearing age had been sterilized on the island, supported initially by private American funds and subsequently by the US government under Johnson. The opinion of an eminent demographer, J.M. Stycos, was that many physicians on the island supported sterilization because 'they thought and still think that contraceptive methods are too difficult for lower-class Puerto Rican women' (quoted in Mass, 1976, p. 95). The contempt for women's ability to make choices implicit in the programme was also revealed by evidence showing that many women had not been informed about the irreversibility of sterilization, that other forms of contraception were either not available or prohibitively expensive, and that doctors were reimbursed financially for every operation conducted.

China also used a strong system of incentives and disincentives to enforce its one-child policy. Between 1975 and 1985, stringent measures taken to implement the policy included forced abortions, compulsory sterilization of one spouse after the second child, and compulsory IUD insertions. It is also believed to have created an increase in female infanticide (*People's Daily* reports, cited in Hillier, 1988). In Bangladesh, a number of major donors, including the Dutch, British, Scandinavians and UNICEF expressed their unhappiness over the incentive system, sterilization abuses and neglect of MCH services, and demanded assurances that the World Bank Population III programme would be reformed and monitored (Hartmann and Standing, 1989). In Kenya, the emphasis on population control in many foreign-funded programmes laid them open to suspicions of 'genocidal intent' (Sai, 1973; Warwick, 1982; Bondestam, 1980).

The effects of pro-natalist policies that pressurize women to have more children than they want have been as repugnant as those which enforce lower fertility. Religion remains a powerful force in denying women the right to contraception and abortion in both First and Third Worlds. The Catholic Church, for instance, maintains an implacable hostility to both. Yet its prohibition on abortion is little more than a hundred years old. Prior to that, a controversy had raged about 'ensoulment': at what point does the foetus become human and receive a soul so that abortion becomes homicide? It had been the Church's position that ensoulment did not take place prior to 'quickening' or foetal movements, which in a first pregnancy occurs around fifteen to seventeen weeks, so that by implication, abortion prior to this period did not constitute a mortal sin. Currently, however, the Church position is that a fertilized ovum constitutes a genuine human person from the moment of conception and therefore possesses an inalienable right to life. However, the Church's own confusion on this matter is suggested by the fact that newly fertilized ova are not regarded as human persons, except in the context of abortion, so that fertilized ova which fail to implant (around 50 per cent) and are discharged normally by the body are not baptised. 'Most significantly, a foetus which miscarries even at a late stage of pregnancy is neither baptised as a matter of ecclesiastical decree nor given a church burial.' As Greer (1984) points out, such rituals would be in keeping with the Church's position that it takes life before birth very seriously: 'The fact that they do not carry out rituals of this kind suggests that in fact they do not really believe what they maintain in polemic' (p. 161).

Despite the almost total lack of abortion in the Republic of Ireland, and its severe restriction in Northern Ireland, Irish women in the twenty-two to twenty-five age group are as likely to have an abortion as their English counterparts, and more Irish women per head of the population have abortions than in Holland or Denmark. Criminalizing abortion has never prevented it; it simply increases its human and material costs to women. (The highly publicized case in 1992 of a fourteen-year-old Irish schoolgirl, pregnant as a result of rape, taken by her parents to England for an abortion and then forced to return by an Irish High Court injunction, drew attention to what some of these costs might be.)

Draconian measures to deny women the right to control their fertility were taken in Romania[1] where, in an effort to curb the decline and ageing of the population, the Ceauşescu regime declared abortion and family planning illegal. Women had to submit to checks every three months to ensure that they were not using birth control. The crude birth rate rose from 14.3 to 27.4 between 1966 and 1967 and total fertility rate increased from 1.9 to 3.7 children. However, as a World Bank report points out, there were high human costs to this 'apparent policy "success"' (World Bank, 1991, p. 128). An illegal abortion industry sprang up as women turned to any means, including self-induced abortions, to control their fertility, and birth rates began a steady decline by 1967. Women also avoided gynaecological examinations and Romania now has the highest rate of cervical cancer mortality in Europe. Maternal mortality rates jumped from under 70 per 100,000 live births in 1965 to over 150 in 1967, with 85 per cent attributable to abortion. Infant mortality rates increased from 46.6 to 59.5 per thousand between 1967 and 1968 largely due to abandonment or neglect of unwanted infants (World Bank, 1991). The other tragic casualties of the policy were the thousands of children placed in institutional care. Most of them came from the economically most vulnerable subgroups: gypsies; young, unmarried or single mothers; the physically and mentally ill. In other words, it appeared that poverty conditions in combination with large family sizes were the key factors associated with the institutionalization of children. A study conducted by UNICEF and the Romanian government comments on the human tragedy of the unwanted child: 'compromised parent–child attachment can lead to abandonment, child abuse and neglect, failure to thrive, depression and mental illness in later life, maternal feelings of incompetence, postpartum depression and development delay' (1991, p. 24).

Feminist Debates and the Politics of
Needs Interpretation

For feminists, the issue of reproductive rights crystallizes in many ways the whole question of women's rights over their own bodies. It is in the area of reproduction that women's bodies and social experiences differ most significantly from those of men. Women's rights to bear or not bear children is considered central to their sense of selfhood: 'our bodies *are* our selves'. Consequently, contraceptive technology appeared to hold out to women the promise of greater control over their own bodies. However, among feminists also, the politics of reproductive needs have led to conflicting positions on the question of reproductive technology. For some, women's ability to adopt family planning was seen as indicative of their greater autonomy over their lives. Writing from Bangladesh, Sattar (1979) suggested that 'any support to the family planning programme is a support to women and children . . . Acceptance of a family planning method means that a woman can control her own fertility. This leads very often to a gain in self-confidence and is the first step to a woman looking outside the home for work' (pp. 13–14).

By and large, however, feminists have perceived official population programmes as an infringement on women's autonomy rather than an enhancement of it. Their opposition to them has generally been aligned with different political perspectives on the women's question in development. Written in the 1970s, Mass's critique cited earlier offers a dependency feminist analysis of population programmes. Her study asked why women's right to birth control, a potentially progressive demand, had long been supported by oppressive states, and whose interests were thus served. She concluded that birth control offered under the aegis of population control served a variety of imperialist interests. She noted that these interests had their own 'dependency theory', viz. the consumption drain on economic growth represented by the large proportion of young dependents in Latin American populations. However, she suggested that this focus on overpopulation as the cause of underdevelopment was an 'elaborate veiling of the system's unequal distribution of wealth and its exploitation of labour power' (p. 3) and its inability to generate sufficient growth in the Third World to be able to feed and provide work for its population. She expressed serious doubts about the possibility of safe family planning in a world where 'self-interested motives for US population programs [are] spread internationally' (p. 181) and concluded that 'only when private property is abolished and the economy produces and reproduces for the entire society, can men and women carefully plan their

futures, their family's future and the future of their country'. As part
of a more immediate strategy, however, she suggested that women
activists needed to struggle for better health care, including access to
safe birth planning in a way which took account of the needs of the
majority rather than those of a privileged minority. Very specific
demands could be made on the state for maternity care, proper
medical services, dependable child care, low-cost and safe birth
control, and abortion with follow-up care, but 'all these demands
should be connected to the right to organize in hospitals for better
wages, working conditions and workers' control . . . not to place birth
control in a context in which it includes the needs of the majority is to
betray women's struggles for complete emancipation' (pp. 12–13). She
concluded that '"Freedom to control our bodies" may one day happen
within the framework of working-class goals, such as quality health
services for everyone – and the prevention of genocidal population/
sterilization programs' (p. 12).

However, mounting evidence that human-rights abuses in population-control programmes were not merely the outcome of US
imperialism but also figured as part of the national agendas of many
Third World and socialist countries has strengthened the view among
other feminists that patriarchal interests, rather than purely capitalist
ones, were at stake in official attempts to establish control over
women's bodies. The politics of the Feminist International Network of
Resistance to Reproductive and Genetic Engineering (FINRRAGE) is
the clearest expression of this position. Described as one of its leading
members, Mies has played an influential role in articulating the
rationale for FINRRAGE's opposition to the population establishment. Flowing logically from her analysis that the interests of the
global capitalist patriarchy are served through their control over the
technologies of destruction is her stance on the question of reproductive technology as yet another manifestation of 'technopatriarchal'
control over women. Mies suggests that the international battle over
women's bodies has entailed a dual strategy of discouraging poor
women from the South from breeding more poor people who might
one day claim a share of the wealth robbed from them, while middle-
class women, particularly those in the North, are encouraged to breed
because they add to consumption demand, which drives capital
accumulation (Mies, 1989). She cites evidence that demonstrates what
FINRRAGE members see as the basically anti-women, aggressive and
sadistic nature of reproductive engineers or 'technodocs'. The
Declaration that emerged out of a conference organized in Bangladesh by FINRRAGE in 1989 poses a stark opposition between
destructive 'man-made' technologies, on the one hand, and female

skills in dealing with nature in a compassionate, humane and ecologi-
cally sustainable way, on the other: 'We want to renew, reaffirm and
build upon this female tradition.'

Akhter (1988) another FINRRAGE member, supports its indict-
ment of the 'anti-natural' effects of modern reproductive technologies: 'From a natural point of view, the human species are endowed
with the power to procreate. It is a vital power that ensures the species'
survival. But contraceptive technologies in this case act against this
power. They mutilate the human body, interfere with the biological
processes, and build barriers with the reproductive organs, disrupting
bodily functions' (p. 153). She also draws attention to the repressive
ways in which international population controllers, supported by
coercive state machineries and the 'technodocs', have identified
women in a deliberate policy to 'depopulate' Bangladesh: 'uteri of
Bangladeshi women have become the direct hit of the population
controllers through the mediation of the state' (p. 156).

While the potential of traditional medicine has certainly been
neglected by the population establishment, and shrugged off by the
pharmaceutical industry, and while reproductive technologies have
been distributed in ways that frequently violate human rights, the
'either/or' politics of FINRRAGE paradoxically also leads to a denial of
choice to women. The blanket condemnation of all forms of reproductive technology frequently leads FINRRAGE members to deny the
legitimacy of the expressed needs and practices of women in many
parts of the world, and to shrug off the possibility that women may
choose contraceptive methods, with full knowledge of the risks. The
militaristic terminology adopted by FINRRAGE members echoes, in
many ways, the language of the population-control establishment,
suggesting that they are also engaged in a war over who should control
women's bodies and reproductive capacity. And, as in many wars, it
appears that there can be only two sides. Akhter suggests that women
are motivated to accept contraceptive methods, specifically those
promoted by the population controllers, by the creation of an
environment in which they are made to think that they are 'stupid' if
they do not accept' (Akhter, 1988, p. 158). Yet the views that she
advances are the mirror image of those she attributes to the population
establishment. If the population controllers created a situation where
women felt 'stupid' if they did not accept reproductive technologies,
FINRRAGE members appear to regard women as dupes of patriarchy
if they do.

The argument that women might want to use reproductive technologies in order to have – or not have – children is given short shrift by
most FINRRAGE members. The 1989 conference devoted some time

to discussing the hopes and despair of women seeking IVF (in vitro fertilization) treatment, but as Ute Winkler (FINRRAGE) declared, such women were 'simply objects of such techniques'.[2] She argued that it was necessary simultaneously to expose the use of IVF and to offer counselling to infertile women to reject IVF:

> We cannot wait until we have convinced all women who are infertile that they should reject IVF before we . . . formulate our position in public. Just knowing that women are opposed to IVF may give these women the support they need to stop or reject IVF treatment. . . . And don't forget: IVF is not a solution for infertility. Women are still infertile when they conceive through IVF.

Equally the argument that women might wish to use reproductive technology to control their fertility is dismissed as merely reflecting coercive male sexuality rather than women's self-identified need. As the 1989 conference report notes:

> Kamaxi of India reported that poor women in the villages do want to get contraception because they do not want to bear so many children. It is not only a demand of the educated women. In reply to that, Farida (Akhter) said, it is because the poor women in the villages do not have the power to say no to the sexual desire of men. We probably need to change our ways of looking at problems.

The question of men's sexual access was brought up elsewhere in the conference report when another Indian participant argued that 'We can change the man–woman relationship in 100 years, but right now we have 20 million people who want contraceptives.' This was challenged by Klein (FINRRAGE), who argued that women's demands for contraception had to be seen in the context of men's belief in their rights to sexual access to women.

The report concluded that, 'There was some disagreement expressed regarding the individuality involved in the act of sexual relationships and many came away with different understandings of what was being said.' One such 'different understanding' of sexuality from that apparently subscribed to by FINRRAGE members would suggest that sexual pleasure is not simply the monopoly of men, that it is not always imposed by men on women, and that the desire to use contraception may also represent a desire by women to enjoy sex without anxieties about unplanned pregnancy. One version of this alternative view is offered in a monograph compiled by three feminists active in the arena of reproductive rights in India: (Chayanika, Swatija and Kamaxi, 1990):

We, as women ourselves and as users of birth control methods have to clearly state loudly and clearly that if we want any contraception it is in order to have some measure of control over our lives. We want it so that we can be free to express ourselves sexually. We need it so that we and our children are not forced upon each other. We have been using it so that our full potential as human beings can be nurtured, so that we are not completely circumscribed by our capacity to procreate. (p. 71)

FINRRAGE puts forward many legitimate criticisms of the current state of reproductive technology and policy, but its arguments betray a disregard for the needs of different women and a lack of respect for women who do not share their views. Its blanket conflation of technology with patriarchy, of use with abuse, undermine what would otherwise have been a powerful critique of the population establishment. In the next section, I would like to argue that policies which promote reproductive technology as an element of reproductive choice can be compatible with, and indeed crucial to, a broader feminist goal of equitable development. We need to consider population policies in terms of two crucial and related dimensions: the problems associated with the technology itself and those stemming from the interests that are promoted through, and the power relations that govern, the formulation, design and implementation of current population policies. Although the population establishment has had considerable power in defining reproductive possibilities for women, it has not been able to do it unchallenged. The issue of reproductive rights has been fought for by a variety of actors and institutions over the past decades and is finally being recognized as a legitimate concern within the development field. It is now essential to carry the politics of needs identification into what Fraser identifies as a second arena of struggle: the politics of needs satisfaction.

The Case for a Feminist Population Policy

A feminist perspective on population policy would have to recognize both the profound social implications of child-bearing as well as its implications for individual women. Women experience motherhood in contradictory ways. It can be experienced as a socially imposed institution, which in some contexts is the only source of social recognition available to them. It is also experienced as a deeply personal relationship between themselves, their bodies and their children (Rich, 1976). At the same time, as Sen and Grown (1985) point out, 'Women know that child bearing is a social, not purely personal, phenomenon; nor do we deny that world population trends are likely to exert considerable pressure on resources and institutions by the end of this century' (p. 42).

It is this interweaving between individual and social dimensions that invests the decision to bear or not to bear children with such complex and far-reaching ramifications. It has become clear that many of the old connections made between public good and private choice in the formulation of official population policy were far too simplistic. As the World Bank acknowledges, 'birth control is not just a technical and demographic issue; it has a moral and a cultural dimension. Becoming a parent is both a deeply personal event and – in virtually all societies – central to community life as well' (1984, p. 160). The 1984 World Bank Report has sought to distance itself from any hint of 'neo-Malthusian descriptions of population as a problem' (p. 184) in its analysis of the link between development and population change. For the next five or six decades, according to the Report, the problem of poverty 'goes beyond one of global resources and is less easily amenable to any technological fix' (p. 184). The report recognizes that, while the social costs of large families may be high in terms of long-term investments in the standard of living and economic growth, poor parents are making a reasonable choice in having many children. The conditions of poverty frequently engender high fertility.

The new danger is that current concerns about possible links between population growth and environmental problems may give fresh life to fertility-reduction arguments for population policy. Here, too, it is clear that there is need for caution (Repetto, 1985; Rodgers, 1984; Commoner, 1988); the study of these interrelationships must also include their mediation by different modes of resource exploitation and consumption patterns. The needs of the world's poor, on the one hand, and the greed of the world's rich, on the other, are the two forces driving the population–consumption–environment connection. One arises out of the search of poor populations seeking to squeeze a livelihood from fragile environments, thereby causing soil depletion, deforestation and other forms of localized destruction of the habitat. The other, which speeds up global warming through 'gas-guzzling' cars and large-scale deforestation for industrial or export-oriented cattle rearing, can be attributed to the consumption patterns of the affluent. It may well be that high fertility rates are a part of the response of poor people to their poverty and therefore implicated in environmental degradation. But it should also be borne in mind, given that a disproportionate amount of the world's resources are consumed by a small minority located mainly in the North, that the greed of a wealthy minority, rather than the need of the world's poor, deserves a disproportionate share of the blame (see Action Aid Development Report No. 5, 1991 for some illustrative figures).

A population policy that is concerned with the needs of the poor, as well as with the preservation of the natural environment, has to break finally with the narrow fertility-reduction goals of the past and address the social conditions in which reproductive choices can be enhanced. When the focus is shifted from the social dimensions of reproductive behaviour to the personal dimensions, the same conclusions emerge. That women (and sometimes men) all over the world want access to reproductive technology is testified to both within statistical surveys as well in the testimony of development and feminist activists (Dixon-Mueller and Germain, 1992; Chayanika et al., 1990; Sen and Grown, 1985; Torres, 1990; Petchesky and Weiner, 1990; Huq, 1992). There are sound reasons for addressing this need. We have noted already the unequal gender division of labour, rights and responsibilities in the area of reproductive behaviour. While it may be in the interests of domestic collectivities to have large numbers of children, the costs and benefits of such a strategy are not equally distributed within the family. Put simply, patriarchally organized families ensure that senior male members reap the benefits of large families while women in the reproductive ages bear the costs in the form of high rates of maternal morbidity and mortality. Surely any notion of social justice, and certainly any notion of gender equity, demands that those who bear the main burden of reproductive responsibilities should also enjoy a measure of reproductive choice.

However, as long as it is in the interests of domestic collectivities to enforce particular patterns of fertility behaviour, women are unlikely to exercise very much control over their reproduction. The slow progress made by family-planning programmes, despite the resources invested in them, in bringing about a change in fertility behaviour highlights the limitations of purely individual solutions. A more promising route forward is suggested by research which shows that birth rates declined most in countries where socio-economic development was relatively advanced and family-planning programmes were strong (Costa Rica, Korea and Singapore), and roughly equal in countries where one, but not the other, of the two conditions held (World Bank, 1984). Thus there were only modest declines in birth rates where (a) development was strong but family planning relatively weak (Brazil and Turkey); and (b) where development levels were low but family-planning provision was strong (India and Indonesia). Clearly family planning works best where it complements and re-inforces certain aspects of developmental change. This is best illus-trated by individual country case studies, notably Kerala, Cuba,

Sri Lanka and South Korea, which, though differing in political orientations and levels of development, all experienced major declines in their fertility rates without intensive population-control efforts. The key factors involved were: income and land redistribution: employment opportunities and education; mass education; improvements in the position of women; accessible health care and family-planning services.

Sen (1989) also confirms a correlation between national fertility rates and a combination of infant mortality rates and selected indicators of women's status (female secondary education, their age at marriage); the correlation is further strengthened by the existence of a strong family-planning effort. What is striking about these findings is the suggestion that reproductive behaviour is most likely to change in conditions of development equity. Wide-ranging social reforms of this kind ensure that the benefits from economic progress are more equitably shared by all sections of the community rather than being concentrated on a privileged few. They provide households with extra-familial resources for their survival and security, thus diminishing the incentive to have large families. Furthermore, the reductions in infant mortality rates that accompany social development reduce the uncertainties surrounding children's chances of survival, which have in the past made large numbers of births so essential. Countries that have high rates of infant mortality generally have not experienced a lowering of birth rates. What this suggests is that if enhancing women's reproductive choice, in their own interests and in the interests of society, is seen as the primary 'end' of population policy, well-thought-through family-planning programmes are only one of the means. Policies which seek to improve women's reproductive choices cannot confine themselves to the narrow parameters of family-planning programmes; they need to address the social conditions in which these choices are made. The problem is that these broader connections have seldom been operationalized within the policy process. National and international policymaking bodies have operated as though there were two different groups of women in the Third World, 'one with reproductive responsibilities who are the target of health and nutrition projects, and another group with productive responsibilities who are the target of agricultural and income generation projects' (Leslie, 1989, p. 6). Among agencies concerned with human resource development, there are further subdivisions; among multilateral agencies, for instance, between those concerned with general health care (WHO), those concerned with women's reproductive capacity (UNFPA), and those concerned with children's health (UNICEF). The consequence of this division of responsibilities is that different sectors have independently devised interventions which require women's participation, without paying adequate attention to overall demands on women's energy, time and health. Furthermore, agencies concerned with human resources have tended to focus on women as the family's health agents and reproducers to the detriment of their health needs and well-being as producers. If the focus is broadened to take account of women's role in production as well as reproduction, it becomes obvious that the productivity of both the present and future generations of a country's labour force depend critically on women's well-being.

Clearly the provision of contraceptive technology should remain on the policy agenda since it is an important element of reproductive well-being. But the manner of provision has to be radically rethought in the light of past abuses. Furthermore, contraceptive provision should be seen as only one element in a broader package of measures whose goal is to enhance women's well-being and rights over their own bodies. The other elements in this broader package have to be determined through country-specific analyses of population–health–development linkages. The rest of this chapter offers a number of principles and guidelines for a population policy that seeks the goal of gender equity and reproductive choice rather than fertility reduction per se. Starting with the question of 'gender-awareness' within family-planning programmes themselves, it progressively broadens its focus to take account of gender relations within societies at large.

A User Perspective on Family-Planning Programmes

The controversy, resistance and setbacks encountered by family-planning programmes in the Third World since their inception in the 1960s have largely been generated in opposition to the interests they are perceived to serve. 'Family planning has been perceived by large numbers of people . . . as being more politically oriented than health attuned . . . Many approaches have favoured top-down efforts with their predominant focus at national and government levels of administration' (Syme, 1987). The two charges most frequently levelled against the population establishment have been insensitivity to women's reproductive rights and indifference to women's reproductive needs. These must be the starting premiss for all interventions in this field. The 'user perspective' developed by the Population Council appears to be an attempt to operationalize this viewpoint. It emphasizes the human factor in family planning (Bruce, 1980), pointing out that sustained use of contraception requires services that take account – *and are seen to be taking account* – of individual needs and well-being. This can be achieved in a number different ways.

First of all, reproductive choice must be operationalized through offering a *choice of methods*. The selective promotion of forms of contraception that remove reproductive control from women (sterilization, injectibles, implants and so on) does little to reassure the population that the interests of users have shaped the provision of services. Reproductive choice means recognizing that women do not have uniform needs and are best served through access to the widest range of contraceptive methods compatible with their health. This would allow different subgroups of women in the reproductive ages to tailor their contraceptive practice to their individual health needs and social circumstances. It would allow them to plan the number and spacing of children, delaying the first birth, terminating reproduction and replacing child loss. It would allow the possibility of switching methods as an alternative to discontinuation when a particular form of contraception proved unsatisfactory. It would recognize that women at different stages of their life cycle have different health requirements.

Safe menstrual regulation and abortion are essential within the choice of methods because of the possibility of contraceptive failure or non-use, as well as to mitigate the more traumatic conditions caused by rape, incest or risks to the mother's life. Wider provision of contraceptives *can* diminish the incidence, but *cannot* prevent all unwanted pregnancies. Abortion remains a major means of fertility control in the world. About 33 million safe, legal abortions are carried out each year. Clandestine procedures raise the total to between 45 to 60 million (Black, 1987). Globally this means that there are between twenty-four and thirty-two induced abortions for every one hundred known pregnancies. It was pointed out at a recent international symposium on women's health that throughout history women have resorted to abortion, whether legal or not, for the sake of themselves and for their children (Mair, 1989) and that restrictive laws do not stop abortions – they simply make them unsafe (Germain, 1989). Indeed, an estimated 200,000 or more Third World women die needlessly each year due to botched abortions; additional uncounted thousands suffer severe morbidity problems, including infertility and chronic ill-health. Unwanted pregnancies threaten women's health, well-being and human rights; they also result in the tragedy of unwanted or abandoned children and infanticide. The slogan of the women's movement in the UK in the 1970s in response to legislative attempts to curtail the availability of abortion remains pertinent today: 'Every child a *wanted* child, every mother a *willing* mother.'

Fortunately, current thinking on abortion appears to be moving from a concentration on its criminality to a concern with women's health and family well-being. Over the past two decades, at least sixty-five jurisdictions have liberalized their abortion laws; only four countries have restricted the grounds for procedure (Cook, 1989). However, 28 per cent of the world's population still lives in countries where abortion is either illegal or can only be performed to save a women's life. The differential rate of abortion-law reform between industrialized and developing countries is an important factor in explaining differential rates of maternal mortality and morbidity between these two regions (Cook, 1989). Legalization alone does not guarantee availability of abortion services (Sai and Nassim, 1989). In India, for instance, where abortion is legal, only one in six abortions are provided by trained personnel in safe conditions. In Bangladesh, menstrual regulation services recognized and supported as a preventive health service reach only 10–20 per cent of the 75,000 women who attempt to terminate pregnancy every year. Enabling legislation together with the provision of widespread low-cost services are therefore integral and complementary components for successful family planning.

Closely related to the question of reproductive choice is that of *reproductive safety*. In general, the population establishment have used efficacy of method as the main criterion guiding research and dissemination in this field. Indeed, as Naripokkho (a women's organization in Bangladesh) found through its dialogues with health and family-planning officials, notions of risk and safety are often used in the official discourse to apply to the likelihood of pregnancy associated with contraceptive failure rather than to the effects on women's health from its use. The pharmaceutical industry has concentrated its efforts on systemic and surgical methods of birth control; female hormonal methods, in particular, have received a disproportionate share of research funds. While these are generally less safe in health terms than barrier methods, they are also more profitable and receive greater recognition and prestige within the medical establishment. In addition, the industry has frequently tried out new methods of contraception on the population of Third World countries before such methods have passed safety regulations in the First World. Thus, in the early 1970s, USAID was accused of 'dumping' high oestrogen (higher risk) pills, which had been obtained at low prices from their manufacturers, on the population of Third World countries. Depo-Provera, an injectable, hormonal contraceptive manufactured by a US firm, has high rates of dissemination in large numbers of Third World countries. However, its use is restricted to specific categories of women in Sweden, West Germany and the UK, and banned in the United States where studies of its effects on humans are deemed insufficient to confirm or refute the risk of cancer. More recently, Norplant (encapsulated hormones inserted under the skin of the arm, which prevent pregnancy for at least five years) has also been promoted in the Third World before having been approved in the United States and some other European countries.

Advocates of population control often justify this apparent indifference to the health risks of contraceptive technology by weighing them against mortality risks from pregnancy. As the journal *Population Reports* claims, 'With all methods, family planning in developing countries is much safer than childbearing.' However, some of the flaws of this position have been summarized by Hartmann and Standing (1989) who note that such an argument penalizes the poor for their poverty. High maternal mortality rates are not only the consequence of high fertility, but also the product of inadequate nutrition, poor health services and other aspects of poverty. Furthermore, the health risks associated with contraceptives are likely to be higher among Third World women, who are, on average, more malnourished, and have poorer sanitary facilities and health services than their counterparts in developed countries.

The insensitivity to women's health concerns that characterizes many family-planning programmes probably accounts for persistent reports of unpleasant side effects associated with many contraceptives and which lead to high drop rates, belying the favourable picture that might be suggested by high contraceptive acceptance rates. An overview of client reactions to family-planning programmes in eight developing countries concluded that 'the most common client reactions were: disinterest in program services; initial acceptance followed by subsequent discontinuation; subversion of the program by rumours: *and in a minority of the cases, full acceptance and use of the service provided*' (Warwick, 1982, p. 164, emphasis in original). A World Bank study in Kenya found that the family-planning programme between 1974 and 1978 had concentrated almost entirely on the dissemination of pills to the neglect of other forms of contraception. Contraceptive side effects led to high drop-out rates so that the programme was more successful in recruiting acceptors than in retaining them (World Bank, 1980b). Zeidenstein cites survey evidence from a number of developing countries which indicated that 44 per cent of IUD acceptors and 71 per cent of pill acceptors had discontinued within twenty-four months of acceptance (1980, p. 26). In view of the vast sums of money spent annually on these programmes and the evidence of unmet need in the population, there are clearly 'important gaps in perception' (Zeiden-stein, 1980, p. 26) that need to be bridged between those who design and develop programmes and those who use them. As Winikoff and Sullivan (1987, p. 135) point out, the short continuation rates and low rates of effectiveness associated with so many family-planning pro-grammes suggest that 'the reality of contraceptive practice is one of a high incidence of failure'. Sporadic use and early discontinuation of contraception does not serve either the narrower objective of fertility reduction or the broader one of reproductive choice. Safety consid-erations require that the provision of contraceptive services should be judged both in terms of their effectiveness as well as their health implications for women. If there is a trade-off, then it is one that women must make an informed choice about for themselves. Further-more, all provision should always include comprehensive screening of potential clients to ascertain their suitability for particular methods, as well as subsequent follow-up procedures to minimize the possibility of adverse side effects.

Finally, the users' perspective in family planning requires channels for *information sharing* between users and providers. The absence of such channels often accounts for the understandable fears, specula-tion, rumours and mutual suspicion that have characterized relations between official providers and users within the community. The formation of user groups, perhaps building on existing cooperatives and women's groups, the use of participatory forms of appraisal and research, and the adoption of institutional mechanisms for communi-cation, feed-back and interaction between users, planners and pro-viders will help ensure greater responsiveness to users' needs and continuous monitoring of programme effectiveness. Such mechan-isms can be used by family-planning workers to provide information about various aspects of their work: the safety and suitability of various forms of contraception; the need to return for follow-up services; the availability of counselling for abortion patients, and so on. They can also be utilized by users to provide evaluative information about the services received.

Indicators of success for family-planning programmes need to go beyond simple target fulfilment or contraceptive acceptance rates. Bruce (1980), for instance, suggests a variety of ways of evaluating such programmes which go beyond measuring 'intentions' (for ex-ample, policy statements, budgets) to results (births spaced or averted). One measure of long-term effectiveness in family-planning pro-grammes worth noting is *extended use-effectiveness* (Tietze and Lewitt,

1968, cited in Bruce, 1980), which measures rates of pregnancy by first method used, ignoring whether pregnancy was accidental or not, and counting only unwanted pregnancies. Here the emphasis is not on the success or failure of individual women in using contraception, but on whether programmes have instructed their clients sufficiently and offered them effective alternatives if they needed to switch for any particular reason.

Greater institutional responsiveness also requires that many more women are involved in decision-making roles at every programme level. At present, women appear mainly as field-level workers or as users of contraceptive techniques. But, as Zeidenstein (1980) points out, 'a program cannot possibly comprehend women's views about availability, choice, self-selection, program responsiveness, learning opportunities or integration into woman's life experiences without women in vital decision-making roles at every level' (p. 28). The challenge, he points out, is to institute some form of affirmative action that will enable the recruitment, training and support for women in decision-making roles, rather than to wait until women with suitable qualifications present themselves.

Factoring Gender In: Making Men Visible in Family-Planning Programmes

Men have been the invisible gender in family-planning discourse and policy: programmes tend to operate as though contraceptive users must necessarily be women. This focus ignores the potential offered by primarily 'male methods' of contraception – condoms, vasectomy and withdrawal – as well as periodic abstinence, a method that requires the cooperation of both partners. It also places the responsibilities and risks of contraception solely with women. Yet until around thirty years ago, the few contraceptive methods available were mostly male methods and it is likely that the 'demographic transition' from high to low fertility regimes in Europe and North America was achieved mainly through the widespread use of withdrawal. Surveys carried out in the US and the UK at the start of the 1960s suggested that 67 per cent and 95 per cent of married women respectively had relied at some stage on male methods (*Population Reports*, 1986). The introduction of oral contraceptives and the IUD shifted patterns of contraceptive use to women although there is some evidence of an increase in vasectomies in some Northern countries.

In developing countries as a whole in the 1970s and early 1980s, around 25 per cent of contracepting couples relied on methods which require male participation. In sub-Saharan Africa, where few people have access to family-planning services and overall contraceptive use is low, around 40 per cent of those using family-planning employ methods that require male cooperation – condoms, rhythm, withdrawal, as well as postpartum abstinence for birth spacing. Vasectomy is virtually non-existent in Africa. In the Asian and Pacific countries, where family-planning programmes are more widespread, male methods are relatively less important and are used by around 25 per cent of contracepting couples.

It appears, therefore, that the presence of family-planning programmes has actually discouraged male responsibility in planned parenthood. There are strong grounds for reversing this trend. The basic criteria of reproductive choice and use-effectiveness in contraceptive methods require that family planning be based on the mutual cooperation of women and men in deciding which method is appropriate for them at each stage of their reproductive lives. It is of course self-evident that the costs of unwanted pregnancies impinge more immediately and directly on women; however, in relationships based on mutual trust, responsibility for averting (or planning) births as well as for parenthood should ideally be shared by both women and men.

Male methods of contraception are often cheaper, safer and simpler than female methods. Condoms, for instance, are simple to use, safe, effective, cheap, easy to distribute and need no medical supervision. Furthermore, in addition to preventing pregnancy, they provide protection against sexually transmitted diseases, including AIDS. As a permanent family-planning method, vasectomy is a far simpler, cheaper and safer alternative than tubectomy, yet there are more female sterilizations in the world. The reasons are probably linked to both lack of motivation among men and the greater orientation of family-planning programmes to female methods of contraception. Coitus interruptus – or withdrawal – is considered the oldest form of contraceptive practice in the world and is widely sanctioned in Islamic countries. Again, compared to most female methods, it has no costs, requires no supplies or medical supervision. However, it is considered less effective than other methods.

Integrating men into family-planning programmes requires adopting many of the same features that should ideally characterize programmes for women. Thus men also require accessible services – widely distributed and available at all times – and a wide choice of methods, offered free or at minimal cost. Condoms in particular lend themselves to these requirements. Vasectomy offered in hygienic, well-organized clinics and centres should be made widely available as an effective way of terminating the reproductive cycle. Greater emphasis should also be placed on research into new forms of male contraception; one estimate suggests that only 8 per cent of the world's contraceptive budget is spent on developing male methods of contraception. However, in addition to these features, family-planning programmes for men may also need to incorporate a greater stress on encouraging men to share responsibility for family planning. It has been widely recognized that a major problem encountered in the dissemination of contraceptives is not women's lack of motivation, but the resistance of men. Since most family-planning programmes behaved as though women make decisions about family planning in a social vacuum, it is necessary to learn from the few examples available of attempts to reach men in the workplace, in the community and in health-care centres. The principle of responsible fatherhood has been promoted through a variety of means in a number of Third World countries (see *Population Reports*, Series J, No. 33, 1986). In Jamaica, the National Family Planning Board organized lectures, panel discussion, motivational seminars, community and workplace-based discussions, booklets, posters and campaigns in the mass media. In Mauritania, the Ministry of Health and Social Affairs organized a school for fathers to encourage men to be sensitive to women's health problems and family planning. Educational outreach programmes for young people have been organized in Hong Kong, Ireland and Sierra Leone, sometimes using telephone hotlines to offer information and advice in safe anonymity. The Caribbean Family Planning Affiliation developed radio spots, posters and videos as a part of male-responsibility campaigns in seven Caribbean islands, while both Nigeria and Zimbabwe have also used the media to address this issue. In India, the Husband Craft programme started by the Malavani Health Centre in Bombay to involve men in family-planning discussions, and in ante- and postnatal care for women found that 71 per cent of people attending the centre adopted family-planning measures after husbands had attended, compared to 15 per cent where husbands had not. Finally, lessons can also be drawn from the Population Education Programme of the International Labour Office, which has been a major promoter of employment-based educational programmes for over a decade. It has assisted employers and trade unions in various developing countries to set up family welfare services at the workplace and introduced population education into the curricula of vocational training courses. It is essential that men's responsibility for family welfare is not seen by policymakers solely in breadwinning terms.

Where is the M in MCH? The Neglect of
Women's Reproductive Health

Along with family planning, the other element in PHC that impinges
directly and specifically on women's health status is MCH (Mother and
Child Health) services. While the interlinkages between the health
status of mother and child are recognized by health policymakers,
their translation into primary health care strategies has tended to be
rather selective. Resources have been most strongly concentrated on
family-planning provision and, within MCH, on children's welfare.
According to World Bank estimates, most developing countries
allocate less than 20 per cent of their health budgets to maternal and
child health programmes and the bulk of these funds goes to child
health (Herz and Measham, 1987). Even information on mothers'
health is sparse. According to the WHO, while fifty out of fifty-two
countries have reported on infant mortality rates, only five have ever
reported on maternal mortality data. There is a general assumption
that 'what is good for the child is good for the mother' (Rosenfield and
Maine, 1985). The reverse relationship – the ramifications of the
mother's health status on the child's – has received far less attention.
Moreover, the causes of maternal mortality differ from those of child
death rates and require different remedies. The net result of this
neglect of the 'M in MCH' has been that primary health-care strategies
have had little impact on certain important aspects of women's
reproductive health and their repercussions on infant health.

Poor maternal health (malnutrition and chronic or acute infections)
combined with heavy manual work during pregnancy result in low-
weight babies with impaired chances of survival and high rates of
morbidity. As we have already noted in Chapter 7, the extremely high
rates of infant and child mortality in The Gambia were attributed by
the World Bank (1980) to 'the unsatisfactory situation of their
mothers, who usually are badly nourished and heavily overworked' (p.
19). In fact, around 18 per cent of children born in the developing
world are of low birth weight, with the highest percentages recorded
for Southern Asia followed by sub-Saharan Africa. Breast-milk
production is also likely to be inferior in malnourished mothers with
detrimental consequences for infant nutrition and immunity to
infection. Furthermore, evidence exists to suggest that a significant
proportion of infants whose mothers die are likely to die before the
age of one (Chen et al., 1974). Maternal health care is therefore a
logical precondition to children's welfare. However, maternal health
should not only be seen as a necessary adjunct to children's health. It is,
above all, an end in itself. An estimated 500,000 maternal deaths occur

annually of which over 99 per cent take place in the Third World, with
ratios of over 800 deaths per 100,000 live births in West Africa, to 55
per 100,000 live births in East Asia, and around 10 in the industrialized countries (Graham et al., 1989). Put differently, a woman's
lifetime chances of pregnancy-related death vary from 1 in 19 in East
and West Africa, to 1 in 34 in south and west Asia, to 1 in 722 in East
Asia, to 1 in 2,089 in Europe (Black, 1987). Whereas a child in the
developing world suffers a risk of death approximately four to ten
times higher than that of a child in Western Europe or North America,
a pregnant woman in the Third World bears approximately fifty to
one hundred times the risk of her counterpart in the developed world
(Winikoff, 1988). Moreover, figures on maternal deaths are likely to be
underestimates (Rosenfield and Maine, 1985). In the US, official data
on maternal mortality are thought to be an underestimate by 20 to 30
per cent. Inaccuracies in the Third World are likely to be even higher.

In any case, maternal deaths are just one aspect of the unnecessary
suffering that follows from the neglect of women's reproductive
health. While data on morbidity rates are rarely available, Rosenfield
and Maine point out that 'it is certain that for every woman who dies,
many more have serious long-term complications' (p. 83). One
estimate claims that for every maternal death that would be prevented
by greater attention to reproductive health facilities, at least ten
women would avoid serious health impairment from illness and
complications (Black, 1987). Some conditions arise directly from
pregnancy: haemorrhage, pregnancy-related hypertension, obstructed
labour, toxaemia. Others are exacerbated by pregnancy: anaemia,
heart disease, renal disease, malaria. Female circumcision is another
cause of avoidable sexual and birth trauma and maternal morbidity in
particular countries. Strong arguments have been put forward for
contraceptive usage as a means of reducing maternal mortality (Black,
1987; Herz and Measham, 1987). Given that deaths from botched
abortions constitute around 25 per cent of all maternal deaths, while
hospitalization costs for complications from abortions represent a
heavy drain on scarce health resources, legalization of abortion would
go far towards eliminating this source of risk. The other maternal
mortality risk factors associated with reproductive activity have been
summarized by Sadik as 'too young, too old, too many and too close'
(1989, p. 11):

- Very young age at pregnancy increases the chance of maternal
  deaths. Studies indicate that pregnancies to girls under 15 resulted
  in maternal mortality rates five to seven times higher than that in the
  20–24 age group.

- Older women are also at risk. Women over 35 are two to five times more likely to die as a result of childbirth as women in their twenties.
- High parity pregnancies are more likely to result in the mother's death than low parity ones; sixth and subsequent births caused maternal mortality that was two to three times higher than for second births.
- Finally, maternal mortality is higher when babies are born in quick succession to a mother whose body has not yet recovered from previous births.

Family planning will clearly have a role to play in reducing maternal mortality rates in the sense that the risk of dying from pregnancy-related complications is likely to be less if there are fewer pregnancies in a population. But reduced fertility rates do not in themselves lower the risk of dying from pregnancy in the same population. This is clearly demonstrated in findings based on the efficient demographic surveillance system in the Matlab district in Bangladesh (Koenig et al., 1988). Here a decade of well-funded family-planning services helped to increase contraceptive use, reduce fertility rates and consequently reduce the number of women in the reproductive ages who died from maternity-related causes. However, there appeared to be very little effect on the mortality risks associated with pregnancy. Thus women who did get pregnant were as much at risk of dying as in other parts of the country, that is, between five and seven deaths per thousand births. The authors of the study concluded that maternal mortality remains a major health problem in the Matlab area, in spite of a decade of successful family planning.

The risks associated with pregnancy are only partly reduced by greater targeting of family-planning services to the high-risk categories of potential mothers. As noted earlier, uncertain rates of continuation and effectiveness among contraceptive users mean that *both* family-planning acceptors and non-acceptors will continue to have need for reproductive health-care services to reduce maternal mortality and morbidity. Indeed, certain forms of family planning may themselves increase reproductive risk if adequate screening, counselling, clinical care and follow-up procedures are not part of the programme. Family planning is therefore only one element in a broader intervention strategy designed to ensure the prevention of unwanted pregnancies and the protection of women's health during wanted ones.

What is needed is the integration of MCH and family planning in place of the separation observed in most contexts. Summarizing from

Taylor and Berelson, (1971), the advantages of a health-backed family-planning service would be that:

- it would provide information and family-planning services through a trusted and knowledgeable system of care with broad and integrated health concerns;
- it could identify and offer services to women most at risk from further pregnancies;
- it has optimal chances of follow-up care and continuing services from the same professional personnel with healthful consequences for both mother and child;
- it could work towards a comprehensive system of vital registration;
- the personnel (midwives, physicians with obstetrical and gynaeco-logical training, community health workers), the facilities, examining rooms and instruments needed for family planning work, are similar to those needed for MCH services, so there are important potential economies of scale.

As Taylor and Berelson stress, the prerequisite for all endeavours in the family-planning/MCH field is 'an infrastructure competent to direct and provide relevant information and services to the people' (p. 22). The World Bank Safe Motherhood proposal points out that the reduction of maternal mortality and morbidity, like all aspects of primary health care, requires a tiered system of health-service provision with as much emphasis as possible on prevention or early treatment of health problems. However, each element of the system must be effective since no health-care programme can really work through action at one level only. In addition, to incorporating a user's perspective, there needs to be sufficient attention to both primary and clinical facilities for an effective reproductive health-care system. Two interrelated elements emerge as the basis for such a system.

The first is the establishment of community-based care through the organization of outreach networks in the community consisting, for example, of satellite and mobile clinics, user groups, community health workers and traditional village midwives, all of whom could be mobilized to provide backup in the referral and educational functions of the health service. While a number of programmes to train traditional birth attendants are underway, they are often one-off efforts and their emphasis on 'technical know-how' without sufficient explanation of 'technical know-why' means that the lessons imparted are rapidly forgotten; more systematic follow-up training might help to avoid this.[3] The second entails ensuring access to clinic-based services. The main clinical causes of maternal deaths – haemorrhage, infection, toxaemia and obstructed labour – cannot be averted by preventive measures on the community level. A referral system to identify those at risk has to be backed up by adequate transportation and clinics or hospitals with the trained staff and essential supplies to deal with blood transfusion, Caesarian section and other surgical procedures and treatment of eclampsia. The Bangladesh non-governmental health organization, Gonoshasthya Kendro, reports mortality risks associated with pregnancy of around one per thousand live births (much lower than both Matlab and national figures reported above) and attributes this to its efficient referral and clinical back-up system (personal communication with Drs Chowdhury and Hashem, 1990).

Beyond Reproduction: The Broader Context of Women's Lives

The policy measures suggested so far fall mainly within the domain of reproductive rights and well-being. Each set of recommendations seeks to broaden the focus of population programmes: the expansion of reproductive choices through comprehensive provision of safe contraceptive methods; the greater involvement of men in the responsibilities of planned reproduction and parenthood; and a greater concern for maternal health to complement the present focus on family planning and children's welfare. This final section puts forward a number of recommendations which should belong in any long-term population planning, but which go beyond immediate reproductive health concerns.

It is important to bear in mind that maternal health and well-being requires attention to women's status long before they become pregnant. A woman's ability to lead a healthy, active life, to bear healthy active children, to choose from a range of productive roles, and to decide the timing of significant life events will depend very crucially on the kinds of constraints she has to operate under. In a graphic, stylized account, Winikoff (1988) illustrates how the constraining factors that help to perpetuate women's low status, high fertility and maternal mortality/morbidity rates across generations are closely intertwined and have to be dealt with simultaneously. The interaction of class and gender inequality makes a young girl, particularly one from a poor, rural household, more likely to suffer from ill-health, anaemia, malnutrition and illiteracy than a young boy. Typically, she is likely to be endowed with fewer resources and opportunities to take care of herself; she is unlikely to be able to acquire new skills and training later on in her life and will have limited possibilities of employment to improve her situation. The route to social security and personal fulfilment lies in early marriage and early, and possibly frequent child-bearing. She will have less access than a woman from a wealthier background to reproductive technology, and to reliable health services during pregnancy and delivery. If she survives, the inadequate care and nutrition she received during her pregnancies put her and her children at risk of continuing poor health. And if any of her children are girls, then the cycle of female disadvantage and high rates of fertility and mortality are likely to be reproduced.

The MCH measures recommended in the previous sections relate only to women in the reproductive age group, when in fact much earlier intervention in a woman's life cycle is needed to break the cycle of disadvantage. As far as health policy is concerned, there is a case for making *women's* health, rather than *maternal* health per se, the main focus of policy. A health-care policy that only recognizes women in their capacity as reproducers is unlikely to promote a social perception of women as empowered social actors. Such policies become part of the problem, rather than a solution, to the restricted life choices open to women. A more gender-aware health policy would have to be two-pronged. The first would require equalizing access to health care; there are many aspects of existing health provision that women would benefit from as much as men, but do not share equal access to. The second would require recognition that there are health problems that are gender-specific. In particular, there has been a 'culture of silence' around problems that women suffer as women, such as reproductive tract infection (Kiseke, 1989, p. 2, cited in Dixon-Mueller and Wasserheit, 1991). A gender-aware health policy may also imply that more attention and resources have to be devoted to identifying and addressing women-specific health problems.

To move beyond the sphere of health, female education has been identified by a large number of studies in a variety of contexts as a key variable in predicting women's status, fertility and autonomy (see Lockwood and Collier, 1988 for a recent review of this literature). There are a number of routes through which education enhances the quality of women's lives. Women with education face expanded opportunities in the labour market; they marry later and have their first birth later. Education gives women greater understanding and access to improved contraceptive practices and information on nutri-tion, sanitation and child care. Less tangibly, the ability to read and write is an important component in communicating and exchanging ideas and in analysing and acting upon one's own problems; thus education can help to empower women within their households and communities (see, for instance, Dighe and Patel, 1993; Batliwala, 1992).

Since women's limited access to education is frequently the product of deep-rooted gender discrimination, there is a strong case for policies which counter this bias. In addition to improving and expanding the physical infrastructure and equipment available for education, educational provision could be made more favourable to female enrolment. Improving the recruitment and training of female teachers might be a positive step in some cultures. Another critical measure is the reform of the formal school curriculum to reflect more accurately the roles and opportunities available to women and girls in a changing world. The educational system is, after all, a primary and early medium through which social 'rules' and practices around gender for both boys and girls are formed. Given parents' reluctance to educate girl children, particularly in the context of scarce resources, some governments have attempted to increase the incentive to encourage greater female participation in schools. Food-for-education schemes (along the lines of food-for-work schemes) could be implemented utilizing the comparative advantages of both governmental and non-governmental agencies in order to encourage women and girls to attend educational centres. Another possibility, being tried out in Bangladesh, is provision of female scholarships to overcome parental bias towards daughters' education. Finally there are innovative outreach programmes for women's literacy, such as Mahila Samakhya in India, which attempt to use education as a tool for empowerment (Batliwala, 1992).

However, the full potential of education for enhancing women's autonomy cannot be realized without addressing their financial dependence. We have noted that marginal income-generating projects for women, characteristic of official WID policy in the early years, did little to improve women's status and were frequently not even economically viable. The rising rates of female labour-force participation in export-oriented manufacturing and in micro enterprises suggest that, where opportunities exist, women will participate in a far wider range of jobs than envisaged by policymakers in the past. If women's autonomy and bargaining power is to be enhanced, it is important that future policy broaden the employment options available to them. Like men, women need well-paid and secure jobs and, as long as they are entrusted with primary responsibility for child care, they need the additional facilities and support services that will make this possible. These include adequate maternity leave, retraining opportunities after a period of absence from the labour market, affordable child-care facilities and non-discriminatory career structures. Unless women's domestic responsibilities are recognized and provided for at the workplace, motherhood may continue to represent the only feasible route to self-realization open to many women.

The third critical, and related, element in policies for gender equity relate to women's collective mobilization around their needs and interests. A stress on group approaches and social-action programmes is increasingly found in studies concerned with gender equity in the development process (Sen and Grown, 1985; Wignaraja, 1990; Commonwealth Secretariat, 1989). Some of these initiatives will be discussed in greater detail in the next chapter, but it is worth noting here that, while there are limits to the extent to which official policymakers can directly empower women, they can play an important enabling role by supporting innovative initiatives that address the crucial issues of women's rights. All of the three elements – education, employment and organization – identified here are necessary, but not sufficient in themselves, to the longer-term goal of women's empowerment. In combination, however, they will go a long way towards ensuring women a more equal place in the development process and to building the preconditions for a greater balance between the planet's human and natural resources.

Conclusion

The measures recommended in this chapter are intended to inform a population policy that is guided by a concern with women's reproductive choice and well-being. Some of the measures proposed represent a rethinking of past interventions and can therefore be implemented with resources released from other areas of population programmes. For instance, a reallocation of resources could be used to fund recommended new areas of research and to expand the mix of birth-control methods on offer. With certain other measures, such as the provision of legal and safe menstrual regulation and abortion facilities, the immediate burden of the costs might have to be shared by the public sector instead of being borne by individuals alone, but the longer-run burden on the health service of dealing with the complications of botched abortions would be diminished.

However, it is important to stress that women's health and reproductive needs are not, and cannot be, costless. This brings us to what Fraser sees as the final 'moment' in the politics of needs interpretation, which is the struggle over resources. A sustainable population policy predicated on a respect for women's reproductive health, rights and choices cannot be done on the cheap. The argument that feminist health activists frequently encounter is that resources are scarce and there are competing demands on the budgets of national and international agencies. However, scarcity of resources is not the main problem. Donor agencies have frequently subordinated their lending policies to short-term concerns with debt repayments; many Third World governments continue to spend large amounts of their budgets on defence, armaments and showpiece projects. According to recent estimates, less than 5 per cent of domestic public budgets in developing countries is devoted to health care (background paper to International Conference on Better Health for Women and Children Through Family Planning, 1987). Unless the different agencies of development can be persuaded to incorporate a more equitable population policy into their objectives, the resources available for such investments will remain inadequate. What is lacking is not resources, but political commitment to women's reproductive health and rights.

The present concern with protecting the environment has focused attention once again on the link between population growth and the deterioration of the world's ecology. There is a danger that alarming predictions of global disaster will stampede the population establishment once again into coercive and narrowly conceived programmes for fertility reduction. But the environmental debate has also highlighted a new and positive concept to add to the lexicon of development, that of sustainability. This chapter argues against the 'quick technological fix' as the solution to growing imbalances between the world's population and resource base. It is suggesting instead that a population policy based on respect for human rights, reproductive choice, male responsibility and women's enfranchisement is likely to lead to *sustainable* changes in reproductive behaviour and a qualitatively better human foundation for the development effort.

Notes

1 My thanks to Rosemary McCreary, UNICEF, for providing this information.
2 Details of and extracts from the FINRRAGE conference are taken from *Conference Khaber*, daily bulletins issued during the 1989 conference.
3 I owe this point to Dr Naila Khan.

9

Empowerment from Below:
Learning from the Grassroots

[M]any victims learn to be helpless, as women often do,
which allows them to evade the conscious status of victim-
hood but at an awful cost to themselves. (Shklar, 1990, p. 39)

[P]eople, especially poor women, are capable of promoting
their own development if their own efforts and initiatives
are recognized and supported. The first steps must be to
build the 'infrastructures', the context in which women can
feel some sense of control over their lives'. (Antrobus, 1987,
p. 112)

Introduction

Along with the dominant paradigms within the development field,
there have always existed alternative ways of viewing development
which have evolved out of grassroots experience. What distinguishes
these alternative views is that they are based on close, face-to-face
interaction between organizations and their constituencies so that
ideas and policies are shaped in the crucible of everyday practice
rather than in the upper echelons of remote and rule-bound bureaucracies. Empowerment is one such contribution from the grassroots. It
signals a recognition by those working at the local level that, despite the
rhetoric of participatory development, the power to define priorities
remains where it has always been, in the hands of a minority at the top.

The idea of empowerment expresses the interests of the
disenfranchised groups of society and, as Shetty (1991) points out, it
represents a confluence of experiences at the grassroots. An early

223

usage is to be found in the American Black radicalism of the 1960s. It has also been employed by community development groups in the North as well as the South. Finally, empowerment has been identified as a key goal of feminist grassroots organizations that want to move beyond the WID focus on formal equality with men. The concept has travelled beyond the grassroots. The major international development agencies now routinely refer in their policy declarations to the empowerment of the poor and of women. However, there is no consensus on the meaning of the term and it is frequently used in a way that robs it of any political meaning, sometimes as no more than a substitute word for integration or participation in processes whose main parameters have already been set elsewhere (Shetty, 1991).

The concept of empowerment is clearly rooted in the notion of power and in its reverse, powerlessness or the absence of power. While earlier analysis tended to focus on powerlessness – the powerlessness of the poor, of women, of ethnic minorities – there has been a shift away from this locution because of its static connotations. Moreover, powerlessness suggests a total absence of power whereas in reality even those who appear to have very little power are still able to resist, to subvert and sometimes to transform the conditions of their lives. The focus has therefore shifted to the more processual aspects of power – empowerment and disempowerment. However, this still leaves un-answered the question of what is meant by *power*, and therefore by empowerment. This is the question I want to explore in this chapter. I want to examine some theoretical concepts of power in relation to gender and then to consider how our understanding of power might be enriched through a study of grassroots attempts to operationalize empowerment for women.

Gender and Power in the Social Sciences

A useful theoretical discussion of power is to be found in Lukes's *Power: A Radical View* (1974) which distinguishes between three different interpretations commonly found in the social-science literature. The first, which he describes as 'the power to', is closely associated with liberal forms of analysis and is concerned with decision-making on issues over which there is an *observable conflict*. It defines power as the capacity of an actor to affect the pattern of outcomes against the wishes of other actors and asks the question 'who prevails in decision-making?' (p. 15). This notion of power as interpersonal decision-making capacity underpins a great deal of the WID literature. It is evident, for instance, in attempts to measure the statistical frequency with which women and men make decisions in different areas of household activity and to demonstrate that women are likely to exercise greater decision-making power in households where they have access to income. Such findings have been used to bolster WID advocacy for greater access for women in development. In practice, however, while these efforts may have succeeded in generating access to income-generating projects for women, few have transformed their position within the household.

One problem is that power analysed solely in terms of individual decision-making fails to capture those aspects which lie outside observable decision-making processes. A broader view of power would focus not only on the enactment of decisions, but also on exclusion of certain issues from the decision-making agenda, so that they are suppressed from being 'decisionable' (Giddens, 1979, p. 90). Power in this view no longer rests only in the ability of some actors to initiate, decide and veto decisions, but also in their ability to confine decision-making to 'safe' issues. Conflict may not be observed simply because it has not been permitted to surface in the arena of decision-making; however, inaction on issues or 'non-decisionmaking' can also be seen as a manifestation of power. This 'power over' (as Lukes terms it) inheres in the implicitly accepted and undisputed procedures within institutions which, by demarcating decisionable from non-decisionable issues, systematically and routinely benefit certain individuals and groups at the expense of others (Bachrach and Baratz, 1962).

Shifting focus in this way from the interpersonal exercise of power to its institutionalized basis comes closer to the way in which power has been conceptualized in the analysis of gender relations offered in earlier chapters. Our discussion of the household division of labour, for instance, highlighted the extent to which the assignment of domestic responsibilities to women is so deeply institutionalized in household rules and practices that it appears non-negotiable. Women who wish to take up employment can only do so by cutting down on their leisure or withdrawing children from school. They rarely do so by renegotiating the division of labour so that husbands undertake a greater share of domestic chores. Similarly, while women may successfully bargain over certain aspects of household expenditure, what remains non-negotiable is men's overall control over household land, capital and other valued resources.

However, the household is by no means the only institutional arena in which male power is exercised through the mobilization of biased norms, rules and procedures. Public organizations are also implicated. Staudt (1985) makes this point in relation to the deeply entrenched norms within public policy concerning the inviolability of the domestic sphere: 'The symbolism of women maintaining a personal and private family refuge provides the normative justification for either policy inaction or the perpetuation of male preferential policies. The "nondecisions" of this broad area of society have perhaps been more prolonged than in any other policy sphere' (p. 7). Male power also operates, as we noted in Chapter 2, through the organizational logic of public institutions, which, by favouring certain kinds of actors, skills, bodies and capacities over others, are typically constituted as class and gender-based hierarchies. To challenge the rules and practices by which such hierarchies are organized would entail challenging the organizational basis of these public bodies. Conformity is safer and carries more tangible rewards. This is pointed out by Goetz (1992) in her review of the experience of senior women in bureaucratic organizations:

> For many of these women, success is both a function and expression of their ability to conform to organizational structures and cultures by taking on sociological characteristics of men in their dress, deportment, managerial styles, and most importantly in their capacity to minimize the demands of the home. . . . As a minority in most organizations, women have least interest in challenging dominant agency practices because of the precariousness of individual career positions, and their effective 'minority status' outside of organizations reinforces their need to conform within them. (p. 14)

An institutional, rather than purely interpersonal, analysis of male power draws attention to the gender biases implicit within the rules and practices of different social institutions. Overt discrimination or patriarchal conspiracies are unnecessary when male privilege can be assured simply by mobilizing routine institutional procedures. However, both notions of power outlined so far deal with conflicts of interest which have been identified and articulated, even if they are then suppressed. Where there is no evidence of conflict, the presumption is that consensus prevails. The assumption is that power and conflict are necessarily linked. There is no room here for the idea that 'interests might be unarticulated or unobservable, and above all, for the idea that people might be mistaken about, or unaware of, their own interests' (Lukes, 1974, p. 14). Lukes offers a third dimension of power to address this gap, one which encompasses, but goes beyond, the previous two. It recognizes that conflicts of interest may be suppressed not only from the decision-making agenda, but also from the consciousness of the various parties involved. Power relations are kept in place because the actors involved – both dominant and subordinate – subscribe to accounts of social reality which deny that such inequalities exist or else assert that they are due to individual misfortune rather than social injustice (Shklar, 1990). This formulation of power is concerned with 'the socially structured and culturally patterned behaviour of groups, and practices of institutions' (Lukes, 1974, p. 22) which help to shape not only whose interests will prevail but also how different actors perceive their interests. It prevents conflicts between dominant and subordinate groups from becoming manifest by shaping wants, needs and preferences in such a way that both accept their role in the existing order 'either because they can see or imagine no alternative to it, or because they value it as divinely ordained and beneficial'. Power relations may appear so secure and well-established that both subordinate and dominant groups are unaware of their oppressive implications or incapable of imagining alternative ways of 'being and doing'.

There is considerable overlap between this third dimension of power and what feminists have called 'the power within'. The feminist analysis draws attention to the fact that, while resources provide the material levers through which gender asymmetries are sustained, social rules, norms, values and practices play a critical role in concealing the reality and pervasiveness of male dominance and defusing gender conflict. Research into household relations in a 'gentrifying area of North London' offers interesting insights into this aspect of power in an urban industrialized context (Wilson, 1991). It notes that all the women interviewed appeared to subscribe to the dominant ideology of equality of shares within marriage, but the majority were reluctant to talk about the actual division of intra-household resources. The problem lay in calculating individual shares. Very few of the women were able to give accurate accounts of their husbands' personal expenditures: 'It was clear that in virtually all marriages there was a conspiracy of silence in an area where inspection would have challenged the dominant ideology of marriage – the shares were not fair' (p. 33). Wilson comments that most of the women preferred not to acknowledge conflict as an aspect of daily life so that the unequal nature of material shares within marriage became in effect a no-go area.

Women may find it strategic to avoid or defuse potentially conflictual situations with men because they recognize that the rules of the game are loaded against them and the costs of confrontation are likely to be high. Or, as the opening quotation from Shklar suggests, they may learn helplessness in order to avoid facing the terrible implications of their disempowerment. It is this aspect of power that Sen is getting at when he suggests that women are less likely to secure favourable outcomes for themselves in household decision-making processes because their longer-term security lies in subordinating their personal well-being to that of male authority figures. This may be a conscious strategy or it may reflect women's actual evaluation of their own self-worth. The injustice of such a state of affairs will not be self-evident if it is presented as the only, the natural or the unalterable way to be. Power thus has an irreducible subjective aspect to it (Shklar, 1990).

Recognition of the complexity of women's experience of gender subordination explains Molyneux's point (1985) that 'the relationship between what we have called strategic gender interests and women's recognition of them and desire to realize them cannot be assumed. Even the "lowest common denominator" of interests (e.g. complete equality with men, control over reproduction, and greater personal autonomy and independence from men) are not readily accepted by all women' (p. 234). There is, of course, the danger with the idea that strategic interests are not transparent, even to women themselves, of posing a 'false consciousness' against the standard of some objectively given set of interests. While Molyneux acknowledges this might be a factor, she also suggests that changes realized in a piecemeal fashion can threaten women's short-term practical interests or entail losses which are not compensated for and are likely to be resisted by women themselves. Attempts at empowerment have to take note of the trade-offs that women make in order to cope with the ramifications of oppressive relationships in their lives.

There are other reasons why positing non-transparency of strategic gender interests does not necessarily imply false consciousness on the part of women. Interests emerge out of different dimensions of social life, but they are always rooted in experience. Some emerge out of the routine practices of daily life – women's practical gender interests are relatively clear cut. Others are only likely to become discernible through engagement in different kinds of practice, which bring about a new basis for experience and knowledge from which to reassess the old one. It is the very restrictions on women's life choices that help to curtail their ability to 'know' other ways of being and to engage in the analytical process by which their structural, rather than individual, interests as a subordinated category come more clearly into view. Women may be aware of the circumscribed nature of their lives without necessarily knowing what to do about it. This awareness is implicit in some of the metaphors women use to describe themselves; in the South Asian context, for instance, women describe themselves as frogs in a well or as oxen blindly turning the grindstone, to emphasize the limitations they see on their vision of the world. A deductive analysis can help sketch out in broad brush strokes the main structural mechanisms by which women's subordination is maintained and reconstituted in specific contexts, but the 'power from within' ultimately entails the experiential recognition and analysis of these issues. Such power cannot be given; it has to be self-generated.

Power, then, is seen to be more fluid, more pervasive and more socially embedded than the conventional focus on individual decision-making would suggest. Power lies not only in men's ability to mobilize material resources from a variety of arenas in order to promote their individual and gender interests, but also in their ability to construct the 'rules of the game' in ways that disguise the operations of this power and construct the illusion of consensus and complementarity. Consequently, while women may successfully pursue their ends, and manage quite significantly to constrain men in the process it is still the case that their goals are likely to be shaped by social systems which deny them ready access to the social privilege, authority, and esteem enjoyed by men of an equivalent class.

The multidimensional nature of power suggests that empowerment strategies for women must build on 'the power within' as a necessary adjunct to improving their ability to control resources, to determine agendas and make decisions. In the rest of this chapter, I will be examining grassroots efforts to empower poor women, using examples from South Asia, in order to give the concept a more operational meaning. This does not mean that the official agencies of development are incapable of taking on aspects of women's empowerment; nor does it mean that empowerment is only relevant to the poor. However, bureaucratic institutions are weighed down by their own histories, by the legacy of rules, practices and ideologies they have inherited from the past. Given the complexity, weight and class bias of such institutions, it is the poor that have been hardest to reach. Grassroots non-governmental organizations tend to be less rule-governed and their face-to-face interactions with their constituencies have given them both a greater advantage in promoting innovative strategies and less scope for sidestepping the issue of women's subordination.

Participatory Agendas and the
Identification of Need

Most poverty-reduction programmes are seen in terms of meeting the basic needs of the poor. They are either designed to meet these needs

through the direct provision of basic services to the poor or by
improving their entitlements to basic resources. The first stage in the
design of such interventions is therefore identifying and prioritizing
basic needs. However, as we noted in the previous chapter, this is not a
neutral process, but one fraught with the 'politics of needs interpretation'. Through what conceptual and methodological lenses do planners 'see' needs? Do they share or have empathy with the experiences
of those whose needs they are defining? Who has the last word in
determining the legitimacy of a particular need within the 'decisionable' agenda?

There is a story that Schumacher is supposed to have told to a
conference he once attended[1] which serves as a poignant allegory for
the disempowering implications of top-down approaches to poverty
eradication. According to this story, Schumacher was sitting in an
airport restaurant waiting for his flight to the conference and observed
a family – a father, a mother and their child – at the next table. The
waitress came to take their order. The mother turned to the father who
was hidden behind his newspaper to ask him what he wanted. Not
bothering to lower his newspaper, he announced that he wanted a
hamburger. The child piped up that she would like spaghetti hoops,
but her mother ignored her and said to the waitress, 'That will be three
hamburgers, please.' The waitress turned in the direction of the
kitchen and shouted, 'Two hamburgers and one spaghetti hoops.' The
child turned to her mother in amazement and said, 'Did you see that,
she thinks I am *real*.' Different meanings can of course be read into an
anecdote like this, but for me it illustrates quite graphically the
disempowering and infantilizing ways in which policymakers have
frequently treated the poor, particularly poor women. By and large,
inasmuch as poverty alleviation has addressed the needs of the poor,
policymakers have tended to prioritize men's needs over women's.
Women are rarely treated as knowing what they need; rather, agencies
seek to think and act on their behalf. Either women's needs and
priorities are subsumed (and then forgotten) within those of the
household collectivity or, when they are addressed separately, they
tend to fall in the category of women's practical gender needs as
mothers, wives and carers within the family.

What emerges from the experience of the innovative NGOs is that
where a space is created for women's own voices to be heard, either
through participatory processes of needs identification or else by
organizational practices that encourage participation in shaping and
changing the 'decisionable agenda', a different set of needs may come
into view. In providing this space, therefore, such organizations have
helped to challenge conventional stereotypes about gender needs, to

make visible hitherto hidden categories of women's needs and to lay bare the interconnections between different aspects of women's lives.

The Grameen Bank in Bangladesh offers an example of how the use of participatory methodologies throws up very different needs and priorities from those which arise out of 'expert'-led analysis. Grameen started out as a poverty-eradication project in 1976 as the result of the findings of action research on poverty carried out by Md Yunus, a professor at Chittagong University. By adopting a participatory and open-ended methodology, the research helped to counter many conventional preconceptions about the rural poor which were en-shrined in the development literature in Bangladesh: that they were primarily landless wage labourers; that their poverty resulted from inadequate access to waged labour; and that they were (implicitly) men (Sultan, 1992). The research revealed instead that the rural poor earned their livelihoods from a variety of self-employed activities rather than relying solely on wage labour, and that their major constraint was the lack of access to financial institutions rather than to the waged labour market. The research also helped to spell out the gender dimension of poverty: it drew attention to women's key contribution in household livelihood strategies among the poor and their greater tendency to devote their incomes to family, rather than personal, welfare. It was evident that self-employment was more important for women, given the paucity of waged-labour opportuni-ties open to them. Yet in terms of access to credit, they were, if anything, more disadvantaged than poor men.

Beginning as a small credit programme in 1976, Grameen became an independent national bank in 1983. Its strategy of providing credit to the poor and landless sought to release the potential contained in their survival skills; it would permit them to move beyond coping strategies by expanding their enterprises and moving into new activities. Grameen is best known today for its success in reaching credit to poor and assetless women. While it started by lending primarily to men, a policy decision to favour women resulted in them forming an increasing percentage of its borrowers since 1983. Today women constitute over 90 per cent of bank borrowers.

The Self Employed Women's Association in India also works with poor self-employed women but, unlike Grameen, it works primarily in urban areas. It emerged in response to the expressed needs of women workers in the unorganized sector who had largely been ignored by the male-dominated trade-union movement. While the union had set up a Women's Wing in 1954, it targeted women only through their relationship to male mill workers. The work of the wing was in the classic welfarist mode. By 1968 it was offering classes in sewing, knitting, embroidery, spinning, press composition, typing and steno-graphy throughout Ahmedebad to wives and daughters of mill workers. At the same time, the union demonstrated total indifference to the drastic displacement of women workers from factory employ-ment: between 1950 and 1970, women working in the mills dropped from 20 per cent to 3 per cent (Sebstadt, 1982, p. 234). Nor did it concern itself with the poor and lower-caste women who worked for the textile industry on a casual piece-rate basis. Within TLA, few women were employed in any post higher than clerk.

A survey carried out in the early seventies by the Women's Wing uncovered the existence of large numbers of a hitherto ignored section of the textile workforce: women tailors in the unorganized sector who complained of exploitation by contractors but who were not repre-sented by the labour movement or protected by labour laws. SEWA was formed to represent the interests of women who were outside formal employer–employee relationships. This itself entailed a strug-gle, since the Labour Department felt that without a recognized employer there was no need for a union. SEWA argued that a union was to defend the interests of workers rather than to struggle against a clearly identifiable employer. Its members were drawn from three categories: home-based workers, petty traders and casual wage labour. To counter the labels of 'unorganized', 'informal', 'unprotected', 'unregistered', 'marginal' and 'black economy', which were applied to a section of the workforce that accounted for nearly 90 per cent of employment in India, and to indicate its centrality to the economy, the organization adopted the term 'self-employed worker'.

In both the Grameen and SEWA cases, the initial set of needs identified were economic ones. Participatory approaches to needs identification can also help to identify welfare needs other than those conventionally assigned to women. Such needs tend to remain hidden in more conventional approaches to policy design because the lower priority, the shame and embarrassment associated with women's bodies in many societies have given rise to the wider problem of the 'culture of silence' around women's sexual, reproductive and general health questions. An example of this comes from a participatory action research project carried out by Jumani (1993) as a preliminary stage in SEWA's outreach to poor rural women. Inadequate sanitation facilities meant that more poor villagers had to use the open spaces. This posed particular problems for poor women who, in the interests of modesty, were forced to use the fields under cover of darkness, either late in the evening or early in the morning; cases of rape were common in the spaces kept apart for toilet facilities. The long periods between relieving themselves caused bowel and bladder problems. Further-more, limited availability of water exacerbated the extra discomfort and hygiene problems faced during menstruation.[2]

The other issue that has remained submerged until recently is that of domestic violence. Here again, deep-rooted beliefs about the sanctity and safety of the domestic sphere, the shame and blame that often attach to women who are beaten, and the male biases of most development agencies have long combined to ensure that this was an issue largely characterized by silence and non-decisionmaking. The significance of organizational practice in allowing domestic violence to surface within the decision-making agenda is described in Price's (1992) case study of SUTRA, which began working in Himachal Pradesh in 1977. In its early years, SUTRA worked within the pre-existing government model of service delivery, concentrating on improving on the efficiency of government targeting and delivery of services and hoping thereby to encourage demands within the local population for improved services from the government. Its targeting practices displayed fairly conventional gender biases: the services for men aimed at improving agricultural production and enhancing market access, while those for women aimed at their familial and domestic roles. An internal review in 1984 raised fundamental questions about the nature of the organization and its achievements in bringing about social change. It was recognized that women expressed greater support for the organization because they saw it as providing a space of their own which was not permitted to them elsewhere in society. It was also recognized that merely offering more efficient replacement services had not resulted in villagers putting pressure on the government to improve its delivery system. Consequently, SUTRA decided to concentrate on building up women's organizations as its main goal, with development implementation as a secondary one.

What was interesting about the shift to this new agenda was the way in which it challenged earlier preconceptions and threw up previously submerged needs. When consulted, women expressed concerns over issues that had earlier been categorized as male areas of interest: drinking-water supplies, irrigation schemes, teachers' non-attendance at schools, corruption among local officials. As the needs that the women members began to articulate expanded into areas of women's health, more women were recruited onto the hitherto largely male staff to cope with some of the cultural barriers entailed in dealing with such needs. The increased numbers of women staff in turn brought further problems out into the open, particularly domestic violence, rape and alcoholism. In the early phase of the organization's life, problems of violence against women had been generally shrouded in silence or denial: 'Women felt the honour of the family was affected by such discussions, and if individual women were beaten or faced other difficulties, there was often a tendency to lay blame on the woman herself for not "suffering in silence"' (p. 55). One of the factors that helped to break down this silence was that some of the women staff had also suffered from these problems. The sharing of these experiences helped to break down the 'them' and 'us' relation between the village women and staff members. Once the taboo on the subject was broken, action could be taken. An increasing number of women came forward on their own or others' behalf to explore ways in which these situations could be dealt with. Thus issues which had been previously defined as private acquired a public and political status in the eyes of the women.

Finally, a third aspect of needs that comes into view if greater participation is built into the planning process is the interdependency between different categories of needs, particularly in the lives of women. There is a 'magic bullet' mentality among many policymakers: the idea that complex issues of gender and poverty can be dealt with through a single 'strategic intervention'. In reality, however, people's lives are such that they cannot be divided into neat compartments which are kept insulated from each other. Rather, what occurs in any one arena will have implications for all other arenas, sometimes to the extent of negating the intended effects of an intervention. Consequently, very few of the innovative NGOs concentrate purely on the delivery of a single 'input'. Even where they may prioritize a single category of need, they generally offer a complementary package of resources or services to ensure the need is actually met. SEWA, for instance, from its inception has recognized that the problems of self-employed women required a struggle on a number of different fronts. Unlike the case of male factory workers whose main struggle was with a single employer, self-employed women have to confront problems arising from exploitative contractors and moneylenders, police harassment and discriminatory laws. As we shall describe in greater detail below, this has entailed the involvement of SEWA in a much broader range of activities than conventional trade unions, straddling both development and union work, and brought it into conflict with the Textile Labour Association.

In its early years, Grameen Bank offered credit for a very narrow range of 'productive' activities which related to market-oriented production. However, it became clear that if credit was intended to enhance household survival and security, it needed to be fungible between different uses of women's time, all of which contributed to the well-being of household members. Loans for health-related activities could act simultaneously as a time-saving measure (since women had to take time off from economic activities to take care of the sick) as well as an asset-preserving one (since families often had to sell off productive assets to pay for medical treatment). Recognizing the fungibility of labour and resources within the household, Grameen has expanded its loan-giving activities. Since the mid-eighties, it has sought to develop viable borrower cooperative groups to undertake such activities as primary health care, child nutrition, sanitation, literacy and family planning. It is also planning to add a health programme to its activities in view of the fact that enterprise profits are often wiped out by expensive medical costs.

Gonoshasthaya Kendra (People's Health Centre), on the other hand, is an NGO in Bangladesh which specializes in primary health-care provision but which also offers income-earning opportunities to women from poorer households. This dates back to 1972 when a woman was brought into the health centre after having tried to kill herself by taking pesticides. She had not been able to provide the necessary post-harvest labour for her family because she was suffering from excessive bleeding following the use of contraceptive pills and had been asked by her husband's family to return to her parental home because she was proving to be a liability for a poor farming family. When the woman regained consciousness, she told the doctor treating her that if all that GK could do was to send her back to her husband, they should have let her die. In other words, her life was not worth saving if she could only live it as a liability. Recognizing that economic dependence was one aspect of the problem that women faced, GK began its vocational training programme, with the emphasis on non-traditional skills (for example, metal work, carpentry, shoe-making, bakery, fibre-glass fabrication, printing, irrigation-pump operation, repair and management). These are not only likely to have higher financial returns, but are also seen to challenge old preconceptions about women's abilities and competences (Gonoshasthaya Kendra, 1991).

To sum up, the space given by an organization to the bottom-up establishment of needs conveys a great deal about how it has positioned women within its programmatic endeavours: as competent, but socially constrained actors who are capable of making choices, articulating priorities and taking responsibility, or as passive clients in need of enlightenment and uplifting. Such space can be created through the use of participatory methodologies in the process of needs identification or by adopting open, rather than closed, decision-making processes so that organizational priorities are constantly monitored and revised in the light of experience. The growing body of literature on PRA can be seen as one attempt to systematize this principle of a participatory approach to needs identification and organizational monitoring. While no set of methods are *in themselves* sensitive to gender difference and inequality – each method is only as good as its practitioner – PRA's qualitative, dynamic and interactive methodology makes it more likely to pick up on gender differences in needs and priorities as well as on categories of need which might remain submerged in more conventional approaches to policy design. PRA techniques not only emphasize more empathetic ways of communicating with the poor, but allow exploration of issues generally considered sensitive: gynaecological problems, sexually transmitted disease, domestic violence and alcoholism (see, for instance, Welbourne, 1992).

Compensating for Institutitional Failure: Alternative Forms of Needs Satisfaction

Once a need has been given recognition within the policy agenda of an organization, it has to be translated into strategies for interpreting and meeting the need. A major factor behind women's disenfranchisement within the development process has been the gender biases entrenched within the routine rules and procedures through which mainstream development agencies distribute resources. Except where the resources in question correspond specifically to 'women's roles', these institutions have been, explicitly or implicitly, targeted at men. By tailoring their rules and procedures to take cognizance of the gender-specific constraints that women from low-income households have to deal with, the innovative NGOs have sought to compensate for the exclusionary implications of mainstream institutional practice. Their own rules and procedures embody a very different set of assumptions about potential 'beneficiaries' and result in very different modes of provision.

First of all, they recognize that gender inequalities in the division of resources and responsibilities within the domestic domain create gender inequalities in the ability to take up opportunities outside the domestic domain. Consequently, along with 'primary' sets of needs around which their interventions are organized, the innovative NGOs have sought to respond to secondary and interrelated sets of needs which derive from the specific constraints that women face in accessing mainstream institutional resources. And second, they have sought to provide this access on terms which position women as agents and participants in the development effort rather than as clients and recipients. This has entailed an emphasis on building a sense of ownership and responsibility among poor women in relation to the organization's activities, rather than on limiting their participation to the more instrumental and limited version of participation as the take-up of services or meeting of project targets.

A comparison of formal credit institutions and alternative modes of credit delivery will illustrate these points. The significance of self-employment in the livelihood strategies of both rural and urban poor has now been established in a variety of different contexts; it has also become abundantly clear that formal financial institutions have failed to provide them with the services that would help them to upgrade the productivity of their enterprises. Even where such institutions have sought to implement special credit schemes for the poor (for example, the Uganda Commercial Bank's Rural Farmer's Scheme; see Musoke and Amajo, 1989) and the Differential Rate of Interest scheme in India (see Everett and Savara, 1991), women's participation in particular has been negligible. A number of studies have pointed out the lack of fit between the norms and procedures of mainstream banking institutions and the circumstances and constraints of women's lives. These include:

- The women's lack of material assets to underwrite the security of loans.
- Inflexible procedures often entailing formidable paper work and requiring basic literacy. A study of the Uganda credit scheme found that the number of visits required to get loan applications processed and approved loans disbursed was a major reason given by women farmers for their lack of participation in the scheme (Musoke and Amajo, 1989).
- Women's enterprises tend to be smaller and are therefore deemed less creditworthy. Smaller loans have relatively higher administrative costs.
- The costs of acquiring information about a group that is generally more isolated and less mobile also inhibit bank lending to poor women.
- Ambiguity of goals for employees in public financial institutions who are required to combine conventional profit-oriented concerns in the majority of their transactions with poverty-oriented concerns in their loans to the poor. Incentive structures tend to reward the former rather than the latter activity. Bank clerks involved in 'weaker section lending' to India complained that they aspired to be bank officers rather than social workers; that involvement in such lending did not prepare them for the bank officer examination and

hence they had less chance of promotion to officer positions than other bank clerks (Everett and Savara, 1991).

- Finally, there are the less tangible obstacles associated with the social distance between educated, middle-class and mainly male bank employees and poor women. As we noted in Chapter 6, their clothing and general appearance, combined with their general lack of experience and confidence in the public domain, ensured that poor rural women were unlikely to obtain entry into mainstream banking institutions, assuming that they attempted it. Devaki Jain quotes from a SEWA publication describing its members' experience of the government's 'weaker section lending' in Ahmedebad:

> Being all women, accompanied by children, filthy in appearance, unaccustomed to manners and business talks, they were annoying to and not much welcome by the bank staff at their premises. Being illiterate they would go to the wrong bank, go at the wrong hours, could not fill in the slips . . . the bank staff has neither time nor understanding to deal with this class of borrowers and would start doubting their bona fides. (Cited in Everett and Savara, 1991, p. 248)

The NGOs have responded in a number of different ways. Some, like the India Development Service in Karnataka, act as financial intermediaries between the formal credit institutions and groups of rural women and men. Others, like the Community Development Fund in Hyderabad, have sought to build credit and thrift cooperatives among poor women and men without seeking assistance from the state. Both SEWA and Grameen have adopted the third option of setting up alternative, poverty-oriented banks. In fact, this is the main area of Grameen activity and it is worth examining some of the innovative practices it has adopted to overcome the constraints that poor women in particular face.

- Grameen has provided *institutional* access by replacing material with social collateral requirements. This has been accomplished through the practice of joint-liability, borrower-solidarity groups. Borrowers are formed into groups of five in order to receive the basic general loans that will enable them to pursue their livelihood strategies. The loan is to individuals, but the choice of activity and the size of the loan is vetted by the group, which is also responsible for monitoring its use and providing support and advice to the borrower. Each borrower knows that default on loans will jeopardize the chances of other group members receiving loans.

- It has achieved *physical* access for poor women through a system of 'barefoot banking'. A dense network of branches and outreach work by bank employees to village centres helps to compensate for the social and financial constraints on women's mobility. To put this point quantitatively, the bank has 781 branches and a staff of 14,000 who put in 40,000 miles of legwork a day to reach its 869,538 members dispersed in 19,536 out of the country's 64,000 villages (Huq and Sultan, 1991).
- Procedures have been simplified and form filling kept to a minimum. Grameen's borrowers undergo a week's training to learn to sign their own names.
- Interest rates are set at commercial levels. Grameen believes that the problem for the poor is lack of access rather than insolvency (Sultan, 1992). The emphasis is on subsidizing administrative costs rather than the loans themselves. The strategy works and repayment rates are an astonishing 98 per cent.
- The costs of information on the multiplicity of small enterprises in which women are involved are minimized by leaving the choice of enterprise to the individual borrower, with the final responsibility for deciding and monitoring resting with her group members. The only condition is that the loan must be for an activity which the borrower can carry out herself, and it must be invested within a week of the loan. The first seeks to ensure that the purchase of assets is not determined by men, while the second ensures that sufficient thought is given to the chosen enterprise before application is made for a loan.

There are other tangible and intangible changes that Grameen has sought to promote in the lives of women through its rules and practices. It has special housing loans which enable poor families to invest in durable, flood-resistant structures. Housing is an asset which is overlaid with many different meanings. It serves a very basic need for shelter in a flood-prone country. It is often the main site of economic activity for people who are self-employed. But, as Huq and Sultan (1991) point out, it has important psychological and symbolic significance: 'A durable shelter is one of the basic requirements for people to be able to organise their thoughts, discipline their actions and undertake plans and programs for creative pursuits. People without a home tend to be uncertain, worried and unstable, which affects their every action' (p. 174). If the loan is given to the woman (and the majority are), the land on which the structure is built has to be registered in her name. As Sultan (1992) points out, this has some very important implications in the context of Bangladesh. It recognizes the reality that increasing impoverishment is often associated with men abandoning their responsibilities to their wives and children in order to better their own situations. Registering land in women's names gives them a stake in the community into which they have married and in which they spend a major portion of their adult lives. It also increases the 'exit costs' of men wishing to dissolve a marriage, since they no longer have automatic claim to all assets accumulated during marriage. Should a husband die, it ensures that some property is retained intact by his widow rather than being redistributed among his entire family. Above all, it seeks to replace widespread perceptions of women as assetless dependents with new ones of them as bearers of valued entitlements.

Finally, Grameen stresses the need to give women a sense of ownership of the Bank. It has members, not clients. Landless women are the major shareholders of the bank, owning of the bulk of its share capital. Nine out of twelve of the Board of Directors are women from its landless groups. In terms of women's positioning within the Grameen agenda, it could be said that Grameen recognizes the practical need of poor women to earn a livelihood and that it seeks to promote their strategic concerns by increasing their access to, and control over, new economic resources.

In the case of SEWA, the institutional failure that it sought to compensate for was that of a conventional trade union which had been organized around male definitions of work and male interests in the workplace. The paridigmatic member of the Textile Labour Association was the male factory worker with a single identifiable employer, fixed work location, regular wages, and protective labour legislation covering his occupation. His major problems related to wages, hours of work, occupational safety, security of employment and retirement benefits. By contrast, women in the unorganized sector tended to be confined to casual contract work or self-employment and enjoyed few of the benefits of protective legislation. They were made up of home-based piece-rate workers, ragpickers, street traders and increasing numbers of casual wage labourers. They shared some of the same problems as industrial workers as far as hours, pay and hazardous working conditions are concerned. But they also faced additional problems related to supplies of raw materials, access to markets, exploitation by moneylenders, middle men, police and public authorities. As poor women, they were often isolated from society and lacked information about training and employment opportunities, legal rights and public provision of services.

It was the interests of this group of workers that SEWA was set up to protect. Consequently, its activities have always been more wide-ranging than conventional male-dominated trade unions and include legal aid, credit provision, workers' rights and representations for higher wages and better working conditions. Union members from various trades are organized as cooperatives to deal with exploitation by middlemen and lack of access to raw materials and markets. Cooperative members contribute the share capital, own the co-operative and elect a managing committee to handle its daily business. Cooperatives have been formed around credit, crafts and artisanal activities, livestock, trading, vending, and services like cleaning and ragpicking. Moreover, given that its members have no access to the social services and social security available to formal sector workers, SEWA has organized child-care and health cooperatives, life-insurance schemes and maternity-benefit schemes. SEWA has now been adopted by the Labour Ministry as a state-wide scheme for agricultural workers (Bhatt, 1989).

SEWA encourages members to take advantage of existing provision wherever possible, linking them to the institutions providing welfare benefits, health services, state housing or governmental training programmes. However, because so many institutions are closed to poor women, SEWA has also sought to build alternative institutions for its members. The prime example of this is SEWA bank. Initially SEWA had sought to act as a financial intermediary between its members and government lending schemes for poorer sections, which operated through mainstream banks. However, the familiar problems associated with the formalized rules and practices of these institutions – time-consuming bank procedures, needlessly complicated application forms, banking hours and attitudes of male bank staff – soon made it clear that credit on its own was not enough. SEWA Bank was set up using deposits and share capital from SEWA members. It is staffed by people who are sensitive to the needs and constraints of poor women, and its procedures, lending schemes and savings programmes are organized around these needs and constraints. In place of a signature, an identity card and pass book are issued to each member, bearing a photograph of her holding a slate showing her account number. Women who need a secure place to keep their passbooks can store them in a locked cabinet in the bank. Loan appraisal and creditworthiness are established through personal dialogue, and decisions generally take less than a week. Repayment rates are around 90 per cent. SEWA bank operates on a comprehension of the lives of its members in their totality rather than purely in economic and credit terms. Like Grameen, its emphasis is on ensuring access rather than subsidizing interest rates.

The broad range of activities that SEWA undertakes in the interests of its members created considerable tension with the main body of the TLA. One of the TLA's complaints against SEWA was over its developmental activities. These were seen as hampering SEWA's trade-union functions. SEWA's argument, however, has been that since it represented unconventional workers, it had to go beyond the conventional range of needs: 'Pressure and development or union and co-operative – by linking the two, both the arms [of SEWA] have been able to uplift the worker from exploitation and unemployment' (Bhatt, 1979, cited in Gandhi and Shah, 1992, p. 282). Tensions between TLA and SEWA came to the fore during the 1981 riots over the reservation of medical college seats for students from the *dalit* castes. SEWA, whose members were drawn primarily from the *dalit* caste, made a public declaration supporting the *dalits*. This went against the silent stance adopted by the TLA, who were aligned with the National Labour Organization, which included many members from higher castes. SEWA was charged with indiscipline and expelled.

SEWA continues to experiment with the attempt to straddle both development and union activities, to address the problems its members face within the family as well as in the marketplace, as women as well as workers. It acknowledges women's reproductive responsibilities, long overlooked by male-dominated trade unions, and has formed child-care and health cooperatives, often using these issues as the basis for reaching women who have not yet been organized. It has helped its members in cases of dowry, bride-price, domestic and sexual harassment, and rape. Its actions include meeting with women's family members, filing petitions in the courts, and issuing summonses to husbands, with the help of police escorts. Lobbying for better legislation has also been an important aspect of SEWA's work.

A very different strategy for compensating for institutional failure is that of Nijera Kori in Bangladesh. This organization was founded by a group of development activists who left BRAC (now one of the largest NGOs in Bangladesh) because of their disillusionment with its practice of providing loans to the poor. Their fear was that NGO involvement in lending to the poor would end up by substituting the old relations of dependence and patronage involving moneylenders and landlords with new forms of such relations with NGO staff. Because NGOs are not politically elected or accountable (except to their donors), there are few safeguards to ensure that they behave in responsible ways. Rather than providing credit and other economic resources to the poor, NK's strategy has been to seek to compensate for the failure of public entitlement systems to reach poor women and men. Nijera Kori argues that there is state commitment in Bangladesh to providing various material resources to the poor – from redistribution of *khas* (unclaimed, publicly owned) land and water bodies to the provision of employment through public works schemes. What prevented disenfranchised groups from claiming their full entitlement was their lack of political clout.

Nijera Kori avoids distributing material resources; it seeks instead to work with more intangible resources, by building the organizational capacity of poor people to press their claims on public institutions. Its activities include group formation, training in human and skill development, meetings between different groups, a legal-aid programme, and collective action and mobilization on social issues. In terms of economic resources, priority is given to the mobilization by the poor of their own resources and includes joint cultivation and aquaculture supported by group savings. Nijera Kori works with both women and men who are organized in separate groups but undertake joint activities. Where public works programmes are undertaken or poverty alleviation strategies implemented, Nijera Kori's group strategy ensures that the 'rules' of resource distribution are equitable and effective.

Like Nijera Kori, the Women's Development Programme (WDP) in Rajasthan avoids the direct distribution of material resources. Unlike the other examples we have used so far, it is a joint government/NGO effort. The WDP was set up by the government of Rajasthan in recognition of the fact that, despite its attempt to channel resources to women, there appeared to have been little change in their condition. 'It also took note of the fact that men had been entrusted with the responsibility for women's development in the family, government and society far too long' (Dighe and Jain, 1989, p. 78). It was to compensate for the institutional failure of the local state to meet women's needs and priorities that the WDP was set up. Its concern was less with putting new mechanisms of delivery in place and more with building alliances and networks that would allow poorer village women to put collective pressure on unresponsive local institutions. The WDP was set up as a collaboration between the local government and the Information Development and Resource Agency (IDARA), a voluntary agency working in the field of adult education and rural development. Monitoring and evaluation for the Programme was to be conducted by the Jaipur Institute of Development Studies, a local research institute. The front-level worker of the WDP was the *sathin* who was responsible for formation of women's fora at the village level. She was selected for her qualities of commitment and courage rather than for any formal qualifications. Clusters of ten village *panchayats* with ten *sathins* were coordinated by a *pracheta*. The government department responsible for district-level coordination received technical advice and support from IDARA.

The principal aim of the WDP was 'to empower women through communication of information, education and training and to enable them to recognize and improve their social and economic status (Jain et al., 1986, p. 6). Its strategy was to use the *sathin*'s access to the local bureaucracy as an important resource in meeting locally defined needs. The *sathin*'s role was to provide necessary information, to link village women up with the appropriate officials who can deal with their demands, and to organize collective responses. Jain et al. (1986) provide some examples of how this function was carried out. In Ajmer district, the *sathin* found that the local official in charge of local famine works was threatening to eliminate from his list of wage earners those women who refused to get sterilized. He had his own 'targets' to meet because of government pressure over family planning. The *sathin* intervened with the support of some senior government officers and the women were reinstated. The *sathin* also assisted a number of women who were interested in sterilization to get the operation. Other women in the famine work helped them to retain their jobs by working extra to ensure that they did not have to undertake taxing physical work straight after the operation. The woman agreed that it was not family planning that they objected to, but the coercive measures which accompanied it.

In Jodhpur district, the *sathins* mobilized women labourers to demand minimum wages for famine works. They found out that they had been putting their thumb impressions to payments of Rs. 11 but receiving only Rs. 3 or Rs. 4. This led to a demand for literacy and numeracy, and adult-education centres were gradually set up in a number of the villages. In Udaipur district, a key problem identified was alcoholism among men, which led to widespread incidence of wife beating. The *sathin* was asked by the men not to interfere, although the women had complained bitterly. A collective decision was taken in a *jajam* to make alcohol consumption illegal. However, the police could only take action against misbehaviour in public, not within the home. The issue was discussed again in the village general meeting, this time involving the men of the village, including the village elders. The police agreed to prosecute men who consumed illicit liquor and beat their wives. Attempts by some of the men in the village to 'excommunicate' the *sathin* failed because of the unanimous support of the women.

Another kind of institutional failure is addressed by the efforts of Saptagram, one of the few examples of an NGO in Bangladesh that is staffed mainly by women at all levels of the organization. As such, it provides a particular challenge to conventional institutions, including other NGOs in the country, which claim that it is impossible to find women prepared to undertake responsibility at the higher levels of management. While most NGOs in Bangladesh today have identified poorer women as a key target group, the number of women they employ on their staff is very limited, and they generally do not stay very long. In Saptagram, flexible service rules taking individual women's family circumstances into account mean that most of the primarily female staff stay on in the organisation, even after marriage. Staff members are allowed to bring their children into the office or project headquarters; time off for family responsibilities is given. In exchange, members will work more intensively when the organization requires it. Members are allowed to use conventional public transport or rickshaws, rather than required to ride bicycles – a rule that has the effect of putting off many potential women applicants to some of the other NGOs in Bangladesh. This emphasis on recruiting committed women staff has had the effect of slowing down Saptagram's rate of expansion, since it can grow only as fast as it can find good female staff. Nevertheless, in its attempt to combine feminist and development principles, it offers a different model of organization to most other NGOs in Bangladesh. Saptagram, as a recent evaluation report suggested, is not about 'including women' in development or about 'the women especially'. It is a development organization that is 'for women' (Arn and Lily, 1992). It offers a glimpse into what would become possible were existing institutions to adapt their rules and practices to the needs of working women rather than requiring working women to adapt to the logic of male-dominated institutions.

The Power Within: Transforming Consciousness and Reinterpreting Need

We have stressed so far the importance of incorporating women's own needs and priorities into the construction of organizational agendas. However, current priorities reflect the current conditions of women's lives. Different priorities might come into view if women were able to review their lives from other vantage points. Strategies of 'empowerment from within' provide women with these other perspectives. They entail reflection, analysis and assessment of what has hitherto been taken for granted so as to uncover the socially constructed and socially shared basis of apparently individual problems. New forms of consciousness arise out of women's newly acquired access to the intangible resources of analytical skills, social networks, organizational strength, solidarity and sense of not being alone.

Although located outside the region we are concentrating on, Shanti Dairiam (1992)[3] provides an excellent case study of an organization's attempt to build battered women's sense of control over their own lives, the 'power within'. It illustrates the kinds of institutional norms and practices that are adopted to achieve this goal. The Malaysian Women's Aid Organization (WAO) was set up in 1982 to provide a range of support services to women with violent husbands, including shelter, counselling, legal advice and support, job placement, housing, and so on. Abused women are given shelter by the WAO, along with their children, for three months during which they have to decide whether they wish to return to their husbands or to lead an independent life. The WAO's philosophy makes the restoration of self-esteem and autonomy to women, whose experience has badly damaged these inner resources, its primary concern. It operates on the principle that every woman has the right to self-determination. However, many processes have to be gone through before this right is exercised: 'She has to come to terms with what has been happening to her within the marital relationship, unlearn the many years of reinforcement that she is an unworthy person, that what has happened to her is her own fault and to feel a sense of outrage at the violation of her bodily integrity.' All WAO's actions are geared to providing an environment in which women feel empowered to take responsibility for their own decisions and own lives.

Women hear about the WAO through various forms of publicity or they may be referred by the police, welfare departments, hospitals or women's organizations, but they must make the approach to WAO on their own. This is to ensure that they are seeking assistance of their own volition and that they are fully aware of and prepared for the kinds of choices and trade-offs facing them. When a woman openly and publicly acknowledges that she is being beaten by her husband and that she wants to do something about it, she is laying herself open to the risk of her husband's wrath as well as alienation from her family and community. It may lead to ultimate separation. Only women who have no friends or family to go to are advised to stay at the shelter. Invariably these are poorer women. At the centre, attempts are made to provide the women with interactions very different from the brutalizing and self-corrosive experiences they have been through. This does not happen automatically or overnight but through a slow and patient process. Many of the women are not accustomed to fending for themselves in public space and even fewer have ever dealt with public officials. They are encouraged to go out on their own, taught bus routes and required to do their own shopping or visits to hospital, though a companion is provided if necessary. They are taught how to make police reports, obtain identity cards for children who are of age, effect the transfer of children from one school to another. They are given support, information and counselling until they are ready to make a decision regarding their own future. WAO helps them to implement this decision, whether it entails returning to their husbands or leading separate lives. If it is the former, the woman is supported in stipulating her terms and conditions for returning. The WAO does not get involved in this process of dialogue and negotiation. It is initiated by the woman, and the services of the state welfare department may be sought. If the woman decides to leave, WAO undertakes to assist her with the legal processes for separation or divorce, maintenance and custody of children. She is also assisted with job placement and housing.

Dairiam suggests that women's action in seeking support at the shelter comes as a shock to many of their husbands since it may be the first time that their wives have offered them any resistance. Men's pride, self-esteem and sense of ownership of their wives are all profoundly affected. Whatever the women decide to do ultimately, the knowledge that there is an alternative safe place where they can take refuge from the violence they experience within their marriages has improved their bargaining power vis-à-vis their husbands. Both parties know that if they do not negotiate an acceptable set of terms for continuing their marriage, the woman no longer has to accept an abusive relationship. She has a supportive institution outside her marriage to back her if she wants to leave. For both women and men, women's ability to resist their husbands' violence, often for the first time in the marriage, can have a profound effect.

The extent to which other more clearly development-oriented NGOs give explicit consideration to transforming consciousness and the modes through which they seek to do so varies considerably. Within the Grameen Bank, there is an emphasis on building new collective identities for women through the process of group formation. Fuglesang and Chandler (1986) describe this approach: 'Quite simply it means to stand together and to move together, to have an intention together and to act together in pursuit of that intention.' They also emphasize the interpersonal dynamics involved in the process. 'Such a formation is expressed both in physical or spatial arrangements and in the thinking, the feeling, the attitudes and the behaviour of the participants, right down to their body language. Most significantly, it is a social design in which people participate in making themselves socially and economically accountable to each other' (p. 52).

Through a series of workshops with its bank workers and women borrowers, culminating in a National Workshop in 1984, a set of Sixteen Decisions were agreed upon as a kind of social development charter that would have to be agreed on by all members of the groups. These decisions act as a focus of group discussions as well as a tool for monitoring and evaluating Grameen's work. Along with conventional development goals (health, water and sanitation, housing, nutrition, family planning, education, savings and investment, environment) they also emphasize some of the more intangible aspects of social development (discipline, unity, responsibility, courage, justice and solidarity). There is also the decision not to give or take dowry, widely regarded as one of the key structural expressions of women's subordination.

There is a great deal of emphasis within the Grameen culture on the personal behaviour and appearance of the poor women that it organizes:

> The culture of poverty is in the stance of the landless. It is expressed in the bent back, the fallen glance, and the low inaudible voice. It is an emotional vote of no-confidence in the self. . . . Grameen recognizes that people's dignity grows out of a straight back. The Bank workers attach great importance to people at centre meetings looking at them directly as they talk, standing straight, and speaking loudly and clearly. (p. 95)

This emphasis on physical deportment explains the role assigned to exercise and discipline within Grameen organizational culture. Meetings and workshops are begun with special salutes, a programme of exercise, shouting of slogans and recitation in unison of the Sixteen Decisions. In the context of Bangladesh, where men monopolize the use of public space, where women's bodies are invested with beliefs about pollution and shame, the emphasis on freedom of body movement has a certain logic. Nevertheless, its form and mode of delivery speak of its origins in a certain class-based view of what constitutes empowerment; it has not evolved from below. It is also a 'male' model of empowerment in that it is masculine deportment and movement that are held up as the standard to emulate. Very little attention is paid to bringing about changes in men's everyday behaviour and practices in the arena of gender, despite the fact that the vast majority of its workers are male, and the vast majority of its membership is female.

The politics of gender, and an explicit concern with 'the power within', figure more centrally in the activities of the WDP. Here, as we saw, the stress was on intangible resources – training and education, communication of information, building of support networks – with a view to improving women's longer-term access to more tangible resources, particularly those distributed by the state. In contrast to the bias towards tangible, quantifiable performance indicators displayed in conventional planning ('such as, so many children immunized, so many made literate, so many given bank loans etc.' Dighe and Jain, 1989, p. 92), the WDP seeks to redefine 'work' to include these more intangible resources: support, solidarity and empowerment. Dighe and Jain (1989) note how one WDP *pracheta* struggled to come to terms with this novel approach to development work:

> *Didi*, we often feel desperate that we cannot see our work. We cannot measure the trust and confidence that we have established with the people. Everything appears so fluid. We go to the Regar women, sit with them and talk to them. It is gradually becoming clear that the dirt and filth for which we despised them is a result of sheer poverty. Now we sit and eat with them and can see why their priorities are different. But I still wonder, is this measurable work? (*Pracheta's* report, Ajmer District, June 1985)

Continuous training forms the backbone of the programme and considerable emphasis is given to the training of the *sathins* who form the basic support network for poorer women in the villages and provide them with a channel of communication with state institutions. Training takes place through *jajams*, the monthly meeting of the *sathins*, organized at the village level, and *shivirs*, three-day camps organized around specific problems identified by women within a district. What is distinctive about WDP's training approach is its emphasis on that neglected dimension in most development efforts – the self. WDP is concerned with the transformation of 'the self' as the key route to women's *self*-empowerment. It seeks to generate experiences which strengthen women's sense of selfhood as well as their perceptions of their place in society. 'Far from being lectures on "cleanliness", "nutrition", and "child-development", the training programmes experiment with the possibility of creating a climate of questioning, reflecting, sharing, choosing, seeking and discovering' (Jain et al., 1986, p. 13). Detailed attention is given to every aspect of interaction during training programmes, including physical arrangements, modes of communication, and the content of the training itself, since each element is seen as a part of the process for rethinking the sense of self that participants bring into any development programme. The actual programmes are devised to respond to local needs in each village, but share the process of moving from individual perceptions of problems to collective identification of priorities. The key issues identified then become the main theme of the training programmes that are used to disseminate relevant information and come up with possible solutions.

Drawing on the idea that 'the struggle to learn, to describe, to understand, to educate is a central and necessary part of our humanity . . . [a] struggle [that] is not begun at second hand after reality has occurred [but that] is in itself a major way in which reality is continually formed and changed', WDP used a range of innovative ways in the struggle to describe and change reality. A great deal of the training is devoted to work with the everyday cultural symbols that underpin, and undermine, women's self-image in different societies. Theatre is also drawn on as a means of communication:

> they did not speak of their analysis and then translate it into a play – they analysed in drama. The play made their thought explicit. The plays covered the functioning of a milk co-operative in one of the villages, they used plays to highlight what was meant by a good woman and a bad woman within the existing value system. They also used stories, anecdotes, riddles. They resorted to songs as a method of documentation and an easy-to-handle system of information retrieval. Songs are easily acceptable, spread and created. They do not need a setting, they can travel from place to place. (Shrivasthava, 1992)

A rather different approach to issues of individual consciousness is that of 'conscientization' as an explicitly political act which forms the basis of the learning processes embodied in Freire's 'pedagogy for the oppressed'. Developed in Latin America, these have been adopted and adapted to a variety of different contexts. The Freirean conscientization process seeks to turn literacy into a political act. While seeking to conscientize through literacy training, it is not illiteracy that is seen as the main problem, but the underlying structures that sustain it. Consequently, teaching literacy may merely have a domesticating function, helping the oppressed to adapt better to the conditions of their oppression. As James (1990, p. 24) points out, many organizations claim 'ingenuous literacy visions', borrowing the political language of transformative literacy but leaving behind the theory.

A number of South Asian organizations (including both Saptagram and Nijera Kori) working with the landless have adopted and adapted Freire's ideas to their local contexts. Their strategy is to build the organizational capacity among landless women and men on the basis of a conscientization process in order that they will mobilize around their self-defined priorities and concerns. If the poor lack the material and political clout to challenge the structure and distribution of entitlements in their society, then conscientization and organization are seen as mobilizing the only resources they do have: their capacity to resist and transform through their collective strength. It could be said that Saptagram's commitments to run a development organization mainly for women, with a primarily female staff in a society where men have typically monopolized institutional power, space and resources, itself signals the significance given to transformatory ways of perceiving and doing development. In addition, conscientization through adult-education classes is an important component in its approach. This takes place through a learning–teaching format in which literacy is taught, not through the convention of using words that have little relevance to the everyday lives of poor people, but rather through dialogue around words and themes that have a deep resonance. These may include class-based themes such as wages, landlords, property, as well as gender-based ones such as dowry, wife-beating, divorce and land rights. The discussions generated allow participants in the training programmes to analyse and question the realities behind these everyday words, to construct alternative visions, and to reflect on the strategies by which these visions might be brought closer. The act of moving beyond acceptance of structures which are so pervasive and deep-rooted that they become invisible to the exploration of how these structures are sustained – and who they benefit – is seen as a politicizing process.

Another important element in this continuing process of building awareness is expanding women's mobility. Women's lives within rural society have been extremely circumscribed in both physical and social terms. As we noted earlier, they frequently liken themselves to oxen turning the grindstone, treading an endless cycle of drudgery, blind to the world beyond. Saptagram organizes group meetings in different village centres so that members from different parts of the region can exchange information and share experiences. Such travel plays an important role in breaking down the sense of isolation and powerlessness that women are often trapped in.

A final, and again different, example of an attempt to empower rural women through a political understanding of their problems is the Bankura experiment, an association between CWDS, a research group, and *samitis* (groups) of poor women in West Bengal (Mazumdar, 1989). These groups were organized around reclamation of waste land donated to them by fellow villagers. This part of Bankura district had few opportunities for wage labour, so that seasonal migration was a critical aspect of the survival strategies of poor and assetless families. In response to demands for work locally expressed at a meeting of women agricultural labourers, the West Bengal Minister for Land

Reform brought in the CWDS in an advisory role. While CWDS emphasized the self-organization of the poor, it also saw a role for a middle-class women's group in setting up the first channels of communication between poorer rural women's organizations and the wider structures of decision-making within development. They stressed the value of such strategic coalitions as a way of overcoming some of the constraints that poorer woman faced.

A critical resource promoted by CWDS was professional management training to enable the women to manage their enterprises. This was provided through training workshops on a quarterly basis for a year for the same group of women. Training was seen by the CWDS organizers both as human resource development but also as a politicizing technique. In the words of the director, 'Wage labour displays a psychology of dependence on work-givers. This is reflected in their language. The psychology of entrepreneurship and self-reliance represents a tremendous transition and challenge to these women' (cited in Singh, 1993, p. 189). Training covers a wide variety of issues. Along with management skills and formal vocation-related training, the workshops focus on policy issues: legal rights, rules governing *samity* assets and membership, the ability to challenge dowry, alcoholism. The agenda is continuously improvised and revised in response to new ideas and new needs. The workshop has also produced training skills in the *samity* members. When the government approached the CWDS to provide training to its officers on rural women's development issues, it was the *samity* members who were brought in to provide the training. As Vina Majumdar notes in her report on the Bankura experiment, women's subordination within rural social relations, their dependent positions within their households, and the drudgery that characterizes their existence had created a structural isolation which prevented the growth of collective forms of consciousness and action to transform their lives. The mastering of new technologies built up women's confidence in their own abilities, and demands for new knowledge of all kinds – from treatment of livestock to laws, to ideas about the bigger world outside their experience – proliferated, 'making [the organizers] wonder who propagated the myth about poor rural women's lack of motivation for education' (Mazumdar, 1989, p. 29). One lesson that CWDS took home from the experiment was the role of particular forms of consciousness-raising in organizing women. 'We found the peasant women fully conscious of the reasons for their poverty and their subordinations.' What they were ignorant of was their 'new rights – as human beings, as workers and as citizens, their rights and responsibilities to participate in all decisions within the family, the community and the state, to influence the process of change and claim a share of state assistance for themselves' (Mazumdar, 1989, p. 29). The emergence of a collective and strategic awareness of the nature of gender subordination in place of earlier 'gender blindness' is described vividly by one of the women that Mazumdar quotes:

> We were like frogs in a dark well. No one had thought of extending our minds. Our idea of *we* meant the family, or at most, the village or the caste in the village. When we became members of a multivillage, multicaste organization, *we* suddenly expanded. Now it has become so much bigger — we are a part of a network of organizations. This, plus the knowledge that we have equal rights, has been like a shot of vitamin in our lives. We are stronger, and more determined today than ever before. (p. 33)

The Power With: Solidarity and Alliances

The preceding quotation echoes the theme of collective identity that underpins most empowerment strategies. This stress on the *collective* has a dual rationale. First, it relates to the ideological basis of gender subordination. The social basis of male domination is often concealed through powerful ideological mechanisms, including the 'naturalization' of the status quo, so that women experience subordination as inevitable and interpersonal. Recognition of the shared aspects of subordination points to its collectively enforced, and hence collectively changeable, character and forms the basis of strategies for change. The second, and related, point is that, given women's disenfranchisement from most sources of institutional power, their collective strength is seen as the most important transformatory resource at their disposal. And in contexts where norms of seclusion and segregation curtail their ability to participate in community-based networks, their leverage to challenge gender hierarchies within the domestic arena is correspondingly curtailed. The organizational capacity of poorer women is seen as a vital instrument for articulating their interests within the development process. However, it has to be built up through a conscious process. If it existed naturally, then the disempowerment of the poor would not be an issue. Many of the organizations we have been discussing in this chapter stress this need to build up or strengthen the networks and alliances among poor people as an aspect of empowerment.

Group formation is critical to Grameen credit disbursement. While loans are to individual group members, the group is actively involved at every stage of the process. It must decide the amount of loans to grant and which borrowers will receive them. The groups have weekly meetings during which weekly instalments of the loan are paid off. Furthermore, the group provides social collateral, the only form of collateral that the bank relies on. Social collateral operates through group accountability processes which members have established among themselves. Saptagram takes the principle of group solidarity further; its women's groups are at the core of its empowerment strategy. Unlike Grameen, it provides loans to the group rather than to individual members (with the exception of special loans for destitute women). This principle is strictly adhered to in the interests of fostering group solidarity. Groups make the decision to save according to their member's ability, and Saptagram provides a matching amount as a loan. While the savings and loan programme is what initially attracts women to form themselves into groups, the formation process with regular meetings and regular savings begins to give the relationship a more proactive character. The choice, planning and management of the group's schemes are the responsibility of the members themselves since they are in the best position to understand their own circumstances. Once a group has been operating successfully for a while, it tends to move away from direct involvement with Saptagram and to run its activities entirely independently, with Saptagram continuing to act as an umbrella organization. Perhaps the most important effect of such a group formation process is that it cuts across traditional vertical alliances, such as those based on kinship or patron–client relationships. It offers a form of organization that they can *choose* to belong to, unlike those based on family, kinship or patronage where their consent is either not required or which entail a trade-off between autonomy and security.

Trade unions are traditionally about building the collective bargaining power of workers vis-à-vis management. However, because of the structures and relations of production within which self-employed women are located, conventional forms of union organization are seen by SEWA as inadequate. At the heart of SEWA's organizational strategy is a model of joint action by unions and cooperatives: 'Cooperatives, by providing alternative forms of production, when complemented by more conventional union actions, offer a stronger chance of eradicating the poverty of these workers' (Sebstadt, 1982).

SEWA attempts to bridge the class as well as gender interests of its membership. It provides a social connection to a section of the work force whose members are either isolated within the home or in dispersed and shifting work locations. Access to these new and collective relationships, built around their shared needs and interests as workers and as women, has given SEWA's members the opportunity to think of themselves in terms other than those imposed by their traditional domestic, caste and community roles. Bhatt (1989) suggests that the attitudes of husbands/family members change when they know the women have the support of a powerful organization. The attitudes of women themselves change as they participate in leadership training and workers' education, and understand organizational processes, communication skills and their rights as workers. The strength of this dual model of organization is that it recognizes that women's ability to organize around more strategic concerns is likely to be most firmly grounded when it emerges out of the organizational strengths acquired through meeting their more practical interests. Acknowledging that union organization requires different skills and strengths to cooperative organization, Jhabvala points out that,

> Nonetheless, the two can work well together. For example, to form a strong trade union, courage, awareness and solidarity are needed. Among the self-employed, women are in such a weak position to begin with, they really cannot talk about solidarity at the very beginning. A co-operative can be an entry point into the community and serve as the center of contact for a union. It also provides a base on which to build up organizers and local leaders. For example, when we were struggling against the *chindi* tax, if SEWA had not already been a part of the community in Dariapur, we never would have gotten the wage increase. You have to be there to grab. You can be there through a co-operative. (cited in Sebstadt, 1982)

Organization on the basis of shared interests can have broader ramifications. The twin goals of the Bankura project of employment generation and organization building for collective empowerment also had the major impact of breaking down social barriers of caste and religion hierarchies among women: 'taboos on inter-communal social relations, eating together, marriage choices, speaking in public, accepting leadership of a person considered to be lower in social status – seem to break down more easily when women acted together. There are occasional confrontations and conflicts, but there is a groundswell of change' (Mazumdar, 1989, p. 33).

The Power To: Mobilizing for Change

We have identified the key components of some of the strategies undertaken by organizations committed to women's empowerment. However, unless these elements are translated into mobilization strategies by women around self-defined concerns and priorities, development organizations are in danger of substituting themselves as the agents of change for those they seek to organize. To this extent, empowerment must entail as an ultimate goal the ability of the disempowered to act collectively in their own practical and strategic interests. As Mazumdar points out in relation to the Bankura experience:

> Neither the organizations nor the employment to be generated were to be ends in themselves. They were merely to be the means of mobilizing poor rural women to participate more effectively in the wider process of socio-political development, to wrest from society the rights, the dignity and the resources to which they were entitled for their own development, through collective action to increase their voice in development decisions that affected their lives. (1989, p. 11)

The development organizations that we have described in this chapter did not arise spontaneously through the efforts of poor women. They came into existence through the efforts of other relatively more powerful actors who had access to the funds, contacts and information necessary to set them up. They are generally not financially self-sufficient but rely on funds from other agencies. They must also retain state approval if they are to remain in existence and must therefore tailor their operations to fit official definitions of what constitutes legitimate developmental activity. This places most innovative development organizations in a very contradictory position. On the one hand, their ability to operate depends on containing their activities within a non-political agenda which does not challenge the existing basis of class and gender entitlements. On the other hand, when empowerment is carried out as a truly transformative project, no organization can set predetermined limits on what is achieved. Attempts to analyse and understand the roots of class and gender oppressions spill inevitably over from the arena of development into that of politics, as oppressed groups seek to move from redefining local project activity to setting the overall policy agenda.

The NGOs we have discussed have undertaken a variety of strategies to deal with the potentially political implications of their work. For Grameen, whose goal is the alleviation of poverty, the main concern is with successful delivery of credit to poor women rather than with challenging the structures of gender subordination. It uses its weight and resources to ensure certain strategic changes occur in women's lives, but it also seeks to defuse confrontation from the outset through a process of meetings with women's families before beginning operations in a new area. Grameen philosophy stresses the familial benefits that are likely to flow from its investments in women members of the family rather than the transformatory potential of its work. Consequently, there may be constraints at work which prevent Grameen's women's groups from taking on a more political role in the process of development.

By contrast, Nijera Kori places at the heart of its strategy the mobilization of landless women and men to press for their entitlements. It sees its long-term goal as encouraging the development of autonomous and democratic organizations of the poor. A review of Nijera Kori's experience stresses conflicts that it has to deal with. It suggests that, while at the household level men frequently oppose the involvement of their women members, such resistance is partly diluted by Nijera Kori's strategy of organizing men alongside women. Less easy to resolve has been the resistance of vested-interest groups within the rural hierarchy. Attempts by Nijera Kori groups to raise the agricultural wage, to resist the appropriation of government *khas* lands by powerful landowners, to undertake their own joint cultivation of such lands, to complain about local government corruption, have all been carried out in the face of harassment, often bordering on violence, of group members. A recent review of the organization (Westergaard, 1992) also notes that in terms of awareness of social issues, group members have taken action against oppressive aspects of gender relations and started to settle disputes among themselves, rather than relying on traditional rural power structures. More recently, Nijera Kori groups have been involved in fielding their own candidates in the local elections.

Working mainly with women, Saptagram attempts to combine an anti-poverty development agenda with the objectives of a women's organization. There is a stress on building the organizational autonomy of its women's groups and their links to wider networks. The organization seeks to monitor group empowerment by the way in which group members take up and participate in *andolons* or movements. These are generally against dowry, illegal divorce and polygamy, violence against women and other forms of social injustice. These movements are generally self-initiated, although Saptagram staff provide support, advice and information when requested. Groups often come to Saptagram centres for support and information when they need it; they do not wait for the staff to come and visit them in their villages. Members have been involved in organizing and leading women labourers in rural public works to down their tools and demand their wage entitlement from the local authorities. Group members are often called on in the local village courts (traditionally the domain of male elite groups) to represent women's viewpoint and interests. In addition, Saptagram has facilitated linkages between its women's groups and wider movements. Its groups have participated in International Women's Day celebrations organized by various feminist organizations, as well as in the national movement for democracy which overthrew the Ershad government in 1990. Recently Saptagram's groups have been involved in a national women's movement protest against the stoning of a woman found guilty of adultery by the local village tribunal.

SEWA, too, can be seen as an organization that represents the interests of women, specifically of women workers. Some of the criticisms levelled at SEWA point to the extent to which 'purist' strategies for women's empowerment still prevail. Radicals continue to criticize SEWA for its links with the government on some development issues and for its distance from the traditional organizations of the working class. However, SEWA emerged out of the failure of the organizational form traditionally espoused by the male left – the trade union – to take the problems of women workers seriously. One of its organizers describes the paternalism of the TLA: 'The TLA looks at SEWA as a daughter; when she conforms to orders she is patted on the back. But when she grows up she is bound to think for herself and question. The TLA could not take this' (cited in Sebstadt, 1982).

The SEWA leadership has remained aware of the limitations of an organization of women workers where leadership is being provided by 'outsiders', but points to the problems of expecting leadership to emerge spontaneously from its rank-and-file membership:

> With our middle class upbringing we have limits to understanding the poor, but they also have limits to taking up leadership. With the demands of their day to day struggle to survive they have little time to assume the responsibility of leadership. They also carry little weight in society. However, with a middle class background, someone like myself has more weight and the ability to communicate with those in the establishment . . . Only creating awareness is not enough. We must also prepare leaders. But until they are ready to assume power, we must assume final responsibility for action. If we don't, we fail. If the poor had that capacity already, they would not have been exploited for so long.

SEWA continues to push for greater participation by its members at all levels of the organization. Both unions and cooperatives are democratic bodies where committee members are elected from the wider membership. Its flexibility and its comitment to its membership have allowed it to meet new challenges and to respond to crisis situations in ways that strengthen the organization. The SEWA Bank, for instance, came into existence in 1974 as a result of the efforts of the SEWA membership. They initiated a campaign to raise the legal minimum share capital required to set up a bank. Within six months they had succeeded in selling shares worth Rs. 10 to over four thousand women. When the campaign organizers learnt only a day in advance of registration that fifteen promoters had to sign the papers, a group of members sat up through the night learning to sign their names.

The subsequent split with the TLA and withdrawal of its deposits presented a major crisis for SEWA. However, women's groups from around the country swung behind SEWA membership in their drive to raise share capital and the Bank continued in existence. As its organizers stress, the Bank is an important resource in its members' lives, not only lending them money but also allowing them a safe place to deposit their savings, thus safeguarding them from appropriation by male family members. As in Grameen, there is a stress on ownership of the bank by its members. Such ownership is not purely symbolic. SEWA Bank belongs to its members; they own the share capital that keeps it in existence and they are represented on its board of members. This gives them a keen interest in its day-to-day operations. This was illustrated for Maitrayee Mukhopadhyay[4] when, in the course of preparing a field report for Oxfam, she interviewed Sumandatanya, a self-employed woman who sold dental twigs in the market for a living and was on the Board of SEWA Bank. She provided Mukhopadhaya with a detailed breakdown of the figures on loan capital, deposit accounts, capital assets, number of borrowers and lenders and the profit position of the bank, entirely from memory. Later that day, Mukhopadhyay interviewed a bank manager who, after some delay in order to consult the records, gave almost identical estimates to those already provided by Sumandatanya.

SEWA has linked its membership up to the wider women's movement in protesting strategic gender issues such as dowry, rape, sati, violence against women. It has also worked with other women's organizations to change policies and laws in India and to oppose sex discrimination tests, which are leading to female foeticide. It has trained its members to produce video films drawing public attention to the lives and problems of poor self-employed women, and provided legal assistance to individuals and groups fighting discriminatory laws and individual injustices.

The experiences of the WDP highlight both the strengths and weaknesses of NGO collaboration with the government. They also point to the artificiality of the separation between development and politics. As government employees, the WDP *sathins* have ease of access to the local bureaucracy, an important resource in meeting women's locally defined needs. The *sathin's* role is to provide necessary information, to link village women up with the appropriate state officials who can respond to their demands and to organize collective responses where such response is not forthcoming. However, recent critiques of the WDP suggest that the class and caste dimensions of poor women's lives have not received the same degree of attention that gender has. Here state involvement appears to have played an important role in limiting the 'decisionable' agenda within which WDP works. As one recent article notes, 'Whenever questions which bring major structural contradictions in society under scrutiny or those which challenge state policies of development are raised, they are dubbed as "political" in the former instance and out of the purview of the WDP charter in the latter' (Malika et al., 1993, p. 374).

Yet, given the explosive potential of challenging traditional gender hierarchies, these status-imposed limitations have left WDP workers bereft of the collective power of the wider women's movement without necessarily guaranteeing them state support either. This came tragically to the fore when a *sathin* was gang-raped by men of the socially dominant Gujar caste while she was campaigning against child marriage in the light of government directives. Despite demands by the women's groups that the men be brought to justice, there has been a reluctance on the part of the state to act. As Malika et al. (1993) observe, the state appears willing to sacrifice the interests of 'one' woman from an economically and numerically weaker caste in order to placate the more powerful constituency represented by the powerful Gujar caste, particularly prior to important local elections. The WDP experience appears to suggest that, while considerable progress in women's conditions can be made under state auspices, once the broader political dimensions of gender subordination are recognized and acted on, women's empowerment can become as destabilizing to the social order as more conventional forms of oppositional politics. One important lesson to be drawn from WDP's experience is that the state is a contradictory force in the process of women's empowerment. It has the power to override certain kinds of local constraints and to provide the enabling conditions for women to mobilize around their own self-defined priorities. But where such activity conflicts with other interests of the state, it is unlikely to prove a reliable ally. Women's empowerment has to be linked up with the struggle of other marginalized groups if it is to be sustainable.

Conclusion

This has been an extremely selective discussion about strategies for empowering women, but it provides a useful context for reflecting once more on the question of empowerment and how it might relate to the question of women's strategic gender interests. Many of the strategies we have discussed here deal with the same basic needs that figure in more conventional poverty-alleviation programmes, namely, income, employment and credit. Where they differ, therefore, is not in the category of needs considered important, but how such needs are identified and met. What also emerges out of this discussion is that women's practical and strategic gender interests are not separate and dichotomous categories, but rather linked through the transformatory aspects of these different strategies for empowerment. This transformatory potential lies in the extent to which strategies seek to open up, rather than foreclose on, the possibilities available to women.

How is this transformatory potential operationalized? First of all, it depends on the extent to which NGO interventions are organized around the participatory modes of needs identification and prioritization rather than through the imposition of their own priorities on those who have traditionally had no voice in influencing the course of development. Second, it depends on the extent to which the rules and practices of NGO interventions succeed in compensating for the exclusionary implications of most conventional institutions of resource distribution. In particular, it depends on the extent to which NGOs are able to provide women with access to new kinds of resources, thereby signalling new potentials and possibilities rather than merely reinforcing old roles and constraints. Third, it depends on how women are positioned within NGO strategies – as needy clients or as socially constrained but competent actors. Grameen, which positioned women as independent entrepreneurs, able to utilize and repay loans; SEWA, with its emphasis on the rights and interests of self-employed women workers to a trade union of their own; Nijera Kori, with its concern to make effective the entitlements that the state offered to the poor; Saptagram, with its commitment to creating an organization mainly for women to be run mainly by women; and WDP, with its goal of improving women's ability to evolve their own agendas rather than merely implementing predetermined ones; all these efforts echo the waitress in Schumacher's story – they seek to treat women as 'real' actors in the development process rather than seeking to act on their behalf.

A further transformatory aspect of NGO strategies is the emphasis on new forms of collective awareness and association. Many NGOs begin from the analysis that women from the dispossessed groups within society suffer the silences imposed by their gender as well as their class, and that empowerment entails 'conscientization' or breaking these silences. This requires that women are able to challenge the belief systems which legitimize their subordination, to analyse their own situations and problems, and to come up with their own strategies. As Dighe and Jain (1989) put it: 'From a state of powerlessness that manifests itself in a feeling of "I cannot", empowerment contains an element of collective self-confidence that results in a feeling of "we can"' (p. 87).

However, all these activities will do little in themselves to address the broader context of women's lives unless they are translated into organizational power. One of the major limitations of the development NGO as a vehicle for women's empowerment is that it tends to be accountable upwards to governments or donors. Consequently, there is a constant pressure to manage its activities around acceptable and predefined agendas. Of course, many of the organizations we have been talking about have managed to escape these restrictive confines, subverting official entitlement policies or reinterpreting officially acceptable concerns in the light of grassroots realities. But there is still the danger that without an organizational commitment to strengthening poor women's own ability to mobilize around their self-defined interests, their participation in development and their access to resources will remain confined to the parameters of local-level projects. Organization and mobilization are a key route by which women can link up with the broader struggle for a more accountable development and start to challenge the allocation of resources at the policy level. Hence the longer-term sustainability of empowerment strategies will depend on the extent to which they envision women struggling within a given set of policy priorities and the extent to which they empower them to challenge and reverse these priorities. It is only when the participation of poorer women goes beyond participation at the project level to intervening in the broader policymaking agenda that their strategic interests can become an enduring influence on the course of development.

Notes

1 I owe this story to Lloyd Mullen.
2 In their study of rural poverty in Bangladesh, Rahman and Sen (1993) also note this hitherto neglected aspect of the sanitation problem and cite a woman who described the suffering created by this inconvenience to Dr Yunus of Grameen Bank as akin to *kabar-azab*, the perpetual punishment suffered by sinners in their graves.
3 My thanks to Shanti Dairiam for allowing me to quote from her case study.
4 Maitrayee Mukhopadhyay, personal communication.

═══ 10 ═══

Triple Roles, Gender Roles, Social Relations: The Political Subtext of Gender Training Frameworks

> What we do in the world reflects what we know about it, and what we know depends on how we go about knowing, or in other words when thinking about change we should start by thinking about thinking. (Bawden and Macadam, 1988, cited in Ison, 1990)[1]

> Only by sharpening the links between equality, development and peace, can we show that the 'basic rights' of the poor and the transformation of the institutions that subordinate women are inextricably linked. They can be achieved together through the self-empowerment of women. (Sen and Grown, 1985, p. 75)

Gender Training as Development Practice

In 1991, an international conference on Gender Training and Development Planning held in Norway highlighted gender training as an important means by which feminist advocates and practitioners were seeking to de-institutionalize male privilege within development policy and planning. Greater awareness of the costs of gender-blindness in past interventions has made policymakers more receptive to the idea of such training as an input into incorporating a gender perspective within their work. However, what is meant by a gender perspective is not uniform across the different training methodologies currently in use. The report from the Bergen conference highlighted both the commonalities as well as some important differences (Rao et al., 1991, p. 11). It suggested that one feature common to most gender training frameworks was 'a systematic analysis of the current and potential roles and responsibilities of both men and women and their access to and control over resources within a particular system' (p. 1). Differences lay in the emphasis given to efficiency, equity and empowerment as the basis for revised policy approaches. Related to this, as Moser pointed out in her conference presentation, were the kinds of objectives pursued through different training approaches. Some addressed the professional dimension: 'skilling professionals in discharging their duties more effectively' (cited in Rao et al., 1991, p. 14). Others introduced the political dimension in their analysis of gender. Less frequently addressed was a third, personal, dimension: challenging the deeply entrenched attitudes and stereotypes about gender difference held by powerful decision-makers within planning institutions.

The conference report suggested that 'to a large extent, these differences in emphasis appear to be a function of differing institutional cultures, rather than difference in underlying commitment to gender equity' (p. 9). There is considerable validity to this observation. The range of issues addressed by different training efforts seems to vary considerably according to the audiences addressed. Northern aid agencies and development banks demonstrate greatest resistance to approaches that stress gender as a power relation and the need for change at the personal level; national development agencies, particularly those working with grassroots constituencies, appear more open to this transformatory agenda (Rao et al., 1991). However, differences in emphasis are not merely externally imposed by institutional cultures. They also reflect the 'different ways of thinking' about gender and development embedded within different training approaches. Internally generated and externally imposed differences in training approaches are not entirely unrelated, of course. Like-minded planners and gender trainers tend to gravitate towards each other because they endorse a common world-view of means and ends. While this tendency is understandable, it is likely to lead to system-conforming, rather than system-transforming, perspectives on gender and development. More challenging in the long run would be to expose gender trainers to planning agencies that do not share their most cherished assumptions, and planning agencies to trainers who challenge their entrenched world-views. One step in this direction reported at the conference was that of the Centre for Women and Development Studies in India, which carried out training of local government officials with the village women they worked with (Sujaya, 1991). This face-to-face encounter was an effective way of persuading officials that poor rural women were experienced and knowledgeable managers of their local environments; in need of material assistance from the government rather than top-down 'educational' instructions.

In this chapter, I want to explore some of the ways in which the political subtexts of different training methodologies are manifested in their treatment of efficiency and equity goals and their positioning of the planner as a possible agent of change. I will be examining the content and implications of three different gender training frameworks that have emerged over the past decade and that may be seen as part of the 'first generation' of efforts in this field: the gender-roles framework (Overholt et al., 1985), the triple-roles framework (Moser, 1989), and the social-relations framework, which has underpinned the analysis in this book. These frameworks emerged as a result of training experiences in response to rather different institutional needs, although all of them share an academic pedigree. The gender-roles framework (GRF) was developed at the Harvard Institute of International Development in collaboration with the Women in Development Office of USAID and subsequently used with the staff of USAID, the World Bank and a number of other donor agencies. The triple-roles framework (the TRF) reflects the author's experience of training at the Development Planning Unit in London with Third World planners from different sectors, some British NGOs and a number of donor agencies. The social-relations framework (SRF) describes the approach that has evolved through the IDS efforts in gender training;[2] a schematic summary of this approach is contained in the Appendix.

The IDS training courses, sometimes run in-country, bring together primarily Third World participants, active in different areas of development: development researchers, planners and grassroots practitioners. The rationale for this mixed audience lies in our belief in the interconnections between the different dimensions of development; ideas, practice, and the institutional contexts in which they are reproduced. The social-relations approach that we employ helps to sketch out some of these interconnections. It also allows us the space to address the 'personal' dimensions of social change: the taken-for-granted ideas about gender relations that we carry around with us and which inform so much of everyday development practice. Like all conceptual efforts, training frameworks seek to draw boundaries around complex empirical realities in order to focus attention on issues considered significant. They therefore involve simultaneously suppressing some, and privileging other, information. This chapter suggests that while both the GRF and the TRF contain different and important insights for planners, they also contain a number of limitations stemming from what is suppressed and what is privileged. It concludes by arguing for analytical frameworks which move beyond the static notions of efficiency favoured by policymakers; which encourage policymakers to examine critically their own roles in the construction and reinforcement of gender inequality; and finally which incorporate a transformative politics premissed on the central notion of women's self-empowerment. The discussion in this chapter will attempt to pull together, at the risk of some repetition, some of the arguments and ideas that have been developed in preceding sections of the book.

The 'Gender Subtext' of Development Policies: Lessons from the Past

We have dealt elsewhere in this book with the reasons why women were assigned such a marginal place in early 'gender-blind' development efforts. The lessons drawn from this experience and the desire to avoid these mistakes in the future provide the rationale for training efforts to encourage planners and policymakers to rethink old assumptions and practices in order to achieve greater gender awareness in the policy process. I will recapitulate some of the main lessons from the WID literature as a starting point for our discussion.

One of the major criticisms of development policy made by feminists in this field has centred on the extremely flawed model of the household that informed policy efforts. As we saw in Chapter 2, this model drew on the ideal-typical household of standard sociological theory: a nuclear family consisting of a male head, primarily responsible for breadwinning, together with his wife and children, with the wife bearing primary responsibility for the care and welfare of the family. Even when planners began to acknowledge, in response to the WID critique, that women (and children), particularly among lower-income households, were engaged in productive work, the latter were mainly perceived in the role of the unpaid family 'helpers'. Women's effort was considered 'subsidiary, literally auxiliary, not crucial to the enterprise' (Roberts, 1979, p. 64); men retained their privileged place within planners' models and practice as heads of households and principal decision-making agents.

The 'gender sub-text' (Fraser, 1989, p. 149) in development thought was manifested in the very different positioning of women and men in the policy domain. As we noted in Chapter 5, Folbre (1986a, 1986b) has drawn attention to the locational dichotomy in individual behaviour posited by liberal economic theory: self-interested and competitive in the market place; altruistic and cooperative within the home. This appears to have been transformed within development policy into a gender dichotomy. Economic policy has both assumed, and sought to promote, the idea of self-interested, free-floating economic man, competing in the marketplace, while social policy has both assumed, and sought to promote, the idea of the altruistic mother, embedded in the moral domain of household and community. The efficiency costs incurred by this misleading depiction of the gender division of labour at household and community levels have been demonstrated in a series of case studies of project misbehaviour. Some of these were discussed in Chapter 7. For instance, Staudt's case study (1978) of the Kenyan government's attempts to promote high-yielding hybrid maize points to the productivity losses that resulted because extension staff assumed that farmers were mainly male, and that only male farmers were innovative. She concluded that male preference in the extension service was likely to erode the long-term productivity of women farmers, undermining their autonomy as economic actors and lowering governmental capacity to raise agricultural output. Elsewhere production targets failed to materialize because planners assumed households functioned as corporate decision-making units under the control of the male head. Research cited earlier, by Dey (1981, 1982) and Jones (1985, 1986), into attempts to introduce irrigated rice production in The Gambia and Cameroon respectively, offered examples of the kind of project misbehaviour that results when such assumptions are not valid. In both contexts, women and men had separate access to land, based on their complementary obligations to contribute to household subsistence needs. This division of obligations and resources provided women with some protection from arbitrary demands on their labour from male household members. In both case studies, they were reluctant to invest their labour in a new male-controlled innovation where the implications for their own economic autonomy were unpredictable, even if the absolute gains for the household might be considerable.

One genre of project misbehaviour documented in the WID literature was therefore associated with attempts to increase economic productivity by targeting incentives at 'the household' or, more specifically, at its male head. Efficiency objectives would have been better served by a greater degree of gender neutrality in the policy design. A different genre of development failures was associated with misconceived notions of 'the community' that figured in a number of social-policy initiatives. Here material incentives were entirely dispensed with. It was assumed that benefits would accrue to the entire community, once information and motivation provided by policy-makers was combined with 'community participation'. However, experience has shown that the solidary community was as much a figment of the policymakers' imagination as was the solidary household. Analyses of community health programmes, for instance, suggested that the concept of community participation was used largely as a euphemism for the unpaid or underpaid labour of women within the community. They pointed out that while such programmes regard the concept of community participation as central to their success, 'the participation they rely upon is predominantly, although not exclusively, that of women' (Leslie et al., 1988, p. 308). In the words of Bruce and Dwyer (1988, p. 18), 'the invisible women of the economic theorist become the all-powerful mothers of the health and welfare advocates'. The casting of women as all-powerful mothers in these highly gender-specific policy interventions had the advantage of dispensing with the need to offer them material incentives. It assumed their 'natural' willingness to undertake more work in the interests of family and community 'with more knowledge, but little more time or money'. The same assumption appeared to underlie one version of the UNICEF case for more 'human' structural adjustment policies: 'there is scope for decentralising many activities in health, nutrition, child care, sanitation etc. to the family (or community) level . . . while such an approach may increase time costs for women, it will place extremely modest monetary costs on the household; and will lead to substantial savings in the public sector' (Cornea, 1987, p. 174, cited in Elson, 1991b, p. 178). The assumption behind this is, in cost–benefit terms, that women's labour has a zero opportunity cost. In the light of widespread findings that suggest that women generally work longer hours than men (Birdsall and McGreevey, 1983; Leslie et al., 1988) the failure of so-called community participation to materialize in many of these programmes is not unexpected.

Other areas of policy research revealed further examples of how an 'imagined community' of interests[3] was used by policymakers to justify attempts to mobilize women's unpaid labour. Rocheleau (1990, p. 4), for instance, notes how a policy view of women-as-resources, as 'fixers' of forestry and resource management problems, has frequently translated into 'a narrow focus on women as free (or cheap) labour to work on forestry projects in the community interest'. Social forestry projects are renamed Women's Social Forestry Projects; road-building projects are renamed Women's Social Infrastructure Projects and so on. The gender-blindness of policy here stems not so much from ignoring women within policy design, but from abstracting them from the social context of their lives.

Putting together this history of misconceived and misdirected interventions, it became clear that compartmentalized modes of development planning have permitted different groups of policy-makers to focus on very specific aspects of women's lives and define their interventions in terms of those aspects alone. Home economists, health planners, agricultural planners, the environment lobby have all targeted women in their plans on the basis of narrowly defined perceptions of what women do. The problem is that women, particularly poor women, do simultaneously undertake many of these roles and responsibilities, often without pay; hence their longer hours of work. Development interventions, designed and implemented by individual sectors with very little coordination between them, generate conflicting demands on women's time and energy. Such interventions are either doomed to failure (thereby confirming planners' worst fears about women's irrational behaviour) or else result in the intensified exploitation of women's labour.

The lack of fit between the sectoral mind-set of development planners and the inter-sectoral realities of women's activities has led to the emergence of conceptual frameworks, like the ones we will be discussing, which seek to demonstrate the *cross-cutting* nature of gender as a development issue. Given the neglect of women's economic agency and productive contributions in past development efforts, it is not surprising that these frameworks gave a central place to the gender division of labour. However, as we noted above, they emerged in response to different needs, addressed different audiences, and offered different perspectives on the conceptualization of gender in the policy process. Thus while all three frameworks seek to achieve a shift from gender-blind to gender-aware policy through a rethinking of assumptions and practices, they are based on very different understandings of the nature of power and inequality. Consequently they give rather different signals to policymakers on the question of gender equity and social transformation. The GRF is intended as a diagnostic tool for project planners concerned with the efficient use of scarce resources. The TRF is aligned more closely to social policy concerns; it promotes gender planning as a distinct planning approach that takes account of gender differences in roles and hence in needs. The SRA offers a methodology for integrating a gender perspective into different aspects of the policy process. It stresses the interconnections between efficiency and welfare and argues for the transformation of current dichotomies in the policy arena in the interests of a more equitable redistribution of resources and responsibilities between women and men. In the rest of this chapter, we will be comparing the treatment of production and power in these frameworks. We will begin with gender divisions in production processes and ask how they deal with the key questions of who does what and how.

The Division of Labour in the
Gender Roles Framework

The gender roles framework offers a methodology for integrating gender-awareness into project design. The framework incorporates a bargaining, rather than an altruistic, model of the household: 'In placing women within the household context . . . we must emphasize that although individuals in households may have *shared* interests, they also have *separate* interests, and they may sometimes have *opposing* interests' (Cloud, 1985, p. 25). Its basic analytical tool is a matrix of questions that focuses attention on gender divisions in production as well as in access and control over resources and benefits. In terms of *what* is produced, two categories of production are distinguished: (a) goods and services, and (b) human resources. The latter activities (which include fuel and water collection, food preparation, birthing, child care, education, health care, and laundry) are undertaken to produce and care for family members and are distinguished from the production of goods and services in that they are often viewed as non-economic and generally carry no financial remuneration. The under-lying distinction between the two categories thus appears to be between market-based and family-based production.

The issue of *who* produces is addressed in the GRF by focusing attention on the age and gender (and class and ethnicity) of the individuals performing different activities. It also addresses certain characteristics of the production process: the time allocated (daily and seasonally) and the location of activity (shops, fields). It makes an important distinction between the question of access (the ability to use) and that of control (the ability to determine use) in the distribution of resources for production and the resulting benefits. In a more detailed formulation of this framework for planning agricultural projects, Cloud (1985) categorizes the different forms that the gender division of labour and management might take. She suggests that five common patterns are:

- Separation by crop. Women and men are responsible for produc-tion and disposal of different crops within the household produc-tion system, viz. women's subsistence crops and men's cash crops; women's horticultural crops and men's cereal crops; women's swamp rice and men's irrigated rice; women's goats and men's cattle.

- Separation by fields. Here women may produce the same crops as those controlled by men, but in different fields and often earmarked for separate destinations.
- Separate tasks. Here some or all tasks within a single cycle are assigned by gender. For instance, men may prepare the ground while women plant or transplant. Ploughing is often done by men. Post-harvest processing and storage of cereals are usually women's tasks. Milking generally, or milking of different animals, may be assigned by gender.
- Shared tasks. Some production systems may be marked by jointness in most tasks; in others, only labour-intensive tasks are shared.
- Separation by gender of household management; that is, depending on whether they are male-managed or de facto or de jure female-managed.

By offering an *open-ended* series of questions around the division of labour, the GRF encourages appreciation of the variety of activities engaged in by household members and highlights some of their logical interconnections. Thus, if a project intervention entails increased demands on adult women's labour time, the GRF points to its possible ramifications for the overall division of labour. Given their existing responsibilities, will the new demand be met by cutting down on women's involvement in other productive activities, by cutting down on their leisure or sleep, or by devolving the responsibilities onto others within the household? Were these others previously idle or was their time only made available by withdrawal from other forms of activity, such as schooling or labour-market participation? What are the resource implications of these cross-substitutions between different categories of labour within the household economy?

The insights provided by the GRF would obviously have gone a long way toward pre-empting the kind of project failures cited earlier in this chapter. However, the GRF has some major limitations in the broader context of planning which derive from its methodological focus on the logical relationship between *activities* rather than the social relationship between *people*. This leads to the treatment of the gender division of labour as a relationship of separation – by activity, field, crops or sector – and to the neglect of its social interconnections within different production processes. It is necessary to recognize that the division of labour is about connection as much as separation (Whitehead, 1991): in assigning women and men to different responsibilities, activities or spheres, it also makes it essential for them to engage in relationships of cooperation or exchange. In so far as women and men are assigned to producing separate products (gender-segregated production processes), they will need to establish some form of exchange in order to gain access to each other's produce. In so far as they are assigned to separate activities within the same production cycle (gender-sequential production processes), they will need to cooperate in order that production is completed and the product divided between the different actors in the process. And, as we noted in Chapter 5, decision-making control in critical stages or activities within the production process can have implications which spill over into other stages or activities. The gender division of labour thus implies both a technical as well as a social interdependence between women and men.

As far as policy design is concerned, the conceptualization of the gender division of labour as a relation of social connection, rather than simply one of separation, implies that women's activities cannot be seen in isolation from the 'upstream', 'downstream' and lateral linkages that make up the production processes in which they are embedded. Neglect of these linkages can undermine the objectives of an intervention. This is illustrated in a review by Goetz (1989) of a fish-smoking project developed by UNIFEM in Guinea. The project was formulated on an understanding of the gender division of labour close to that put forward in the GRF. It identified the different activities undertaken by women and men in a fishing community in Konakry-Guinea and sought to introduce labour-saving technology into the stages of production in which women were concentrated, with a view to increasing their productivity. In Konakry, it was primarily men who caught fish; the fish were smoked and sold by women. The UNIFEM project sought to introduce *chorkor* fish-smoking ovens because they were more efficient than the existing methods used in Konakry. Women were organized into groups in order to make use of this new technology.

Despite its good intentions, the project did not succeed in its goals. This, Goetz points out, could be attributed to its treatment of women's activities in isolation from the context of the social relations of production in fishing. Not only was the focus of the project entirely on women-specific activities, but there was an implicit assumption that project intervention at one stage of the production process would have no repercussions on other stages. Consequently, little thought was given to how the supply of fish for smoking was to be assured to women involved in the project. The assumption appeared to be that it would be forthcoming from the usual sources. In reality, not only did the women experience major supply problems, but these differed according to the kinds of social networks they had prior access to. Women who had experience in fish smoking usually secured their supplies by cultivating *kostamente* relations with specific fishermen. These *kostamente* relationships took a variety of forms. They could, for instance, be between spouses. Alternatively, fishermen established such arrangements with women in a series of ports along the coast through an initial gift to ensure the women's loyalty. Women either paid directly for the fish or supplied the fishermen with fuel purchased through their trading activities or else provided cash advances. *Kostamente* relationships carried mutual benefits for both parties. They assured men of regular outlets for processing and marketing their fish, while they provided women with an established supply of fish for their activities. The project disrupted these interdependencies without offering anything in their place. Perceiving women as beneficiaries of outside funds, the fishermen were led to raise their prices beyond what individual women or project groups could afford. Those women in secure *kostamente* relationships were reluctant to expand their operations through the project for fear of jeopardizing these contacts. As Goetz points out, 'while the project focused in the decade-honoured way on women's productive activities, women were no more autonomous than the men. They relied on men to initiate the production process while men relied on them to complete the process. Both men and women invested a great deal of time, energy and resources in establishing *kostamente* relationships.'

A second error that the project made was to assume that because fish smoking had been identified as a 'women's activity', it could automatically be taken up by all women in the locality. In fact, it could only be effectively undertaken by those who had already invested in the requisite human and social resources. Those women who had no previous experience in this activity had neither the skills nor the supply connections necessary. In the absence of contacts in the fishing community, this group had to purchase fish at unprofitably high prices in the market or use frozen fish rejected from the catch provided by the Russian fleet to the Guinea government. The need to defrost the fish added to the labour inputs of the activity. As Goetz concludes, focusing on the gender *division* of tasks in the production process without considering their *interdependencies* thus fractured a smoothly running system without providing an alternative that might have enhanced women's control over their activities.

The Division of Labour in the
Triple Roles Framework

The TRF is intended to analyse the gender distribution of roles within households and is mainly concerned with low-income households. Moser (1989) uses the 'triple role' formulation to draw attention to the multiplicity of demands on women's time in low-income households in the Third World. *Productive* and *reproductive* roles refer to 'income-earning activities' and 'children/domestic labour' respectively, while *community management* roles cover the 'collective' aspect of production (community organization and provision of items of collective consumption). While women and men within the household may be engaged in all three areas of activity, the division of roles between them is neither uniform nor symmetrical. Women are seen to have primary responsibility in reproductive activities, but are also engaged in productive work, earning incomes through agricultural labour and in informal-sector enterprises. Furthermore, often as an extension of their gender-ascribed roles as wives and mothers, they are involved in community management work. Faced with inadequate state provision of housing and basic services, they may take on responsibility at the community level to allocate scarce resources in the interests of the survival of their households or to put pressure on local institutions for infrastructural provision. In contrast, men's roles within the household are largely perceived in breadwinning terms, whether or not this meshes with the reality of their situations. Men do not have a clearly defined reproductive role, though they may assist women in domestic activities. Like women, men are also involved in community activities, but mainly in leadership roles at the formal political levels, rather than at the level of organizing collective consumption.

Moser's formulation of the household division of labour seeks to raise gender awareness in the planning process by drawing attention to the fact that women have to balance triple roles and that this will have implications for their ability to participate in planned interventions:

> Because the triple role of women is not recognised, the fact that women, unlike men, are severely constrained by the burden of simultaneously balancing these roles of reproductive, productive and community managing work is ignored. (p. 1801)

In addition, by virtue of its exchange value, only productive work is recognized as work. Women's community management and reproductive work is seen as 'natural' and effortless and therefore ignored by men within their communities as well as planners who have to assess different needs within the community. By contrast, the bulk of men's work is valued, either directly through paid remuneration or indirectly through status and political power.

The TRF was a timely response to the need to recognize the multiple demands on women's time, now that they have been discovered by development agencies as cheap labour for a variety of interventions. Like the GRF, it seeks to make visible those aspects of women's work that had been hitherto invisible to planners because they were carried out as their unpaid familial responsibilities. However, it goes beyond the individualistic focus of the GRF in its recognition of the community basis of many aspects of household survival and reproduction. Nevertheless, the analytical usefulness of the triple-roles concept is somewhat curtailed by its failure to separate out different dimensions of the gender division of labour. To some extent, this weakness in Moser's framework stems from the fact that the concept of 'roles' is itself an imprecise one, lending itself to different levels of meaning: descriptive as well as analytical, referring sometimes to prescribed norms (what people ought to be doing) and sometimes to observed behaviour (what they actually do).

There is a tendency within the TRF to conflate resources (the outputs of the production process) with relations (the organization of the production process). Separating out the different dimensions of the division of labour – *what* is produced, *who* produces it and *how* – would add to the conceptual clarity of the framework without sacrificing the main points Moser is attempting to make. It would help to spell out the different goals of human activity; the multiplicity of labour processes by which these goals are met; and the hierarchies of authority, power and values that these different labour processes embody. It would also draw attention to the fact that the same resources can be produced through different social relations, within and outside the household, with very different values and rewards accruing to the producer.

Focusing on the question of who does what, some inconsistencies are apparent in the way in which the question is addressed in the triple-roles framework. Productive and reproductive roles are defined in relatively straightforward terms by the kinds of resources they generate. So productive roles can be seen as relating to the 'income-earning' activities, while reproductive roles deal with child care and domestic activities. The confusion arises in relation to community roles, where Moser appears to switch between specific kinds of *resources* as the basis of role-definition and the *relations* through which these resources are produced. It is not clear here whether community roles are simply the production of goods and services through *collective* rather than *individual* effort so that the emphasis is on *how* production is organized; or whether they relate to *what* is produced, viz. a category of claims made possible by virtue of membership of community-based organizations. This confusion becomes clearer by looking at Moser's own examples. As an example of women's community roles, Moser points to their frequent initiatives at local community level in allocating scarce resources to the survival needs of their households. Here, what distinguishes community roles is not what is produced, but the specific relations through which it is produced. Shelter, water and health could, after all, be produced in a variety of institutional contexts – states, markets, households as well as communities. It is the fact that they are produced in this case through collective rather than individual effort that leads to their categorization as a community role.

Elsewhere, however, Moser appears to associate 'community roles' with certain intangible resources generated by community participation and action. Thus, as a second example of women's community roles, she points to situations where they come together to put pressure on local institutions for infrastructural provision. There is, however, a difference between the previous set of activities which directly produced resources and this set which seeks to acquire them through a redistributive process. 'Pressure on local institutions' can be seen as a *claim* on future tangible resources rather than a tangible resource in itself. Women's community roles, in this example, refer to those activities through which they seek to change resource allocation at community level by exerting collective pressure. If their efforts are successful, their collective and intangible 'claims' on local institutions will ultimately be transformed into individual and tangible benefits. The examples that Moser gives of men's community roles also relate mainly to intangible resources (authority, leadership) through community participation, which again can produce material and individual benefits as a subsequent outcome. The main differentiation made by Moser between women's community roles and those of men appears to be that women tend to be located at the level of unpaid production and provision, often within informal associations, while men are more likely to be located in remunerated leadership positions in more formally constituted community organizations.

We can, therefore, distinguish two different principles at work in Moser's definitions of roles. In the case of productive and reproductive roles, the defining principle is the kind of resources that are produced: income and human resources respectively. 'Community roles', however, appear to encompass both a specific category of resources (formally and informally constituted claims) and the kinds of social relations through which resources are produced (community rather than household based). The confusion may arise from the fact that participation in certain kinds of social relationships is in itself about access to resources (the *kostamente* relationships mentioned above are one example), but the distinction nevertheless needs to be clarified. The failure to do so leads to a truncated view of production processes. As in the GRF, insufficient attention is paid to the fact that most resources can be produced in a variety of institutional locations (households, markets, states and communities) so that the same resource may be produced through very different social relations. Women's reproductive work is likely to have very different implications for issues of access and control when it is carried out as unpaid family labour compared to when it is carried out through community-based associations. It is not just what women do, but how they do it that should inform the planning process.

A further implication of ignoring the relational aspect of production is that there is little in the triple-roles framework to suggest that characteristics such as authority and command are properties of social relations other than those associated with community roles. Because Moser touches on the question of social relations only in her discussions of 'community roles', it is only in this context that gender differences in authority and control in the relations of production are referred to. In reality, all labour activities can be analysed in terms of relationships that carry quite different connotations of authority, control, recognition and remuneration for the different social actors involved. There is, for instance, some indication within the literature that women's ability to participate in extra-household networks may not only strengthen their bargaining power within the household, but also provide them with political clout within the community.

It is also not clear how relevant the assumption of women's triple roles is for all low-income contexts. In fact, it is women's disenfranchisement from the market and community in many parts of South and West Asia (and men's privileged access to both) that constitutes the basis of their subordination. To impose the assumption of triple roles as a generalization for *all* women in low-income households across the world can close off policy attention to the constraints that prevent some categories of women in poverty from participating in community and market activities.

To sum up, Moser's work makes a useful contribution in drawing attention to the multiple roles that women play, but fails to give systematic attention to the multiplicity of social relations through which these roles are performed. The activities she discusses can be carried out in a broader set of institutional locations than recognized in her framework. Her focus on low-income households is partly

responsible for this oversight since it precludes consideratic
production possibilities through different institutional relation:
their implications for women's triple roles within the house
Moser's reason for focusing on gender roles in low-income households
is, she explains, precisely because gender tends to be subsumed within
class in so much of policy and planning. However, as Murthy notes in
her critique of the TRF and GRF, equally pervasive in policy and
planning has been the tendency to treat women as a homogenous and
unproblematic category, 'isolating gender from other sources of
oppression, and reducing the complexity of women's oppression'
(Murthy, 1993, p. 13). As we noted at the end of Chapter 2, the
absence of attempts to devise theories of race roles or class roles is
precisely because the language of roles cannot capture the exercise of
power implicit in racial interactions and class relations. The reliance on
roles as an *analytical* concept surfaces primarily in relation to gender
(rather than race or class) and testifies to a tendency within policy
circles to treat gender in isolation from the structural perspectives that
inform the analysis of these other forms of social inequality.

The Division of Labour in the
Social Relations Framework

It should be clear from the preceding discussion that the SRF places
considerable importance on distinguishing between what is produced
and how it is produced, between the different ends of the development effort and the means by which they are realized. In its narrowest
sense, development policy can be thought of in terms of the technical
logic by which means are translated into ends. However, once we start
to elaborate what these means and ends are, this technical logic is seen
to be embedded in a broader institutional context in which the social
relationships between different means and ends become a critical
focus of analysis, since some means contribute more effectively than
others to the desired ends of development. A social-relations framework attempts to outline some of the steps by which we move from the
technical logic of means and ends in policy design to its social logic.

As we noted in Chapter 4, the human factor in development is
unique in that it enters as both means and ends: human well-being is
the final goal of development, and human resources are one of the key
means for achieving this goal. Human beings thus have both intrinsic
and instrumental value in the process of development. The underlying rationale for the SRF is the premise that all policy and planning
has to be judged in terms of its contribution to the final 'end' of

development, which is the achievement of human well-being. On the basis of some of the earlier discussion in this book, human well-being is taken to encompass certain basic goals: survival, security and autonomy.[4] Consequently, production is defined as encompassing all activities that produce the means by which these final goals are met. The 'means' of production can be classified as human resources (the labour power, health and skills of individuals), tangible resources (assets, money, commodities) and intangible resources (solidarity, contacts, information, political clout). As we have noted in earlier chapters, the latter category occupies a far more important place in productive endeavours than is recognized in conventional economic planning, precisely because such planning is biased towards individualized production and discrete, tangible resources rather than more fluid 'social' or 'relational' resources (Berry, 1986; Fleming, 1991; Guyer, 1981 and 1986; March and Taqqu, 1986). Participation in informal networks and associations has been identified as a particularly critical means of creating these intangible resources through which people defend or improve on their material resource base. Such resources may take the form of 'claims' on others to be turned into tangible resources in times of crisis, or they may take the form of group solidarity and group pressure, political contacts, information channels. Like other categories, intangible resources can be a means to an end (as in claims and so forth) or they may be valued as ends in themselves (solidarity, status, participation). Access to such resources is likely to be particularly critical in situations where market or state provision of social security is missing or where access to these institutions is imperfectly distributed.

Most productive activities, whether concerned with human, tangible or intangible resources, can be carried out through a variety of social relations and in a variety of institutional contexts. Gender relations refer specifically to those aspects of social relations which create and reproduce systematic differences in the positioning of women and men in relation to institutional processes and outcomes. Material inequalities other than those of gender are also likely to be significant, but take different forms (class, caste, race or religion) in different contexts. Gender relations are therefore interwoven into the broader set of social relations structuring the division of resources and responsibilities, claims and obligations between different social groups of women and men within any given society.

Gender-awareness in policy and planning requires a prior analysis of the social relations of production within relevant institutions of family, market, state and community[5] in order to understand how gender and other inequalities are created and reproduced through their separate and combined interactions. While these different institutions may operate with their own distinct ideologies and procedures, they also share certain common norms and assumptions which lead to the systematic creation and reinforcement of social inequalities across institutional sites. As we noted in Chapter 3:

> Despite the separation of domestic institutions from the public domains of production and exchange, familial norms and values are constantly drawn on in constructing the terms women and men enter, and participate, in public life and in the market place. At the same time, because different social institutions are organized around quite specific objectives and have their own rules and practices, gender hierarchies are not seamlessly and uniformly woven into institutional structures but produced dynamically through the interaction of familial gender ideologies and distinct institutional rules and practices.

However, few institutions profess to ideologies of gender (or any other form of) inequality, and the analysis of institutions requires going beyond their official goals and ideologies, to 'unpacking' them by examining the actual relationships and processes by which they are constituted. An examination of the considerable social-science literature on institutions (Giddens, 1979; Berger and Luckmann, 1966; Hodgson, 1988; Connell, 1987; North, 1990) is helpful here. It suggests that, while institutions vary from each other and across cultures, what is generic to them is that they are 'patterned sets of activities organized around the meeting of specific needs in accordance with certain rules of conduct and practice' (Hodgson, 1988). We need to analyse different institutional sites of production, both to assess their implications for efficiency and equity goals and to determine the most appropriate institutional mechanisms for meeting various policy objectives. Five distinct but interrelated dimensions of social relationships within institutions can be identified as significant to the analysis of social inequality in general and gender inequality in particular: rules, activities, resources, people and power.

Rules: how things get done   What is distinctive about institutional behaviour is that it is rule-governed rather than random. Distinct institutional patterns of behaviour inhere in the official and unofficial norms, values traditions, laws and customs which constrain or enable what is done, how it is done, by whom and who will benefit. The institutionalization of rules has the advantage that it allows recurring decisions to be made with an economy of effort; their disadvantage is that they entrench the ways things get done to the extent of giving them the appearance of being natural or immutable.

Resources: what is used, what is produced   The other side of the coin to the 'rules' of an institution is the generation of distinct patterns of resource distribution. Such resources include those which are desired for their direct contribution to human well-being (the 'direct' means we talked about in Chapter 4) and those whose value is derived rather than direct, the 'indirect means' of production.

People: who is in, who is out, who does what   Institutions are constituted by quite specific categories of people; few are totally inclusive, despite their official ideologies. Rather, they select quite specific categories of individuals (and exclude others) and assign them to specific tasks and responsibilities within their production processes or to specific benefits within their distributional processes. Institutional patterns of inclusion, exclusion, placement and progress express class, gender and other social patterns.

Activities: what is done   Institutions are organized around specific objectives and carry out certain tasks and activities in pursuit of these objectives. These activities can be productive, distributive or regulative, but their rule-governed nature means that institutions generate routinized patterns of practice and are reconstituted through such practice. Institutional practice is therefore a key factor in the reconstitution of gender and class inequalities. In the final analysis, it is institutional practice that will have to be changed if gender relations are to be transformed.

Power: who decides, whose interests are served   Finally, institutions generally embody relations of authority and control. Few are entirely egalitarian, regardless of their official ideologies. Instead, the unequal distribution of resources and responsibilities, together with the official and unofficial rules which promote and legitimize this distribution, ensure that some institutional actors have authority and control over others and promote practices that are likely to reconstitute their privileged positions within the institutional hierarchy. Thus power is constituted as an integral feature of institutional life through its norms, its distribution of resources and responsibilities and its practices. Those whose interests are served by the institutional configuration of rules and resources are also most likely to resist, and have the capacity to resist, change, but this does not mean that institutions are static constructs. They have to be constantly re-created by the practice of different institutional actors through processes of bargaining and negotiation; and they can be transformed once a sufficient proportion of those with a stake in change are prepared to challenge institutional rules and practice.

A narrow version of this framework would help to highlight the gender implications of the interrelated elements making up different institutions; a broader focus would help to reveal how gender and other social inequalities are mutually constituted. The household is a logical starting point for such analysis because of its central role in enabling, constraining and differentiating its members' participation in the economy and society at large. It brings out the point made in different ways in the other two frameworks, that women's unpaid – and frequently unacknowledged – domestic responsibilities represent a prior set of demands on their labour time. Their ability to participate in other, more remunerative, forms of production is likely to be conditioned by the degree of flexibility in their domestic labour overheads as well as by the norms and rules which govern access to extra-domestic institutions.

Most households display an asymmetry in the division of resources, labour and claims through which they secure their members' well-being. Women, by and large, are given primary responsibility for the care and maintenance of human resources. The extent to which men also participate in this work varies across cultures and classes. Similarly, men are generally associated with breadwinning responsibilities and resources while the extent to which women are active in this category varies across culture and class. The extent to which men and women engage in activities which produce the more intangible resources – autonomy, solidarity, status within the community, claims on others – will depend, in particular, on their access to social networks and extra-domestic associations, and the nature and potentials of these relationships. Since the household is not the only site where these resources are produced, the analysis must also consider the relations governing other institutional sites: the community, the market and the state. Gender divisions within the household are obviously important in determining the terms on which women and men enter or have access to these other institutions. However, each of these institutions also has its own set of rules and resources, its own norms, values, allocational patterns and authority structures that help to assign women and men, as bearers of class and gender characteristics, to appropriate places within the institution or as beneficiaries of institutional activity. We therefore need to move beyond the analysis of households to examine who does what and how within these extra-household institutions, while recognizing that these will be affected by the extent and form of institutional interconnectedness. Using some of Whitehead's ideas (1990), we can further disaggregate our analysis of gender relations to consider how it is woven into the institutional fabric through:

- the culturally constructed *rules* about the differing aptitudes and capacities of women and men, often ascribed to biological differ-ence, which underpin the structure of claims and obligations, rights and responsibilities. These rules may be contractually specified or normatively upheld but they have considerable power in determin-ing the character of institutional practice.
- the assignment of women and men to particular *tasks, activities and responsibilities* within the family and in the broader economy on the basis of these gender-ascribed characteristics. Thus the greater association of women with the tasks of caring for the young, the sick and the elderly both within the household and within state and market institutions is often explained in terms of their 'natural' maternal predispositions.
- the distribution of *resources* between women and men to reflect their culturally assigned roles and responsibilities. Thus in societies where women are required to contribute to family food provisions, they are more likely to enjoy independent access to land and other resources. By contrast, in societies where the male breadwinning role is seen to encompass responsibility for feeding the family, men are given privileged access to productive resources within the household, but also within state and market institutions.
- the distribution of *skills and capabilities*. The routinized practice of certain tasks and activities helps to build the skills that go with these tasks. In this sense, the gender division of labour has the effect of a self-fulfilling prophesy. The attributes which give women an advantage in certain jobs and occupations – nurturing skills, patience, docility, 'nimble fingers', managing budgets – are acquired through their cultural assignment to the kinds of tasks and responsibilities within which these traits are likely to be developed.
- the allocation of *authority and control* between women and men within the institutional structures. As we suggested in our discussion of empowerment in the previous chapter, the implications of institu-tional rules, access to resources (including organizational resources), skills and capabilities, the organization of the division of labour and responsibilities converge to produce unequal gender relations in

which men are more likely than women to command authority and resources.

- the division of *claims* between women and men on the outputs produced or distributed by different institutions. Such claims are based on formal and informal evaluations by these institutions of differing needs and contributions of women and men. Thus cultures where women are both perceived as economic producers and provided with the resources to carry out their roles are also less likely to display gender biases in intra-household food distribution. However, the distribution of claims also depends on the distribution of bargaining power between the genders and their resulting capacity to uphold or contest pre-existing cultural evaluations. From a policy point of view, improving women's access to extra-household resources may not translate immediately into improved claims within their households, but it may 'improve their powers of persuasion' in the process of renegotiation.

For a social-relations framework to be useful, it is important that the institutional analysis of gender relations is linked to the design and evaluation of policy and planning. At the most general level, the analysis suggests that all planning, whether concerned with general macroeconomic policy or with specific micro-level interventions, has to be informed by this broader set of social relations through which production is organized and human needs are met. The gender impact of policy interventions is likely to vary considerably, according to which sectors, occupations and activities are affected, who predominates in them and through what kinds of institutional relations. The policy component of the analysis, therefore, draws attention to the different kinds of resources through which policy goals can be translated into practical outcomes; the different institutional rules and practices through which these resources are produced and distributed; and the implications of different institutional relations for the gender division of resources, responsibilities and decision-making power. Some examples might make clearer how an institutional analysis can contribute to the design and assessment of policy from a gender perspective.

The discussion of credit programmes in the previous chapter offered an example of how an institutional analysis of gender relations might inform the formulation of a new intervention. A comparison of gender relations within the household and the 'gender-subtext' of apparently neutral financial organizations helped to highlight the lack

of fit between women's circumstances and constraints and the organizational logic of formal credit delivery. The need for economic
collateral, the urban location of most banks, the bias towards large-
scale enterprises; the reliance on influential contacts and networks; the
need for literacy and time to complete bank procedures: all these
militated against loans to poor rural women without any need for overt
discrimination. The Grameen Bank can be seen as an institutional
innovation which seeks to revise these biases against the poor.

Similarly, the gender implications of new technologies cannot be
predicted *a priori* but have to be assessed on the basis of rules, resources
and practices within different contexts. Take the example of food-
processing technologies. Where female seclusion and highly segmented labour markets coexist with a large class of landless labour, as
in Bangladesh and parts of northern India, home-based processing of
crops is generally carried out in wealthy households by hired, rather
than family, female labour. In this situation, the introduction of rice
mills will have very different implications for women from different
classes (Greeley, 1987; Whitehead, 1985). For women who have to
undertake crop processing as unpaid family labour along with their
other domestic chores, mechanization represents a lessening of their
labour burdens. For women from wealthy households who merely
supervise hired female labour in rice processing, the introduction of
mechanized processing will simply cut down on supervisory time. But
for women from the landless households, for whom rice processing for
wealthy households represents one of the few wage-earning
opportunities for women in a traditionally secluded culture, mechanization imposes an enormous loss of income.

In the West African context, where landlessness is not a significant
feature, the processing of staple crops is a regular component of the
household chores carried out by the 'unpaid family labour' of women
in the household. It is an extremely time- and energy-consuming
aspect of women's domestic work. Here mechanization represents not
the displacement of employed female labour, but the easing of a major
domestic chore. Thus different categories of women involved in
ostensibly the same productive activity will experience technological
change differently because they are involved through different
institutional relations with different implications for the division of
resources and responsibilities.[6]

The relevance of a gender-relations analysis to the production of
tangible economic resources such as credit and agricultural technology
may be clear enough since it is more easily recognized that 'economic'
production is carried out through a variety of social relations: unpaid
family labour, self-employment, waged employment, tenancy and

sharecropping relations, and so on. It is less frequently recognized that the reproduction and care of *human* resources requires a similar analysis. The main distinction between health care produced at home by women in their capacity as mothers and wives, and the work performed by professional health providers in state or private health service delivery, differs not in the kind of resources produced – both are concerned with different aspects of human resource (re)production – but in the very different institutional relationships which govern this form of activity. While women are, as Moser points out, frequently associated with the production and care of human resources, their contribution is not always undertaken in the same capacity or 'role'. Important aspects of health-care production are carried out by unpaid family labour within the 'moral' economy of household and kinship organization, but others are undertaken through the social relations of the market and the state. Still others are organized through formal and informal community-based initiatives.

Here again, different categories of women involved in the production of health care may have conflicting interests because of their specific institutional locations. This was evident in the following example, which comes from personal discussion with Gerry Bloom. He points out that, given the gender and race segmentation of the labour market in Zimbabwe, nursing offered one of the few opportunities available to educated black women for professional employment. Since independence they have created a powerful professional niche for themselves in nursing. In this context, the class and gender implications of sporadic attempts by a male-dominated medical establishment to increase the role of sub-professional cadres at the expense of the professional nurses are by no means clear cut. The resistance of the nursing profession to this move may be seen as an assertion of power by elite women and inimical to the interests of low-income women who, as the users of health services, may find it harder to gain access to highly professionalized systems of health-service provision. It may be seen as inimical to the interests of less-educated women who would benefit from the expansion of job opportunities in a more decentralized health-care system. Alternatively it could be argued that decentralization is simply a bid by a male-dominated medical entitlement to hire cheaper, if less-qualified nurses, and that it is inimical to the interests of women as users since it lowers the quality of care on offer. Because women – and men – participate in human resource production in a variety of social relations (purchasers of health services, waged and unwaged producers of health care), their needs and interests cannot be read off from either their class or their gender, but have to be analysed in the context of these intersecting social relations within different institutional sites.

Finally, access to *intangible resources*, the most elusive category in policy terms, has important development implications, particularly in relation to empowerment strategies. Discussing the informal networks and associations through which women generally improve their political clout within the community and their bargaining power within the home, March and Taqqu distinguish between women's 'defensive' associations' as a form of enforced solidarity which is based solely on women's mutual exclusion from male society (Bujra, 1979, p. 31, cited in March and Taqqu, 1986, p. 33) and 'active' associations which establish new resources and provide real alternatives to women. As an example of 'defensive' associations, Stoler's work (1977) in Java indicates that women from landless families typically find opportunities for wage labour by entering into patron–client relations with women from wealthy households. These 'vertical, dyadic' relationships, while of mutual benefit to both wealthy and landless women, 'cross-cut the possible strength that women might gain by exerting collective pressure on a wealthy landlord' (Stoler, 1977, p. 83; cited in March and Taqqu, 1986, p. 42). A contrasting example was cited in Chapter 5 from Hart's work in Malaysia. Hart pointed to the way female agricultural labourers, by working in gangs, were able to drive up their wages.

In general, investment in extra-household associations and networks is important to both women and men, but it carries a special significance for poorer women on at least two grounds. First, they tend to be most disadvantaged in their access to state and market mechanisms of resource distribution; such networks offer them possibly their only route to material resources and claims. As March and Taqqu (1986, p. 65) point out, 'The interpersonal bonds underlying these informal associations are so crucial to the survival of marginal women that the claims they make on these women's resources can be effective at creating pools of capital or labour where other formal claims might fail.' Second, while community participation may indeed be, as Moser suggests, an extension of women's ascribed gender roles within the family, it also offers women a measure of autonomy from male authority within the household and can help furnish them with 'serious powers of persuasion in their dealings with men' (March and Taqqu, 1986, p. 41). Intangible resources – a collective consciousness, the building of group solidarity and organizational skills – were central to attempts by innovative NGOs discussed in the previous chapter to empower poor and landless women to participate in community life, to improve their bargaining power within the household, and to exercise some control over their own lives.

The Political Subtext of Gender Training

The discussion so far has dealt with primarily informational issues; the adequacy or otherwise of information conveyed about the gender division of resources and responsibilities by different training frameworks. Sensitivity to gender differences and asymmetries within households, markets and communities is clearly essential if development interventions are to be tailored to local capabilities. Gender-awareness requires rethinking old taken-for-granted assumptions and practices so that policies are better informed by an understanding of the social context in which they are taking place. However, the asymmetrical nature of gender relations also raises questions about power and privilege that impinge on the planned distribution of resources. Development planning is not simply a technocratic response to neutrally determined imperatives; it is also a process of struggle over concepts, meanings, priorities and practices which themselves arise out of competing world-views about the final goals of development. Nor are all the potential constituencies within the development process equally represented in this struggle. Just as 'effective demand' in the marketplace refers to claims backed by purchasing power, rather than those based on equity or need, so too 'effective demand' in the policy process is more likely to reflect claims based on political power rather those based on equity or need.

Gender training efforts can promote quite different approaches to policy, depending on the nature of the analytical framework used. Some forms of analysis may lead to a concern with neutrality. Others may seek to influence planners in more fundamental ways. They may seek to alert planners to differences in what women and men do, and concomitant differences in what they are likely to need; they may point to the inequities arising out of current divisions of labour and responsibilities and encourage a more dynamic view of women's needs; and they may encourage planners to analyse the reasons for the missing voices in the planning process. The frameworks under discussion offer different routes to the articulation of women's needs and priorities and therefore contain different 'political subtexts' concerning question of social change. Implicit in these political subtexts are different views about planners: the extent to which they are treated as benign and neutral arbiters of conflicting interests, and the extent to which they are perceived as actors in the conflict.

Equity and Empowerment in the Gender Roles Framework

The view of the planner implicit in the GRF suggests an essentially benign and neutral agent who, with sufficiently accurate information, can be relied on to implement the universal good. The aim of the GRF is therefore to draw the attention of planners to who does what and who enjoys access and control. However, while access and control are useful ways of characterizing activities, they are also unnecessarily static and dichotomous. They suggest that individuals are either able to make use of given resources or else they are able to decide how these resources are to be used. However, there is usually a range of possibilities between access to resources/benefits and control over resources/benefits, with differing implications for the exercise of decision-making power. These possibilities may offer a route by which planners can attempt to counter the unequal division of resources and responsibilities and to enhance women's control over their own lives. However, the framework is silent on issues of equity and empowerment other than those associated with the efficient allocation of resources. Its aim is the promotion of gender-neutral interventions. Equity within this framework lies in ensuring that resources and responsibilities are channelled in accordance with pre-existing gender divisions in the interests of efficiency. While passing reference is made to the desirability of consulting women, it is clear that the parameters within which this consultation might take place are already established. In other words, women are to be consulted about the implementation of a predetermined agenda which has evolved out of particular development priorities and practices. The reluctance to take on issues of gender equity, except as a by-product of efficiency considerations, is explained by Cloud (1985):

> While many development professionals are sensitive to cultural differences and unwilling to be accused of cultural imperialism for proposing change in the social relationships between the sexes, it is commonly accepted that development projects can appropriately attempt to intensify economic change and move it in desired directions. Shifting discussion of farm women's roles from social to economic terms has the advantage of permitting rational discussion using commonly accepted analytic tools and arguments. It *pays* to deliver resources to women in agricultural systems. This argument is easily understood, and, one hopes, persuasive. (p. 18)

It is true that there are strategic payoffs for certain categories of development professionals in using 'rational discussion, using commonly accepted analytic tools' to argue the efficiency case for investing in women. The payoffs relate to the hegemony of certain discourses within their institutions. For instance, a NORAD-commissioned review of the World Bank by Lexow and McNeill (1989) comments: 'The language of the Bank is economics . . . those who are not trained as such generally acquire the economic way of thinking quite quickly, whether because they believe in its merits, or because of its dominance within the bank' (p. 74). However, there are also strategic limitations to adopting this discourse. As Lexow and McNeill go on to note, it is not clear that the issue of women and development can be dealt with in purely economic terms. They point to the 'constraints that this imposes on those who promote issues other than pure economic efficiency; and the dangers that may arise in falling too readily in line with such an approach' (p. 87). These dangers are evident in the GRF's incorporation of the discourse of efficiency borrowed from neo-classical welfare economics, a tradition in which issues of power, domination and equity occupy a notoriously marginal and ambivalent place. 'Efficiency' in this tradition is defined in narrow, technocratic terms (equalizing the marginal returns to the resources invested in different projects) and has little to do with efficacy in meeting needs. To rely purely on efficiency arguments as the main criterion for allocating development resources will do little to challenge structural inequalities in production, distribution and consumption. At a more general level, efficiency arguments may facilitate the distribution of resources to women in those areas of sub-Saharan Africa where they have been documented as playing significant roles in agricultural production. But the productivity rationale is unlikely to offer arguments for redirecting resources in the context of the Middle East and northern India where gender relations constrain women's activities and resources, undermining their ability to contribute to planners' definitions of production. Metaphorically speaking, if women have to compete for development resources with one hand tied behind their backs, it would be more efficient in the long run to untie their hands than to allocate resources on the basis of calculations which leave this prior disadvantage intact. However, this would require thinking about efficiency in a dynamic way rather than as a static response to a given and unequal division of labour, and would have to be built into frameworks for raising gender-awareness among policymakers.

On a different point, accusations of cultural imperialism are more likely to be levelled at some agencies than others. The absence of any explicit recognition of this in the GRF makes 'the planner' appear as an abstract, disembodied and universal figure. In reality, of course, the northern development agencies and international financial institutions operate with very different criteria, constraints and politics to these of national and local planning institutions. It is important for gender trainers to acknowledge explicitly the heterogeneity of the planning universe and the consequent diversity of opportunities it contains, both as a reminder to themselves and for the benefit of those they train. It is also worth noting that the question of cultural imperialism seems to figure more often when development policies impinge on intra-household power relations in favour of women. Yet policies which have altered women's customary rights to land and other resources, or men's customary obligations to the family, have rarely been challenged or labelled cultural imperialism. While it is true that culture and tradition are important components of individual and community identities, not all members of the community have an equal stake in defending all aspects of culture. As Obbo points out, 'Traditions that break women's backs, that take women's work for granted without any regard, that keep women at home, that insist on morality for women only, these traditions must be forgotten' (Obbo, 1980, p. 28, cited in Maguire, 1984, p. 3). Democratic consultation within a community can assist in building up local support for designing and evaluating interventions which may entail social change.

A final problem with the GRF is that it comes uncomfortably close to promoting the view that any new resource offered to women is automatically in their interests. One of the case studies (Pyle, 1985) used by Overholt et al. to illustrate the application of the GRF in practice helps to highlight this point. The case study is from Java where the World Bank, in collaboration with the Indonesian Family Planning Association, set up a credit scheme for women in order to promote family planning. Two resources were therefore being offered to rural women: reproductive technology and credit.

A preliminary GRF analysis might suggest that the project would benefit women: the resources on offer related to women's responsibilities in reproduction and production; women were given specific access to these resources and presumably controlled the benefits that resulted. However, further analysis reveals other considerations which undermine this preliminary conclusion. First of all, neither of the resources on offer in the Indonesian project were intended for all women, or even for all poor women. They were intended only for women in the reproductive ages. Clearly, in the case of reproductive technology this was a logical choice, but the need for credit was common to most poorer women, not just those in reproductive ages.

However, access to credit was made conditional on acceptance of contraceptives, so that the distribution of credit was guided by planners' priorities rather than need or even creditworthiness. Nor was the promotion of reproductive technology necessarily prompted by a concern for women's needs. Although reproductive technology has the potential to expand women's control over their bodies, the terms on which it is offered will determine the extent to which this potential is realized. In this case, there was a number of problems. First of all, to promote a single contraceptive technology geared entirely to use by women was to ignore male roles and responsibilities in the area of family planning and to place the burden and risks entirely on to women. The scheme was thus premissed on a very narrow view of reproductive responsibilities. Furthermore, there was already wide-spread use of contraceptives in Java. The rationale for the new intervention was described by the author of the case study as follows: 'Having attained a high level of contraceptive prevalence, the [National Family Planning Coordinating Board] was concerned with achieving high continuation rates and making the promised "small, happy, prosperous family" norm a reality' (Pyle, 1985, p. 135). In other words, along with high acceptance of contraceptives, there were also high drop-out rates. A high continuation rate was therefore to be achieved through 'special emphasis' on a single type of contraceptive, the IUD. Among the distinguishing characteristics of the IUD as a form of contraception is that, along with injectibles and implants, it cannot be discontinued at will. While this lack of control may make it less attractive to many women, it does make it more attractive to planners bent on fertility reduction.

The Indonesian project did not utilize direct coercion to force women to use IUDs, but the tying of credit to its use distorted the ability of women to make reproductive choices guided by their own needs and priorities. Such a distortion was likely to have been most serious for poorer women, for whom the absence of alternative sources of credit would make the pressure to adopt IUDs more compelling.

There are, therefore, some important questions raised by the GRF case study which are not clearly brought out by the underlying framework. Why do interventions in reproductive behaviour, surely one of the most personal spheres of people's lives, escape donor agency concerns about 'cultural imperialism'? Whose 'norms' and priorities guide the allocation of development resources and to what extent do equity considerations enter into the process? The fact that the dissemination of a particular kind of reproductive technology had to be tied to the additional incentive of credit suggests that such technology by itself was not perceived as appropriate by women themselves. Rather, a policy of fertility reduction had been prioritized by the World Bank and the Indonesian government and implemented through the promotion of a technology which reduced women's reproductive choices rather than expanding them.

There is little in the GRF that would prompt planners to consider the need to realign their priorities with the disempowered sections of the communities they serve. It thus offers a 'safe' option to those who use this framework. Indeed, Brouwer's experience with the use of the GRF for project planning in the Australian bilateral aid programme leads her to warn that the framework was becoming the development consultant's answer to the critique that women had been ignored in the development process (Brouwer, 1989). The danger with this reliance on the GRF was that it was a specifically project-oriented analytical tool. It was insensitive to broaden community dynamics and cultural values. Finally, it oversimplified women's lives, abstracting them from their relationships and networks and treating them as an entity separate from men. The GRF, she concludes, should not be use to substitute for proper and sensitive social analysis at key stages of the policy process.

Equity and Empowerment in the Triple Roles Framework

The TRF offers a very different route into the discussion of planning goals. It seeks to establish 'gender planning' as a planning tradition in its own right, establishing a bridge between women's needs and planning process. However, it notes that the issue of women's needs has to be rooted in an analysis of their specific situations. Here Moser draws on Molyneux's analysis of the place assigned to women in various categories of state intervention. To recapitulate, strategic gender interests are derived deductively, 'from the analysis of their subordination and from the formulation of an alternative, more satisfactory set of arrangements to those which exist' (p. 232), while practical gender interests can be analysed inductively and 'arise from the concrete conditions of women's positioning within the gender division of labour . . . Practical interests are usually a response to an immediate perceived need, and they do not generally entail a strategic goal such as women's emancipation or gender equality' (p. 233).

By adopting Molyneux's distinction between practical and strategic gender interests and adapting it to a planning discourse, Moser shifts her conceptual framework out of the more technocratic planning domain occupied by the GRF and closer to a concern with gender politics. The adaptation to planning discourse is achieved by translating the language of interests into the language of needs. Moser suggests that planning for low-income women in the Third World must be based on their interests, in other words, 'on their prioritized concerns':

> By identifying the different interests women have, it is possible to translate them into planning needs, in other words, the means by which their concerns may be satisfied. From this the requirements for gender policy and planning can be formulated, and the tools and techniques for implementing them clarified. (p. 1802).

Just as 'women's interests' are a problematic concept, Moser suggests that the widespread use of 'women's needs' within the planning context must also be challenged. 'Women's needs' are likely to vary widely, 'determined not only by the specific socio-economic context, but also by the particular class, ethnic and religious structures of individual societies' (p. 1803). Moser suggests, therefore, that Molyneux's distinction between strategic and practical can be usefully applied to clarify the possibilities and limitations of planning as a tool for change. The issue of women's practical gender needs then links up to the earlier discussion on women's triple roles; they are seen as arising out of the multiple responsibilities assigned to women by the gender division of labour – child care, family health, food provision, income earning and the community management of basic services. Social policies geared to meeting needs must take cognizance of women's triple roles and be sensitive to the possibility that meeting needs arising out of any one role may have ramifications on their other roles.

Moser points out that a great deal of women's practical needs are in response to the requirements of the family (for example, food, shelter, health care, water) but tend to be identified by both women and policymakers with 'women's needs'. Meeting women's practical needs may lighten the burden of responsibilities that women carry, but does little to challenge their subordinate position. Practical needs tend to be the ones most readily recognized by planners because they fit in best with conventional development concerns. Indeed a great deal of the now discredited 'welfare' approach focused on women's practical needs, defined primarily in relation to their reproductive roles. While strategic gender needs require a more complex and structural analysis, Moser points out that the distinction between the two may be helpful for policymakers who are open to more challenging ways of meeting women's practical needs. For instance, locating child-care facilities at the father's place of work rather than the mother's helps to challenge the gender division of labour in which nurturing and caring are seen as primarily women's responsibilities; joint tenure in planning housing and human settlement offers women protection in violent or unstable domestic situations.

Moser's analysis succeeds in signalling a broader transformatory agenda to planners, something not attempted in the GRF, while at the same time recognizing some of the constraints different planners may face in implementing such an agenda. For planners working in politically conservative environments, recognition of the frequent convergence between women's practical needs and the needs of their families provides an alibi for channelling resources to women without such actions being labelled 'feminist'. On the other hand, for those able to take on more innovatory approaches, the concept of women's strategic needs provides a set of useful guidelines.

These contributions notwithstanding, it is worth speculating on some of the political implications of replacing the language of gender interests with the language of gender needs. As Moser notes, while Molyneux does not define 'interests' as such, or distinguish between 'needs' and 'interests', her analysis is clearly located in a particular Marxist-structuralist tradition in which the concept of interest is counterposed to liberal notions of tastes, wants, needs and preferences which are defined as functions of individual experience. Interests, by contrast, are seen as arising out of the structural patterning of individual life-chances by virtue of their belonging to particular social groups. They refer to the idea of having a stake in supporting or opposing some state of affairs, but encompass the possibility that individuals are not aware of that stake. Objective interests exist, in other words, regardless of whether they are subjectively perceived or not (Balbus, 1971). Strategic gender interests arise, to go back to the discussion in the previous chapter, out of power relations in the structural sense of the word.

Moser's use of the concept of needs, on the other hand, is drawn from the dominant planning discourse. Interpreting 'interests' as 'prioritized concerns', she suggests that they can be translated into planning needs, that is, 'the means by which their concerns may be satisfied'. Planners are thus seen as providing the means by which women meet their strategic gender interests. However, in moving from interests to needs, we are moving between very different views about the roles and relationships of different actors in society. The vocabulary of needs emerges out of a very different discourse to that of interests, and consequently gives very different signals to policy-makers.[7] The language of needs is generally a perspective from above, 'the perspective of socially engaged experts, of the political elite and administrators' (Jonasdottir, 1988); those who are affected do not necessarily have to be where the decisions are taken. Consequently, 'to speak politically – that is, with reference to authoritative decisions – only in terms of needs leaves open the question of who is to define what those needs are and who is to act on behalf of them' (p. 35).

The 'interests' perspective, on the other hand, denotes a view taken from below. The term 'interests' comes from the Latin *inter+esse* meaning 'between' or 'among', and the core of this perspective is 'the demand of persons to "be among" – the demand to be present, literally (physically), or with own wants represented' (Jonasdottir, 1988, p. 48). The language of need is thus associated with a top-down planning approach which constructs, in this case, women as clients of bureau-cratic provisioning, while that of interests positions them as social actors, disempowered but not powerless, capable of being 'agents of their own development, able to exercise choices and set their own agendas' (Elson, 1991b, p. 14). This distinction between needs and interests would be a purely semantic one if all planning processes were transparent, participatory, democratic and accountable. Planners could then be relied on to act neutrally and for the universal good. But, as we have sought to stress in earlier chapters, national and inter-national bureaucracies are also actors in a struggle for resources and power. The extent to which they have played an independent role in the struggle and the extent to which they have merely reflected the broader balance of forces cannot be determined *a priori*, but the evidence shows that policymakers at both national and international levels have frequently played the role of active agents, rather than innocent bystanders, in the creation and exacerbation of gender inequality (Connell, 1990; Staudt, 1990; Charlton and Everett, 1989; Mukhopadhyay, 1992; Kandiyoti, 1991).

Moser's adoption of the concept of women's strategic gender needs, in place of the language of interests, serves to obscure important aspects of gender politics common to many institutions. First of all, it underplays the conflictual aspects of gender relations and the fact that men, too, have strategic gender interests which may often be diametrically opposed to those of women. Men's strategic gender interests account for the resistance, noted in earlier chapters, to redistributive policies in favour of women. Such resistance is as likely to be located within the planning apparatus itself as it is to be located 'out there'. We have already noted the very narrow and technocratic discourse considered acceptable by some of the major institutional actors in development; this operates to set very narrow limits on the kinds of change that can consider within their policymaking agendas. Compare, for instance, the possibilities embodied in the World Bank's emphasis on market solutions to poverty (1990) with the UNDP's stress on 'judicious' mix of institutional mechanisms. Compare also the promotion of efficiency approaches to women and development associated with USAID with the notion of autonomy contained in the Dutch government's policy document for development where the stress is on 'control over one's own life and body' through control over sexuality and fertility, equal access to and control over the means of production, political self-determination and the right to an independent identity and self-respect (Jan Pronk, cited in Lycklama a Nijeholt, 1992, p. 20).

However, it is not just a question of the 'correct' vocabulary. Take the examples contained in Staudt's analysis of bureaucratic resistance within USAID (1987), Rogers' documentation of male bias within the international agencies (1980), Carney's account of how local planners in The Gambia were able to subvert the stated gender equity goals of their government and their funding agencies (1988), Goetz's discussion of the way in which class and gender norms shape the implementation of official and non-governmental policies to work with rural women in Bangladesh (1991): all make it difficult to see how male-dominated, top-down agencies can hope to address women's strategic gender interests without some transformation also occuring in their own rules, practices and perceptions.

To sum up, Moser's contribution does succeed in bringing planners closer to the domain of gender politics, but it offers a bureaucratized version of this politics. It does not challenge the mainstream institutions to reflect on the class and gender interests which may shape their own practices and which may seriously curtail their ability to identify and translate the 'prioritized concerns' of women from low-income households into a set of means for addressing them. As long as planning goals and procedures remain entrenched within hierarchical and bureaucratic structures, the discourse of needs will at best promote 'an enlightened top-down' approach to the question of women in development.

Equity and Empowerment in the
Social Relations Framework

A social-relations approach does not seek to add women to existing planning traditions, nor does it seek to establish a distinct and separate planning approach based on differences in gender roles and needs. Rather, it attempts to *rethink* existing policy approaches, concepts and tools from a gender perspective in order to reveal their biases and limitations and to discard, modify and transform them in the interests of achieving development with gender equity; the goal, therefore, is *gender-aware* policy and planning.

To summarize some of the earlier discussions in this book, gender as a power relation derives from institutional arrangements which provide men, of a given social group, with greater capacity than women from that group to mobilize institutional rules and resources to promote and defend their own interests. In most contexts, men enjoy, by and large, greater access to food, political positions or land; greater physical mobility; lesser responsibilities in terms of self-maintenance or of care of the young and the old; a privileged position in term of command of labour, particularly women's labour; less confined sexuality (Young et al., 1981, p. viii). Since the power relations between women and men are the product of institutional practice, genuine change entails institutional transformation. The differing strategic gender interests of men and women derive out of their positioning within these unequal social relations and shape their attitudes to change. To the extent to which such relations embody male privilege, it is likely to be in men's strategic interests to resist the idea that gender inequities exist, that such inequities might be socially constructed, rather than naturally given, and that they can consequently be challenged and transformed. However, the fact that women may have a longer-term strategic interest in such transformation does not mean that these interests are transparent to them in the way that needs emerging out of existing daily routines and responsibilities might be.

This lack of transparency reflects the fact that there are differences between women, as well as between women and men. Because women are positioned within their societies through a variety of different social relations (class and ethnicity, as well as gender), the interests they share as a gender category will also be shaped in 'complex and sometimes conflicting' ways. It also reflects the fact that women, along with men, are likely to subscribe to prevailing ideas about gender inequality as either divinely ordained, biologically given or economic-ally rational. Consequently, women's strategic gender interests are not given *things*; they are likely to emerge only through a process of struggling 'against the grain' of commonsense notions about gender inequality. 'Conscientization', as we saw in the previous chapter, is an important step in the struggle through which women increase their capacity to define and analyse their subordination, to construct a vision of the kind of world they want, and to act in pursuit of that vision.

Young's reformulation of Molyneux's ideas in terms of strategic gender interests and practical gender needs is useful in this context (1986). At one level, it retains the tension that Molyneux identifies between the immediate and the underlying, between what 'is' and what 'could be', in the formulation of policies and programmes. It reminds us that women's practical gender needs, arising as they do out of their pre-assigned, routine responsibilities for family welfare within the existing gender division of labour, are likely to be more easily accommodated within the policy-making agenda than their strategic concerns which threaten the existing status quo.

At another level, the language of needs and interests signals some of the tensions that characterize the relationships between policymakers and those for whom policy is made. As we have seen, the rules, resources and practices of largely male-dominated and elitist policy-making agencies are themselves implicated in the reproduction of gender and other social inequalities. Policymakers routinely focus on the identification and satisfaction of 'needs' as the basis of their interventions. However, what never enters into the policy-making process are questions around who is to determine which needs are decisionable within the policy agenda and which are not; how decisionable needs are to be met and what resources are to be allocated to meeting them. These are retained firmly in the hands of the authorized decision-makers within the policymaking agencies. As Jonasdottir points out, 'the needs perspective, if applied separately from an interest perspective, does not require the existence of any channel of influence from below other than for positive or negative responses to decisions which have been taken and policies which are already worked out' (1988, p. 49).

Retaining both needs and interests as distinctive elements of a social-relations analysis helps to carve out an autonomous space for women in the planning process, and allows them to be perceived as actors competent to interpret their own needs rather than as merely recipients of officially defined provision. It reminds us there are certain gender 'needs' that are unlikely to be given any status within bureaucratic planning processes unless women empower themselves to identify and establish their legitimacy as a policy concern. However, for this to happen, they must have access to the enabling resources of space and time. Women's practical gender needs, and the ways in which they are met, thus become interrelated dimensions of strategic interests: needs point in the direction of satisfying choices, while interests refer to expanding control over the interpretation of needs and the conditions of choice.

Returning to Molyneux's examples of women's strategic gender interests – abolition of the gender division of labour; removal of institutionalized forms of discrimination; establishment of political equality; reproductive choice; measures against male violence, the sexual exploitation of women and coercive forms of marriage – what characterizes all of them is that they entail a challenge to the structural basis of women's disempowerment. They seek to enhance women's control over their own lives in the crucial areas of politics, work, play, love, sex and reproduction. They are the measures through which a gender-transformative project is to be implemented. However, going as they do to the very heart of the power relations of gender, they are also likely to meet with profound resistance. The capacity to withstand this resistance has to be built up; it cannot be taken for granted. Consequently, the idea of strategic gender interests can also be given a processual interpretation. Meeting daily practical needs in ways that transform the conditions in which women make choices is a crucial element of the process by which women are empowered to take on the more deeply entrenched aspects of their subordination. In our earlier discussion of empowerment strategies we emphasized those elements of basic needs provision that appeared to link women's practical gender needs with their strategic gender interests. These include the provision of new economic resources; participation in systems for establishing, prioritizing and addressing needs and opportunities; new analytical skills and awareness; building new and collective relationships; and mobilization around self-defined concerns and priorities.

The concept of strategic gender interests has a useful role to play in gender training. An analysis of women's strategic gender interests can help to 'conscientize' policymakers to critical points of intervention in different contexts – legal reform, reproductive choice, employment promotion, access to new extra-household resources, organizational activity. It can also help to shape the delivery of services to meet women's practical needs in ways which have *transformatory* or *redistributive* potential, that is, which help build up the enabling infrastructures essential for the process of self-empowerment.[8] At the same time, the analysis of male gender interests will serve to remind policymakers of the likelihood of resistance both within and outside the bureaucracies to any genuinely redistributive policies. It highlights the need for those committed to gender equity within the policymaking structures to build strategic alliances on different issues at different points of the planning process, across sectors and with non-governmental organizations and researchers, so that they can 'review and possibly do things differently from the present, and . . . renew their vision of development and their contact and communications with the key grassroots players in the process (Heyzer, 1989, p. 17).

In the final analysis, planning for women's empowerment is most likely to succeed when the process is seen as the responsibility of those who are planned for; when social action groups and grassroots movements help to counter the top-down logic of the planning process and to open it up to what Sharada Jain calls 'movements from below'. Until that happens, however, a final component in the social relations approach we have been attempting to develop would be a gender audit (of the kind suggested, for instance, in Jahan, 1989) to be carried out on all interventions with human resource, and therefore gender, implications. Such a gender audit would provide a bottom-up flow of evaluative information into the planning process – either directly if there are appropriate mechanisms of accountability or else indirectly, through informal channels of advocacy and pressure, including the media and local grassroots organization. Such an audit could ask:

1 What are the goals of the intervention? Are they shared by both women and men? Equally by all women and men? If not, what are the grounds for supporting the intervention?
2 Whose needs or potentials are being addressed through the proposed intervention? Who identified and prioritized them and who was consulted in designing implementation strategies?
3 Who is being targeted by the proposed interventions? Is the targeted group defined in generic, abstract terms, in gender specific or gender inclusive terms? As household units or as individuals? How is the target group being conceptualized: as producers, consumers, experts, agents, victims, clients, participants, beneficiaries?
4 What assumptions are being made by the intervention about the gender division of resources and responsibilities? What evidence is there that these assumptions are well-informed?
5 What resources are being made available through this intervention? Who is likely to have access to these resources, who is likely to manage them, and who is likely to control them? If extra responsibilities are entailed, are extra resources being made available to match them?
6 What benefits or gains flow from this intervention? Who is likely to have access to them, who is likely to manage them, and who is likely to control them? Who is likely to lose from this intervention (which men and which women)?
7 Does this intervention address women's strategic gender interests? Does it have the potential to do so and how can such potential be

realized? What kinds of resistances is it likely to meet and how can they be dealt with?

Conclusion

There is, as we noted in the first section of this book, an intimate relationship between ways of thinking and ways of doing. In particular, the inclusions and exclusions that characterize different ways of thinking will help to determine what is considered worth thinking about and what is considered worth doing. This chapter – and this book – have been about ways of thinking about the institutionalized nature of gender inequalities in the rules, resources, practice and power structures of different societies, and the implications for ways of doing development. The world-views underpinning different analytical frameworks for analysing gender and development bear critically, not only on how policy is formulated, designed, implemented and evaluated, but also on which issues are considered important and who are identified as the main actors in the development process.

What we have sought to do in this book is to extend the analysis of gender relations beyond their operations within the family and the market to examine their construction within the planning agencies themselves. Receptivity to transformative ideas about gender vary considerably between different institutions. These differences do not reduce to an issue of numbers of women within the bureaucracy, though more women within these organizations would certainly help to challenge the gender ideologies and institutional practices that are taken for granted within most bureaucracies. Rather, they relate to a combination of factors which help to constitute gender hierarchies within any organization: the forms of knowledge that it privileges; the professional training of its actors; its operating styles, norms and culture; the resources that it commands; its degree of interaction with different constituencies; and the political interests that are dominant within it. Gender-equity goals would be more effectively addressed through gender training if it could be used to encourage more critical self-examination among planners as to how exclusionary structures work within their own institutions, through their hierarchies of authority and knowledge, rules of recruitment and divisions of resources and responsibilities.

To conclude, therefore, planning institutions are neither monolithic nor uniform. Their governance structures and the opportunities they offer have to be subjected to critical scrutiny like any other institution, when thinking strategically about gender equity. However, if women's self-empowerment is seen as a key route to gender equity, an important first step is the efficient provision of space, resources and time that will allow women to articulate their own interests rather than having them anticipated and met on their behalf. Planners can be valuable and powerful allies in this process of enfranchisement, but in the final analysis the main actors must be those whose voices have been suppressed for so long within the different arenas of development.

Notes

1 I owe this quote to Robin Mearns.
2 The IDS course 'Women, Men and Development' has been running roughly annually since 1985. Clearly many of the ideas in this chapter are the product of collaborative work on the course with colleagues from the Institute, earlier with Kate Young, and more recently with Alison Evans and Ann Marie Goetz. In addition, I have benefited from my training collaborations with Shireen Huq, Maitreyee Mukhopadhyay, Ramya Subramaniyam, Kiran Bhatia, Deborah Kasente, Elinor Dionisio, Vasanta Kannabiran, Emelina Quintillan, Kumudhini Rosa, Letitia Mukurasi, Helen Dalton, Shanti Dairiam, Razia Aziz, Faustina Ward-Osborne, Pamela Chikoti, Meera Shah and Judy Pointing.
3 The phrase comes from Anderson, 1983.
4 I have opted for the term 'autonomy' rather than 'self-esteem' as used in Chapter 6 because it appears to be a broader concept. I use the term autonomy in the sense of 'the power to' which emerges out of the processes of empowerment discussed in Chapter 9. It is not intended to imply an individualistic notion of disembodied free choice but rather the ability of people to participate fully in those decisions that shape their life choices and their life chances at both personal and collective levels.
5 'Community', strictly speaking, includes local governments and local markets as well as households, but it is being used here in a rather loose, residual sense to refer to those organizations, networks, village structures and inter-household associations which make up local civic society. Non-governmental and women's organizations are also included within this category.
6 A social cost–benefit analysis carried out in Bangladesh found that the social costs of mechanizing the processing stages outweighed the social benefits because the loss of income suffered by landless women outweighed the overall productivity gains. A similar exercise for the West African context might reach very different conclusions. Haswell (1988) noted for instance the concern of local women's pressure groups in The Gambia with securing grinding mills, while in neighbouring Senegal, Nath (n.d.) reported that village women lined up with their mortars and pestles in the path of a

visiting minister to demonstrate against the daily drudgery of pounding millet and sorghum.

7 There is an interesting discussion about the distinction between wants, needs and interests within official policy discourses to be found in Plant et al., 1980. As they point out, social welfare services are seldom devised to meet people's wants or serve their interests. In general, the market is seen as the institutional framework within which individual economic agents satisfy their wants and preferences through mutually beneficial transactions where a quid is exchanged for a quo. Similarly, it is in the political arena that people seek to articulate their rights and interests as citizens or as members of interest groups. The concept of need, on the other hand, demarcates a very different arena of distribution and is fundamental to understanding the normative nature of social welfare provision. Social welfare policies generally entail a unilateral transfer of resources to a group of recipients on the basis of a perceived moral, as opposed to a positive legal, entitlement, something to which they have a right. It is generally made by a more powerful group within a society to those perceived as its least advantaged members and least able to meet their own needs. The problem of stigma and dependence arises within social welfare provision because of the relationships of inequality within which they are normally made and their association with needs rather than rights.

8 Young (1986) applies the concept of 'transformatory potential' to specific categories of needs: 'in identifying women's needs, those with tranformatory potential would be sought, so that they can become the focus of gender equality strategies' (p. 16). While I am also using the concept as a bridge between the idea of practical needs and strategic gender interests, my usage differs in that it is not the needs as such that are seen to have transformatory potential, but the way in which needs are identified, prioritized and satisfied.

Appendix

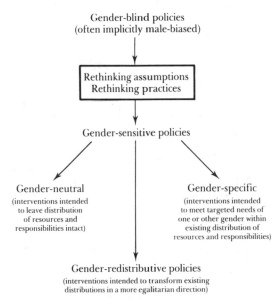

Gender-blind policies
(often implicitly male-biased)

Rethinking assumptions
Rethinking practices

Gender-sensitive policies

Gender-neutral
(interventions intended
to leave distribution
of resources and
responsibilities intact)

Gender-specific
(interventions intended
to meet targeted needs of
one or other gender within
existing distribution of
resources and responsibilities)

Gender-redistributive policies
(interventions intended to transform existing
distributions in a more egalitarian direction)

Figure 1 Policy Review (A)

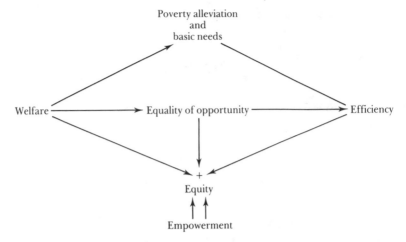

Figure 2 Policy Review (B)

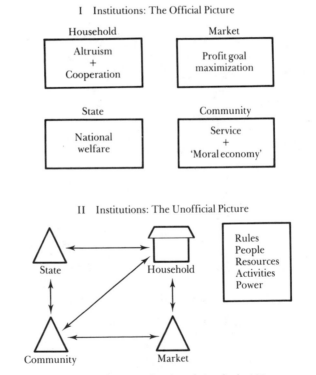

Figure 3 Institutional Analysis (A)

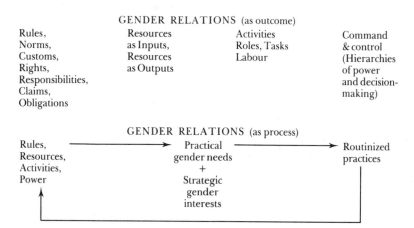

Figure 4 Institutional Analysis (B)

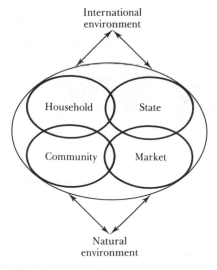

Figure 5 Institutional Analysis (C)

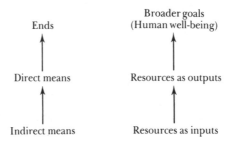

Figure 6 Analysing Interventions (A)

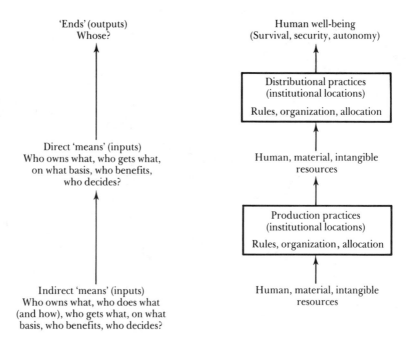

Figure 7 Analysing Interventions (B)

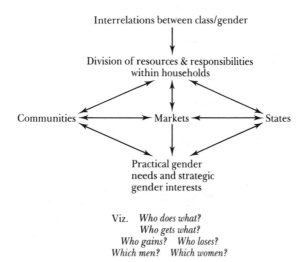

Figure 8 Analysing Interventions (C)

Figure 9 Analysing Interventions (D)

Bibliography

AAWORD (1982) 'The Experience of the Association of African Women for Research and Development (AAWORD)'. *Development Dialogue*, 1–2, pp. 101–13.

Abdullah, T. and S. Zeidenstein (1982) *Village Men of Bangladesh: Prospects for Change*. Oxford, Pergamon Press.

Acharya, M. and L. Bennett (1982/83) 'Women in the Subsistence Sector: Economic Participation and Household Decision-making in Nepal'. *World Bank Staff Working Paper, No. 256*. Washington D.C.

Acker, J. (1990) 'Hierarchies, Jobs, Bodies: A Theory of Gendered Organizations'. *Gender and Society*, vol. 2, no. 4, pp. 139–58.

Action Aid (1991) *Lifestyle Overload? Population and Environment in the Balance*. Action Aid Development Report No. 5. London.

Adnan, S. (1988) 'Birds in a Cage: Institutional Change and Women's Position in Bangladesh'. Paper presented at conference, *Women's Position and Demographic Change in the Course of Development*, IUSSP, at Asker, Norway, 15–18 June.

Agarwal, A. (1985) 'Ecological Destruction and the Emerging Patterns of Poverty and People's Protests in Rural India'. *Social Action: A Quarterly Review of Social Trends*, January–March.

Agarwal, B. (1974) 'Women and Technological Change in Agriculture: The Asian and African Experience'. In *Technology and Rural Women*, ed. I. Ahmed, pp. 67–114. London, Allen and Unwin.

Agarwal, B. (1990) 'Social Security and the Family in Rural India: Coping with Seasonality and Calamity'. *Journal of Peasant Studies*, vol. 17, no. 3, pp. 341–412.

Akhter, F. (1988) 'The State of Contraceptive Technology in Bangladesh'. *Reproductive and Genetic Engineering*, vol. 1, no. 2, pp. 153–8.

Alam, S. (1985) 'Women and Poverty in Bangladesh'. *Women's Studies International Forum*, vol. 8, no. 4, pp. 361–71.

312

Alamgir, M. (1980) *Famine in South Asia: Political Economy of Mass Starvation*. Cambridge, Mass., Oelgeschlager and Hain Publishers.

Amsden, A., ed. (1980) 'Introduction'. *The Economics of Women and Work*, pp. 11–38. Harmondsworth, Penguin.

Anderson, B. (1983) *Imagined Communities*. London, Verso.

Antrobus, P. (1987) 'A Journey in the Shaping: A Journey without Maps'. Bunting Institute, Radcliffe College. Mimeo.

Antrobus, P. (1989a) *Women in Development*. Paper presented at the XVth Annual General Assembly of Development Non-Governmental Organizations, Brussels. April.

Antrobus, P. (1989b) 'The Empowerment of Women'. In *The Women and International Development Annual*, vol. 1. ed. R.S. Gallin, M. Aronoff and A. Ferguson, pp. 189–207. Boulder, Colorado, Westview Press.

Antrobus, P. (1989c) *Women and Planning: The Need for an Alternative Analysis*. Paper presented at the Second Disciplinary Seminar, Social Sciences, Women and Development Studies, The University of West Indies, Barbados. 3–7 April.

Appadurai, A. (1984) 'How Moral is South Asia's Economy? A Review Article'. *Journal of Asian Studies*, vol. 43, no. 3, pp. 81–97.

Appleton, S., P. Collier and P. Horsnell (1990) *Gender, Education and Employment in Côte d'Ivoire*. Social Dimensions of Adjustment Working Paper No. 8. World Bank, Washington.

Arn, A.-L. and F. Banu Lily (1992) *Evaluation Report of Saptagram Nari Swanirvar Parishad*. Dhaka.

Arndt, H.W. (1987) *Economic Development. The History of an Idea*. Chicago, University of Chicago Press.

Ayalew, S. (1985) 'Time Budget Analysis as a Tool for PHC Planning (with examples from Ethiopia)'. *Social Science and Medicine*, vol. 21, no. 8, pp. 865–72.

Aziz, K.M.A. (1979) *Kinship in Bangladesh*. International Centre for Diarrhoeal Disease Research, Bangladesh. Dhaka.

Bachrach, P. and M.S. Baratz (1962) 'The Two Faces of Power'. *American Political Science Review* 56. pp. 947–52.

Balbus, I. (1971) 'The Concept of Interest in Pluralist and Marxist Analysis'. *Politics and Society*, vol. 1, no. 2, pp. 151–77.

Bandarage, A. (1984) 'Women in Development: Liberalism, Marxism and Marxist-Feminism'. *Development and Change*, vol. 15, no. 3, pp. 495–515.

Banerji, D. (1980) 'Political Economy of Population Control in India'. In *Poverty and Population Control*, ed. L. Bondestam and S. Bergstrom, pp. 83–101. London, Academic Press.

Bardhan, K. (1985) 'Women's Work, Welfare and Status'. *Economic and Political Weekly*. vol. XX, no. 50, pp. 2207–17 and continued in vol. XX, nos. 51 and 52, pp. 2261–9.

Bardhan, P.K. (1974) 'On Life and Death Questions'. *Economic and Political Weekly*, Special Number, vol. 9, nos. 32–34, pp. 1293–1303.

Basu, K. (1986) 'Markets, Power and Social Norms'. *Economic and Political Weekly*, vol. XXI, no. 43, pp. 1893–6.

Batliwala, S. (1992) 'The Mahila Samakhya Strategy for Women's Mobilization and Empowerment'. Translated from Mahila Samakhya Journal *Samakhya Samvada*, vol. 1, no. 3.

Bawden, R. and R. Macadam (1988) 'Towards a University for People-Centred Development: A Case History of Reform'. Paper prepared for Winrock International, Washington.

Beall, J., S. Hassim and A.Todes (1989) ' "A Bit on the Side"? Gender Struggles in the Politics of Transformation in South Africa'. *Feminist Review*, no. 33, pp. 30–56.

Becker, G. (1965) 'A Theory of the Allocation of Time'. *Economic Journal*, vol. LXXX, no. 200, pp. 493–517.

Becker, G. (1974) 'A Theory of Marriage: Part I'. In *Economics of the Family: Marriage, Children and Human Capital*, ed. T. W. Schultz. Chicago, University of Chicago Press.

Becker, G. (1976) *The Economic Approach to Human Behaviour*. Chicago, University of Chicago Press.

Becker, G. (1981) *Treatise on the Family*. Cambridge, Mass., Harvard University Press.

Beneria, L. and M. Roldan (1987) *Crossroads of Class and Gender*. Chicago, University of Chicago Press.

Beneria, L. and G. Sen (1981) 'Accumulation, Reproduction and Women's Role in Economic Development: Boserup Revisited'. *Signs*, vol. 7, pp. 279–98.

Beneria, L. and G. Sen (1982) 'Class and Gender Inequalities and Women's Role in Economic Development – Theoretical and Practical Implications'. *Feminist Studies*, vol. 8, no. 1, pp. 157–76.

Benholdt-Thomsen, V. (1981) 'Subsistence Production and Extended Reproduction'. In *Of Marriage and Market. Women's Subordination in International Perspective*, ed. K. Young, C. Wolkowitz and C. McCullagh, pp. 30–48. London, CSE Books.

Bennet, L. and M. Acharya (1981) *The Rural Women of Nepal*. Report of the Project on the Status of Women in Nepal, Vol. II, part 9.

Berger, P. and T. Luckmann (1966) *The Social Construction of Reality*. London, Penguin Social Sciences.

Bernstein, H. (1979) 'Sociology of Underdevelopment versus Sociology of Development?'. In *Development Theory. Four Critical Studies*, ed. D. Lehman, pp. 77–106. London, Frank Cass and Co.

Berry, S. (1986) 'Macropolicy Implications of Research on Rural Household and Farming Systems'. In *Understanding Africa's Rural Households and Farming Systems*, ed. J. L. Moock, pp.199–215. Boulder, Colorado, Westview Press.

Berry, W. (1977) *The Unsettling of America: Culture and Agriculture*. New York, Avon Books.

Bhatt, E. (1979) 'Organizing the Self-employed Workers (An Experiment)'. Paper presented at the Regional Consultation on Strategies for Women's Development, Colombo.

Bhatt, P. (1989) 'Women's Organizations: Issues and Debates'. M.A. dissertation, Institute of Development Studies, Sussex.

Bhatty, Z. (1980) *Economic Role and Status of Women: A Case Study of Women in the Beedi Industry in Allahabad*. ILO Working Paper, Geneva.

Birdsall, N. and W.P. McGreevey (1983) 'Women, Poverty and Development'. In *Women and Poverty in the Third World*, ed. M. Buvinic, M.A. Lycette and W.P. McGreevey, pp. 3–13. Johns Hopkins Press, Baltimore, Maryland.

Birke, L. (1986) *Women, Feminism and Biology. The Feminist Challenge*. Brighton, Harvester Press.

Black, M. (1987) 'Family Planning: An Essential Ingredient of Family Health'. In *Basic Documents* from the International Conference on Better Health for Women and Children through Family Planning, Nairobi, Kenya, 5–9 October.

Blanchet, T. (1988) *Maternal Mortality in Bangladesh. Anthropological Assessment Report*. NORAD Office, Dhaka.

Bohme, G. (1984) 'Midwifery as Science: An Essay on the Relation between Scientific and Everyday Knowledge'. In *Society and Knowledge*, ed. N. Stehr and V. Meja, pp. 365–85. New Brunswick, Transaction Books.

Bondestam, L. (1980) 'The Foreign Control of the Kenya Population'. In *Poverty and Population Control*, ed. L. Bondestam and S. Bergstrom. Academic Press, London.

Boserup, E. (1970) *Women's Role in Economic Development*, New York, St Martin's Press.

BRAC (1980) *The Net. Power Structure in Ten Villages*, Dhaka: BRAC Publications.

Braun, J. von, D. Puetz and P. Webb (1989) *Irrigation Technology and Commercialization of Rice in the Gambia: Effects on Income and Nutrition*. Research Report 75. International Food Policy Research Institute, Washington.

Brouwer, E. (1989) 'AIDAB and the Use of Gender Analysis in Project Design'. In *Gender Sensitivity in Development Planning, Implementation and Evaluation*, ed. R. Raj-Hashim and N. Heyzer. Report of the APDC Sub-Regional Workshops, Kuala Lumpur.

Bruce, J. (1980) 'Implementing the User Perspective'. *Studies in Family Planning*, vol. 11, no. 1, pp. 29–34.

Bruce, J. and D. Dwyer (1988) *A Home Divided: Women and Income in the Third World*. Stanford, Calif., Stanford University Press.

Bujra, J.M. (1979) 'Introductory: Female Solidarity and the Sexual Division of Labour'. In *Women United, Women Divided: Comparative Studies of Ten Contemporary Cultures*, ed. P. Caplan and J.M. Bujra, pp. 13–45. Bloomington, Indiana University Press.

Bunch, C. and R. Carrillo (1990) 'Feminist Perspectives on Women in Development'. In *Persistent Inequalities. Women and World Development*, ed. I. Tinker, pp. 70–82. Oxford, Oxford University Press.

Burawoy, M. (1979) *Manufacturing Consent: Changes in the Labor Process Under Monopoly Capitalism*. Chicago, University of Chicago Press.

Burfisher, M.E. and N. Horenstein (1985) *Sex Roles in the Nigerian Tiv Farm Household*. West Hartford, Conn., Kumarian Press.

Butler, J. (1987) 'Variations on Sex and Gender: Beauvoir, Wittig and Foucault'. In *Feminism as Critique*, ed. S. Benhabib and D. Cornell, pp. 128–42. Cambridge, Polity Press.

Buvinic, M. (1983) 'Women's Issues in Third World Poverty: A Policy Analysis'. In *Women and Poverty in the Third World*, ed. M. Buvinic, M. Lycette and W.P. McGreevey, pp. 14–33. Baltimore, Johns Hopkins University Press.

Buvinic, M. (1986) 'Projects for Women in the Third World: Explaining their Misbehaviour'. *World Development*, vol. 14, no. 5, pp. 653–64.

Cain, M.C. (1984) *On Women's Status, Family Structure and Fertility in Developing Countries*. Background paper for the World Development Report. World Bank, Washington D.C.

Cain, M.C., S.R. Khanum and S. Nahar (1979) 'Class, Patriarchy and the Structure of Women's Work in Rural Bangladesh'. *Population and Development Review*, vol. 5, no. 3, pp. 405–38.

Caldwell, J.C. (1982) *Theory of Fertility Decline*. London, Academy Press.

Caldwell, J.C., P.H. Reddy and P. Caldwell (1982) 'Demographic Change in Rural South India'. *Population and Development Review*, vol. 8, no. 4, pp. 689–727.

Campioni, M. and E. Grosz (1991) 'Love's Labours Lost. Marxism and Feminism'. In *A Reader in Feminist Knowledge*. ed. S. Gunew, pp. 366–98. London, Routledge.

Carney, J. (1988) 'Struggle over Land and Crops in an Irrigated Rice Scheme in the Gambia'. In *Agriculture, Women and Land. The African Experience*, ed. J. Davison, pp. 59–78. Boulder, Colorado, Westview Press.

Carney, J. and M. Watts (1990) 'Manufacturing Dissent: Work, Gender and the Politics of Meaning in a Peasant Society'. *Africa*, vol. 60, no. 2, pp. 207–41.

Cassen, R.H. (1978) *India. Population, Economy, Society*. London, Macmillan Press.

Chambers, J. (1990) 'Gender and Anxiety'. *The Adminstrator*, vol. XXXV, no. 1, pp. 38–42.

Chambers, R. (1978) 'Project Selection for Poverty-Focused Rural Development: Simple is Optimal'. *World Development*, vol. 6, no. 2, pp. 209–19.

Chambers, R. (1983) *Rural Development. Putting the Last First*. Harlow, Longman Scientific and Technical.

Chambers, R. (1988) *Poverty in India: Concepts, Research and Reality*. IDS Discussion Paper 241, Institute of Development Studies, Sussex.

Chambers, R. (1989) 'Editorial Introduction: Vulnerability, Coping and Policy'. *IDS Bulletin*, vol. 20, no. 2, pp. 1–7.

Chambers, R. (1992) 'Rural Appraisal: Rapid, Relaxed and Participatory'. IDS Discussion Paper No. 311. Institute of Development Studies, Sussex.

Charlton, S.E.M. and J. Everett, eds. (1989) *Women, the State and Development*. Albany, New York, State University of New York Press.

Chaudhury, R.H. and N.R. Ahmed (1980) *Female Status in Bangladesh*, Bangladesh Institute of Development Studies, Dhaka.

Chayanika, Swatija and Kamaxi (1990) *We and our Fertility*. Research Centre for Women's Studies, SNDT Women's University, Bombay.

Chen, L.C., A.K.M. Chowdhury and S.L. Huffman (1980) 'Anthropometric Assessment of Energy-Protein Malnutrition and Subsequent Risk of Mortality among Pre-school aged Children'. *American Journal of Clinical Nutrition*, vol. 33, pp.1836–45.

Chen, L.C., M.C. Gesche, S. Ahmed, A.I. Chowdhury and W.H. Mosley (1974) 'Maternal Mortality in Rural Bangladesh'. *Studies in Family Planning*, vol. 5, no. 11, pp. 334–41.

Chen, L.C., E. Huq and S. D'Souza (1981) 'Sex Bias in the Family Allocation of Food and Health Care in Rural Bangladesh'. *Population and Development Review*, vol. 7, no. 3, pp. 435–74.

Chen, M. and R. Ghuznavi (1979) *Women in Food-for-Work: The Bangladesh Experience*. World Food Programme, Bangladesh.

Chenery, H.B., M.S. Ahluwalia, C.L.G. Bell, J.H. Duloy and R. Jolly (1974) *Redistribution with Growth*. Oxford, Oxford University Press.

Chhachhi, A. (1983) 'The Case of India'. In *Of Common Cloth*, ed. W. Chapkis and C. Enloe, pp. 39–45. Amsterdam: Transnational Institute.

Chodorow, N. (1978) *The Reproduction of Mothering: Psychoanalysis and the Sociology of Gender*. Berkeley, University of California Press.

Choudhury, O.H. (1991) 'Nutritional Dimensions of Poverty'. In *Rethinking Poverty: Dimensions, Process, Options*, ed. H.Z. Rahman, B. Sen, M. Hossain, O.H. Choudhury and S. Hamid. Bangladesh Institute of Development Studies, Dhaka.

Chowdhury, A.K.M.A., S.L. Huffman and L.C. Chen (1981) 'Agriculture and Nutrition in Matlab Thana, Bangladesh'. In *Seasonal Dimensions to Rural Poverty*, ed. R. Chambers, R. Longhurst and A. Pacey. London, Francis Pinter.

Chowdhury, M.K., A. Razzaque, S. Becker, A.M. Sarder, and S. D'Souza (1982) *Demographic Surveillance System – Matlab. Volume Nine. Vital Events and Migration – 1979*. International Centre for Diarrhoeal Disease Research Bangladesh. Dhaka.

Ciancanelli, P. and B. Berch (1987) 'Gender and the GNP'. In *Analyzing Gender. A Handbook of Social Science Research*, ed. B.B. Hess and M.M. Ferree, pp. 244–66. London, Sage Publications.

Cleave, J.H. (1974) *African Farmers: Labor Use in the Development of Smallholder Agriculture*. New York, Praeger Special Studies in International Economics and Development.

Cloud, K. (1985) 'Women's Productivity in Agricultural Systems: Considerations for Project Design'. In *Gender Roles in Development Projects*, ed. C. Overholt, M.B. Anderson, K. Cloud, and J.E. Austin, pp. 57–78. West Hartford, Kumarian Press.

Coale, A.J. and E.M. Hoover (1958) *Population Growth and Economic Development in Low Income Countries: A Case Study in Indian Prospects*. Princeton, Princeton University Press.

Cockburn, C. (1983) *Brothers. Male Dominance and Technological Change*. London, Pluto Press.

Coeytax, F.X. (1984) *The Role of the Family in Health: Appropriate Research Methods*. World Health Organisation, Geneva.

Colclough, C. and J. Manor, eds. (1991) *States or Markets? Neo-liberalism and the Development Policy Debate*. Oxford, Clarendon Press.

Commoner, B. (1988) *Rapid Population Growth and Environmental Stress*. Paper presented to the United Nations Expert Group on Consequences of Rapid Population Growth, 24–26 August. New York, United Nations.

Commonwealth Secretariat (1989) *Engendering Adjustment for the 1990s*. London, Commonwealth Secretariat.

Connell, R.W. (1987) *Gender and Power*. Cambridge, Polity Press.

Connell, R.W. (1990) 'The State, Gender, and Sexual Politics'. *Theory and Society*, 19, pp. 507–44.

Cook, R.J. (1989) 'Abortion Laws and Policies: Challenges and Opportunities'. In *Women's Health in the Third World: The Impact of Unwanted Pregnancy*, ed. A. Rosenfield, M.F. Fathalla, A. Germain and C.L. Indriso. Special Issue of *International Journal of Gynecology and Obstretrics*.

Coreil, J. (1991) 'Maternal Time Allocation in Relation to Kind and Domain of Primary Health Care'. *Medical Anthropology Quarterly*, vol. 5, no. 3, pp. 221–35.

Cornea, G.A. (1987) 'Social Policymaking: Restructuring, Targetting, Efficiency'. In *Adjustment with a Human Face* Vol. 1, ed. G.A. Cornea, R. Jolly and F. Stewart, pp. 165–82. Oxford, Oxford University Press.

Dairiam, S. (1992) 'Violence against Women: A Development Issue'. Paper prepared for Gender Training Workshop held at the National Planning Academy. December. Mimeo.

Dex, S. (1985) *The Sexual Division of Work*. Brighton, Wheatsheaf.

Dey, J. (1981) 'Gambian Women: Unequal Farmers in Rice Development Projects'. *Journal of Development Studies*, vol. 17, no. 3, pp. 109–22.

Dey, J. (1982) 'Development Planning in the Gambia: the Gap between Planners' and Farmers' Perceptions. Expectations and Objectives'. *World Development*, vol. 10, no. 5, pp. 377–96.

Dighe, A. and S. Jain (1989) 'Women's Development Programme: Some Insights in Participatory Evaluation'. *Prashasnika*, vol. XVIII, nos. 1–4, pp. 77–98.

Dighe, A. and I. Patel (1993) 'Gender Equity in Literacy in India: Some Issues'. *Perspectives in Education*, vol. 9, no. 1, pp. 3–14.

Dinnerstein, D. (1977) *The Mermaid and the Minotaur. Sexual Arrangements and Human Malaise*. New York, Harper and Row.

Dixon, R.B. (1985) 'Seeing the Invisible Women Farmers in Africa: Improving Research and Data Collection Methods'. In *Women as Food Producers in Developing Countries*, ed. J. Monson and M. Kalb, pp. 19–35. Los Angeles, University of California Press.

Dixon-Mueller, R. and A. Germain (1992) 'Stalking the Elusive "Unmet Need" for Family Planning'. *Studies in Family Planning* vol. 23, no. 5, pp. 330–35.

Dixon-Mueller, R. and J. Wasserheit (1991) *The Culture of Silence. Reproductive Tract Infections among Women in the Third World*. International Women's Health Coalition, New York.

Donahue, J.D. (1980) 'Cost–benefit Analysis and Project Design: Objectives, Options and Opportunity Costs'. In *Cost–benefit Analysis and Project Design*, ed. J.D. Donahue pp.1–8. USAID and the Program of Advanced Studies in Institution Building and Technical Assistance Methodology, USA.

Dreze, J. (1988) *Famine Prevention in India*. Development Economics Paper No. 3, Suntory Toyota International Centre for Economics and Related Disciplines, London School of Economics and Political Science.

D'Souza, S. and L.C. Chen (1980) 'Sex Differentials in Mortality in Rural Bangladesh'. *Population and Development Review*, vol. 6, no. 2, pp. 257–70.

Dyson, T. and M. Moore (1983) 'On Kinship Structure, Female Autonomy and Demographic Behaviour'. *Population and Development Review*, vol. 9, no. 1, pp. 35–60.

Edholm, F., O. Harris and K. Young (1977) 'Conceptualising Women'. *Critique of Anthropology*, vol. 3, nos. 9 and 10, pp.101–130.

Ehrlich, P. (1968) *The Population Bomb*. Published under the auspices of the Sierra Club by Ballantine Books, New York.

Eichler, M. (1991) *Nonsexist Research Methods. A Practical Guide*. London, Routledge.

Eisenstein, H. (1984) *Contemporary Feminist Thought*. London, Unwin Paperbacks.

Elliot, C. (1977) 'Theories of Development: An Assessment'. In *Women and National Development: The Complexities of Change*, ed. Wellesley Editorial Committee, pp. 1–8. Chicago, University of Chicago Press.

Ellis, F. (1988) *Peasant Economics Farm Households and Agrarian Development*. Cambridge, Cambridge University Press.

Elson, D. (1988a) 'Market Socialism or Socialization of the Market?'. *New Left Review*, no. 172, pp. 3–44.

Elson, D. (1988b) 'Review of Joekes, 1987'. *Journal of Development Studies*, pp. 139–42.

Elson, D. (1991a) 'Male Bias in the Development Process: An Overview'. In *Male Bias in the Development Process*, ed. D. Elson, pp. 1–28. Manchester, Manchester University Press.

Elson, D. (1991b) 'Male Bias in Macro-Economics: The Case of Structural Adjustment'. In *Male Bias in the Development Process*, ed. D. Elson, pp. 164–90. Manchester, Manchester University Press.

Elson, D. and R. Pearson (1981) 'The Subordination of Women and the Internationalization of Factory Production'. In *Of Marriage and Market. Women's Subordination in International Perspective*, ed. K. Young, C. Wolkowitz and C. McCullagh, pp. 144–66. London, CSE Books.

Emmerji, L. (1992) 'Worlds of Difference'. In *International Governance*. IDS Silver Jubilee Papers 1966–1991, pp. 37–68. Institute of Development Studies, Sussex.

Engels, F. (1972) *The Origin of the Family, Private Property and the State*. London, Lawrence and Wishart.

Enke, S. (1969) 'Birth Control for Economic Development'. *Science*, vol. 164.

Epstein, T.S. and D. Jackson, eds. (1977) 'The Feasibility of Fertility Planning. Micro Perspectives'. London, Pergamon Press.

Evans, A. (1991) 'Gender Issues in Household Rural Economics'. *IDS Bulletin*, vol. 22, no. 1, pp. 51–9.

Evans, A. (1993) ' "Contracted-out": Some Reflections on Gender, Power and Agrarian Institutions'. *IDS Bulletin*, vol. 24, no. 3, pp. 21–30.

Evenson, R.E. (1976) 'On the New Household Economics'. *Journal of Agricultural Economics and Development*, vol. 6, pp. 87–103.

Evenson, R.E. (1978) 'Philippine Household Economics: An Introduction to the Symposium Papers'. *The Philippine Economic Journal*, vol. XVII, nos. 1 and 2, pp. 1–31.

Everett, J. and M. Savara (1983) *Bank Credit to Women in the Informal Sector: A Case Study of the DRI in Bombay City*. SNDT Women's University Research Unit on Women's Studies, Bombay.

Everett, J. and M. Savara (1991) 'Institutional Credit as a Strategy towards Self-Reliance for Petty Commodity Producers in India: A Critical Evaluation'. In *Women, Development and Survival in the Third World*, ed. H. Afshar, pp. 239–59. Macmillan Press, London.

Farouk, A. (1976) *The Vagrants of Dhaka City*. Bureau of Economic Research, Dhaka University, Dhaka.

Feldman, S. and F.E. McCarthy (1984) *Rural Women and Development in Bangladesh*. NORAD, Oslo.

Fergany, N. (1981) *Monitoring the Condition of the Poor in the Third World: Some Aspects of Measurement*. ILO/WEP Research Working Paper WEP 10–6/WP52. ILO, Geneva.

Fernandes, W. and R. Tandon (1981) *Participatory Research and Evaluation*. New Delhi, Indian Social Institute.

Ferree, M.M. and B.B. Hess (1987) 'Introduction'. In *Analyzing Gender. A Handbook of Social Science Research*, ed. B.B. Hess and M.M. Ferree, pp. 9–30. London, Sage Publications.

Feurstein, M. (1986) *Partners in Development*. London, Macmillan.

FINRRAGE (1989) *The Declaration of Comilla*. FINRRAGE-UBINIG International Conference, Comilla.

Fleming, S. (1991) 'Between the Household: Researching Community Organization and Networks'. *IDS Bulletin*, vol. 22, no. 1, pp. 37–43.

Folbre, N. (1984a) 'Market Opportunities, Genetic Endowments and Intra-family Resource Distribution: Comment'. *American Economic Review*, vol. 74, no. 3, pp. 518–20.

Folbre, N. (1984b) 'Household Production in the Philippines: A Non-neoclassical Approach'. *Economic Development and Cultural Change*, vol. 32, no. 2, pp. 303–30.

Folbre, N. (1986a) 'Hearts and Spades: Paradigms of Household Economics'. *World Development*, vol. 14, no. 2, pp. 245–55.

Folbre, N. (1986b) 'Cleaning House: New Perspectives on Households and Economic Development'. *Journal of Development Economics*, vol. 22, pp. 5–40.

Fraser, N. (1989) *Unruly Practices. Power, Discourse and Gender in Contemporary Social Theory*. Cambridge, Polity Press.

Friedmann, H. (1979) 'Household Production and the National Economy: Concepts for the Analysis of Agrarian Formations'. *Journal of Peasant Studies*, vol. 7, no. 2, pp. 158–84.

Fuglesang, A. and D. Chandler (1986) *Participation as Process – What Can We Learn from Grameen Bank, Bangladesh?* Oslo, NORAD.

Galbraith, J.K. (1974) *Economics and the Public Purpose*. London, André Deutsch.

Gandhi, N. and N. Shah (1992) *The Issues at Stake. Theory and Practice in the Contemporary Women's Movement in India*. New Delhi, Kali for Women.

Germain, A. (1989) 'The Christopher Tietze International Symposium: An Overview'. In *Women's Health in the Third World: The Impact of Unwanted Pregnancy*. Supplement 3 to *International Journal of Gynecology and Obstetrics*, ed. A. Rosenfield, M.F. Fathalla, A. Germain and C.L. Indriso, pp. 1–8.

Germain, A. and J. Ordway (1989) *Population Control and Women's Health: Balancing the Scales*. International Women's Health Coalition/Overseas Development Council.

Giddens, A. (1979) *Central Problems in Social Theory*. London, Macmillan.

Glendinning, C. and J. Millar, eds. (1987) *Women and Poverty in Britain*. Brighton, Harvester.

Goetz, A.M. (1989) 'Misbehaving Policy: A Feminist Analysis of Assumptions Informing A Project For Women Fish-Smokers in Guinea'. Paper presented to the Canadian Association of Africa Scholars Annual Meeting, Queen's University, Kingston, Ontario. May.

Goetz, A.M. (1991) *The Institutional Politics of Gender in Rural Development Policy for Women in Bangladesh*. Ph.D. dissertation, Cambridge.

Goetz, A.M. (1992) 'Gender and Administration'. *IDS Bulletin*, vol. 23, no. 4, pp. 6–17.

Gonoshasthaya Kendra (1991) 'Development of Narikendra: Vocational Training Centre for Women'. Nayarhat, Dhamrai. Bangladesh. Mimeo.

Goody, J. (1976) *Production and Reproduction: A Contemporary Study of the Domestic Domain*. Cambridge University Press, Cambridge.

Gordon, S., ed. (1984) *Ladies in Limbo. The Fate of Women's Bureaux – Case Studies from the Caribbean*. London, Commonwealth Secretariat.

Government of Bangladesh (1992) *Women and Men in Bangladesh: Facts and Figures 1992. An Executive Summary*. Bangladesh Bureau of Statistics, Dhaka.

Government of India (1974) *Towards Equality: Report of the Committee on the Status of Women in India*. New Delhi.

Graham, W., W. Brass and R.W. Snow (1989) 'Estimating Maternal Mortality: The Sisterhood Method'. *Studies in Family Planning*, vol. 20, no. 3, pp. 125–35.

Greeley, M. (1987) *Postharvest Losses, Technology and Employment: the Case of Rice in Bangladesh*. Westview Press, Boulder, Colorado.

Greeley, M., N. Kabeer, S. Davies and K. Hussein (1992) *Measuring the Poverty Reduction Impact of Development Interventions*. Prepared for the Overseas Development Administration, London.

Greenough, P.R. (1982) *Prosperity and Misery in Modern Bengal: The Famine of 1943–44*. Oxford, Oxford University Press.

Greer, G. (1984) *Sex and Destiny. The Politics of Human Fertility*. London, Secker and Warburg.

Greiner, T. (1983) 'Some Economic and Social Implications of Breastfeeding'. Appendix 2 in M. Thomas, *Investment Appraisal of Supportive Measures to Working Women in Developing Countries*, pp. 51–5. Report prepared for the Commonwealth Secretariat and World Health Organisation.

Guyer, J.I. (1981) 'Household and Community in African Studies'. *African Studies Review* 24, pp. 87–137.

Guyer, J.I. (1986) 'Intra-household Processes and Farming Systems Research: Perspectives from Anthropology'. In *Understanding Africa's Rural Households and Farming Systems*, ed. J. L. Moock, pp. 92–104. Westview Press, Boulder, Colorado.

Guyer, J.I. (1988) 'Dynamic Approaches to Domestic Budgeting: Cases and Methods from Africa'. In *A Home Divided. Women and Income in the Third World*, ed. J. Bruce and D. Dwyer, pp. 155–72. Stanford University Press, Stanford, Calif.

Guyer, J. I. and P.E. Peters (1987) 'Introduction' in *Development and Change*, vol. 18, no. 2, pp. 197–214.

Gwatkin, D. R. (1979) 'Political Will and Family Planning: The Implications of India's Emergency Experience'. *Population and Development Review*, vol. 5, no. 1.

Haddad, L. and J. Hoddinott (1991) 'Gender Aspects of Household Expenditures and Resource Allocation in the Côte d'Ivoire'. University of Oxford. Mimeo.

Hamid, S. (1989) 'Women's Non-Market Work and GDP Accounting: The Case of Bangladesh', *Bangladesh Institute of Development Studies Research Report No. 116*. Dhaka.

Hamid, S. (1991) 'Female-headed households'. In *Rethinking Poverty. Dimensions, Process, Options*. Report submitted to the Like-minded Group of Donors. Bangladesh Institute of Development Studies, Dhaka.

Hannan, M.T. (1982) 'Families, Markets and Social Structures: An Essay on Becker's *A Treatise on the Family'. Journal of Economic Literature*, vol. 20, no. 1, pp. 65–72.

Harris, O. (1981) 'Households as Natural Units'. In *Of Marriage and Market. Women's Subordination in International Perspective*, ed. K. Young, C. Wolkowitz and C. McCullagh, pp. 49–68. London, CSE Books.

Hart, G. (1991) 'Engendering Everyday Resistance: Politics, Gender and Class Formation in Rural Malaysia'. *Journal of Peasant Studies*, vol. 19, no. 1, pp. 93–121.

Hart, G. (1992) 'Household Production Reconsidered: Gender, Labor Conflict, and Technological Change in Malaysia's Muda Region'. *World Development*, vol. 20, no. 6, pp. 809–23.

Hartmann, B. (1987) *Reproductive Rights and Wrongs. The Global Politics of Population Control and Contraceptive Choice*. Harper and Row, New York.

Hartmann, B. and J. Boyce (1983) *A Quiet Violence. View from a Bangladesh Village*. London, Zed Books.

Hartmann, B. and H. Standing (1989) *The Poverty of Population Control: Family Planning and Health Policy in Bangladesh*. Bangladesh International Action Group, London.

Hartmann, H. (1986) 'The Unhappy Marriage of Marxism and Feminism: Towards a More Progressive Union'. In *The Unhappy Marriage of Marxism and Feminism. A Debate on Class and Patriarchy*, ed. Lydia Sargent, pp. 1–41. London, Pluto Press.

Hartsock, N. (1987) 'The Feminist Standpoint. Developing the Ground for a Specifically Feminist Historical Materialism'. In *Feminism and Methodology*, ed. S. Harding, pp.157–80. Milton Keynes, Open University Press.

Hartsock, N. (1990) 'Rethinking Modernism: Minority vs. Majority Theories'. In *The Nature and Context of Minority Discourse*, ed. A. R. JanMohammed and D. Lloyd, pp.17–36. New York, Oxford University Press.

Harvey, D. (1982) *The Limits to Capital*. Chicago, Chicago University Press.

Haswell, M. (1981) *Energy for Subsistence*. Macmillan, London.

Haswell, M. (1988) *Population and Change in a Gambian Rural Community 1947–87*. Mimeo.

Haverman, R.H. (1976) 'Benefit–Cost Analysis and Family Planning Programs'. *Population and Development Review*, vol. 2, no. 1, pp. 37–64.

Herz, B. and A. Measham (1987) *The Safe Motherhood Initiative: Proposals for Action*. World Bank, Washington.

Heyzer, N. (1989) 'Issues and Methodologies for Gender Sensitive Planning'. In *Gender Sensitivity in Development Planning, Implementation and Evaluation*, ed. R. Raj-Hashim and N. Heyzer, pp. 13–17. Report of the APDC Sub-Regional Workshops. Kuala Lumpur.

Hill, P. (1975) 'The West African Farming Household'. In *Changing Social Structure in Ghana*, ed. J. Goody, pp. 119–36. London, International African Institute.

Hillier, S. (1988) 'Women and Population Control in China: Issues of Sexuality, Power and Control'. *Feminist Review*, no. 29, pp. 101–13.

Hoddinott, J. (1992) 'Household Economics and the Economics of the Household'. Paper presented at the IFPRI/World Bank conference on Intra-household Resource Allocation, IFPRI, Washington, 12–14 February.

Hodgson, G.M. (1988) *Economics and Institutions*. Cambridge, Polity Press.

Hokesbergen, R. (1986) 'Approaches to Evaluation of Development Interventions: The Importance of World and Life Views'. *World Development*, vol. 14, no. 2, pp. 283–300.

Horenstein, N.R. (1985) 'Factoring Gender into the Development Equation'. *Horizons*, vol. 4, no. 3, pp. 26–30.

Hossain, M. (1987) *The Assault that Failed: A Profile of Absolute Poverty in Six Villages of Bangladesh*. UNRISD, Geneva.

Hoyle, F. and G. Hoyle (1971) *The Molecule Men*. New York, Harper and Row.

Humphrey, J. (1987) *Gender and Work in the Third World. Sexual Divisions in Brazilian Industry*. London, Tavistock Publications.

Humphrey, J., S. Joekes, N. Kabeer and J. Pointing (1991) *Gender and Households as Factors in Adapting to Economic Change*. Report to ILO Geneva. Mimeo.

Huq, M. and M. Sultan (1991) ' "Informality" in Development: the Poor as Entrepreneurs in Bangladesh'. In *The Silent Revolution. The Informal Sector in Five Asian and Near Eastern Countries*, ed. A.L. Chickering and M. Salahdine, pp. 145–83. International Center for Economic Growth, San Francisco.

Huq, N. (1992) 'The Realities of Women's Lives in Bangladesh and Fertility Regulation Technologies'. Paper prepared for the Asian Regional Meeting on Women's Perspectives in the Introduction of Fertility Regulating Technologies. World Health Organization, Manila.

International Labour Organisation (1976) *Employment, Growth and Basic Needs: A One-World Problem*. ILO, Geneva.

Institute of Development Studies (1979) *IDS Bulletin*, vol. 10, no. 3.

Institute of Development Studies (1991) *WDP – Emerging Challenges*. Jaipur.

Irvin, G. (1978) *Modern Cost–Benefit Analysis*. London, Macmillan Press.

Ison, R.L. (1990) *Teaching Threatens Sustainable Agriculture*. IIED Sustainable Agricultural Programme Gatekeeper Series SA 21, London.

Jackson, C. (1978) 'Hausa Women on Strike'. *Review of African Political Economy* 13, pp. 21–36.

Jackson, D. (1977) 'Paradigms and Perspectives. A Cross-cultural Approach to Population Growth and Rural Poverty'. In *The Feasibility of Family Planning. Micro Perspectives*, ed. T. Scarlett Epstein and D. Jackson, pp. 3–20. London, Pergamon Press.

Jagger, A. (1983) *Politics and Human Nature*. Brighton, Harvester.

Jahan, R. (1989) *Women and Development in Bangladesh: Challenges and Opportunities*. Ford Foundation, Dhaka.

Jahangir, B.K. (1986) 'Women and Property in Rural Bangladesh'. *Journal of Social Studies*, no. 34.

Jain, D. (1983) *Development as if Women Mattered*. Lecture delivered at OECD DAC meeting, Paris. Available from Institute of Social Studies Trust, New Delhi.

Jain, D. and N. Banerjee, eds. (1985) *Tyranny of the Household*. New Delhi, Shakti Books.

Jain, S., K. Srivastava, K. Mathur, M. Jaitly and N. Nair (1986) *Exploring Possibilities. A Review of the Women's Development Programme*. Institute of Development Studies, Jaipur.

James, M. (1990) 'Demystifying Literacy: Reading, Writing, and the Struggle for Liberation'. *Convergence*, vol. XXIII, no. 1, pp. 14–26.

Jaquette, J.S. (1982) 'Women and Modernization Theory: A Decade of Feminist Criticism'. *World Politics*, vol. XXXIV, no. 2, pp. 267–84.

Jaquette, J.S. (1990) 'Gender and Justice in Economic Development'. In *Persistent Inequalities*, ed. I. Tinker, Oxford, Oxford University Press. pp. 54–69.

Jaquette, J.S. and K.A. Staudt (1988) 'Politics, Population and Gender: A Feminist Analysis of US Population Policy in the Third World'. In *The Political Interests of Gender. Developing Theory and Research with a Feminist Face*, ed. K.B. Jones and A.G. Jonasdottir, pp. 214–33. London, Sage.

Jiggins, J. (1986) 'Women and Seasonality: Coping with Crisis and Calamity'. *IDS Bulletin*, vol. 17, no. 3, pp. 9–18.

Jodha, N.S. (1985) 'Social Science Research on Rural Change: Some Gaps'. Paper presented at Conference on Rural Economic Change in South Asia: Differences in Approach and in Results between Large-Scale Surveys and Intensive Micro-Studies, Bangalore, India 5–8 August.

Johnson, M.M. (1989) 'Feminism and the Theories of Talcott Parsons'. In *Feminism and Sociological Theory*, ed. R. Wallace, pp. 101–18. London, Sage Publications.

Jonasdottir, A.G. (1988) 'On the Concept of Interest, Women's Interests and the Limitations of Interest Theory'. In *The Political Interests of Gender. Developing Theory and Research with a Feminist Face*, ed. K.B. Jones and A.G. Jonasdottir, pp. 33–65. London, Sage Publications.

Jones, C.W. (1983) 'The Impact of the Semry I Irrigated Rice Production Project on the Organisation of Production and Consumption at the Intra-Household Level'. Harvard University, Prepared for USAID. September.

Jones, C.W. (1985) 'The Mobilization of Women's Labor for Cash Crop Production: a Game-Theoretic Approach'. In *Women in Rice Farming*. Published proceedings of the Conference on Women in Rice Farming Systems, pp. 445–454. London, Gower Press.

Jones, C.W. (1986) 'Intrahousehold Bargaining in Response to the Introduction of New Crops: A Case Study of Northern Cameroon'. In *Understanding Africa's Rural Households and Farming Systems*, ed. J. L. Moock, pp. 105–23. Boulder, Colorado, Westview Press.

Joshi, H. (1983) *Note*. Mimeo. Contribution to Working Group on Investment Appraisal of Supportive Measures to Working Women in Developing Countries, London 21–24 November.

Jumani, U. (1993) *Dealing with Poverty: Self-Employment for Poor Rural Women*. New Delhi, Sage.

Kabeer, N. (1985) 'Organising Landless Women in Bangladesh'. *Community Development Journal*, vol. 20, no. 3, pp. 203–11.

Kabeer, N. (1986) *The Functions of Children in the Household Economy and Levels of Fertility: A Case Study of a Village in Bangladesh.* Ph.D. dissertation, London School of Economics and Political Science.

Kabeer, N. (1987) *Women's Employment in the Newly Industrialising Countries: a Case Study of India and the Philippines.* Report prepared for the IDRC, Canada.

Kabeer, N. (1990) 'Poverty, Purdah and Women's Survival Strategies in Rural Bangladesh'. In *The Food Question: Profits versus People*, ed. H. Bernstein, B. Crow, M. Mackintosh and C. Martin, pp. 134–48. London, Earthscan.

Kabeer, N. and R. Aziz (1990) *Gender Divisions in Food Production and Food Entitlements: Case Studies from Bangladesh and the Gambia.* Training Module, Population and Development Unit, Institute of Social Studies, The Hague.

Kakar, S. (1978) *The Inner World: A Psychological Study of Childhood and Society in India.* Delhi, Oxford University Press.

Kandiyoti, D. (1985) *Women in Rural Production Systems: Problems and Policies.* Paris, UNESCO.

Kandiyoti, D. (1988) 'Bargaining with Patriarchy'. *Gender and Society*, vol. 2, no. 3, pp. 274–90.

Kandiyoti, D., ed. (1991) *Women, Islam and the State.* London, Macmillan.

Kardam, N. (1989) 'Gender and Development Agencies'. In *The Women and International Development Annual*, Vol. 1, ed. R.S. Gallin, M. Aronoff and A. Ferguson, pp. 133–54. Boulder, Colorado, Westview Press.

Keller, B. and D.C. Mbewe (1991) 'Policy and Planning for the Empowerment of Zambia's Women Farmers'. *Canadian Journal of Development Studies*, vol. XXII, no. 1, pp. 75–88.

Keller, F.E. (1985) *Reflections on Gender and Science.* New Haven, Yale University Press.

Kennedy, E. (1989) *The Effects of Sugarcane Production on Food Security, Health and Nutrition in Kenya: A Longitudinal Analysis.* Research Report No. 78, International Food Policy Research Institute, Washington.

Kennedy, E. and B. Cogill (1987) *Income and Nutritional Effects of the Commercialization of Agriculture in Southwestern Kenya.* Research Report No. 63, International Food Policy Research Institute, Washington.

Kiseke, M. (1989) 'Reproductive Health Research and Advocacy: Challenges to Women's Associations in Nigeria'. Paper presented at the Conference of the Society of Obstetrics and Gynecology of Nigeria, Calabar. September.

Kloppenburg, Jr., J. (1991a) 'Alternative Agriculture and the New Biotechnologies'. *Science as Culture*, vol. 2, no. 4.

Kloppenburg, Jr., J. (1991b) 'Social Theory and the De/reconstruction of Agricultural Sciences: Local Knowledge for an Alternative Agriculture'. *Rural Sociology*, vol. 56, no. 4, pp. 519–48.

Koenig, M.A., V. Faveau, A.I. Chowdhury, J. Chakraborty and M.A. Khan. (1988) 'Maternal Mortality in Matlab, Bangladesh: 1975–85'. *Studies in Family Planning*, vol. 19, no. 2, pp. 69–80.

Kumar, R. (1982) *City Lives: women workers in the Bombay cotton textile industry, 1919–1939*. M.Phil. thesis, Centre for Historical Studies, Jawarhalal Nehru University, New Delhi.

Kynch, K. and A.K. Sen (1983) 'Indian Women: Wellbeing and Survival'. *Cambridge Journal of Economics* 7, pp. 363–80.

Layard, R.G., ed. (1972) 'Introduction', *Cost–Benefit Analysis*. Harmondsworth, Penguin.

Leach, M. (1990) 'Gender, Resource Management and Agroecological Change: Perspectives from West Africa'. Paper presented at IDS retreat, *Environmental Change, Development Challenges*, 17–18 December.

Leach, M. (1991) 'Locating Gendered Experience: An Anthropologist's View from a Sierra-Leonean Village'. *IDS Bulletin*, vol. 22, no. 1, pp. 44–50.

Leacock, E. (1977) 'Reflections on the Conference on Women and Development'. In *Women and National Development: The Complexities of Change*, Wellesley Editorial Committee, pp. 320–22. Chicago, University of Chicago Press.

Lebergott, S. (1964) *Manpower in Economic Growth: The American Record since 1800*. New York, McGraw-Hill.

Leng, C.H. and C.C. Khoon (1984) *Designer Genes: I.Q., Ideology and Biology*. Institute for Social Analysis, Selangor, Malaysia.

Leslie, J. (1989) 'Women's Time: A Factor in the Use of Child Survival Technologies?' *Health Policy and Planning*, vol. 4, no. 1, pp. 1–16.

Leslie, J. (1992) 'Women's Time and the Use of Health Services'. *IDS Bulletin*, vol. 23, no. 1, pp. 4–7.

Leslie, J., M. Lycette and M. Buvinic (1988) 'Weathering Economic Crisis: The Crucial Role of Women in Health'. In *Health, Nutrition and Economic Crises. Approaches to Policy in the Third World*, ed. D.E. Bell and M.R. Reich, pp. 307–48. Dover, Mass., Auburn House.

Levine, N.E. (1988) 'Women's Work and Infant Feeding: A Case from Rural Nepal'. *Ethnology*, vol. 27, no. 3, pp. 231–51.

Levinson, F.J. (1974) *Morinda: An Economic Analysis of Malnutrition among Young Children in Rural India*. Cornell–MIT International Nutrition Policy Series. Cambridge, Mass.

Lewis, W.A. (1955) *The Theory of Economic Growth*. London, Allen and Unwin.

Lexow, J. (1988) *WID Issues in Nordic Development Assistance*. Oslo, DECO Development Consulting A.S.

Lexow, J. and D. McNeill (1989) 'The Women's Grant. Desk Study Review (including case studies of the World Bank and UNIDO'. Prepared for NORAD. Development Consulting A.S. (DECO), Oslo. February.

Lipman-Blum, J. (1979) 'The Dialectic Between Research and Social Policy: the Difficulties from a Research Perspective – Rashomon Part II'. In *Sex Roles and Social Policy*, ed. J. Lipman-Blum and J. Bernard, pp. 39–60. Beverly Hills, Sage.

Lipton, M. (1986) 'Seasonality and Ultrapoverty'. *IDS Bulletin*, vol. 17, no. 2, pp. 4–8.

Lipton, M. and M. Ravallion (forthcoming) 'Poverty and Policy'. In *Handbook of Development Economics* vol. 3, ed. J. Behrman and T.N. Srinivasan. Amsterdam, North-Holland Press.

Lockwood, M. and P. Collier (1988) *Maternal Education and the Vicious Cycle of High Fertility and Malnutrition*. World Bank Population and Human Resources Department WPS 130.

Longhurst, R. (1988) 'Cash Crops, Household Food Security and Nutrition'. *IDS Bulletin*, vol. 19, no. 2, pp. 28–36.

Lukes, S. (1974) *Power. A Radical View*. London, Macmillan.

Lycklama a Nijeholt, G. (1992) 'Women and the Meaning of Development: Approaches and Consequences'. Silver Jubilee Paper 6. Institute of Development Studies, Sussex.

McAllister, E. (1984) *Managing the Process of Change. Women in Development*. Presentation to President's Committee Policy Branch, CIDA. January.

Mackintosh, M. (1990) 'Abstract Markets and Real Needs'. In *The Food Question. Profits versus People*, ed. H. Bernstein, B. Crow, M. Mackintosh and C. Martin, pp. 43–5. London: Earthscan.

Maguire, P. (1984) *Women in Development: An Alternative Analysis*. Amherst, Mass., Centre for International Education.

Mahmud, W. and S. Mahmud (1985) *Aspects of the Food and Nutritional Problem in Rural Bangladesh*. ILO/WEP Research Working Paper 10–6/WP74.

Maine, D., A. Rosenfield, M. Wallace, A.M. Kimball, B. Kwast, E. Papiernik and S. White (1987) *Prevention of Maternal Deaths in Developing Countries: Program Options and Practical Considerations*. Paper prepared for the International Safe Motherhood Conference, Nairobi, 10–13 February.

Mair, L.M. (1989) 'Commentary on the Ethics of Induced Abortion from a Feminist Perspective'. In *Women's Health in the Third World: The Impact of Unwanted Pregnancy*. Special Issue of *International Journal of Gynecology and Obstetrics*, ed. A. Rosenfield, M.F. Fathalla, A. Germain and C.L. Indriso, pp. 57–60.

Malika, A. and other members of Mahila Samuh (1993) 'Women's Development: What is the State's Intention?' *Economic and Political Weekly*. 6 March, pp. 373–6.

Mamdani, M. (1972) *The Myth of Population Control*. New York, Monthly Review Press.

Manser, M. and M. Brown (1980) 'Marriage and Household Decision-Making: A Bargaining Analysis'. *International Economic Review* 21, pp. 31–44.

March, K.S. and R.L. Taqqu (1986) *Women's Informal Associations in Developing Countries. Catalysts for Change?* Boulder, Colorado, Westview Press.

Marsden, D. and P. Oakley, eds. (1990) *Evaluating Social Development Projects*. Oxford, Oxfam Publications.

Marx, K. (1968) 'Preface to The Critique of Political Economy'. In K. Marx and F. Engels, *Selected Works*. New York, International Publishers.

Marx, K. (1970) *Capital. A Critical Analysis of Capitalist Production* Vol. 1. Moscow, Progress Publishers.

Mass, B. (1976) *Population Target. The Political Economy of Population Control in Latin America*. Toronto, Women's Press.

Mazumdar, V. (1989) *Peasant Women Organize for Empowerment: The Bankura Experiment*. Occasional Paper No. 13. Centre for Women's Development Studies, New Delhi.

Merchant, C. (1980) *The Death of Nature: Women, Ecology and the Scientific Revolution*. New York, Harper and Row.

Mies, M. (1980) 'Capitalist Development and Subsistence Production: Rural Women in India'. *Bulletin of Concerned Asian Scholars*, vol. 12, no. 1, pp. 2–14.

Mies, M. (1981) 'Social Origins of the Sexual Division of Labour'. ISS Occasional Papers, No. 85. The Hague, Institute of Social Studies.

Mies, M. (1982) *The Lacemakers of Narsapur. Indian Housewives Produce for the World Market*. London, Zed Books.

Mies, M. (1986) *Patriarchy and Accumulation on a World Scale. Women in the International Division of Labour*. London, Zed Books.

Mies, M. (1988) 'From the Individual to the Dividual'. *Reproductive And Genetic Engineering*, vol. 1, no. 3, pp. 225–37.

Mies, M. (1989) 'What Unites, What Divides Women from the South and from the North in the Field of Reproductive Technologies?'. Paper presented at the FINRRAGE-UBINIG International Conference on Reproductive and Genetic Engineering and Reproductive Health, Comilla, Bangladesh.

Mies, M., V. Bennholdt-Thomsen and C. Von Werlhof (1988) *Women. The Last Colony*. London, Zed Books.

Miller, B.D. (1981) *The Endangered Sex. Neglect of Female Children in Rural North India*. Ithaca, Cornell University Press.

Mincer, J. (1980) 'Labor Force Participation of Married Women: A Study of Labor Supply'. In *The Economics of Women and Work*, ed. A. Amsden, pp. 41–51. Harmondsworth, Penguin.

Miranda, A. (1982) *The Demography of Bangladesh*. DERAP Publications. No. 144. Chr. Michaelsen Institute. Bergen, Norway.

Mitra, S. (1982) 'Ecology as Science and Science Fiction'. *Economic and Political Weekly* 17. pp. 147–52.

Mitter, S. (1986) *Common Fate, Common Bond*. London, Pluto Press.

Molyneux, M. (1985) 'Mobilisation without Emancipation: Women's Interests, State and Revolution in Nicaragua'. *Feminist Studies*, vol. 11, no. 2, pp. 227–54.

Moore, H. (1988) *Feminism and Anthropology*. Cambridge, Polity Press.

Morgan, R. (1977) *Going Too Far: the Personal Chronicles of a Feminist*. New York, Random House.

Morishima, M. (1976) *The Economic Theory of Modern Society*. Cambridge, Cambridge University Press.

Moser, C.O.N. (1989) 'Gender Planning in the Third World: Meeting Practical and Strategic Gender Needs'. *World Development*, vol. 17, no. 11, pp. 1799–1825.

Moser, C.O.N. (1992) 'From Residual Welfare to Compensatory Measures: the Changing Agenda of Social Policy in Developing Countries'. Silver Jubilee Paper 6. Institute of Development Studies, Sussex.

Mukhopadhyay, M. (1992) 'Women, the State and Personal Laws in India'. Paper presented at the Twelfth European Conference on Modern South Asian Studies, Berlin. Mimeo.

Murthy, R.K. (1993) 'Gender Concepts in Training and Planning'. Paper presented in the Tools for Trainers Workshop, Amsterdam, 6–12 June. Organized by Population Council and Royal Tropical Institute.

Musoke, M.G.N. and M. Amajo (1989) *Women's Participation in Credit Schemes: Case Studies from Uganda*. Research Report prepared for UNIFEM.

Nakajima, C. (1970) 'Subsistence and Commercial Family Farms: Some Theoretical Models of Subjective Equilibrium'. In *Subsistence Agriculture and Economic Development*, ed. C. Wharton, pp.165–85. London, Frank Cass.

Nandy, A. (1986) *The Intimate Enemy*. Delhi, Oxford University Press.

Nash, J. and H. I. Safa (1980) 'Introduction' and 'Introduction to Part I'. In *Sex and Class in Latin America. Women's Perspectives on Politics, Economics and the Family in the Third World*, ed. J. Nash and H.I. Safa, pp. x–xiii and 25–9. New York, J.F. Bergin Publishers.

Nath, K. (n.d.) 'Labour-Saving Techniques in Food-processing: Rural Women and Technological Change in the Gambia'. *Boston University African Studies Centre Working Papers*, No. 108.

New Internationalist (1985) *Women. A World Report*. London, Methuen.

Newland, K. (1977) *Women and Population Growth: Choice Beyond Childbearing*. Worldwatch Paper 16, Washington.

Nicholson, L. (1987) 'Feminism and Marx. Integrating Kinship with the Economic'. In *Feminism as Critique*, ed. S. Benhabib and D. Cornell, pp. 16–30. Cambridge, Polity Press.

NORAD (1988) *Report on Feasibility Study on Training and Rehabilitation of Socially Handicapped Women (Prostitutes)*. Prepared by Engineering Science Ltd, Dhaka.

North, D.C. (1990) *Institutions, Institutional Change and Economic Performance*. Cambridge, Cambridge University Press.

Oakley, P. (1990) 'The Monitoring and Evaluation of Popular Participation in Development'. Paper presented at the Conference of the European Association of Development Research and Training Insitutes, Oslo, Norway. June.

Obbo, C. (1980) *African Women*. London, Zed Books.

Overholt, C., M.B. Anderson, K. Cloud, and J.E. Austin, eds. (1985) *Gender Roles in Development Projects*. West Hartford, Kumarian Press.

Palriwala, R. (1989) 'Reaffirming the Anti-Dowry Struggle'. *Economic and Political Weekly*, April, pp. 942–4.

Payne, P. and P. Cutler (1984) 'Measuring Malnutrition'. *Economic and Political Weekly*, August, pp. 1485–91.

Pearse, A. (1974) *The Social and Economic Implications of Large-Scale Introduction of New Varieties of Food Grain: Summary of Conclusions of the Global Research Project*. Geneva, UNRISD Report No. 74.

Petchesky, R. and J.A.Weiner (1990) *Global Feminist Perspectives on Reproductive Rights and Reproductive Health*. Report on Special Sessions held at the Fourth Interdisciplinary Congress on Women, Hunter College, New York City. 3–7 June.

Phillips, A. and B. Taylor (1980) 'Sex and Skill: Notes Towards a Feminist Economics'. *Feminist Review*, no. 6, pp. 79–88.

Pietila, H. and J. Vickers (1990) *Making Women Matter. The Role of the United Nations*. London, Zed Books.

Pike, M. (1982) 'Segregation by Sex, Earnings Differentials and Equal Pay: An Application of the Crowding Model to U.K. Data'. *Applied Economics*, vol. 14, no. 5, pp. 503–14.

Pirsig, R.M. (1974) *Zen and the Art of Motorcycle Maintenance*. New York, William Morrow.

Pittin, R. (1987) 'Documentation of Women's Work in Nigeria. Problems and Solutions'. In *Sex Roles, Population and Development in West Africa*, ed. C. Oppong, pp. 25–44. New Hampshire, Heinemann Educational Books.

Plant, R., H. Lesser and P. Taylor-Gooby (1980) *Political Philosophy and Social Welfare. Essays on the Normative Provision of Welfare Provision*. Routledge and Kegan Paul, London.

Pollak, R.A. (1985) 'A Transaction Cost Approach to Families and Households'. *The Journal of Economic Literature*, vol. XXIII, no. 2, pp. 581–609.

Popkin, B. (1983) 'Rural Women, Work, and Child Welfare in the Philippines'. In *Women and Poverty in the Third World*, ed. M. Buvinic, M. Lycette and W.P. McGreevey, pp. 157–76. Baltimore, Johns Hopkins University Press.

Population Crisis Committee (1988) *Poor, Powerless and Pregnant*. Population Briefing Paper No. 20. Washington, D.C.

Population Reports (1986) *Family Planning Programs. Men – the New Focus for Family Planning Programs*, Series J, no. 33. The Johns Hopkins University, Baltimore, Maryland.

Price, J. (1992) 'Who Determines Need? A Case Study of a Woman's Organization in North India'. *IDS Bulletin*, vol. 23, no. 1, pp. 50–57.

Psacharopoulos, G. and A. Tzannatos (1991) *Female Employment and Pay in Latin America. A Regional Study*. Human Resources Division, Technical Department, Latin America and Caribbean Region. The World Bank, Washington.

Pyle, D. (1985) 'Indonesia: East Java Family Planning, Nutrition, and Income Generation Project'. In *Gender Roles in Development Projects*, ed. C. Overholt, M.B. Anderson, K. Cloud and J.E. Austin, pp. 135–62. West Hartford, Kumarian Press.

Rahman, A. (1986a) *The Socio-Economic Disadvantages and Development Perspectives of the Poor in Bangladesh Agriculture*. BIDS Research Report No. 52. Dhaka.

Rahman, A. (1986b) *Peasants and Classes. A Study in Differentiation in Bangladesh*. Dhaka, University Press.

Rahman, A., T. Haque and S. Mahmud (1987) *A Critical Review of the Poverty Situation in Bangladesh in the Eighties*. Bangladesh Institute of Development Studies, Dhaka.

Rahman, H.Z. (1991) 'Crisis and Insecurity: The "Other" Face of Poverty'. In *Rethinking Poverty. Dimensions, Process, Options*. Report submitted to the Like-minded Group of Donors. Bangladesh Institute of Development Studies, Dhaka.

Rahman, H.Z. and B. Sen. (1993) *Rural Poverty Update, 1992. Improvement, but . . .* Bangladesh Institute of Development Studies, Dhaka.

Rahman, M.A. (1982) 'The Theory and Practice of Participatory Action Research'. Paper presented at the Tenth World Congress of Sociology, Mexico. August.

Ramu, G.N. (1989/90) ' "Men Don't Cry and Men Don't Cook and Clean" – A Study of Housework among Urban Couples'. *Samya Shakti*, vols. IV and V, pp. 156–74.

Rao, A. (1991) 'Introduction'. In *Gender Analysis in Development Planning*, ed. A. Rao, M.B. Anderson and C.A. Overholt, pp. 1–8. New York, Kumarian.

Rao, A., H. Feldstein, K. Cloud and K. Staudt (1991) 'Introduction', *Gender Training and Development Planning: Learning From Experience*. The Population Council, New York.

Rathgeber, E.M. (1990) 'WID, WAD, GAD: Trends in Research and Practice'. *The Journal of Developing Areas*, vol. 24, pp. 489–502.

Repetto, R., ed. (1985) *The Global Possible: Resources, Development and the New Century*. New Haven, Conn., Yale University Press.

Rich, A. (1976) *Of Woman Born: Motherhood as Experience and Institution*. W.W. Norton, New York.

Robbins, L. (1935) *An Essay on the Nature and Significance of Economic Science*. London, Macmillan.

Roberts, P. (1979) ' "The Integration of Women into the Development Process": Some Conceptual Problems'. *IDS Bulletin*, vol. 10, no. 3, pp. 60–66.

Roberts, P. (1988) 'Rural Women's Access to Labour in West Africa'. In *Patriarchy and Class: African Women in the Home and Workforce*, ed. S. Strichter and J. Partpart, pp. 97–114. Westview Press, Boulder, Colarado.

Roberts, P. (1989) 'The Sexual Politics of Labour in Western Nigeria and Hausa Niger'. In *Serving Two Masters. Third World Women in Development*, ed. K. Young, pp. 27–47. New Delhi, Allied Publishers.

Roberts, P. (1991) 'Anthropological Perspectives on the Household'. *IDS Bulletin*, vol. 11, no. 1, pp. 60–64.

Robinson, J. (1962) *Economic Philosophy*. London, C.A. Watts.

Robinson, J. (1975) *Collected Economic Papers* Vol. II. Oxford, Basil Blackwell.

Rocheleau, D. (1990) 'Gender Complementarity and Conflict in Sustainable Forest Development: a Multiple User Approach'. Paper presented to IVRO World Congress Quinquennial, Montreal, 5–11 August.

Rodgers, G. (1984) *Poverty and Population: Approaches and Evidence*. International Labour Office, Geneva.

Rogers, B. (1980) *The Domestication of Women: Discrimination in Developing Societies*. Kogan Page, London.

Rosaldo, M.Z. (1980) 'The Use and Abuse of Anthropology. Reflections on Feminism and Cross-Cultural Understanding'. *Signs: Journal of Women in Culture and Society*, vol. 5, no. 3, pp. 389–417.

Rosen, B. and A. LaRaia (1972) 'Modernity in Women: An Index of Social Change in Brazil'. *Journal of Marriage and the Family*, xxxiv, pp. 353–60.

Rosenfield, A. and D. Maine (1985) 'Maternal Mortality – A Neglected Tragedy. Where is the M in MCH?', *The Lancet*, vol. 2, pp. 83–85.

Rosenhead, J. and C. Thunhurst (1979) 'Operational Research and Cost Benefit Analysis: Whose Science'. In *Demystifying Social Statistics*, ed. J. Irvine, I. Miles and J. Evans, pp. 289–304. Pluto Press, London.

Rosenzweig, M.R. (1986) 'Program Interventions, Intrahousehold Distribution and the Welfare of Individuals: Modelling Household Behaviour'. *World Development*, vol. 14, no. 2, pp. 233–43.

Rosenzweig, M.R. and T.P. Schultz (1982) 'Market Opportunities, Genetic Endowments and Intrafamily Resource Distribution: Child Survival in Rural India'. *American Economic Review*, vol. 72, no. 4, pp. 803–15.

Rosenzweig, M.R. and T.P. Schultz (1984) 'Market Opportunities, Genetic Endowments and Intrafamily Resource Distribution: Reply'. *American Economic Review*, vol. 74, no. 3, pp. 521–2.

Rubin, G. (1975) 'The Traffic in Women: Notes on the "Political Economy" of Sex'. In *Towards an Anthropology of Women*, ed. R. R. Reiter, pp. 157–210. New York, Monthly Review Press.

Rutabanzibwa-Ngaiza, J., K. Heggenhougen and G. Watt (1985) *Women and Health in Africa*. London School of Hygiene and Tropical Medicine, Evaluation and Planning Centre, London.

Sabir, N.I. and G.J. Ebrahim (1984) 'Are Daughters More at Risk Than Sons in Some Societies?' *Journal of Tropical Paediatrics*, no. 30.

Sadik, N. (1989) *The State of the World Population*. New York, UNFPA.

Safa, H.I. (1980) 'Class Consciousness among Working-Class Women in Latin America: Puerto Rico'. In *Sex and Class in Latin America. Women's Perspectives on Politics, Economics and the Family in the Third World*, ed. J. Nash and H. I. Safa, pp. 69–85. New York, J.F. Bergin Publishers.

Saffiotti, H. (1977) 'Women, Mode of Production, and Social Formations'. *Latin American Perspectives*, vol. IV, nos. 1 and 2, pp. 27–37.

Safilios-Rothschild, C. (1974) *Women and Social Policy*. Englewood Cliffs, N.J., Prentice-Hall.

Safilios-Rothschild, C. and S. Mahmud (1989) *Women's Roles in Agriculture: Present Trends and Potential for Future Growth*. Bangladesh, UNDP/UNIFEM.

Sai, F.T. (1973) 'Perspectives on the Genocide Issue'. *International Journal of Health Services*, vol. 3, no. 4, pp. 753–8.

Sai, F.T. and J. Nassim (1989) 'The Need for a Reproductive Health Care Approach'. In *Women's Health in the Third World: The Impact of Unwanted Pregnancy*. Special Issue of *International Journal of Gynecology and Obstetrics*, ed. A. Rosenfield, M.F. Fathalla, A. Germain and C.L. Indriso, pp. 103–13.

Saith, A. and A. Tankha (1972) 'Economic Decision-Making of the Poor Peasant Household'. *Economic and Political Weekly*. February.

Samuelson, P.A. (1956) 'Social Indifference Curves'. *Quarterly Journal of Economics*, vol. 70, no. 1, pp. 1–22.

Sattar, E. (1979) 'The Demographic Situation'. In *The Situation of Women in Bangladesh*, ed. Women for Women, pp. 1–34. Dhaka, Women for Women and UNICEF.

Schultz, Theodore W. (1973) 'The Value of Children: An Economic Perspective'. *Journal of Political Economy*, vol. 81, no. 2, part II, pp. S2–S13.

Scott, A. (1986) 'Economic Development and Urban Women's Work: the Case of Lima, Peru'. In *Sex Inequalities in Urban Employment in the Third World*, ed. R. Anker and C. Hein, pp. 13–369. London, Macmillan Press.

Scott, A. (1991) 'Informal Sector or Female Sector? Gender Bias in Urban Labour Market Models'. In *Male Bias in the Development Process*, ed. D. Elson, pp. 105–32. Manchester, Manchester University Press.

Seager, J. and A. Olson (1986) *Women in the World. An International Atlas*. London, Pluto Press.

Sebstadt, J. (1982) *Development and Struggle Amongst Self-Employed Women: A Report on Self-Employed Women's Association of India*. Washington, USAID.

Seers, D. (1979) 'The Meaning of Development'. In *Development Theory. Four Critical Studies*, ed. D. Lehmann, pp. 9–24. London, Frank Cass.

Sen, A.K. (1982a) *Choice, Welfare and Measurement*. Oxford, Basil Blackwell.

Sen, A.K. (1982b) *Poverty and Famines. An Essay on Entitlement and Deprivation*. Oxford, Oxford University Press.

Sen, A.K. (1984) *Resources, Values and Development*. Cambridge, Mass., Harvard University Press.

Sen, A.K. (1987) *The Standard of Living*. Cambridge, Cambridge University Press.

Sen, A.K. (1990) 'Gender and Cooperative Conflicts'. In *Persistent Inequalities*, ed. I. Tinker, pp.123–49. Oxford, Oxford University Press.

Sen, G. (1989) 'Fertility Decline and Women's Autonomy. Another Look'. Paper presented at the Ninth World Congress of the International Economics Association, Athens, Greece. 28 August–1 September. Mimeo.

Sen, G. and C. Grown (1985) *Development, Crises and Alternative Visions: Third World Women's Perspectives*. Bangalore, DAWN Secretariat. 1985. Subsequently published by Monthly Review Press, New York.

Sen, G. and C. Sen (1985) 'Women's Domestic Work and Economic Activity'. *Economic and Political Weekly*, vol. 20, no. 17, pp. 49–56.

Senauer, B. (1990) 'The Impact of the Value of Women's Time on Food and Nutrition'. In *Persistent Inequalities*, ed. I. Tinker, pp. 150–61. Oxford, Oxford University Press.

Shah, M. (1993) 'Impact of Technological Change in Agriculture: Women's Voices From a Tribal Village in South Gujerat, India'. Term paper for MA in Gender and Development, Institute of Development Studies, Sussex.

Shatrugna, V., U. A. Maheshwari and T. Sujata (1987) *Women and the Health Care System in Zaheerabad – Towards a New Paradigm of Health*. Report submitted by Anveshi Research Centre for Women's Studies, Hyderabad, to the National Council on Self-Employed Women, Task Force on Health, Ministry of Human Resources Development, New Delhi. December.

Shetty, S. (1991) 'The Assessment of "Empowerment" in Development Projects – An Enquiry'. MA. Dissertation, London School of Economics and Political Science.

Shiva, V. (1989) *Staying Alive. Women, Ecology and Development*. London, Zed Books/Delhi, Kali for Women.

Shklar, J.N. (1990) *The Faces of Injustice*. New Haven, Yale University Press.

Shrivasthava, K. (1992) 'The WDP Experience: Training'. Text of seminar presented at the Institute of Development Studies, Sussex.

Singh, N. (1993) 'The Bankura Story: Rural Women Organize for Change'. In *Women and the Environment: A Reader*, ed. S. Sontheimer, pp. 179–205. London, Earthscan.

Sivard, R.L. (1985) *Women . . . A World Survey*. Washington D.C., World Priorities.

Smith, D. (1987) 'Women's Perspective as a Radical Critique of Sociology'. In *Feminism and Methodology*, ed. S. Harding, pp. 84–96. Milton Keynes, Open University Press.

Snell, M. (1979) 'The Equal Pay and Sex Discrimination Acts: Their Impact in the Workplace'. *Feminist Review*, no. 1, pp. 37–58.

Solow, R.M. (1963) *Capital Theory and the Rate of Return*. Amsterdam, North-Holland Press.

Sprey, J. (1990) 'Theoretical Practice in Family Studies'. In *Fashioning Family Theory. New Approaches*, ed. J. Sprey, pp. 9–33. Sage Press, London.

Standing, H. (1991) *Dependence and Autonomy. Women's Employment and the Family in Calcutta*. London, Routledge.

Staudt, K. (1978) 'Agricultural Productivity Gaps: A Case Study of Male Preference in Government Policy Implementation'. *Development and Change*, vol. 9, no. 3, pp. 439–57.

Staudt, K. (1982) 'Bureaucratic Resistance to Women's Programs: The Case of Women in Development'. In *Women, Power and Policy*, ed. E. Boneparth, pp. 263–81. New York, Pergamon Press.

Staudt, K. (1985) *Women, Foreign Assistance and Advocacy Administration*. New York, Praeger.

Staudt, K. (1986) 'Women, Development and the State: On the Theoretical Impasse'. *Development and Change*, vol. 7, pp. 325–33.

Staudt, K. (1990) 'Gender Politics in Bureaucracy: Theoretical Issues in Comparative Perspective'. In *Women, International Development and Politics. The Bureaucratic Mire*, ed. K. Staudt, pp. 3–34. Philadelphia, Temple University Press.

Staudt, K. (1991) *Managing Development. State, Society and International Contexts*. London, Sage Publications.

Stewart, F. (1975) 'A Note on Social Cost–Benefit Analysis and Class Conflict in LDCs'. *World Development*, vol. 3, no. 1, pp. 31–9.

Stigler, G.J. and G.S. Becker (1977) 'De Gustibus Non Est Disputandum'. *American Economic Review*, vol. 7, no. 2.

Stoler, A. (1977) 'Class Structure and Female Autonomy in Rural Java'. In *Women and National Development: The Complexities of Change*, ed. Wellesley Editorial Committee, pp. 74–89. Chicago, University of Chicago Press.

Sujaya, C.P. (1991) 'Letting Grassroots Women Speak: Center for Women's Development Studies (CWDS) Workshops in India'. In *Gender Training and Development Planning: Learning From Experience*, ed. A. Rao, H. Feldstein, K. Cloud and K. Staudt, Conference Report, The Population Council.

Sultan, M. (1992) 'Changing Gender Roles through Credit: A Case Study of Grameen Bank'. Conference paper prepared for Study Course 23, Women, Men and Development. Institute of Development Studies, Sussex.

Svedberg, P. (1988) 'Undernutrition in Sub-Saharan Africa: Is there a sex bias?' Institute for International Economic Studies, Seminar Paper No. 421. Stockholm.

Swedberg, R. (1991) *Economics and Sociology. Redefining their Boundaries*. Oxford, Oxford University Press.

Syme, D. (1987) 'Population and Political Issues in Implementing Family Planning Programmes in LDCs: a PVO Perspective' in *Family Planning Within Primary Health Care*. National Council for International Health, Washington D.C.

Taylor, H.C. and B. Berelson (1971) 'Comprehensive Family Planning Based on Maternal/Child Health Services: A Feasibility Study for a World Program'. *Studies in Family Planning*, vol. 2, no. 2, Special Issue.

Thomas, D. (1990) 'Intra-household Resource Allocation: An Inferential Approach'. *Journal of Human Resources*, vol. 25, no. 4, pp. 635–64.

Thomas, M. (1984) *Investment Appraisal of Supportive Measures to Working Women in Developing Countries*. Report prepared for the Commonwealth Secretariat and World Health Organisation, pp. 51–5.

Tiano, S. (1984) 'The Public–Private Dichotomy: Theoretical Perspectives on "Women and Development" '. *Social Science Journal*, vol. 21, no. 4, pp. 11–28.

Tietze, C. and S. Lewitt (1968), 'Statistical Evaluation of Contraceptive Methods: Use-Effectiveness and Extended Use-Effectiveness'. *Demography*, vol. 5, no. 2, pp. 931–40.

Tinker, I. (1976) 'The Adverse Impact of Development on Women'. In *Women and World Development*, ed. I. Tinker and M. Bramsen. Washington, D.C., Overseas Development Council.

Tinker, I. (1982) *Gender Equity in Development: A Policy Perspective*. Washington D.C., Equity Policy Centre.

Tinker, I. (1990a) 'A Context for the Field and for the Book'. In *Persistent Inequalities. Women and World Development*, ed. I. Tinker, pp. 3–13. Oxford, Oxford University Press.

Tinker, I. (1990b) 'The Making of a Field: Advocates, Practitioners, and Scholars'. In *Persistent Inequalities*, ed. I. Tinker, pp. 27–53. Oxford, Oxford University Press.

Todaro, M.P. and E. Fapohunda (1987) *Family Structure, Implicit Contracts, and the Demand for Children: A Consideration of Southern Nigerian Data*. Centre for Policy Studies Working Papers No. 136. New York, The Population Council.

Torres, C. (1990) 'Making Plans for 1991'. *Women's Health Journal*, no. 19.

Tzannatos, Z. (1988) 'The Long-run Effects of the Sex Integration of the British Labour Market'. *Journal of Economic Studies*, vol. 15, no. 1, pp. 5–18.

Tzannatos, Z. (1990) 'The Economics of Discrimination: Theories and British Evidence'. In *Current Issues in Labour Economics*, ed. D. Sapford and Z. Tzannatos, pp. 177–207. London: Macmillan.

UBINIG (1987) *Health and Illness in Two Villages of Commilla: An Interim Report of the On-going Study on Illness Behaviour in Rural Bangladesh.* Dhaka.

United Nations (1980a) *Report of the World Conference of the United Nations Decade for Women, Copenhagen*, A/CONF.94/35.

United Nations (1980b) *Report of the World Conference of the UN Decade for Women: Equality, Development and Peace.* New York, United Nations.

United Nations (1989a) *Elements of an International Development Strategy for the 1990s.* New York, United Nations.

United Nations (1989b) *World Survey on the Role of Women in Development.* New York, United Nations.

UNDP (1990) *Human Development Report 1990.* Oxford, Oxford University Press.

UNFPA (1989) *Global Population Assistance Report 1982–1988.* New York.

UNICEF (1987) *Analysis of the Situation of Children in Bangladesh.* Dhaka.

UNICEF–Ministry of Health–Institute of Mother and Child Care (1991) *Causes of Institutionalization of Romanian Children in Leagane and Sectii do Distrofici.* Bucharest.

USAID (1982) *AID Policy Paper: Women in Development.* Bureau for Program and Policy Coordination, USAID Bureau for Program and Policy Co-ordination, Washington.

Van der Laan, J. and S. Krippendorf (1981) *Remember the Words of the Poor.* Report of the Mission on Women and Emancipation to Bangladesh for the Netherlands Ministry for Foreign Affairs.

Visaria, P.M. (1967) 'The Sex Ratio of the Population of India and Pakistan and Regional Variation during 1901–1961'. In *Pattern of Population Change in India 1951–61*, ed. A. Bose, pp. 334–71. New York, Allied Publishers.

Ware, H. (1981) *Women, Demography and Development.* Development Studies Centre, Canberra.

Waring, M. (1989) *If Women Counted: A New Feminist Economics.* London, Macmillan.

Warwick, D.P. (1982) *Bitter Pills: Population Policies and their Implementation in Eight Developing Countries.* Cambridge University Press, Cambridge.

Weisband, E. (1989) 'Statement of Purpose: Toward a Pedagogy'. In *Poverty amidst Plenty: World Political Economy and Distributive Justice*, ed. E. Weisband, pp. 1–5. Boulder, Colorado, Westview Press.

Welbourne, A. (1992) 'Rapid Rural Appraisal, Gender and Health – Alternative Ways of Listening to Needs'. *IDS Bulletin*, vol. 23, no. 1, pp. 8–18.

Westergaard, K. (1992) *NGOs, Empowerment and the State in Bangladesh.* CDR Working Paper 92.2. Centre for Development Research, Copenhagen.

White, S.C. (1992) *Arguing with the Crocodile. Gender and Class in Bangladesh.* London, Zed Books.

Whitehead, A. (1979) 'Some Preliminary Notes on the Subordination of Women'. *IDS Bulletin*, vol. 10, no. 3, pp. 10–13.

Whitehead, A. (1981) '"I'm hungry, mum" The Politics of Domestic Budgeting'. In *Of Marriage and Market. Women's Subordination in International Perspective*, ed. K. Young, C. Wolkowitz and C. McCullagh, pp. 88–111. London, CSE Books.

Whitehead, A. (1985) 'Effects of Technological Change on Rural Women: A Review of Analysis and Concepts'. In *Technological and Rural Women*, ed. I. Ahmed, pp. 27–64. London, Allen and Unwin.

Whitehead, A. (1990) 'Food Crisis and Gender Conflict in the African Countryside'. In *The Food Question: Profits Versus People?* ed. H. Bernstein, B. Crow, M. Mackintosh and C. Martin, pp. 54–68. Earthscan, London.

Whitehead, A. (1991) *Module 7: Gender-aware Planning in Agricultural Production.* Institute of Development Studies, Sussex.

Wignaraja, P. (1990) *Women, Poverty and Resources.* New Dehli, Sage Publications.

Wilensky, H. and Lebeaux, C. (1965) *Industrial Society and Social Welfare.* New York, Free Press.

Willis, R.J. (1973) 'A New Approach to the Economic Theory of Fertility Behaviour'. *Journal of Political Economy*, vol. 81, no. 2, part II, pp. S14–S64.

Wilson, G. (1991) 'Thoughts on the Co-operative Conflict Model of the Household in Relation to Economic Method'. *IDS Bulletin*, vol. 22, no. 1, pp. 31–36.

Winikoff, B. (1988) 'Women's Health: An Alternative Perspective for Choosing Interventions'. In *Studies in Family Planning*, vol. 19, no. 4, pp. 197–214.

Winikoff, B. and M. Sullivan (1987) 'Assessing the Role of Family Planning in Reducing Maternal Mortality'. *Studies in Family Planning*, vol. 18, no. 3, pp. 128–43.

Wolf, D. L. (1990) 'Daughters, Decisions and Domination: An Empirical and Conceptual Critique of Household Strategies'. *Development and Change*, vol. 21, no. 1, pp. 43–74.

World Bank (1975) *The Assault on World Poverty.* Baltimore, Johns Hopkins University Press.

World Bank (1977) *Agricultural Project Analysis*, vol. 2, EDI, Washington D.C.

World Bank (1979) *Recognizing the 'Invisible' Woman in Development: the World Bank Experience.* The World Bank, Washington D.C.

World Bank (1980a) *Basic Needs in the Gambia.* Report No. 2656–GM, Washington D.C.

World Bank (1980b) *Kenya, Population and Development.* The World Bank, Washington D.C.

World Bank (1983) *Bangladesh. Selected Issues in Rural Development.* Washington D.C.

World Bank (1984) *World Development Report*, Oxford, Oxford University Press.

World Bank (1985) *World Development Report*, 1985 Oxford, Oxford University Press.

World Bank (1990) *World Development Report*, 1990 Oxford, Oxford University Press.

World Bank (1991) *Romania. Accelerating the Transition: Human Resource Strategies for the 1990s*.

World Health Organisation (1980) *Health and Status of Women*, WHO/FHE/ 80.1, Geneva.

World Health Organisation (1987) *Maternal Mortality: The Dimensions of the Problem*. Paper circulated at the Safe Motherhood Conference, Nairobi, 10–13 February.

Young, K. (1986) 'Introduction'. In *Women's Concerns and Planning: A Methodological Approach for Their Integration into Local, Regional and National Planning*. Socio-economic studies. UNESCO, Paris.

Young, K., C. Wolkowitz and C. McCullagh, eds. (1981) 'Introduction'. In *Of Marriage and Market. Women's Subordination in International Perspective*, pp.vii– xi. London, CSE Books.

Youssef, N. (1974) *Women and Work in Developing Societies*. Population Monograph Series, No. 15. Institute of International Relations, University of California at Berkeley.

Zeidenstein, G. (1980) 'The User Perspective: An Evolutionary Step in Contraceptive Service Programme' *Studies in Family Planning*, vol. 11, no. 1, pp. 24–9.

Index

340